THE NEW OXFORD BOOK OF LITERARY ANECDOTES

THE NEW OXFORD BOOK OF LITERARY ANECDOTES

Edited by

JOHN GROSS

OXFORD
UNIVERSITY PRESS

OXFORD
UNIVERSITY PRESS

Great Clarendon Street, Oxford OX2 6DP

Oxford University Press is a department of the University of Oxford.
It furthers the University's objective of excellence in research, scholarship,
and education by publishing worldwide in

Oxford New York

Auckland Cape Town Dar es Salaam Hong Kong Karachi
Kuala Lumpur Madrid Melbourne Mexico City Nairobi
New Delhi Shanghai Taipei Toronto

With offices in

Argentina Austria Brazil Chile Czech Republic France Greece
Guatemala Hungary Italy Japan Poland Portugal Singapore
South Korea Switzerland Thailand Turkey Ukraine Vietnam

Published in the United States
by Oxford University Press Inc., New York

First published 2006

British Library Cataloguing in Publication Data
Data available

Library of Congress Cataloging in Publication Data
The new Oxford book of literary anecdotes / edited by John Gross.
p. cm.
Includes index.
ISBN-13: 978-0-19-280468-6 (acid-free paper)
ISBN-10: 0-19-280468-5 (acid-free paper)
1. Authors, English—Anecdotes. 2. English literature—Anecdotes.
I. Gross, John J.
PR108.N49 2006
820.9—dc22 2005033698

Typeset in Adobe Caslon
by RefineCatch Limited, Bungay, Suffolk
Printed in Great Britain
on acid-free paper by
Clays Ltd., St Ives plc

ISBN 0-19-280468-5 978-0-19-280468-6

1 3 5 7 9 10 8 6 4 2

CONTENTS

INTRODUCTION

The urge to exchange anecdotes is as deeply implanted in human beings as the urge to gossip. It is hard to believe that cavemen didn't practise their skills as anecdotalists as they sat around the fire. The word 'anecdote' itself, on the other hand, was imported into the English language comparatively late in the day. Elizabethans and Jacobeans, Roundheads and Cavaliers all seem to have got by without it. It didn't make its appearance in England until the second half of the seventeenth century, after the Restoration, and even then it took a generation or two to establish itself in the full modern sense. It is a word that comes, via French, from the Greek. It originally meant 'something unpublished', and first achieved regular literary status when the Byzantine historian Procopius applied it, in the plural, to his 'secret history' of the reign of the Emperor Justinian, a confidential and often scandalous chronicle of life at the imperial court.

When English writers began to speak of anecdotes, they initially used the term in the same way, to mean glimpses behind the political scenes, intimate revelations about rulers and ministers. In the early eighteenth century Swift, in Book Three of *Gulliver's Travels*, could still talk about 'those who pretend to write anecdotes or secret history', as though the two things were the same. But by then the word had begun to acquire the looser sense which it has had ever since—as the *Concise Oxford Dictionary* puts it, that of 'a short account of an entertaining or interesting incident'. To most people, an anecdote simply means a good story.

On that definition, it can be about anyone or anything. Most of us like to tell stories about our friends, our enemies, our neighbours, and (not least) ourselves. The heroes of many classic anecdotes are obscure; others remain anonymous. Yet at the same time, a high proportion of anecdotes—certainly published ones—have always been about prominent figures. To some extent the explanation for this lies no deeper than the cult of celebrity. Anecdotes about the famous often reflect their fame, and little else; an incident which would be considered commonplace if it involved a bit-player is assumed to be fascinating when it involves a star. But there are better reasons too. Many famous figures fully merit our curiosity—and high among them come writers.

The public appetite for anecdotes increased throughout the eighteenth century, especially towards the end. In the first seventy years of the century, some twenty titles containing the word 'Anecdote' were published; between 1770 and 1800 there were over a hundred, some of them works running to several volumes. In the handful of these later collections that I have dipped into, authors are well represented (along with lawyers, clergymen, and other public figures). But then as early as 1758, an anonymous contributor to the *Annual Register*—it was in fact Edmund Burke—noted that 'there never was a time in which anecdotes, especially literary anecdotes, were read with greater eagerness than they are now'. And when, a generation later, in 1789, we find Boswell announcing in a letter that his forthcoming life of Johnson will be 'full of literary and characteristical anecdotes', he is obviously confident that those anecdotes will constitute a major part of its appeal.

In the nineteenth century, the fashion for big collections of anecdotes passed, but the taste for anecdotes themselves was if anything even stronger. It was satisfied by biographies, memoirs, letters, diaries, and a mass of journalism. In an age which cherished the picturesque (you only have to think how many Victorian paintings are anecdotal, for instance), a nimbus of popular legend formed around almost every major writer and lots of lesser ones.

There has been no let-up in more recent times. It is true that literature no longer occupies as commanding a place in our culture as it once did. In the twentieth century it found itself competing with new forms of communication and entertainment. Other social changes, too, have helped to switch the spotlight to new kinds of cultural hero. But as against this, the sources of literary anecdote have multiplied. Authors are still news. The attention they receive from the media, relative to other groups, may have diminished, but the media machine itself is far more powerful than it used to be. Or consider the popularity of literary biographies. They flow from the presses, month after month. Sometimes it seems as though people have become more interested in reading about authors than in reading their work. But we can't be sure; and meanwhile, any sign of intelligent interest is better than none.

Like its predecessors, James Sutherland's *Oxford Book of Literary Anecdotes* (1975) and Donald Hall's *Oxford Book of American Literary Anecdotes* (1981), the present book is restricted in its range to authors writing in English (although unlike them, it includes material from outside the British Isles and the United States). I have also followed Sutherland and Hall in equating literary anecdotes with anecdotes about authors. This seems to be both a reasonable working definition—especially if 'being about authors' is stretched to include being about their books and their readers—and a handy organizing principle.

But it still leaves open the question of at what point, if any, a story about an author ceases to qualify as literary. James Sutherland took a fairly firm line about this: he believed that ideally a literary anecdote 'should relate to a writer in his capacity of author'. Donald Hall, on the other hand, allowed himself more latitude. He was ready to include anecdotes irrespective of their explicit literary content, and I feel he was right: his policy is one I have tried to follow myself. Many of the anecdotes in this collection illustrate the working habits of authors, their sources of inspiration, their attitude to colleagues, their dealings with publishers, a dozen different aspects of their careers. Many others, however, have no direct bearing on authorship or literary life.

Boswell gave the warrant for such a mixed approach when he described his Johnson anecdotes as 'literary and characteristical', without drawing any particular distinction between the two categories. (Indeed, he virtually seems to be running them together.) We value anecdotes about a writer, beyond their immediate point, because they bear the stamp of his or her personality. How did Jane Austen face death? How did Joseph Conrad respond when the *Daily Mail* asked if he would write an article about Dr Crippen? What did C. S. Lewis think was the best thing about F. R. Leavis? What did Norman Mailer do when he first joined the US army? The answers to such questions are bound to contain some detail, at the very least, which surprises us. Circumstances are unpredictable. But in most cases there will also be satisfaction at seeing writers react in character, and relating that reaction to what we already know about them from their work.

This is scarcely less true of those anecdotes where the protagonist's reaction is not on record. An ordinary man slips on a banana skin. A celebrated author slips on a banana skin. Is there any essential difference between the two incidents, assuming that is all we are told about them? Perhaps not. But if the writer is someone whom we have read, or whose legend has touched our imagination, we are likely to bring a whole complex of feelings to bear on the story. It takes on its own distinctive tone. (No one slips on a banana skin in the pages that follow, I should add; but there is an account of one of the greatest English writers falling fully clothed into his bath.)

Many anecdotes show writers acting out of character. Such stories are the reverse side of the coin: they get their piquancy from defeating our expectations. And they remind us, incidentally, that it is in the nature of human beings to be inconsistent. All human beings, that is. It would be the same if we were studying any social group.

Still, the inconsistencies of authors have a particular fascination. The gulf between real and ideal can seem so great. In their work, writers take us into a world which is more compelling than the one we are used to, more coherent, more satisfying, more fully realized. They themselves, or so we like to think, have a special aura. And then we meet them, and find that they are often no better than other people. Sometimes they are worse. It is not so much a question of their acting out of character, in fact, as of their having two characters—the one who writes the books, and the one who gets through the rest of the day. And while the one who gets through the rest of the day may be admirable or formidable, he may equally well be vain, jealous, mean, cantankerous, or plain weird. There is an excellent chance that he will drink too much. He may not always tell the truth.

The sins of writers are a recurrent theme in this book. So are their weaknesses and misfortunes. But then anecdotalists thrive on such material. The anecdote may have lost its connection with 'secret history', but it is still a natural home for disabused views and unflattering close-ups, for the ludicrous or disreputable detail which you won't find in official tributes.

I must admit that there were times when I was tempted to add little notes at the end of the less heroic or less edifying items I had chosen, reminders of how much more there was to the authors in question. But then I reflected that I ought to have faith in my readers, that they would be far too wise not to recognize that an anecdote isn't the whole story. And in any case, there are many more anecdotes in the book from which writers emerge with their reputations strengthened—stories in which you can feel the force of their wit, their originality and (when it is there to be felt) their greatness.

The New Oxford Book of Literary Anecdotes is a successor to James Sutherland's and Donald Hall's anthologies, rather than a revised version. I owe a great deal to Sutherland and Hall's editorial example, but in terms of content the overlap between us is relatively small: less than 10 per cent of the material in the new book can be found in the earlier ones.

My selection reflects my personal preferences. I haven't steered clear of classic anecdotes, but neither have I felt any obligation to include them. When there didn't seem much to choose between a familiar and an unfamiliar item, it is the unfamiliar one that I have usually opted for. I have, however, followed Sutherland and Hall in building the book around a succession of what would once have been called standard authors. Roughly speaking, they are the names you would expect to find in a general history of English-language literature. But 'roughly speaking' covers a multitude of exceptions and variations.

In the first place, the earlier centuries are strikingly under-represented. There is no mystery about why this should be so: until we get to the eighteenth century, the most obvious sources of anecdotes—memoirs, letters, diaries, and the like—aren't available on anything like the scale we have become accustomed to since. This doesn't mean that there aren't individual treasures. The stories in Aubrey's *Brief Lives* are as good as any in English. But one can only dream of the anecdotes about Chaucer, Skelton, Dunbar, Marlowe, Webster, and a host of others which ought to be there, but aren't.

The situation is very different in later periods. By the time we get to the era of Swift and Pope, we begin to be spoilt for choice. From then on, for much of the book, the list of authors who are included approximates to what it would have been if I had been compiling an anthology of literature in general. But it doesn't run exactly parallel. A few big names are missing. So are many lesser names whom I admire quite as much as the ones I have chosen—some of whom, indeed, are personal favourites. The fact that a writer doesn't appear in the book shouldn't necessarily be construed as a literary judgement. Considerations of space have weighed heavily, and while I have occasionally come down in favour of an anecdote on the grounds of historical interest, the quality of those available has been far and away the most important determining factor.

From the outset, I had no doubt that I ought to find a place for popular authors (of a kind that would once have been considered sub-literary), and for authors who, whatever their literary qualities, don't primarily belong in a history of literature—philosophers, statesmen, scholars, and the like. In both cases, in practice, I have had to settle for a token (though, I hope, rewarding) selection. The demands on space have been enough to see to that. And on a broader scale, taking the book as a whole, disagreements over my choice of material are likely to multiply (or so I would imagine) as we approach the present.

It isn't only the eternal difficulty of getting contemporaries and near-contemporaries into perspective, before time has done its editorial work. The past fifty years or so have also seen an unprecedented diffusion of literary activity. There are even more contenders for literary fame than there used to be, and at the same time less sense of a literary hierarchy. Above all, there is a much stronger awareness that the local, English-based product is only one variety of literature in English among others. Under such circumstances, even the most conscientious selection of contemporary work is liable to seem somewhat arbitrary. And perhaps a selection of anecdotes shouldn't be too conscientious, anyway. Good anecdotes spring up at random. An anthology ought to preserve something of their haphazard spirit.

Anecdotes are also dynamic. Ideally, they describe the unfolding of a short, self-contained action—'an interesting or entertaining incident'. Certainly a static description doesn't qualify as an anecdote, no matter how striking it is, and when I first began work on this anthology, I decided to confine myself to incidents pure and simple. But before long I had relaxed the rules a bit. On the one hand I found I was depriving myself of valuable material. On the other, there was something faintly dispiriting about laying out one neat little drama after another: it was like compiling a collection of jokes. As a result, the selection presents a more varied face than was originally planned. Straightforward anecdotes take their place alongside what might be called anecdotal material—oddities of behaviour, items which weave two or three incidents together. Many of the stories hinge on something that someone said, but only when it arises out of the immediate situation. Witty observations in themselves are not enough.

Sooner or later anyone who works his way through a collection of anecdotes is likely to find himself asking whether a particular anecdote is true. Did the incident actually happen? Did it happen in the manner described? In most cases the answer is unlikely to be a straight yes or no. Some anecdotes are no doubt as accurate as an honest legal deposition. Some have been deliberately manufactured. But the majority are probably true stories which have been to a greater or lesser degree improved in the telling. They take their inspiration from the truth, and then they build on it.

Does it matter? In the case of vicious stories, a great deal (but then one doesn't really want to call them something as innocuous-sounding as anecdotes). In the case of most other stories, not very much. It partly depends on context. A biographer who points out minor inaccuracies in an anecdote is simply doing his job, helping to establish a reliable record. Someone who points out those same inaccuracies while a friend is telling the anecdote at a dinner party is barely fit for polite society. Anecdotes are a form of entertainment—at their best, an art form. Most of the time it is enough if they are broadly true (and even some of the whoppers are acceptable, as long as nobody takes them too seriously).

Still, I must admit that the question of getting the facts right occasionally nags at me. In the introduction to his anthology, Donald Hall writes that 'in the matter of accuracy, I have been careful to be unscrupulous; if a story achieves print it is grist for this mill.' I admire the spirit in which this is written, but when it came to my own book I didn't altogether live up to it. Every so often I felt moved to point out, in an accompanying note, that the truth of an anecdote had been denied or called in question. I could have added more comments along the same lines, but I was afraid of boring the reader, and of suggesting that I set more store by accuracy—accuracy in anecdotes, that is—than I do.

The anecdotes I have chosen are taken from printed texts. In many cases I have gone for the original source: it is often so powerful that anything else would be out of the question. When I draw on later sources, such as biographies, and there is a choice, I have opted for what seems to me the most concise and readable version. (This isn't always the most scholarly one.) The source is given at the end of each item.

Spelling and punctuation have been modernized, except in a few minor cases. Many of the authors who are the subject of anecdotes are introduced by a headnote briefly explaining who they were (or are). Where there isn't such a note, it is either because I have assumed the great majority of my readers don't need to be told, or because the anecdote itself supplies the necessary explanation. In the former case, there is obvious room for disagreement: a familiar name in some quarters may well seem an obscure one in others. I can only plead that I have tried to strike a balance, to be reader-friendly without becoming reader-patronizing.

I owe a considerable debt to the biographies, biographical collections, and critical studies where I first encountered some of the older texts which I cite. I would like to thank David Kynaston for some helpful suggestions, Judith Luna for editorial advice and support, and Vivien Minto for invaluable assistance in preparing the manuscript.

THE NEW OXFORD BOOK OF LITERARY ANECDOTES

Geoffrey Chaucer · *c.*1343–1400

I find this Chaucer fined in the Temple two shillings for striking a Franciscan friar in Fleet Street; and it seemed his hands ever itched to be revenged, and have his pennyworth's out of them, so tickling religious orders with his tales, and yet so pinching them with his truths, that friars, in reading his books, know not how to dispose their faces between crying and laughing. He lies buried in the south aisle of St Peter's, Westminster; and since hath got the company of Spenser and Drayton, a pair royal of poets, enough almost to make passengers' feet to move metrically, who go over the place where so much poetical dust is interred.

Thomas Fuller, *The Church History of Britain*, 1655

Sir Thomas More · 1478–1535

In his *Utopia* his law is that the young people are to see each other stark naked before marriage. Sir William Roper, of Eltham, in Kent, came one morning, pretty early, to my lord, with a proposal to marry one of his daughters. My lord's daughters were then both together abed in a truckle-bed in their father's chamber, asleep. He carries Sir William into the chamber and takes the sheet by the corner and suddenly whips it off. They lay on their backs, and their smocks up as high as their armpits. This awakened them, and immediately they turned on their bellies. Quoth Roper, 'I have seen both sides,' and so gave a pat on the buttock he made choice of, saying, 'Thou art mine.' Here was all the trouble of the wooing.

John Aubrey, *Brief Lives*, late seventeenth century

Among his Latin books his *Utopia* beareth the bell, containing the idea of a complete commonwealth in an imaginary island, but pretended to be lately discovered in America, and that so lively counterfeited, that many at the reading thereof mistook it for a real truth; insomuch that many great learned men, as Budaeus, and Johannes Paludanus, upon a fervent zeal, wished that some excellent divines might be sent thither to preach Christ's Gospel; yea, there were here amongst us at home sundry good men and learned divines, very desirous to undertake the voyage, to bring the people to the faith of Christ, whose manners they did so well like.

Thomas Fuller, *The Worthies of England*, 1662

Sir Walter Ralegh · 1552?–1618

He loved a wench well; and one time getting one of the Maids of Honour up against a tree in a wood ('twas his first lady) who seemed at first boarding to be something fearful of her honour, and modest, she cried, 'Sweet Sir Walter, what do you me ask? Will you undo me? Nay, sweet Sir Walter! Sweet Sir Walter! Sir Walter!' At last, as the danger and the pleasure at the same time grew higher, she cried in the ecstasy, 'Swisser Swatter, Swisser Swatter!' She proved with child, and I doubt not but this hero took care of them both, as also that the product was more than an ordinary mortal.

John Aubrey, *Brief Lives*, late seventeenth century

On the morning of his execution, according to an eyewitness, Ralegh was very 'cheerful . . . ate his breakfast heartily, and took tobacco, and made no more of his death, than it had been to take a journey; and made a great impression in the minds of those that beheld him.' He dressed himself richly for the occasion, but not ostentatiously, as he had done in his days of royal favor. On account of the fever he had contracted on the Guiana voyage and had never completely shaken, he wore under his hat a wrought nightcap. Seeing a bald-headed old man in the crowd that thronged about him on the way to the scaffold, Ralegh asked him whether he wanted anything. 'Nothing,' said the old man, 'but to see you, and to pray God to have mercy on your soul.' 'I thank thee, good friend,' answered Ralegh, 'and I am sorry to have no better thing to return thee for thy good will; but take this nightcap . . . for thou hast more need of it now than I.'

Stephen J. Greenblatt, *Sir Walter Ralegh*, 1973

Stephen Greenblatt adds that 'the allusion to Sir Philip Sidney's "Thy necessity is yet greater than mine" (see p. 5) would not have been wasted on an audience that treasured such scenes'.

Edmund Spenser · 1552?–1599

It is said that upon his presenting some poems to the Queen she ordered him a gratuity of one hundred pounds, but the Lord Treasurer Burleigh objecting to it, said with some scorn of the poet, of whose merit he was totally ignorant, 'What, all this for a song?' The Queen replied, 'Then give him what is reason.' Spenser for some time waited, but had the mortification to find himself disappointed of Her Majesty's bounty. Upon this he took a proper opportunity to present a paper to Queen

Elizabeth, in which he reminded her of the order she had given, in the following lines:

I was promised on a time
To have reason for my rhime.
From that time, unto this season,
I received nor rhime, nor reason.

The paper produced the intended effect, and the Queen, after sharply reproving the Treasurer, immediately directed the payment of the hundred pounds she had first ordered.

Theophilus Cibber, *The Lives of the Poets*, 1753

Sir Philip Sidney · 1554–1586

Sidney spent the last year of his life in the Netherlands. In October 1586 he joined the forces led by his uncle, the Earl of Leicester, in an attack on a Spanish relief column trying to reach the besieged town of Zutphen, and in the course of the fighting he was wounded in the thigh:

The horse he rode upon was rather furiously choleric than bravely proud, and so forced him to forsake the field, but not his back, as the noblest and fittest bier to carry a martial commander to his grave. In which sad progress, passing along by the rest of the army where his uncle the General was and being thirsty with excess of bleeding, he called for drink, which was presently brought him; but as he was putting the bottle to his mouth, he saw a poor soldier carried along who had eaten his last at the same feast, ghastly casting up his eyes up at the same bottle. Which Sir Philip perceiving, took it from his head before he drank and delivered it to the poor man with these words, 'Thy necessity is yet greater than mine.' And when he had pledged this poor soldier, he was presently carried to Arnheim.

Fulke Greville, Lord Brooke, *The Life of Sir Philip Sidney*, first published 1652

A similar story is told about Alexander the Great.

Francis Bacon · 1561–1626

Mr Hobbes told me that the cause of his lordship's death was trying an experiment: viz. as he was taking the air in a coach with Dr Winterborne (a Scotchman, physician to the King) towards Highgate, snow lay on the ground, and it came into my Lord's thoughts why flesh might not be preserved in snow, as in salt. They were resolved they would try the experiment presently. They alighted out of the coach and went into a poor woman's house at the bottom of Highgate Hill, and bought a hen, and made the woman disenterate [eviscerate] it, and then stuffed the body with snow, and my Lord did help to do it himself. The snow so chilled him that he immediately fell so extremely ill that he could not return to his lodgings (I suppose then at Gray's Inn), but went to the Earl of Arundel's house at Highgate, where they put him into a good bed warmed with a pan, but it was a damp bed that had not been laid in about a year before, which gave him such a cold that in two or three days, as I remember he [Thomas Hobbes] told me, he died of suffocation.

John Aubrey, *Brief Lives*, late seventeenth century

Hobbes had been one of the younger men who waited on Bacon in his country house at Gorhambury, equipped with pen and ink to take down his thoughts. According to Aubrey, Bacon praised him for being the only one who always understood what he wrote, 'which the others not understanding, my Lord would many times have a hard task to make sense of what they writ'.

In their 1998 biography of Bacon, Hostage to Fortune, *Lisa Jardine and Alan Stewart suggest that he may in fact have died as a result of experimenting with drugs in an attempt to alleviate his ill health.*

William Shakespeare · 1564–1616

His father was a butcher, and I have been told heretofore by some of the neighbours that when he was a boy he exercised his father's trade, but when he killed a calf he would do it in a high style, and make a speech. There was at this time another butcher's son in this town that was held not at all inferior to him for a natural wit, his acquaintance and coetanean [contemporary], but he died young.

John Aubrey, *Brief Lives*, late seventeenth century

Over the years a number of traditions became firmly attached to Shakespeare's name. One of them was recounted by Dr Johnson, who said that the information came, via Alexander Pope, from Shakespeare's early eighteenth-century editor Nicholas Rowe:

In the time of Elizabeth, coaches being yet uncommon, and hired coaches not at all in use, those who were too proud, too tender, or too idle to walk, went on horseback to any distant business or diversion. Many came on horseback to the play and when Shakespear fled to London from the terrour of a criminal prosecution, his first expedient was to wait at the door of the playhouse and hold the horses of those that had no servants, that they might be ready again after the performance. In this office he became so conspicuous for his care and readiness, that in a short time every man as he alighted called for Will Shakespear, and scarcely any other waiter was trusted with a horse while Will Shakespear could be had. This was the first dawn of better fortune. Shakespear, finding more horses put into his hand than he could hold, hired boys to wait under his inspection, who, when Will Shakespear was summoned were immediately to present themselves, *I am Shakespear's boy, Sir.* In time Shakespear found higher employment, but as long as the practice of riding to the playhouse continued, the waiters that held the horses retained the appellation of Shakespear's Boys.

Samuel Johnson, note appended to the reprint of Rowe's life of Shakespeare, 1765

Shakespeare's modern biographer S. Schoenbaum described this legend as 'pure nonsense'.

Schoenbaum was almost equally sceptical about a pleasing tradition recorded by Rowe himself:

HIS acquaintance with Ben Johnson [*sic*] began with a remarkable piece of humanity and good nature. Mr Johnson, who was at that time altogether unknown to the world, had offered one of his plays to the players, in order to have it acted; and the persons into whose hands it was put, after having turned it carelessly and superciliously over, were just upon returning it to him with an ill-natured answer, that it would be of no service to their Company, when Shakespear luckily cast his eye upon it, and found something so well in it as to engage him first to read it through, and after this to recommend Mr Johnson and his writings to the publick. After this they were professed friends; tho' I don't know whether the other ever made him an equal return of gentleness and sincerity.

Nicholas Rowe, 'Some Account of the Life of Mr William Shakespear' (preface to Rowe's edition of Shakespeare), 1709

Benjamin Robert Haydon writes to Keats in March 1818, and Keats replies:

MY dear Keats,—I shall go mad! In a field at Stratford-upon-Avon, that belonged to Shakespeare, they have found a gold ring and seal, with the initials W. S. and a true lover's knot between. If this is not Shakespeare, who is it?—A true lover's knot! I saw an impression today, and am to have one as soon as possible: as sure as that you breathe, and that he was the first of beings, the seal belonged to him.

O Lord!

MY dear Haydon,—In sooth I hope you are not too sanguine about that seal, in sooth I hope it is not Brummagem, in double sooth I hope it is his, and in triple sooth I hope I shall have an impression . . .

Ben Jonson · 1572?–1637

He was delated [informed against] by Sir James Murray to the King for writing something against the Scots in a play *Eastward Ho!*, and voluntarily imprisoned himself with Chapman and Marston, who had written it amongst them. The report was, that they should then have their ears cut and noses. After their delivery, he banqueted all his friends; there was Camden, Selden and others. At the midst of the feast, his old mother drank to him, and showed him a paper which she had (if the sentence had taken execution) to have mixed in the prison among his drink, which was full of lusty strong poison; and that she was no churl, she told him she minded [intended] first to have drunk of it herself.

Ben Jonson, *Conversations with William Drummond of Hawthornden*, recorded 1618–19

He can set horoscopes, but trusts them not. He with the consent of a friend cozened a lady, with whom he had made an appointment to meet an old astrologer, in the suburbs, which she kept; and it was himself disguised in a long gown and a white beard at the light of dim-burning candles, up in a little cabinet reached unto by a ladder.

Conversations with Drummond

He hath consumed a whole night in lying looking to his great toe, about which he hath seen Tartars and Turks, Romans and Carthaginians, fight in his imagination.

Conversations with Drummond

John Donne · 1573?–1631

Dr Donne, the poet, in 1602 married the daughter of Sir George Moore privately against her father's consent, who was so enraged that he not only turned him and his wife out of his house, but got Lord Chancellor Egerton to turn him out of his office as Secretary to the Great Seal. Donne and his wife took refuge in a house in Pyrford, in the neighbourhood of his father-in-law, who lived at Losely, in the county of Surrey, where the first thing he did was to write on a pane of glass—

John Donne
An Donne
Undone.

These words were visible at that house in 1749. It should be remembered that Donne's name was formerly pronounced Dun.

James Prior, *Life of Edmond Malone*, 1860; 'Maloniana'

In 1611 Donne was invited to accompany Sir Robert Drury and his wife on a three-year journey to Europe. Donne's wife Anne, who was pregnant, asked him not to go but he accepted the invitation nonetheless. The party stopped at Amiens and then went on to Paris:

Two days after their arrival there, Mr Donne was left alone in that room in which Sir Robert and he and some other friends had dined together. To this place Sir Robert returned within half an hour; and as he left, so he found Mr Donne alone; but in such an ecstasy and so altered as to his looks as amazed Sir Robert to behold him. Insomuch that he earnestly desired Mr Donne to declare what had befallen him in the short time of his absence. To which Mr Donne was not able to make a present answer. But after a long and perplexed pause, did at last say, 'I have seen a dreadful vision since I saw you. I have seen my dear wife pass twice by me through this room with her hair hanging about her shoulders and a dead child in her arms. This I have seen since I saw you.' To which Sir Robert replied, 'Sure, Sir, you have slept since I saw you; and this is the result of some melancholy dream, which I desire you to forget, for you are now awake.' To which Mr Donne's reply was, 'I cannot be surer that I live now than that I have not slept since I saw you, and am as sure that at her second appearing she stopped and looked me in the face and vanished.' Rest and sleep had not altered Mr Donne's opinion the next day. For he then affirmed this vision with a more deliberate and so confirmed a confidence that he inclined Sir Robert to a faint belief that the vision was true.

It is truly said that desire and doubt have no rest. And it proved so with Sir Robert, for he immediately sent a servant to Drury House with a charge to hasten back and bring him word whether Mrs Donne were alive, and if alive, in what condition she was as to her health. The twelfth day the messenger returned with this account: that he found and left Mrs Donne very sad and sick in her bed, and that after a long and dangerous labor she had been delivered of a dead child. And upon examination the abortion proved to be the same day and about the very hour that Mr Donne affirmed he saw her pass by him in his chamber.

Izaak Walton, *The Life of Dr John Donne*, 1640

The child in fact died while the travellers were still in Amiens which shows that the last part of Walton's story at least cannot be correct.

Shortly before his death Donne had his portrait drawn:

DR DONNE sent for a carver to make for him in wood the figure of an urn, giving him directions for the compass and height of it, and to bring with it a board of the just height of his body. These being got, then without delay a choice painter was got to be in a readiness to draw his picture, which was taken as followeth: Several charcoal fires being first made in his large study, he brought with him into that place his winding-sheet in his hand and, having put off all his clothes, had this sheet put on him and so tied with knots at his head and feet and his hands so placed as dead bodies are usually fitted to be shrouded and put into their coffin or grave.

Upon this urn he thus stood with his eyes shut and with so much of the sheet turned aside as might show his lean, pale, and death-like face, which was purposely turned toward the East, from whence he expected the second coming of his and our Saviour, Jesus. In this posture he was drawn at his just height; and when the picture was fully finished, he caused it to be set by his bed-side, where it continued and became his hourly object till his death and was then given to his dearest friend and executor, Doctor Henry King, then chief residentiary of St Paul's, who caused him to be thus carved in one entire piece of white marble, as it now stands in that church.

Walton, *Life of Dr John Donne*

The monument was the only one to survive the destruction of old St Paul's in the Great Fire of London. It can still be seen in the cathedral today.

ROBERT BURTON · 1577–1640

(author of *The Anatomy of Melancholy*)

THE author is said to have laboured long in the writing of this book to suppress his own melancholy, and yet did but improve it; and that some readers have found the same effect. In an interval of vapours he could be extremely pleasant, and raise laughter in any company. Yet I have heard that nothing at last could make him laugh but going down to the Bridge-foot in Oxford, and hearing the barge-men scold and storm and swear at one another, at which he would set his hands to his sides and laugh most profusely. Yet in his college and chamber so mute and mopish that he was suspected to be *felo de se* [to have committed suicide].

White Kennett, *A Register and Chronicle*, 1728

In writing The Anatomy of Melancholy, *Burton adopted the persona of Democritus Junior—the modern counterpart of Democritus of Abdera, 'the laughing philosopher'. Kennett's story, if true, shows how closely he was prepared to follow his model. Democritus is supposed to have gone down to the harbour at Abdera whenever he was depressed to amuse himself by what he saw there.*

The Earl of Southampton went into a shop, and inquired of the bookseller for Burton's *Anatomy of Melancholy*. Mr Burton sat in a corner of the shop at that time. Says the bookseller, 'My Ld. if you please I can show you the author.' He did so. 'Mr Burton,' says the Earl, 'your servant.' 'Mr Southampton,' says Mr Burton, 'your servant,' and away he went.

Thomas Hearne (1678–1735), *Reliquiae Hearnianae*, first published 1857

Anthony à Wood was a great admirer of Mr Burton, and of the books he bequeathed to the Bodleian Library, a great many of which were little historical diverting pamphlets, now grown wonderful scarce, which Mr Burton used to divert himself with, as he did with other little merry books, of which there are many in his benefaction, one of which is *The History of Tom Thumb*.

Hearne, *Reliquiae Hearnianae*

Richard Corbet · 1582–1635

(Bishop of Oxford and subsequently of Norwich; poet; author of 'Farewell rewards and fairies')

He was a student of Christ-church in Oxford. He was very facetious and a good fellow. One time he and some of his acquaintance being merry at Friar Bacon's Study (where was good liquor sold) they were drinking on the leads of the house, and one of the scholars was asleep, and had a pair of good silk stockings on. Dr Corbet (then M.A., if not B.D.) got a pair of scissors and cut them full of little holes.

John Aubrey, *Brief Lives*, late seventeenth century

Thomas Hobbes · 1588–1679

He was forty years old before he looked on geometry, which happened accidentally. Being in a gentleman's library Euclid's Elements lay open and 'twas the *47 El libri I.* He read the proposition. *By G—*, said he (he would now and then swear an emphatical oath by way of emphasis) *this is impossible!* So he reads the demonstration of it which referred him back to such a proposition; which proposition he read. That referred him back to another, which he also read. And so on that at last he was demonstratively convinced of that truth. This made him in love with geometry.

John Aubrey, *Brief Lives*, late seventeenth century

AT night, when he was abed, and the doors made fast, and was sure nobody heard him, he sang aloud, not that he had a very good voice, but for his health's sake: he did believe it did his lungs good, and conduced much to prolong his life.

Aubrey, *Brief Lives*

ROBERT HERRICK · 1591–1674

In 1809 Charles Lamb's friend, the writer Barron Field, visited the village of Dean Prior in Devon where Herrick had served as minister from 1630 until he was ejected by Parliament in 1647, and again from 1660 to his death. Field found that many of the villagers could repeat some of his lines and that the person who knew most about him was 'a poor woman in the ninety-ninth year of her age' named Dorothy King:

SHE repeated to us, with great exactness, five of his *Noble Numbers*. These she had learnt from her mother, who was apprenticed to Herrick's successor in the vicarage. She called them her prayers, which, she said, she was in the habit of putting up in bed, whenever she could not sleep. She had no idea that these poems had ever been printed, and could not have read them if she had seen them.

She is in possession of few traditions as to the person, manners and habits of life of the poet; but in return, she has a whole budget of anecdotes respecting his ghost; and these she details with a careless but serene gravity, which one would not willingly discompose by any hints at a remote possibility of their not being exactly true. Herrick, she says, was a bachelor, and kept a maid-servant, as his poems, indeed, discover; but she adds, what they do not discover, that he also kept a pet pig, which he taught to drink out of a tankard.

Barron Field, *Quarterly Review*, 1810

GEORGE HERBERT · 1593–1633

HIS chiefest recreation was musick, in which heavenly art he was a most excellent master, and composed many divine hymns and anthems, which he set and sung to his lute or viol and though he was a lover of retiredness, yet his love of musick was such, that he went usually twice every week, on certain appointed, days, to the cathedral church in Salisbury; and at his return would say, that his time spent in prayer, and cathedral music, elevated his soul, and was his heaven upon earth. But before his return thence to Bemerton, he would usually sing and play his part at an appointed private musick meeting; and, to justify this practice, he would often say, Religion does not banish mirth, but only moderates and sets rules to it.

And, as his desire to enjoy his heaven upon earth drew him twice every week to Salisbury, so, his walks thither were the occasion of many accidents to others; of which I will mention some few.

In one of his walks to Salisbury he overtook a gentleman, that is still living in that city; and in their walk together, Mr Herbert took a fair occasion to talk with him, and humbly begged to be excused, if he asked him some account of his faith; and said, I do this the rather, because though you are not of my parish, yet I receive tithe from you by the hand of your tenant; and, sir, I am the bolder to do it, because I know there be some sermon-hearers that be like those fishes, that always live in salt water, and yet are always fresh.

After which expression, Mr Herbert asked him some needful questions, and having received his answer, gave him such rules for the trial of his sincerity, and for a practical piety, and in so loving and meek a manner, that the gentleman did so fall in love with him, and his discourse, that he would often contrive to meet him in his walk to Salisbury, or to attend him back to Bemerton; and still mentions the name of Mr Herbert with veneration, and still praiseth God that he knew him.

In another walk to Salisbury, he saw a poor man with a poorer horse, that was fallen under his load: they were both in distress and needed present help; which Mr Herbert perceiving, put off his canonical coat, and helped the poor man to unload, and after to load his horse. The poor man blessed him for it, and he blessed the poor man; and was so like the good Samaritan, that he gave him money to refresh both himself and his horse; and told him, that if he loved himself, he should be merciful to his beast. Thus he left the poor man and at his coming to his musical friends at Salisbury, they began to wonder that Mr George Herbert, which used to be so trim and clean, came into that company so soiled and discomposed; but he told them the occasion. And when one of the company told him, he had disparaged himself by so dirty an employment, his answer was, that the thought of what he had done, would prove musick to him at midnight; and that the omission of it would have upbraided and made discord in his conscience, whensoever he should pass by that place: for if I be bound to pray for all that be in distress, I am sure that I am bound, so far as it is in my power to practise what I pray for. And though I do not wish for the like occasion every day, yet let me tell you, I would not willingly pass one day of my life, without comforting a sad soul, or showing mercy; and I praise God for this occasion. And now let us tune our instruments.

Izaak Walton, *The Life of Mr George Herbert*, 1670

Sir Thomas Browne · 1605–1682

(physician and scholar; author of *Religio Medici* and *Urn Burial*)

He married in 1641 Mrs Mileham, of a good family in Norfolk; 'a lady (says Whitefoot) of such symmetrical proportion to her worthy husband, both in the graces of her body and mind, that they seemed to come together by a kind of natural magnetism.'

This marriage could not but draw the raillery of contemporary wits upon a man who had just been wishing in his new book, 'that we might procreate like trees, without conjunction,' and had lately declared, that 'the whole world was made for man, but only the twelfth part of man for woman;' and, that 'man is the whole world, but woman only the rib or crooked part of man.'

Whether the lady had been yet informed of these contemptuous positions, or whether she was pleased with the conquest of so formidable a rebel, and considered it as a double triumph, to attract so much merit, and overcome so powerful prejudices; or whether, like most others, she married upon mingled motives, between convenience and inclination; she had, however, no reason to repent, for she lived happily with him one-and-forty years, and bore him ten children, of whom one son and three daughters outlived their parents: she survived him two years, and passed her widowhood in plenty, if not in opulence.

Samuel Johnson, 'Sir Thomas Browne', 1756

He appears indeed to have been willing to pay labour for truth. Having heard a flying rumour of sympathetic needles, by which, suspended over a circular alphabet, distant friends or lovers might correspond, he procured two such alphabets to be made, touched his needles with the same magnet, and placed them upon proper spindles: the result was, that when he moved one of his needles, the other, instead of taking by sympathy the same direction, 'stood like the pillars of Hercules.' That it continued motionless, will be easily believed; and most men would have been content to believe it, without the labour of so hopeless an experiment.

Johnson, 'Sir Thomas Browne'

Sir William Davenant · 1606–1668

(dramatist and Poet Laureate)

Mr William Shakespeare was wont to go into Warwickshire once a year, and did commonly in his journey lie at this house in Oxon, where he was exceedingly respected. (I have heard Parson Robert say that Mr William Shakespeare has given him a hundred kisses.) Now Sir William would sometimes, when he was pleasant over a glass of wine with his most intimate friends—e.g. Sam Butler, author of *Hudibras*, etc, say that it seemed to him that he writ with the very spirit that did Shakespeare, and seemed contented enough to be thought his son. He would tell them the story as above in which way his mother had a very light report, whereby she was called a whore.

John Aubrey, *Brief Lives*, late seventeenth century

Edmund Waller · 1606–1687

(poet and politician)

Waller had a reputation for what Dr Johnson called 'insinuation and flattery'. Johnson believed that it was well founded:

Ascham, in his elegant description of those whom in modern language we term Wits, says, that they are *open flatterers, and privy mockers.* Waller shewed a little of both, when, upon sight of the Duchess of Newcastle's verses on the death of a Stag, he declared that he would give all his own compositions to have written them; and, being charged with the exorbitance of his adulation, answered, that 'nothing was too much to be given, that a Lady might be saved from the disgrace of such a vile performance.'

Samuel Johnson, *Lives of the Poets*, 1779–81

John Milton · 1608–1674

There is reason to suspect that he was regarded in his college [Christ's College, Cambridge] with no great fondness. That he obtained no fellowship is certain; but the unkindness with which he was treated was not merely negative. I am ashamed to relate what I fear is true, that Milton was one of the last students in either university that suffered the publick indignity of corporal correction.

Samuel Johnson, *Lives of the Poets*, 1779–81

Johnson's friend Mrs Thrale improved on his account by recording in her journal for 1777 that Milton was flogged at Cambridge 'for a Frolick'.

The earliest source for the story is in John Aubrey's notes on Milton (subsequently published in Brief Lives*). After a reference to the 'unkindness' shown the poet by his first Cambridge tutor, the words 'whipt him' have been inserted. Whether the incident actually took place is open to doubt, but Milton's most thorough modern biographer, William Riley Parker, allows that 'it may be so'.*

In a later journal, in 1800, Mrs Thrale (by now Mrs Piozzi) amused herself by devising a number of anagrams. One of them was 'Solemnity—yes, Milton'.

He rendered his studies and various works more easy and pleasant by alloting them their several portions of the day. Of these the time friendly to the Muses fell to his poetry; and he waking early (as is the use of temperate men) had commonly a good stock of verses ready against his amanuensis came. Which if it happened to be later than ordinary, he would complain, saying *he wanted to be milked.*

Anon., *The Life of Mr John Milton*, *c.*1686. (This has been attributed to John Phillips and also to Cyriack Skinner.)

After some common discourses had passed between us, he called for a manuscript of his; which being brought, he delivered to me; bidding me, 'Take it home with me, and read it at my leisure; and, when I had so done, return it to him, with my judgement therupon.' When I came home, and had set myself to read it, I found it was that excellent poem which he entitled *Paradise Lost*. After I had, with the best attention, read it through: I made him another visit, and returned him his book; with due acknowledgment of the favour he had done me in communicating it to me. He asked me, how I liked it, and what I thought of it; which I modestly but freely told him. And, after some further discourse about it, I pleasantly said to him, Thou has said much, here, of *Paradise Lost*: but what hast thou to say of *Paradise Found*? He made me no answer, but sate some time in a muse: then brake off that discourse, and fell upon another subject.

Afterwards he shewed me his second poem, called *Paradise Regained*: and, in a pleasant tone, said to me, *This is owing to you! For you put it into my head, by the question you put to me at Chalfont, which, before, I had not thought of.*

Thomas Ellwood, *History of his Life*, 1714

Milton's sight began to fail in the 1640s, and by 1652 he was totally blind:

In relation to his love of musick, and the effect it had upon his mind, I remember a story I had from a friend I was happy in for many years, and who loved to talk of Milton, as he often did. Milton hearing a lady sing finely, 'Now will I swear' (says he) 'this lady is handsome.' His ears now were eyes to him.

Jonathan Richardson, *The Life of Milton*, 1734

Sir John Suckling · 1609–1642

(poet and Royalist)

Sir John Suckling invented the game of Cribbidge. He sent his cards to all gaming places in the country, which were marked with private marks of his: he got £20,000 by this way.

John Aubrey, *Brief Lives*, late seventeenth century

Sir John was a man of great vivacity and spirit. He died about the beginning of the Civil War, and his death was occasioned by a very uncommon accident. He entered warmly into the King's interests and was sent over by him into France with some letters of great consequence to the Queen. He arrived late at Calais, and in the night his servant ran away with his portmanteau, in which was his money and papers. When he was told of this in the morning he immediately inquired which way his servant had taken, and ordered horses to be got ready instantly. In pulling on his boots he found one of them extremely uneasy to him, but as the horses were at the door he leaped into his saddle and forgot his pain. He pursued his servant so eagerly that he overtook him two or three posts off, recovered his portmanteau, and soon after complained of a vast pain in one of his feet, and fainted away with it. When they came to pull off his boots to fling him into bed, they found one of them full of blood. It seems his servant (who knew his master's temper well and was sure he would pursue him as soon as his villainy should be discovered) had driven a nail up into one of his boots in hopes of disabling him from pursuing him. Sir John's impetuosity made him regard the pain only just at first, and his pursuit hurried him from the thoughts of it for some time after. However, the wound was so bad and so much inflamed that it flung him into a violent fever which ended his life in a very few days.

Joseph Spence, *Observations, Anecdotes, and Characters of Books and Men*; first published 1820, ed. James M. Osborne, 1966

This story is probably apocryphal. According to another version, Suckling committed suicide.

Sir Thomas Urquhart · 1611–1660

(Scottish author, landowner and traveller; translator of Rabelais; fought for the Royalists in the Civil War)

Urquhart died in Rabelaisian fashion—*car le rire est le propre de l'homme* [for laughter is proper to man]. Exiled in France, secure from Presbyterians and creditors, he took such a fit of laughing when he heard of the Restoration of Charles II that he expired therewith. Dullards have doubted the truth of this story; but, as Mr Willcock [Urquhart's Victorian biographer] says, 'we have to keep in mind that Sir Thomas was not alone in his folly, if folly it were; for a great wave of exultation swept over the three kingdoms at that time. Our author had, like many of his fellow Royalists, staked and lost everything he possessed in the defence of the House of Stuart, and one can have little difficulty in understanding how the announcement of the triumph of the cause, which was so dear to him, should have agitated him so profoundly.'

Hugh MacDiarmid, *Scottish Eccentrics*, 1936

James Harrington · 1611–1677

(political theorist; author of *Oceana*)

Anno Domini 1660, he was committed prisoner to the Tower; then to Portsea Castle. His durance in these prisons (he being a gentleman of a high spirit and a hot head) was the procatractic [originating] cause of his deliration or madness; which was not outrageous, for he would discourse rationally enough and be very facetious company, but he grew to have a fancy that his perspiration turned to flies, and sometimes to bees; and he had a versatile [rotating] timber house built in Mr Hart's garden (opposite to St James's Park) to try the experiment. He would turn it to the sun and sit towards it; then he had his fox-tails there to chase away and massacre all the flies and bees that were to be found there, and then shut his window.

Now this experiment was only to be tried in warm weather, and some flies would lie so close in the crannies and cloth (with which it was hung) that they would not presently show themselves. A quarter of an hour after perhaps, a fly or two, or more, might be drawn out of the lurking holes by the warmth; and then he would cry out, 'Do not you see it apparent that these come from me?' 'Twas the strangest sort of madness that ever I found in anyone: talk of anything else, his discourse would be very ingenious and pleasant.

John Aubrey, *Brief Lives*, late seventeenth century

Samuel Butler · 1613–1680

Butler's famous satire Hudibras *was published in 1663–4. It was applauded by the Royalist party, and Butler might reasonably have hoped for a monetary award from the king or from leading courtiers, but none was forthcoming. One friend who tried to intercede for him was the dramatist Wycherley*:

Mr Wycherley had always laid hold of an opportunity which offered of representing to the Duke of Buckingham how well Mr Butler had deserved of the royal family, by writing his inimitable Hudibras; and that it was a reproach to the Court, that a person of his loyalty and wit should suffer in obscurity, and under the wants he did. The Duke always seemed to hearken to him with attention enough; and, after some time, undertook to recommend his pretensions to his Majesty. Mr Wycherley, in hopes to keep him steady of his word, obtained of his Grace to name a day, when he might introduce that modest and unfortunate poet to his new patron. At last an appointment was made, and the place of meeting was agreed to be the Roebuck. Mr Butler and his friend attended accordingly: the Duke joined them; but, as the d—l would have it, the door of the room where they sat was open, and his Grace, who had seated himself near it, observing a pimp of his acquaintance (the creature too was a knight) trip by with a brace of Ladies, immediately quitted his engagement, to follow another kind of business, at which he was more ready than in doing good offices to men of desert; though no one was better qualified than he, both in regard to his fortune and understanding, to protect them; and, from that time to the day of his death, poor Butler never found the least effect of his promise!

Memoir by Richardson Pack, quoted in Samuel Johnson, *Lives of the Poets*, 1779–81

Abraham Cowley · 1618–1667

I believe I can tell the particular little chance that filled my head first with such chimes of verse as have never since left ringing there: for I remember when I began to read, and to take some pleasure in it, there was wont to lie in my mother's parlour (I know not by what accident, for she herself never in her life read any book but of devotion), but there was wont to lie Spenser's works. This I happened to fall upon, and was infinitely delighted with the stories of the knights, and giants, and monsters, and brave houses which I found everywhere there (though my understanding had little to do with all this), and by degrees with the tinkling of the rhyme and dance of the numbers; so that I think I had read him all over before I was twelve years old, and was thus made a poet as immediately as a child is made an eunuch.

'Of My Self', 1668

John Bunyan · 1628–1688

He may be supposed to have been always vehement and vigorous in delivery, as he frequently is in his language. One day when he had preached 'with peculiar warmth and enlargement', some of his friends came to shake hands with him after the service, and observed what 'a sweet sermon' he had delivered. 'Aye,' he replied, 'you need not remind me of that; for the Devil told me of it before I was out of the pulpit.'

Robert Southey, *Life of John Bunyan*, 1830

Isaac Barrow · 1630–1677

(theologian and mathematician)

Meeting Lord Rochester [the poet] one day at court, his lordship, by way of banter, thus accosted him: 'Doctor, I am yours to my shoe tie.' Barrow, seeing his aim, returned his salute as obsequiously, with 'My lord, I am yours to the ground.' Rochester, improving his blow, quickly returned it with 'Doctor, I am yours to the centre'; which was as smartly followed by Barrow with 'My lord, I am yours to the antipodes'; upon which Rochester, scorning to be foiled by a musty old piece of divinity (as he used to call him), exclaimed, 'Doctor, I am yours to the lowest pit of hell!' on which Barrow, turning on his heel, answered, '*There*, my lord, I leave you.'

Anonymous MS, British Museum, quoted in *The Debt to Pleasure*, ed. John Adlard, 1974

John Dryden · 1631–1700

Dryden was often at loggerheads with his publisher, Jacob Tonson. Tonson, who was a Whig, particularly annoyed him by asking him to dedicate his translation of Virgil to the Whig hero King William III:

Dryden refused, as obdurately as he had refused to write an elegy on the death of Queen Mary in 1694. Tonson at once became even less co-operative than before; one day he refused point-blank to do Dryden some small service, and the poet sat down and gave these three lines to a messenger with the injunction: 'Tell the dog that he who wrote these can write more'. The lines were:

> With leering looks, bull-faced and freckled fair,
> With two left legs, and Judas-coloured hair,
> And frowsy pores that taint the ambient air.

Tonson hastened to comply—but in the end got his own back, for although he did not get the desired dedication to the King, he cunningly altered each picture of Aeneas to resemble His Majesty whose hook-nose was one of his most notable features.

Dryden, for all his tweaking of Tonson's ear, was half afraid of him; after all, it was his livelihood that was at stake in these exchanges. One day at home Dryden was entertaining a young man, Henry St John, later to become famous as Viscount Bolingbroke; St John heard someone else enter the house. Dryden broke off his conversation and said to him: 'This is Tonson; you will take care not to depart before he goes away: for I have not completed the sheet which I promised him; and if you leave me unprotected, I shall suffer all the rudeness to which his resentment can prompt his tongue'.

Kenneth Young, *John Dryden*, 1954

In 1697, at the request of a society of music-lovers, the Musical Meeting, Dryden wrote an ode for St Cecilia's Day, 'Alexander's Feast':

It was set to music by Jeremiah Clarke and performed with great success by the society; its success in critical circles was equally great. The young man, who later became Lord Chief Justice Marlay, took the opportunity shortly after the poem's appearance to pay his court to the author at Will's [a celebrated coffee-house]. Marlay congratulated Dryden on having produced 'the finest and noblest ode that had ever been written in any language'. To which Dryden, who had already drunk a few 'brimmers', replied: 'You are right, young gentleman, a nobler ode never *was* produced, nor ever *will*'.

Young, *John Dryden*

Kate Meyrick was the nightclub queen of London in the 1920s:

IN 1921 she had founded the famous '43'—at 43 Gerrard Street, where Dryden once lived. In her memoirs, *Secrets of the 43 Club* (1933), Mrs Meyrick wrote: 'I could picture the old poet so clearly sitting at his desk, with sheets of paper strewn around him and more lying about on the floor, his hand clasping his brow in the effort of thought. I could follow the shifting expressions of his long, mobile face with its noble forehead, its neat little Van Dyke beard, and its frame of silky hair, once light brown, now transmuted by age into silver.'

Robert Graves and Alan Hodge, *The Long Week-End*, 1940

KATHERINE PHILIPS · 1631–1664

(poet; the 'Matchless Orinda')

SHE was very religiously devoted when she was young; prayed by herself an hour together, and took sermons verbatim when she was but ten years old.

She was when a child much against the Bishops, and prayed to God to take them to him, but afterwards was reconciled to them.

John Aubrey, *Brief Lives*, late seventeenth century

SAMUEL PEPYS · 1633–1703

Pepys gave up writing his diary in 1669, because of an unfounded fear that he was going blind. It is tantalizing not to have his own intimate account of many episodes in his later life—the highway robbery of which he was a victim, for instance:

ON 29 September 1693, the feast of Michaelmas, Pepys was driven by his coachman out of London and into the country towards the riverside village of Chelsea; they may have been on their way to dine with friends, or simply going to take the air. With him in the coach were some ladies and his nineteen-year-old nephew John, who was sporting a silver-hilted sword. The road ran through meadowland and past isolated farms and a few large villas. When three men on horseback, armed and wearing masks, appeared and put one pistol to the breast of the coachman and another to Pepys, there could be no thought of putting up a fight. The men asked what he had, and he handed over his purse with about £3 in it and the various necessaries he carried with him, his silver ruler, his gold pencil, his magnifying glass and five mathematical instruments. It made an impressive collection, and when he asked to have back one particular instrument he was told that, since he was a gentleman, as his assailant claimed to be also, if he sent to the Rummer Tavern in Charing Cross the following day he should have it. John gave up his sword and hatband. Pepys asked the highwaymen to be civil to the ladies and not to frighten them; and some of the ladies were frightened, but one kept her wits about her: 'My Lady Pepys saved a Bag of Money that she had about her.' So read the law report from which this story comes, because two of the men were tried for the crime at the Old Bailey in December. The men, Thomas Hoyle and Samuel Gibbons, were found guilty partly through the evidence of a witness who saw their faces as they pulled off their masks, and partly because Hoyle was taken at the Rummer Tavern with Pepys's pencil in his possession. Pepys gave evidence at the trial but he would not swear they were the men concerned because he had not seen their faces. Both, however, were found guilty of felony and robbery, condemned to death and hanged. The most quick-witted member of the party seems to have been Mary Skinner—Lady Pepys for the occasion—who managed to keep her money safe under her skirts. She was not asked to be a witness, but she was clearly a force to be reckoned with.

Claire Tomalin, *Samuel Pepys: The Unequalled Self*, 2002

Mary Skinner was Pepys's mistress.

Thomas Traherne · 1637–1674

(poet and visionary; author of *Centuries of Meditations*)

Another time, as he was in bed, he saw a basket come sailing in the air, along by the valance of his bed; I think he said there was fruit in the basket. It was a Phantom.

John Aubrey, *Miscellanies*, 1696

Sir Charles Sedley · 1639–1701

(poet, dramatist, friend of Rochester and Dryden)

Thence by water with Sir W. Batten to Trinity House, there to dine with him, which we did; and after dinner we fell in talking, Sir J. Mennes and Mr Batten [the son of Sir William] and I—Mr Batten telling us of a late trial of Sir Charles Sedley the other day, before my Lord Chief Justice Foster and the whole Bench—for his debauchery a little while since at

Oxford Kate's [an establishment at the sign of the Cock in Bow St]; coming in open day into the balcony and showed his nakedness—acting all the postures of lust and buggery that could be imagined, and abusing of scripture and, as it were, from thence preaching a mountebank sermon from that pulpit, saying that there he hath to sell such a powder as should make all the cunts in town run after him—a thousand people standing underneath to see and hear him.

And that being done, he took a glass of wine and washed his prick in it and then drank it off; and then took another and drank the King's health.

It seems my Lord and the rest of the Judges did all of them round give him a most high reproof—my Lord Chief Justice saying that it was for him and such wicked wretches as he was that God's anger and judgments hung over us—calling him 'Sirrah' many times. It is said they have bound him to his good behaviour (there being no law against him for it) in 5000*l* . . .

Upon this discourse, Sir J. Mennes and Mr Batten both say that buggery is now grown almost as common among our gallants as in Italy, and that the very pages of the town begin to complain of their masters for it. But blessed be God, I do not to this day know what is the meaning of this sin, nor which is the agent nor which the patient.

Samuel Pepys, *Diary*, ed. Robert Latham and William Matthews, 1971; entry for 1 July 1663

John Wilmot, Earl of Rochester · 1647–1680

For his other studies, they were divided between the comical and witty writings of the Ancients and Moderns, the Roman authors, and books of physic; which the ill state of health he was fallen into made more necessary to himself: and which qualified him for an odd adventure, which I shall but just mention. Being under an unlucky accident, which obliged him to keep out of the way, he disguised himself, so that his nearest friends could not have known him, and set up in Tower Street for an Italian mountebank, where he had a stage and practised physic for some weeks, not without success.

Gilbert Burnet, *Some Passages of the Life and Death of the Right Honourable John Earl of Rochester*, 1680

Once the wild Earl of Rochester, and some of his companions, a little way from Woodstock, meeting in the morning with a fine young maid going with butter to market, they bought all the butter of her, and paid her for it, and afterwards stuck it up against a tree, which the maid perceiving, after they were gone, she went and took it off, thinking it pity that it should be quite spoiled. They observed her, and riding after her, soon overtook her, and as a punishment, set her upon her head, and clapped the butter upon her breech.

Thomas Hearne, *Remarks and Collections*, note made in 1725

LAST night also, Du Puis, a French cook in the Mall, was stabbed for some pert answer to one Mr Floyd, and because my Lord Rochester and my Lord Lumley were supping in the same house, though in both different rooms and companies, the good nature of the town reported it all this day that his Lordship was the stabber. He desired me therefore to write to you to stop that report from going northward, for he says if it once get as far as York the truth will not be believed under one or two years.

Henry Savile, letter to Viscount Halifax, May 1677

DANIEL DEFOE · 1660–1731

In the 1690s Defoe established a factory at Tilbury in Essex making bricks and tiles:

ACCORDING to his own statement he was at one time employing no less than a hundred poor families on his brickfields, and making a profit of £600 per annum. Mr William Lee, one of his nineteenth-century biographers, made a special excursion down to Tilbury in 1860 to see whether the excavations which were then being made for the new railway had laid bare any of Defoe's handiwork. They had:

Large quantities of bricks and tiles had been excavated, and thrown into heaps, to clear the land for its intended purpose. The pantiles appeared to have attracted very little notice; but the narrowness of the bricks, and the peculiar forms of certain tobacco-pipes, found mixed with both, had excited some little wonderment among the labourers. I asked several how they thought these things came there, and was answered by an ignorant shake of the head. But when I said, 'These bricks and tiles were made 160 years since by the same man that made "Robinson Crusoe"!' I touched a chord that connected these railway 'navvies' with the shipwrecked mariner, and that bounded over the intervening period in a single moment. Every eye brightened, every tongue was ready to ask or give information, and every fragment became interesting. Porters, inspector, and stationmaster soon gathered round me, wondering at what was deemed an important historical revelation.

James Sutherland, *Defoe*, 1937; the quotation is from William Lee, *Daniel Defoe*, 1869

MATTHEW PRIOR · 1664–1721

(poet and diplomat)

Prior was sent to Paris in 1711 to help conduct the negotiations which led to the Treaty of Utrecht:

DURING his embassy, he sat at the opera by a man, who, in his rapture, accompanied with his own voice the principal singer. Prior fell to railing at the performer with all the terms of reproach that he could collect, till the Frenchman, ceasing from his song, began to expostulate with him for his harsh censure of a man who was confessedly the ornament of the stage. 'I know all that,' says the ambassador, '*mais il chante si haut, que je ne sçaurois vous entendre*' ['but he sings so loudly that I couldn't hear you'].

Samuel Johnson, *Lives of the Poets*, 1779–81

JONATHAN SWIFT · 1667–1745

I NEVER wake without finding life a more insignificant thing than it was the day before . . . I remember when I was a little boy, I felt a great fish at the end of my line which I drew up almost on the ground, but it dropped in, and the disappointment vexeth me to this very day, and I believe it was the type of all my future disappointments.

Letter to Lord Bolingbroke, 1729

Between 1701 and 1709 Swift spent part of the year in the small Irish parish of Laracor:

HIS Sunday services seldom drew more than a dozen persons, and the prayer-meetings could only depend on a congregation of one, his clerk and bell-ringer Roger Cox. It is recorded that at the first of these he commenced the exhortation: 'Dearly beloved Roger, the Scripture moveth you and me in sundry places . . .'

Hesketh Pearson, *Lives of the Wits*, 1962

Roger Cox was a genial personality, who enjoyed bringing out the more genial side of Swift himself. He wrote verses, including a poem about a wedding in Laracor:

The Doctor smiled upon you both;
I love to see the Doctor smile,
For it's the sunshine of our isle . . .

A MARRIAGE held not in a church, and without banns, or witnesses, or a ring, or a licence, or registration, was perfectly legal. Swift is believed to have conducted at least one such marriage himself, on one of his journeys between London and Chester, and to have issued this rhyming marriage certificate:

Under an oak, in stormy weather,
I join'd this rogue and whore together;
And none but he who rules the thunder
Can put this whore and rogue asunder.

Victoria Glendinning, *Jonathan Swift*, 1998

DR SWIFT has an odd, blunt way that is mistaken by strangers for ill-nature. 'Tis so odd that there's no describing it but by facts. I'll tell you one that first comes into my head.

One evening Gay and I went to see him; you know how intimately we are all acquainted. On our coming in, 'Hey-day, gentlemen,' says the Doctor, 'what's the meaning of this visit? How come you to leave all the great lords that you are so fond of to come hither to see a poor dean?'

Because we would rather see you than any of them.

'Aye, anyone that did not know you so well as I do might believe you. But since you are come I must get some supper for you, I suppose.'

No, Doctor, we have supped already.

'Supped already! That's impossible—why, 'tis not eight o'clock yet.'

Indeed we have.

'That's very strange. But if you had not supped I must have got something for you. Let me see, what should I have had? A couple of lobsters? Aye, that would have done very well—two shillings. Tarts—a shilling. But you will drink a glass of wine with me, though you supped so much before your usual time, only to spare my pocket?'

No, we had rather talk with you than drink with you.

'But if you had supped with me as in all reason you ought to have done, you must then have drank with me: a bottle of wine—two shillings. Two and two is four, and one is five: just two and sixpence a piece. There, Pope, there's half a crown for you, and there's another for you, Sir, for I won't save anything by you. I am determined.'

This was all said and done with his usual seriousness on such occasions, and in spite of everything we could say to the contrary, he actually obliged us to take the money.

Alexander Pope in Joseph Spence, *Observations, Anecdotes, and Characters of Books and Men*; first published 1820, ed. James M. Osborn, 1966

Laetitia Pilkington (1709–50) was a friend of Swift's during his later years in Dublin. She admired him and learned from him, but her remarkable

Memoirs *make it clear that he was 'a very rough sort of tutor'—'for whenever I made use of an inelegant phrase, I was sure of a deadly pinch, and frequently received chastisement before I knew my crime'.*

SHE tells even more curious stories. Dining at Delany's house one Christmas, Swift set the wine before a hot fire, which melted the pitch and resin that sealed the corks. Swift rubbed his fingers in the black sticky mess and smeared it on Laetitia's face. She merely told him he did her great honour in 'sealing me for his own'. Determined to get a reaction out of her, he asked the company if they had ever seen 'such a dwarf', and insisted she take off her shoes ('Why, I expected you had either broken stockings or foul toes, and in either case should have delighted to have exposed you') and stand against the wainscot. He pressed his hand down hard on her head until she half-crumpled, 'then making a mark with a pencil, he affirmed I was but three feet two inches high'. Laetitia was unable to eat her dinner. She was pregnant at the time.

Laetitia also recalls Swift summoning her to the Deanery very early one morning, and after two hours' badinage but no breakfast instructing her to open a low drawer in his cabinet and take from it a flat bottle containing rum. She knelt down and tried to open the drawer,

> but he flew at me, and beat me most immoderately; I again made an effort, and still he beat me, crying: 'Pox take you! *open* the drawer!' I once more tried, and he struck me so hard that I burst into tears, and said: 'Lord, sir, what must I do?' 'Pox take you for a slut!' said he; 'would you spoil my lock, and break my key.' 'Why, sir, the drawer is locked.' 'Oh! I beg your pardon', said he. 'I thought you were going to pull it out by the key: well, open it and do what I bid you.'

Laetitia found the flat bottle. Swift produced a piece of gingerbread and tried to make her eat some. He always breakfasted between the Deanery and the cathedral, he said, 'and I carry my provision in my pocket'. As the pregnant Laetitia was 'terribly afflicted with the heartburn', she declined, but he insisted; also that she took a sup from the bottle. She held it to her mouth, pretending to drink. He then 'threw me down, forced the bottle into my mouth, poured some of the liquor down my throat, which I thought would have set my very stomach on fire'.

'He then gravely went to prayers'—presumably munching on his gingerbread—'and I returned home, not greatly delighted, but, however, glad to have come off no worse.' Laetitia is writing of events a quarter of a century earlier. Yet the very pettiness and inconsequentiality of the scenes she describes lend them verisimilitude. (The cabinet is still in the Deanery. The one lockable drawer is the bottom left-hand one.)

Glendinning, *Jonathan Swift*

EVEN the broad-minded Mrs Pilkington remarked that 'with all the reverence I have for the Dean, I really think he sometimes chose subjects unworthy of his Muse, and which could serve for no other end except that of turning the reader's stomach, as it did my mother's, who, upon reading the "Lady's Dressing Room", instantly threw up her dinner'.

Glendinning, *Jonathan Swift*

ONE day in mid-March 1744, as Swift sat in his chair, he reached towards a knife, but Mrs Ridgeway [his housekeeper] moved it away from him. He shrugged his shoulders, rocked himself, and said, 'I am what I am, I am what I am'; some minutes later he repeated the same thing two or three times. About a fortnight afterwards, he tried to speak to his servant, whom he sometimes called by name. Not finding words to tell him what he meant, he showed some uneasiness and said, 'I am a fool'—his last recorded words.

Irvin Ehrenpreis, *The Personality of Jonathan Swift*, 1958

WILLIAM CONGREVE · 1670–1729

BUT he treated the Muses with ingratitude; for, having long conversed familiarly with the great, he wished to be considered rather as a man of fashion than of wit; and, when he received a visit from Voltaire, disgusted him by the despicable foppery of desiring to be considered not as an author but a gentleman; to which the Frenchman replied, 'that if he had been only a gentleman, he should not have come to visit him.'

Samuel Johnson, *Lives of the Poets*, 1779–81

In his last years Congreve became closely involved with Henrietta, second Duchess of Marlborough. He left her the bulk of his estate, money which Dr Johnson says ought to have gone to members of the Congreve family, which was then in distress. The Duchess reciprocated by arranging for him to be buried and commemorated in a spectacular fashion:

THE great lady buried her friend with a pomp seldom seen at the funerals of poets. The corpse lay in state under the ancient roof of the Jerusalem Chamber, and was interred in Westminster Abbey. The pall was borne by the Duke of Bridgewater, Lord Cobham, the Earl of Wilmington, who had been Speaker, and was afterwards First Lord of the Treasury, and other men of high consideration. Her Grace laid out her friend's bequest in a superb diamond necklace, which she wore in honour of him, and, if report is to be believed, showed her regard in ways much more extraordinary. It is said that a statue of him in ivory, which moved by clockwork, was placed daily at her table, that she had a wax doll made in imitation of him, and that the feet of the doll were regularly blistered and anointed by the doctors, as poor Congreve's feet had been when he suffered from the gout.

Lord Macaulay, 'Comic Dramatists of the Restoration', 1841

Colley Cibber · 1671–1757

(Poet Laureate; actor, playwright, and joint manager of the Theatre Royal, Drury Lane)

Colley Cibber, they say, was extremely haughty as a theatrical manager, and very insolent to dramatists. When he had rejected a play, if the author desired him to point out the particular parts of it which displeased him, he took a pinch of snuff, and answered in general terms—'Sir, there is nothing in it *to coerce my passions*.'

George Colman the Younger, *Random Records*, 1830

Joseph Addison · 1672–1719

Dr Johnson relates that at Mr Addison's birth he appeared so weak and unlikely to live, that he was christened the same day; but Mr Tyers goes still further, and says that he was actually laid out for dead as soon as he was born.

Addisoniana, 1803

One slight lineament of his character Swift has preserved. It was his practice when he found any man invincibly wrong, to flatter his opinions by acquiescence, and sink him yet deeper in absurdity. This artifice of mischief was admired by Stella; and Swift seems to approve her admiration.

Samuel Johnson, *Lives of the Poets*, 1779–81

Mr Collins of Magd. Coll. tells me that Mr Joseph Addison of their college (who was afterwards Secretary of State) used to please himself mightily with this prologue to a puppet-show—

A certain king said to a beggar,
What hast to eat? Beans, quoth the beggar.
Beans? quoth the king. Yea, beans, I say;
And so forthwith we straight begin the play.
Strike up, player.

Thomas Hearne (1678–1735), *Reliquiae Hearnianae*, first published 1857

AFTER a long and manly, but vain, struggle with his distemper, he dismissed his physicians, and, with them, all hopes of life; but with his hopes of life he dismissed not his concern for the living, but sent for a youth nearly related (the earl of Warwick), and finely accomplished, but not above being the better for good impressions from a dying friend. He came; but, life now glimmering in the socket, Addison was silent: after a decent and proper pause, the youth said, 'Dear Sir, you sent for me; I believe, and I hope, you have some commands; I shall hold them most sacred.' May distant ages not only hear, but feel the reply! Forcibly grasping the earl's hand, he softly said, 'See in what peace a *Christian* can die!'

Edward Young, quoted in *Addisoniana*, 1803

SIR RICHARD STEELE · 1672–1729

BISHOP Hoadley was once invited, and was present, when bishop of Bangor, at one of the whig meetings at the Trumpet in Sheer-lane, where Steele rather exposed himself in his zeal, having the double duty of the day upon him, as well to celebrate the immortal memory of king William, it being the 4th of November, as to unite in company with a party of private friends, so soon as this commemoration was over.

John Sly, the hatter, of facetious memory, was in the house; and when pretty mellow, took it into his head to come into the company on his knees, with a tankard of ale in his hand, to drink it off to the immortal memory, and to retire in the same manner. Steele whispered to the bishop, who sat next him, 'Do laugh; 'tis humanity to laugh.'

Addisoniana, 1803

HENRY ST JOHN, VISCOUNT BOLINGBROKE · 1678–1751

(statesman and political thinker; author of *The Idea of a Patriot King*)

THE Bishop of Peterborough said he saw an odd scene once. The famous Lord Bolingbroke had invited many of the young French nobility to partake of an English dish—a shoulder of mutton baked upon onions—which was to be the admiration of all Paris for excellence; and his maître d'hôtel, a Scotchman, had undertaken to prepare it properly. It was not eatable, however, being spoiled in the dressing, so that St John leaped up in a rage from the table, and fell to beating the maître d'hôtel with it. When he had exhausted his breath with passion and exclamation, his countryman Lord Chesterfield calls out from the other end of the table, in a steady voice—

Nobly done, philosopher!

'I thank you most heartily,' replied the other, and in a transport of passion not unequal to that just over, dropped down on his knees, and formally asked pardon of the company.

Hester Thrale, *Thraliana*, entry for 5 June 1779

Alexander Pope · 1688–1744

In 1715 Lady Mary Wortley Montagu wrote three satirical poems, mock-pastorals in which she lampooned friends and associates of the Prince and Princess of Wales. They circulated in manuscript; the bookseller Edmund Curll got hold of them and published them as Court Poems, *with a preface implying that they were the work of Pope (or possibly his friend John Gay):*

Curll issued the volume on 26 March 1716. Two days later, while visiting Lintot's shop on a matter of business, where he also found Pope, he is said to have been first roundly scolded by the poet for this knavery and then, in what purported to be a peace-making 'Glass of Sack', given some sort of violent emetic. Or, as Pope put it laconically in a letter to Caryll: 'I contrived to save the fellow a beating by giving him a vomit.'

Maynard Mack, *Alexander Pope*, 1985

The *Iliad* took me up six years, and during that time, and particularly the first part of it, I was often under great pain and apprehensions. Though I conquered the thoughts of it in the day, they would frighten me in the night. I dreamed often of being engaged in a long journey and that I should never get to the end of it. This made so strong an impression upon me that I sometimes dream of it still: of being engaged in that translation and got about half way through it, and being embarrassed and under dreads of never completing it.

Pope in Joseph Spence, *Observations, Anecdotes, and Characters of Books and Men*; first published 1820, ed. James M. Osborn, 1966

The famous Lord Halifax was rather a pretender to taste than really possessed of it. When I had finished the two or three first books of my translation of the *Iliad*, that Lord 'desired to have the pleasure of hearing them read at his house'. Addison, Congreve, and Garth were there at the reading. In four or five places Lord Halifax stopped me very civilly, and with a speech each time of much the same kind: 'I beg your pardon, Mr Pope, but there is something in that passage that does not quite please me. Be so good as to mark the place and consider it a little at your leisure. I'm sure you can give it a better turn.'

I returned from Lord Halifax's with Dr Garth in his chariot, and as we were going along was saying to the Doctor that my Lord had laid me under a good deal of difficulty by such loose and general observations; that I had been thinking over the passages almost ever since, and could not guess at what it was that offended his lordship in either of them. Garth laughed heartily at my embarrassment, said I had not been long enough acquainted with Lord Halifax to know his way yet, that I need not puzzle myself in looking those places over and over when I got home. 'All you need do', says he, 'is to leave them just as they are, call on Lord Halifax two or three months hence, thank him for his kind observation on those passages, and then read them to him as altered. I have known him much longer than you have, and will be answerable for the event.'

I followed his advice, waited on Lord Halifax some time after, said 'I hoped he would find his objections to those passages removed,' read them to him exactly as they were at first, and his lordship was extremely pleased with them and cried out: 'Ay, now they are perfectly right! Nothing can be better.'

Spence, *Observations*

WHEN he wanted to sleep he *nodded in company*; and once slumbered at his own table while the Prince of Wales was talking of poetry.

Samuel Johnson, *Lives of the Poets*, 1779–81

The best known of Pope's dogs was Bounce (described by Joseph Spence as 'a great faithful Danish dog'), who accompanied him on his solitary walks—especially when he was threatened by people who had been lampooned in the Dunciad. *According to the poet's half-sister, Mrs Rackett,*

WHEN my brother's faithful dog, and companion in these walks, died, he had some thoughts of burying him in his garden and putting a piece of marble over his grave, with the epitaph: O RARE BOUNCE! And he would have done it, I believe, had not he apprehended that some people might take it to have been meant as a ridicule of Ben Jonson.

Spence, *Observations*

I SEND you a very odd thing, a paper printed in Boston in New England, wherein you'll find a real person, a member of their Parliament, of the name of Jonathan Gulliver. If the fame of that Traveller has travelled thither, it has travelled very quick, to have folks christened already by the name of the supposed Author. But if you object, that no child so lately christened could be arrived at years of maturity to be elected into Parliament, I reply (to solve the Riddle) that the person is an *Anabaptist*, and not christened till full age, which sets all right. However it be, the accident is very singular, that these two names should be united.

Pope, letter to Jonathan Swift, March 1727

Gulliver's Travels *was published in 1726.*

IT was reported, with such confidence as almost to enforce belief, that in the papers entrusted to his executors was found a defamatory Life of Swift, which he had prepared as an instrument of vengance to be used, if any provocation should be ever given. About this I enquired of the Earl of Marchmont, who assured me that no such piece was among his remains.

Samuel Johnson, *Lives of the Poets*, 1779–81

LADY MARY WORTLEY MONTAGU · 1689–1762

(celebrated letter writer; wit; minor poet; friend and then enemy of Alexander Pope; champion of inoculation)

Lady Mary accompanied her husband when he was sent as ambassador to Constantinople:

ONE of the highest entertainments in Turkey is having you to their baths. When I was introduced to one, the lady of the house came to undress me, which is another high compliment that they pay to strangers. After she had slipped off my gown, and saw my stays, she was very much struck at the sight of them and cried out to the other ladies in the bath: 'Come hither, and see how cruelly the poor English ladies are used by their husbands. You need boast indeed of the superior liberties allowed you, when they lock you up thus in a box!'

Quoted by Joseph Spence, *Observations, Anecdotes, and Characters of Books and Men*; first published 1820, ed. James M. Osborn, 1966

AND now I must tell you a little story about Lady Mary which I heard lately. Upon her travels (to save charges), she got a passage in the Mediterranean, on board a Man of War, I think it was Commodore Barnet. When he had landed her safe she told him, she knew she was not to offer him money, but entreated him to accept of a ring in memory of her, which (as she pressed him) he accepted: it was a very large emerald. Some time after, a friend of his taking notice of its beauty, he told him how he came by it; the man smiled, and desired him to show it to a jeweller. He did so; it was unset before him and proved a paste worth 40 shillings.

Thomas Gray, letter to James Brown, 1761

Samuel Richardson · 1689–1761

Richardson had a kind of club of women about him—Mrs Carter, Mrs Talbot, etc.—who looked up to him as to a superior being; to whom he dictated and gave laws; and with whom he lived almost entirely. To acquire a facility of epistolary writing he would on every trivial occasion write notes to his daughters even when they were in the same house with him.

James Prior, *Life of Edmond Malone*, 1860; 'Maloniana'

The extreme delight which he felt on a review [revision] of his own works, the works themselves witness. Each is an evidence of what some will deem a violent literary vanity. To *Pamela* is prefixed a letter from the editor (whom we know to be the *author*) consisting of one of the most minutely laboured panegyrics of the work itself, that ever the blindest idolater of some ancient classic paid to the object of his frenetic imagination. To the author's own edition of his *Clarissa* is appended an alphabetical arrangement of the sentiments dispersed throughout the work; and such was the fondness that dictated this voluminous arrangement, that such trivial aphorisms as, 'habits are not easily changed,' 'men are known by their companions,' etc. seem alike to be the object of their author's admiration. And in *Sir Charles Grandison*, is not only prefixed a complete *index*, with as much exactness as if it were a History of England, but there is also appended a list of the similes and allusions in the volume.

Literary history does not record a more singular example of that self-delight which an author has felt on a revision of his works. It was this intense pleasure which produced his voluminous labours.

Isaac D'Israeli, *Curiosities of Literature*, 1791–1823

Lord Chesterfield · 1694–1773

In the 1730s Chesterfield was active in parliamentary opposition to Sir Robert Walpole:

The late Lord Raymond, with many good qualities and even learning and parts, had a strong desire of being thought skillful in physic, and was very expert in bleeding. Lord Chesterfield who knew his foible, and on a particular occasion wished to have his vote, came to him one morning, and, after having conversed upon indifferent matters, complained of the headache and desired his lordship to feel his pulse. It was found to beat high, and a hint of losing blood given. 'I have no objection, and as I hear your lordship has a masterly hand, will you favour me with trying your lancet upon me?' 'A propos,' said Lord Chesterfield, after the operation, 'do you go to the House today?' Lord Raymond answered, 'I did not intend to go, not being sufficiently informed of the question which is to be debated; but you who have considered it, which side will you be of?' The earl, having gained his confidence, easily directed his judgment; he carried him to the House, and got him to vote as he pleased. He used afterwards to say that none of his friends had done as much as he, having literally bled for the good of his country.

Dr Maty, *Memoirs of Lord Chesterfield*, 1778

THE late Lord Chesterfield's *bons mots* were all studied. Dr Warren, who attended him for some months before his death, told me that he had always *one* ready for him each visit, but never gave him a second on the same day.

James Prior, *Life of Edmond Malone*, 1860; 'Maloniana'

LORD CHESTERFIELD had retained his memory and his presence of mind to his latest breath. Mr Dayrolles having come to pay him his usual visit only about half an hour before he expired, the earl had just strength enough to say in a faint voice: 'Give Dayrolles a chair.' These were the last words he was heard to speak. 'His good breeding,' said Dr Warren, who was present, 'only quits him with his life.'

Maty, *Memoirs of Lord Chesterfield*

Solomon Dayrolles was one of Chesterfield's closest friends.

Towards the end of his life, when he was asked how his contemporary Lord Tyrawley was faring, Chesterfield replied, 'To tell you the truth, we have both been dead this twelve-month, but we do not own it.'

Literary influence can exert itself in strange ways. In 1924 a young girl called Catherine McMullen, who worked in the laundry in a workhouse on Tyneside, came across a reference to Chesterfield's letters to his son in a romantic novel by Elinor Glyn. The working-class heroine of the novel had been recommended to read them as part of a programme of self-education:

FOR Catherine McMullen it was the equivalent of being struck down by the blinding light of revelation on the road to Damascus. 'When I read this story . . . my desires, my craving to be different were compressed into a simple fact. I, too, wanted to be a lady.' At the earliest opportunity she went down to South Shields library and borrowed the letters of Lord Chesterfield. It was a simple act that was to change her life. Lord Chesterfield spoke directly to her. 'If you improve and grow learned everyone will be fond of you, and desirous of your company.' He was a father writing to his illegitimate child about self-improvement and education and the letters became the basis of Catherine's own education—'I would fall asleep reading the letters and awake round three o'clock in the morning my mind deep in the fascination of this new world, where people conversed, not just talked. Where the brilliance of words made your heart beat faster.' She read so much that she was often late for work and her eyes became sore. But the letters answered her deepest desire and throughout her life Lord Chesterfield remained her mentor; the tattered volumes were as often consulted as the Bible.

Catherine McMullen later achieved fame as the novelist Catherine Cookson. The passage quoted is from Kathleen Jones, Catherine Cookson: The Biography, *1999.*

James Thomson · 1700–1748

(poet; author of *The Seasons*)

Among his peculiarities was a very unskilful and inarticulate manner of pronouncing any lofty or solemn composition. He was once reading to Doddington, who being himself a reader eminently elegant, was so much provoked by his odd utterance that he snatched the paper from his hand, and told him that he did not understand his own verses.

Samuel Johnson, *Lives of the Poets*, 1779–81

Henry Fielding · 1707–1754

In 1754 Fielding set out for Portugal in the hope of improving his health. It was not to be. He died in Lisbon shortly after completing his account of the voyage, from which the following episode comes:

A most tragical incident fell out this day at sea. While the ship was under sail, but making, as will appear, no great way, a kitten, one of four of the feline inhabitants of the cabin, fell from the window into the water: an alarm was immediately given to the captain, who was then upon deck, and received it with the utmost concern. He immediately gave orders to the steersman in favour of the poor thing, as he called it; the sails were instantly slackened, and all hands, as the phrase is, employed to recover the poor animal. I was, I own, extremely surprised at all this; less, indeed, at the captain's extreme tenderness than at his conceiving any possibility of success; for, if puss had had nine thousand, instead of nine lives, I concluded they had been all lost. The boatswain, however, had more sanguine hopes; for, having stript himself of his jacket, breeches, and shirt, he leapt boldly into the water, and, to my great astonishment, in a few minutes, returned to the ship, bearing the motionless animal in his mouth. Nor was this, I observed, a matter of such great difficulty as it appeared to my ignorance, and possibly may seem to that of my fresh-water reader: the kitten was now exposed to air and sun on the deck, where its life, of which it retained no symptoms, was despaired of by all.

The captain's humanity, if I may so call it, did not so totally destroy his philosophy, as to make him yield himself up to affliction on this melancholy occasion. Having felt his loss like a man, he resolved to shew he could bear it like one; and, having declared, he had rather have lost a cask of rum or brandy, betook himself to threshing at backgammon with the Portuguese friar, in which innocent amusement they passed their leisure hours.

But as I have, perhaps, a little too wantonly endeavoured to raise the tender passions of my readers, in this narrative, I should think myself unpardonable if I concluded it, without giving them the satisfaction of hearing that the kitten at last recovered, to the great joy of the good captain.

The Journal of a Voyage to Lisbon, 1755

Samuel Johnson · 1709–1784

One day when my son was going to school, and dear Dr Johnson followed as far as the garden gate, praying for his salvation, in a voice which those who listened attentively could hear plain enough, he said to me suddenly, 'Make your boy tell you his dreams: the first corruption that entered into my heart was communicated in a dream.' What was it, Sir? said I. '*Do* not ask me,' replied he with much violence, and walked away in apparent agitation.

Hester Lynch Piozzi, *Anecdotes of the Late Samuel Johnson*, 1786

He called to us with a sudden air of exultation, as the thought darted into his mind, 'O! Gentlemen, I must tell you a very great thing. The Empress of Russia has ordered the *Rambler* to be translated into the Russian language: so I shall be read on the banks of the Wolga. Horace boasts that his fame would extend as far as the banks of the Rhone; now the Wolga is farther from me than the Rhone was from Horace.' Boswell: 'You must be pleased with this, Sir.' Johnson: 'I am pleased, Sir, to be sure.' I have since heard that the report was not well founded; but the elation discovered by Johnson in the belief that it was true, shewed a noble ardour for literary fame.

James Boswell, *Life of Johnson*, 1791

THE first time I was in company with Dr Johnson I remember the impression I felt in his favour, on his saying that as he returned to his lodgings about one or two o'clock in the morning, he often saw poor children asleep in thresholds and stalls, and that he used to put pennies into their hands to buy them a breakfast.

Frances Reynolds, 'Recollections of Dr Johnson', in *Johnsonian Miscellanies*, ed. G. Birkbeck Hill, 1897

A YOUNG fellow, lamenting one day that he had lost all his Greek—'I believe it happened at the same time, Sir (said Johnson), that I lost all my large estate in Yorkshire.'

Piozzi, *Anecdotes*

HE proceeded: 'Demosthenes Taylor, as he was called (that is, the editor of Demosthenes), was the most silent man, the merest statue of a man that I have ever seen. I once dined in company with him, and all he said during the whole time was no more than *Richard*. How a man should say only Richard, it is not easy to imagine. But it was thus: Dr Douglas was talking of Dr Zachary Grey, and was ascribing to him something that was written by Dr Richard Grey. So, to correct him, Taylor said (imitating his affected sententious emphasis and nod), *"Richard."*'

Boswell, *Life of Johnson*

ON the night before the publication of the first edition of his Shakespeare, he supped with some friends in the Temple, who kept him up, 'nothing loth', till past five the next morning. Much pleasantry was passing on the subject of commentatorship; when, all of a sudden, the Doctor, looking at his watch, cried out: 'This is sport to you, gentlemen; but you do not consider there are at most only four hours between me and criticism.'

George Steevens, 'Anecdotes'; in *Johnsonian Miscellanies*

JOHNSON having argued for some time with a pertinacious gentleman, his opponent, who had talked in a very puzzling manner, happened to say, 'I don't understand you, sir'; upon which Johnson observed, 'Sir, I have found you an argument, but I am not obliged to find you an understanding.'

Boswell, *Life of Johnson*

MISS JOHNSON, one of Sir Joshua's nieces (afterwards Mrs Deane), was dining one day at her uncle's with Dr Johnson and a large party: the conversation happening to turn on music, Johnson spoke very contemptuously of that art, and added, 'that no man of talent, or whose mind was capable of better things, ever would or could devote his time and attention to so idle and frivolous a pursuit.' The young lady, who was very fond of music, whispered her next neighbour, 'I wonder what Dr Johnson thinks of King David.' Johnson overheard her, and, with great good humour and complacency, said, 'Madam, I thank you; I stand rebuked before you, and promise that, on one subject at least, you shall never hear me talk nonsense again.'

From J. W. Croker's edition of Boswell, in *Johnsonian Miscellanies*

MR BOSWELL has mentioned in his *Journal of a Tour to the Hebrides*, that Johnson once met with an Italian in London who did not know who was the author of the Lord's Prayer. The Italian, whom Mr Boswell out of tenderness forbore to name, was Baretti. As I walked home with him from Mr Courtenay's, he mentioned that the story as told gave an unfair representation of him. The fact he said was this. In a conversation with Dr Johnson concerning the Lord's Prayer, Baretti observed (profanely enough) that the petition, *lead us not into temptation*, ought rather to be addressed to the tempter of mankind than a benevolent Creator who delighted in the happiness of his creatures. 'Pray, sir,' said Johnson (who could not bear that any part of our holy religion should be spoken lightly of), 'do you know who was the author of the Lord's Prayer?' Baretti (who did not wish to get into any serious dispute, and who appears to be an Infidel), by way of putting an end to the conversation, only replied,—'Oh, sir, you know by *our* religion (Roman Catholic), we are not permitted to read the Scriptures. You can't therefore expect an answer.'

James Prior, *Life of Edmond Malone*, 1860; 'Maloniana'

SOMEBODY said the life of a mere literary man could not be very entertaining. JOHNSON: 'But it certainly may. This is a remark which has been made, and repeated, without justice; why should the life of a literary man be less entertaining than the life of any other man? Are there not as interesting varieties in such a life? As *a literary life* it may be very entertaining.' BOSWELL: 'But it must be better, surely, when it is diversified with a little active variety—such as his having gone to Jamaica; or—his having gone to the Hebrides.' Johnson was not displeased at this.

Boswell, *Life of Johnson*

IN early youth I knew Bennet Langton, *of that ilk*, as the Scotch say. With great personal claims to the respect of the public, he is known to that public chiefly as a friend of Johnson. He was a very tall, meagre, long-visaged man, much resembling, according to Richard Paget, a stork standing on one leg, near the shore, in Raphael's cartoon of the miraculous draught of fishes. His manners were in the highest degree polished; his conversation mild, equable, and always pleasing. He had the uncommon faculty of being a good reader. I formed an intimacy with his son, and went to pay him a visit at Langton. After breakfast we walked to the top of a very steep hill behind the house. When we arrived at the summit, Mr Langton said, 'Poor, dear Dr Johnson, when he came to this spot, turned to look down the hill, and said he was determined "to take a roll down." When we understood what he meant to do, we endeavoured to dissuade him; but he was resolute, saying, he had not had a roll for a long time; and taking out of his lesser pockets whatever might be in them—keys, pencil, purse, or pen-knife, and laying himself parallel with the edge of the hill, he actually descended, turning himself over and over till he came to the bottom.'

Henry Digby Beste, *Personal and Literary Memorials*, 1829; in *Johnsonian Miscellanies*

ONCE when somebody produced a newspaper in which there was a letter of stupid abuse of Sir Joshua Reynolds, of which Johnson himself came in for a share,—'Pray (said he), let us have it read aloud from beginning to end'; which being done, he with a ludicrous earnestness, and not directing his look to any particular person, called out, 'Are we alive after all this satire?'

Boswell, *Life of Johnson*

NOR could he patiently endure to hear that such respect as he thought due only to higher intellectual qualities, should be bestowed on men of slighter, though perhaps more amusing, talents. I told him that one morning when I went to breakfast with Garrick, who was very vain of his intimacy with Lord Camden, he accosted me thus: 'Pray now, did you—did you meet a little lawyer turning the corner, eh?' 'No, sir (said I). Pray what do you mean by the question?' 'Why (replied Garrick, with an affected indifference, yet as if standing on tip-toe), Lord Camden has this moment left me. We have had a long walk together.' JOHNSON: 'Well, sir, Garrick talked very properly. Lord Camden *was* a *little lawyer* to be associating so familiarly with a player.'

Boswell, *Life of Johnson*, 1791

SOON after Garrick's purchase at Hampton Court he was showing Dr Johnson the grounds, the house, Shakespeare's Temple etc.; and concluded by asking him, 'Well, Doctor, how do you like all this?' 'Why, it is pleasant enough,' growled the Doctor, 'for the present; but all these things, David, make death very terrible.'

William Cooke, *Memoirs of Samuel Foote*, 1805

DR MUDGE used to relate, as a proof of Dr Johnson's quick discernment into character:—When he was on a visit to Dr Mudge at Plymouth, the inhabitants of the Dock (now Devonport) were very desirous of their town being supplied with water, to effect which it was necessary to obtain the consent of the corporation of Plymouth; this was obstinately refused, the Dock being considered as an upstart. And a rival, Alderman Tolcher, who took a very strong part, called one morning, and immediately opened on the subject to Dr Johnson, who appeared to give great attention, and when the alderman had ceased talking, replied, 'You are perfectly right, Sir; I would let the rogues die of thirst, for I hate a Docker from my heart.' The old man went away quite delighted, and told all his acquaintances how completely 'the great Dr Johnson was on his side of the question'.

Mrs Rose, quoted in J. W. Croker's edition of Boswell and in *Johnsonian Miscellanies*

HIS knowledge in manufactures was extensive, and his comprehension relative to mechanical contrivances was still more extraordinary. The well-known Mr Arkwright pronounced him to be the only person who, on a first view, understood both the principle and the powers of his most complicated piece of machinery.

George Steevens, 'Anecdotes', in *Johnsonian Miscellanies*

10TH. This day at noon I saw him again. He said to me, that the male nurse to whose care I had committed him, was unfit for the office. 'He is,' said he, 'an idiot, as awkward as a turnspit just put into the wheel, and as sleepy as a dormouse.'

Sir John Hawkins, *Life of Samuel Johnson*, 1787

This was three days before Johnson died.

DAVID HUME · 1711–1776

ON Sunday forenoon the 7 of July 1776, being too late for church, I went to see Mr David Hume, who was returned from London and Bath, just a-dying. I found him alone, in a reclining posture in his drawing-room. He was lean, ghastly and quite of an earthy appearance. He was dressed in a suit of grey cloth with white metal buttons, and a kind of scratch wig. He was quite different from the plump figure which he used to present. He had before him Dr Campbell's *Philosophy of Rhetoric*. He seemed to be placid and even cheerful. He said he was just approaching to his end. I think these were his words . . .

I had a strong curiosity to be satisfied if he persisted in disbelieving a future state even when he had death before his eyes. I was persuaded from what he now said, and from his manner of saying it, that he did persist. I asked him if it was not possible that there might be a future state. He answered it was possible that a piece of coal put upon the fire would not burn; and he added that it was a most unreasonable fancy that we should exist for ever. That immortality, if it were at all, must be general; that a great proportion of the human race has hardly any intellectual qualities; that a great proportion dies in infancy before being possessed of reason; yet all these must be immortal; that a porter who gets drunk by ten o'clock with gin must be immortal; that the trash of every age must be preserved, and that new universes must be created to contain such infinite numbers. This appeared to me an unphilosophical objection, and I said, 'Mr Hume, you know spirit does not take up space.'

James Boswell, Journal, July 1776

Laurence Sterne · 1713–1768

Sterne recalls an incident during his schooldays in Yorkshire:

My master had the ceiling of the schoolroom new whitewashed; the ladder remained there. I, one unlucky day, mounted it and wrote with a brush, in large capital letters, LAU. STERNE, for which the usher severely whipped me. My master was very much hurt at this, and said, before me, that never should that name be effaced, for I was a boy of genius, and he was sure I should come to preferment. This expression made me forget the stripes I had received.

Memoir written for his daughter Lydia, 1767

I am not so much surprised as probably some of your readers at the mortifying account which has been published in your work of the brutality of Sterne to his mother. For, above forty years ago, as I was travelling in a coach from Bath to London, my companion, a Dr Marriot, who was his near neighbour, gave me such a character of the man as filled me with unfavourable impressions of him ever since. Being then a young man, and, like most other young men, being too forward to show my opinion of men and books, I began to express my high admiration of the writings of Sterne, and to pass unqualified eulogiums upon him, as a man possessed of the finest feelings and philanthropy.

As soon as I had ended my frothy declaration, the Doctor very placidly told me that I did not know the man as well as he did; that he was his very near neighbour; and that of all the men he ever knew he was the most devoid of the feelings of humanity, or of everything that we call sympathy.

As one proof of this, the Doctor told me that his daughter had some acquaintance with Miss Sterne, and therefore that she frequently passed an afternoon at his house; that Miss Sterne was subject to violent epileptic fits, that she had been lately seized with one of these, which was accompanied with such alarming symptoms, as made him and his daughter apprehend that she was dying; that they therefore sent to Mr Sterne to apprise him of the circumstance, and to come to them immediately.

After waiting for some time in anxious expectation, the gentleman made his appearance, and seeing his daughter agonized upon the floor, and seemingly ready to expire, he coolly observed that she would be well again presently and that he could not stop a moment, being engaged to play the first fiddle at York that night. Thus he took his leave, and hastily hurried out of the house.

We cannot therefore conclude with any certainty what a man feels from the pathos of his writings, unless we have an intimate acquaintance with the man himself; unless we can prove from his actions that his high-wrought descriptions are the index of his mind.

'Anecdote told by Dr Marriot to W. Hazlett', *Monthly Repository*, 1808

The otherwise unknown Hazlett to whom this anecdote was told has sometimes been identified with William Hazlitt, but the dates make this impossible.

In February 1768 Laurence Sterne, his frame exhausted by long debilitating illness, expired at his lodgings at Bond Street, London. There was something in the manner of his death singularly resembling the particulars detailed by Mrs Quickly, as attending that of Falstaff, the compeer of Yorick for infinite jest, however unlike in other particulars. As he lay on his bed totally exhausted, he complained that his feet were cold, and requested the female attendant to chafe them. She did so, and it seemed to relieve him. He complained that the cold came up higher; and whilst the assistant was in the act of chafing his ankles and legs, he expired without a groan. It was also remarkable that his death took place much in the manner which he himself had wished; and that the last offices were rendered him, not in his own house, or by the hand of kindred affection, but in an inn and by strangers.

Sir Walter Scott, *Lives of the Novelists*, 1821–4

Thomas Gray · 1716–1771

Gray had a morbid fear of fire. His rooms at Pembroke College, Cambridge, where he was a Fellow—he had previously been at Peterhouse—were on the second floor, and he arranged to have a rope-ladder installed with an iron bar outside his window to hold it:

His precautions were not unobserved, and in fact invited the practical joke which Williams and Forrester and their friend Lord Perceval, a fellow-commoner of Magdalene, decided to play upon him. Its outcome was described in a letter written to a friend shortly afterwards by the Reverend John Sharp, a Fellow of Corpus.

Mr Gray, our elegant Poet, and delicate Fellow Commoner of Peterhouse, has just removed to Pembroke-hall, in resentment of some usage he met with at the former place. The case is much talked of, and is this. He is much afraid of fire, and was a great sufferer in Cornhill; he has ever since kept a ladder of ropes by him, soft as the silky cords by which Romeo ascended to his Juliet, and has had an iron machine fixed to his bed-room window. The other morning Lord Perceval and some Petrenchians, going a hunting, were determined to have a little sport before they set out, and thought it would be no bad diversion to make Gray bolt, as they called it, so ordered their man Joe Draper to roar out fire. A delicate white night-cap is said to have appeared at the window; but finding the mistake, retired again to the couch. The young fellows, had he descended, were determined, they said, to have whipped the butterfly up again.

This is the only contemporary account of the affair that has survived; and it was later corroborated by William Cole, who knew all the current gossip of Cambridge, in a note in his copy of Mason's *Memoirs of Gray*. Nor does the tone of Sharp's letter suggest that he would have withheld any circumstance that might have added further to Gray's humiliation: it was only later that the two men became on friendly terms. Before long, however, much more highly coloured versions of the story were gaining ground. It was said that Gray had actually clambered down his rope-ladder; that he had landed in a tub of water placed in readiness under his window; that as he stood shivering in the cold March air, a kindly watchman wrapped him in his greatcoat until the college porter could be aroused. There is no truth in any of these versions. But Sir Edmund Gosse included them all, with embellishments of his own, in his life of Gray, and they were repeated by Sir Leslie Stephen in the *Dictionary of National Biography*, with the consequence that they are often believed today.

R. W. Ketton-Cremer, *Thomas Gray*, 1955

A young man named John Robison served on board one of the ships which took part in General Wolfe's expedition to Quebec in 1759. In later life Robison became Professor of Natural Philosophy at Edinburgh. He sometimes told his students a story which one of them set down in a letter:

HE told me that General Wolfe kept his intention of attacking Quebec a most profound secret; not even disclosing it to the Second-in-Command, and the night before the attack nothing was known. The boats were ordered to drop down the St Lawrence, and it happened that the boat which Professor Robison, then a midshipman, commanded, was very near the one General Wolfe was in. A gentleman was repeating Gray's *Elegy* to the latter, and Mr Robison heard him (the General) say 'I would rather have been the author of that piece than beat the French tomorrow;' and from this remark guessed that the attack was to be made the next day.

James Currie, letter to his father, 1804

In December 1769 Gray entertained his young Swiss friend Charles-Victor de Bonstetten in London. As they were walking through the city,

A LARGE uncouth figure was rolling before them, upon seeing which Gray exclaimed, with some bitterness, 'Look, look, Bonstetten!—the great bear!—There goes *Ursa Major*!'

Sir Egerton Brydges, quoted in Ketton-Cremer, *Thomas Gray*

Johnson was one of the severest critics of Gray's poetry; Gray disliked Johnson's prose style. This is the only occasion on which the two are known to have been in each other's presence.

HORACE WALPOLE · 1717–1797

WHEN he was in France, during his father's administration, passing through Amiens, in warm weather, he stopped to view the beautiful front of the Cathedral: he got out of his carriage—a favourite little dog followed him. The creature being thirsty, looked around for drink, and while his master was engaged in surveying the building, he discovered the vessel of holy water in the porch, and began to lap it. Mr Walpole took him away with all speed, and thought himself fortunate that no one passed by at the moment, as a construction of a very serious nature, might have been put on the son of the Prime Minister of England, suffering such an affront to be offered to the religion of the country.

Laetitia-Matilda Hawkins, *Anecdotes, Sketches and Memoirs*, 1822

ALTHOUGH Voltaire, with whom I had never had the least acquaintance, had voluntarily written to me first, and asked for my book, he wrote a letter to the Duchesse de Choiseul, in which, without saying a syllable of his having written to me first, he told her I had officiously sent him my works, and declared war with him in defence '*de ce bouffon de Shakespeare*', whom in his reply to me he pretended so much to admire. The Duchesse sent me Voltaire's letter, which gave me such a contempt for his disingenuity, that I dropped all correspondence with him.

Horace Walpole, short autobiographical notes, 1769

HE felt, or pretended to feel, great disgust at the practice adopted by the bookmaking admirers of Johnson, who scrupled not to commit to print whatever they heard in private conversation. Hence he would suddenly purse up his mouth in a pointed but ludicrous manner whenever Boswell came into the room, and sit as mute as a fish till that angler for anecdote and repartee had left it.

Lord Holland, *Further Memoirs of the Whig Party*, 1826

SAMUEL FOOTE · 1720–1777

(actor and playwright)

FOOTE, at times, spared neither friend nor foe. He had little regard for the feelings of others: if he thought of a witty thing that would create laughter, he said it. He had never availed himself of the good advice given by Henry the Fifth to Falstaff, 'Reply not to me with a fool-born jest;' and of this I can give one notable example. If Foote ever had a serious regard for any one, it was for Holland, yet at his death, or rather indeed after his funeral, he violated all decency concerning him. Holland was the son of a baker at Hampton, and on the stage was a close imitator of Garrick, who had such a respect for him, that he played the Ghost to his Hamlet merely to serve him at his benefit. Holland died rather young, and Foote attended as one of the mourners. He was really grieved; and the friend from whom I had the account, declared that his eyes were swollen with tears; yet when the gentleman said to him afterwards, 'So, Foote, you have just attended the funeral of our dear friend Holland;' Foote instantly replied, 'Yes we have just shoved the little baker into his oven.'

Joseph Cradock, *Literary and Miscellaneous Memoirs*, 1828

Elizabeth Montagu · 1720–1800

(scholar and author; leading member of the Blue Stocking circle)

There came out books called Every Man His Own Broker, and Every Man His Own Brewer, and such trash; it was that year that Beauclerc married Lady Bolingbroke, and Lord Ossory the Duchess of Grafton. 'Why have we not a book called Every Man His Own Cuckold?', says Mrs Montagu.

Hester Thrale, *Thraliana*, entry for July 1778

Christopher Smart · 1722–1771

His eldest sister Margaret has often repeated to me his first essay in numbers when about 4 years old . . . The young rhymester was very fond of a lady of about three times his own age who used to notice and caress him. A gentleman old enough to be her father to teaze the child would pretend to be in love with his favourite and threatened to take her for his wife—'You are too old,' said little Smart; the rival answered if that was an objection he would send his son; he answered in verse as follows, addressing the lady,

Madam if you please
To hear such things as these
Madam I have a rival sad
And if you don't take my part it will make me mad.
He says he will send his son;
But if he does I will get me a gun.
Madam if you please to pity
O poor Kitty, O poor Kitty.

Letter from Mrs Le Noir, the poet's daughter, undated

Edmund Burke · 1729–1797

In the eighteenth century the ethics of the press had scarcely been discovered, and those able to hire the venal pens of professional slanderers could print nearly what they chose about their political opponents, with virtual impunity. As Burke told Shackleton, the libelee's best protection was the cynicism of the public, which usually discounted newspaper vituperation. Sometimes the commercialized nature of the attacks was accidentally made obvious. Burke's biographer James Prior reports that on one occasion a printer hired by one of Burke's enemies got into a quarrel with his employer and '. . . disclosed a bill which excited some amusement when made public, the items regularly marked and charged running thus—"Letters against Mr Burke," "Strictures upon the Conduct of Mr Burke," "Attacking Mr Burke's veracity," the latter being charged at five shillings . . .'

Thomas Copeland, *Edmund Burke: Six Essays*, 1950

Burke had a notorious weakness for puns:

LORD MULGRAVE called to Burke one day at our table with a—'so, Burke, you riot in puns now Johnson's away.' This made good sport for my lord and for the company, but Burke changed colour and looked like Death.

Hester Thrale, *Thraliana*, entry for August 1777

Burke began writing Reflections on the Revolution in France *early in 1790. Philip Francis, to whom he showed the proofs, found the celebrated encomium of Marie Antoinette extravagant, but Burke insisted that it was exactly what he felt:*

JUST one year later—one year nearer to the guillotine—Marie Antoinette herself, 'through the means of Miss Wilkes', John Wilkes's daughter then in France, was shown the French translation of Burke's already almost elegiac reflections upon her fate. 'One of the Queen's bedchamber women', Burke was told, 'carried it to the Queen, who before she had read half the lines, she burst into a flood of tears, and was a long time before she was sufficiently composed to peruse the remainder.'

Stanley Ayling, *Edmund Burke*, 1988

THERE is a curious but well-authenticated report about Burke's burial. His bones are not now under the slab which marks them in Beaconsfield church. They are not even in the same coffin in which they were originally buried. By his own direction they were first put in a wooden coffin but later transferred to a leaden one placed in a different spot. Burke did not wish it to be known exactly where he was buried. He feared that the French revolutionaries, if they triumphed in England, might dig up and dishonor his corpse.

Copeland, *Edmund Burke*

IGNATIUS SANCHO · ?1729–1780

Sancho had a remarkable career. Born a slave, he was brought to England from the West Indies as a child and handed over to three unmarried sisters (who gave him the name Sancho because he was plump and pudgy and reminded them of Sancho Panza). Subsequently he attracted the interest and support of the Duke and Duchess of Montagu. He worked for the Montagus as a butler and a valet, and then set up in business as a grocer, but he also had wide-ranging artistic ambitions. He tried to establish himself as an actor, playing Othello and Oroonoko. He wrote poems, plays, and musical works. He was a lively letter writer, and the collection of his letters published after his death enjoyed considerable success.

Sancho's friends included such notable figures as Sterne, Gainsborough, and Garrick. He was the first African, or Afro-Briton, to receive an obituary in the British press. But he also encountered frequent displays of hostility:

ALTHOUGH Stevenson [a friend, William Stevenson] tells us that he had 'often witnessed Sancho's patient forbearance, when the passing vulgar have given vent to their prejudice against his ebon complexion, his African features and his corpulent person', he recounts an incident in which Sancho demonstrated 'manly resentment' in the face of such prejudice. Insulted by a 'fashionable' man in the street with the shout 'Smoke [out of the way] Othello!', 'Sancho, immediately placing himself across the path, before him, exclaimed with a thundering voice, and a countenance which awed the delinquent, "Aye, Sir, such Othellos you meet with but once in a century," clapping his goodly round paunch. "Such Iagos as you, we meet in every dirty passage. Proceed, Sir!"'

Vincent Carretta, in *Oxford Dictionary of National Biography*, 2004

OLIVER GOLDSMITH · 1730–1774

HE would frequently preface a story thus: 'I'll now tell you a story of myself, which some people laughed at, and some do not.'

At the breaking up of an evening at a tavern, he entreated the company to sit down, and told them if they would call for another bottle they should hear one of his *bons mots*: they agreed, and he began thus: 'I was once told that Sheridan the player, in order to improve himself in stage gestures, had looking glasses, to the number of ten, hung about his room, and that he practised before them; upon which I said, then there were ten ugly fellows together.' The company were all silent: he asked why they did not laugh, which they not doing, he, without tasting the wine, left the room in anger.

In a large company he once said, 'Yesterday I heard an excellent story, and I would relate it now if I thought any of you able to understand it.' The company laughed, and one of them said, 'Doctor, you are very rude'; but he made no apology.

He once complained to a friend in these words: 'Mr Martinelli is a rude man: I said in his hearing, that there were no good writers among the Italians, and he said to one that sat near him, that I was very ignorant.'

'People,' said he, 'are greatly mistaken in me: a notion goes about, that when I am silent I mean to be impudent; but I assure you, gentlemen, my silence arises from bashfulness.'

Sir John Hawkins, *Life of Samuel Johnson*, 1789

Shortly after first meeting him, Goldsmith's future biographer Thomas Percy (later Bishop of Dromore) visited him in his lodgings in Green Arbour Court, near the Old Bailey:

THE Doctor was writing his Enquiry, etc. [*An Enquiry into the Present State of Polite Learning in Europe*] in a wretched dirty room, in which there was but one chair, and when he, from civility, offered it to his visitant, he himself was obliged to sit in the window. While they were conversing, someone gently rapped at the door, and being desired to come in, a poor ragged little girl, of very decent behaviour, entered, who, dropping a curtsey, said, 'My mamma sends her compliments, and begs the favour of you to lend her a chamber-pot full of coals.'

Thomas Percy, *The Life of Goldsmith*, 1801

Dr Johnson was present at a dinner given by Thomas Percy at which Goldsmith recalled his reactions on the first night of his play The Good-Natur'd Man*:*

RETURNING home one day from dining at the chaplain's table, he told me that Dr Goldsmith had given a very comical and unnecessarily exact recital there, of his own feelings when his play was hissed; telling the company how he went indeed to the Literary Club at night, and chatted gaily among his friends, as if nothing had happened amiss; that to impress them still more forcibly with an idea of his magnanimity, he even sang his favourite song about an old woman tossed in a blanket seventeen times as high as the moon; but all this while I was suffering horrid tortures (said he), and verily believe that if I had put a bit into my mouth it would have strangled me on the spot, I was so excessively ill.

Hester Lynch Piozzi, *Anecdotes of the Late Samuel Johnson*, 1786

Despite the hissing, The Good-Natur'd-Man *had been reasonably well received and had enjoyed a respectable run. Johnson took a hard line with Goldsmith's revelations: according to Percy, 'he declared unfeelingly that "no man should be expected to sympathise with the sorrows of vanity".'*

HE considered him as a friend indeed who would ask him to tell a story or sing a song, either of which requests he was always very ready to comply with, and very often without being asked, and without any preparation, to the great amazement of the company. His favourite songs were *Johnny Armstrong*, *Barbara Allen*, and *Death and the Lady*. In singing the last he endeavoured to humour the dialogue by looking very fierce and speaking in a very rough voice for Death, which he suddenly changed when he came to the lady's part, putting on what he fancied to be a lady-like sweetness of countenance, with a thin, shrill voice. His skill in singing those ballads was no ways superior to the professors of this art which are heard every day in the streets, but whilst he was thus employed he was a conspicuous figure at least and was relieved from that horror which he entertained of being overlooked by the company.

Joshua Reynolds, in *Portraits by Sir Joshua Reynolds*, ed. Frederick W. Hilles, 1952

I WAS only five years old when Goldsmith took me on his knee, while he was drinking coffee, one evening, with my father, and began to play with me; which amiable act I return'd with the ingratitude of a peevish brat, by giving him a very smart slap in the face,—it must have been a tingler—for it left the marks of my little spiteful paw upon his cheek. This infantile outrage was followed by summary justice; and I was locked up by my indignant father, in an adjoining room, to undergo solitary imprisonment, in the dark. Here I began to howl and scream, most abominably; which was no bad step towards liberation, since those who were not inclined to pity me might be likely to set me free, for the purpose of abating a nuisance.

At length a generous friend appeared to extricate me from jeopardy; and that generous friend was no other than the man I had so wantonly molested, by assault and battery—it was the tender-hearted Doctor himself, with a lighted candle in his hand, and a smile upon his countenance, which was still partially red, from the effects of my petulance—I sulked and sobbed, and he fondled and soothed—till I began to brighten. Goldsmith, who, in regard to children, was like the Village Preacher he has so beautifully described—for

Their welfare pleased him, and their cares distress'd,

seized the propitious moment of returning good-humour—so he put down the candle, and began to conjure. He placed three hats, which happened to be in the room, upon the carpet, and a shilling under each:—the shillings, he told me, were England, France, and Spain. 'Hey, presto, cockolorum!' cried the Doctor—and, lo! on uncovering the shillings which had been dispersed, each beneath a separate hat, they were all found congregated under one. I was no politician at five years old and, therefore, might not have wondered at the sudden revolution which brought England, France, and Spain, all under one crown; but, as I was also no conjuror, it amazed me beyond measure. Astonishment might have amounted to awe for one who appeared to me gifted with the power of performing miracles, if the good-nature of the man had not obviated my dread of the magician; but, from that time, whenever the Doctor came to visit my father,

I pluck'd his gown, to share the good man's smile;

a game at romps constantly ensued, and we were always cordial friends, and merry playfellows.

George Colman the Younger, *Random Records*, 1830

Colman's father, the theatre manager and dramatist George Colman the Elder, was responsible for the original productions of The Good-Natur'd Man *and* She Stoops to Conquer.

Erasmus Darwin · 1731–1802

(poet, physician, botanist, pioneer of evolutionary ideas)

He stammered greatly, and it is surprising that this defect did not spoil his powers of conversation. A young man once asked him in, as he thought, an offensive manner, whether he did not find stammering very inconvenient. He answered, 'No, Sir, it gives me time for reflection, and saves me from asking impertinent questions.'

Ernst Krause, *Life of Erasmus Darwin*, 1879

William Cowper · 1731–1800

On Monday morning last, Sam brought me word that there was a man in the kitchen who desired to speak with me. I ordered him in. A plain, decent, elderly figure made its appearance, and being desired to sit, spoke as follows: 'Sir, I am clerk of the parish of All Saints, in Northampton: brother of Mr Cox the upholsterer. It is customary for the person in my office to annex to a bill of mortality, which he publishes at Christmas, a copy of verses. You would do me a great favour, Sir, if you would furnish me with one.' To this I replied, 'Mr Cox, you have several men of genius in your town, why have you not applied to some of them? There is a namesake of yours in particular, Cox the statuary, who, everybody know, is a first-rate maker of verses. He surely is the man of all the world for your purpose.' 'Alas! Sir, I have heretofore borrowed help from him, but he is a gentleman of so much reading, that the people of our town cannot understand him.' I confess to you, my dear, I felt all the force of the compliment implied in this speech, and was almost ready to answer, 'Perhaps, my good friend, they may find me unintelligible too for the same reason.' But, on asking him whether he had walked over to Weston on purpose to implore the assistance of my Muse, and on his replying in the affirmative, I felt my mortified vanity a little consoled, and, pitying the poor man's distress, which appeared to be considerable, promised to supply him. The waggon has accordingly gone this day to Northampton loaded in part with my effusions in the mortuary style. A fig for poets who write epitaphs upon individuals! I have written *one*, that serves *two hundred* persons.

Letter to Lady Hesketh, November 1787

Edward Gibbon · 1737–1794

While living in Switzerland, Gibbon became engaged to Suzanne Curchod, but he broke off the engagement on account of the opposition of his father: 'I sighed as a lover, I obeyed as a son.' The following year he saw her again. By this time she was married to Jacques Necker, the French banker and future minister:

The Curchod (Madame Necker) I saw at Paris. She was very fond of me, and the husband particularly civil. Could they insult me more cruelly? Ask me every evening to supper; go to bed and leave me alone with his wife—what an impertinent security! It is making an old lover of very little consequence.

Letter to Lord Sheffield, 1763

Gibbon took very little exercise. He had been staying some time with Lord Sheffield in the country; and when he was about to go away, the servants could not find his hat. 'Bless me,' said Gibbon, 'I certainly left it in the hall on my arrival here.' He had not stirred out of doors during the whole of the visit.

Samuel Rogers, *Table Talk*, 1856

You will be diverted to hear that Mr Gibbon has quarrelled with me. He lent me his second volume in the middle of November. I returned it with a most civil panegyric. He came for more incense; I gave it, but alas! with too much sincerity; I added, 'Mr Gibbon, I am sorry *you* should have pitched on so disgusting a subject as the Constantinopolitan History. There is so much of the Arians and Eunomians and semi-Pelagians; and there is such a strange contrast between Roman and Gothic manners, and so little harmony between a Consul Sabinus and a Ricimer, Duke of the Palace, that, though you have written the story as well as it could be written, I fear few will have patience to read it.' He coloured; all his round features squeezed themselves into sharp angles; he screwed up his button-mouth, and rapping his snuff-box, said, 'It had never been put together before'—*so well*, he meant to add—but gulped it. He meant *so well*, certainly, for Tillement, whom he quotes on every page, has done the very thing. I well knew his vanity, even about his ridiculous face and person, but thought he had too much sense to avow it so palpably.

Horace Walpole, letter to William Mason, 1781

THE picture of him painted by Sir J. Reynolds, and the prints made from it, are as like the original as it is possible to be. When he was introduced to a blind French lady, the servant happening to stretch out her mistress's hand to lay hold of the historian's cheek, she thought, upon feeling its rounded contour, that some trick was being played upon her with the *sitting* part of a child, and exclaimed, 'Fi donc!' ['Fie for shame!']

Mr Gibbon is very replete with anecdotes and tells them with great happiness and fluency.

James Prior, *Life of Edmond Malone*, 1860; 'Maloniana'

BEFORE my departure from England, I was present at the august spectacle of Mr Hastings's trial in Westminster Hall. It is not my province to absolve or condemn the Governor of India; but Mr Sheridan's eloquence commanded my applause; nor could I hear without emotion the personal compliment which he paid me in the presence of the British nation.

From this display of genius, which blazed four successive days, I shall stoop to a very mechanical circumstance. As I was waiting in the manager's box, I had the curiosity to inquire of the shorthand writer, how many words a ready and rapid orator might pronounce in an hour? From 7,000 to 7,500 was his answer. The medium of 7,200 will afford 120 words in a minute, and two words in each second. But this computation will only apply to the English language.

Edward Gibbon, *Autobiography*, 1796

Gibbon considered that what he called the 'persecution' of Warren Hastings—his impeachment for alleged murder and extortion during his time as governor-general of India—was prompted by party politics.

In the course of his speech Sheridan spoke of atrocities which went beyond anything that could be found 'either in ancient or modern history, in the correct periods of Tacitus or the luminous page of Gibbon'.

THOMAS PAINE · 1737–1809

In 1793 Paine's support for the French Revolution put him in danger, and he left for France. He was warmly received, but during the Terror he was arrested, sentenced to death and held in the Luxembourg prison:

THE room in which I lodged was on the ground floor, and one of a long range of rooms under a gallery, and the door of it opened outward and flat against the wall; so that when it was open the inside of the door appeared outward, and the contrary when it was shut. I had three comrades, fellow-prisoners with me, Joseph Vanheule of Bruges, Charles Bastini and Michael Robyns of Louvain. When persons by scores and by hundreds were to be taken out of the prison for the guillotine it was always done in the night, and those who performed that office had a private mark or signal by which they knew what rooms to go to, and what number to take. We, as I have said, were four, and the door of our room was marked, unobserved by us, with that number in chalk; but it happened, if happening is the proper word, that the mark was put on when the door was open and flat against the wall, and thereby came on the inside when we shut it at night; and the destroying angel passed by it.

'Letters to the Citizens of the United States': Letter III, 1802

In 1802 Paine returned to America, but by now his earlier work on behalf of American independence tended to be overshadowed by his attack on conventional Christianity in The Age of Reason*:*

HIS after-dinner snooze was still a regular feature of his day's programme. One afternoon an old lady dressed in a scarlet cloak knocked at the door and inquired for him. Jarvis said that he was asleep.

'I am very sorry for that, as I want to see him very particularly,' said the old lady.

Jarvis took her into Paine's room and woke him up. He hated being disturbed on these occasions and looked so fiercely at the lady in scarlet that she retreated a step or two.

'What do you want?' he demanded.

'Is your name Paine?'

'Yes.'

'Well, then, I come from Almighty God, to tell you that if you do not repent of your sins and believe in our blessed Saviour, Jesus Christ, you will be damned, and—'

'Poh, poh! it is not true. You were not sent with any such impertinent message. Jarvis, make her go away. Pshaw! God would not send such a foolish, ugly old woman as you about with his messages. Go away—be off—and shut the door.'

His visitor raised her hands in astonishment and left without a word.

Hesketh Pearson, *Tom Paine*, 1937

JAMES BOSWELL · 1740–1795

I WENT to Love's to try to recover some of the money which he owes me. But, alas, a single guinea was all I could get. He was just going to dinner, so I stayed and eat a bit, though I was angry at myself afterwards. I drank tea at Davies's in Russell Street, and about seven came in the great Mr Samuel Johnson, whom I have so long wished to see. Mr Davies introduced me to him. As I knew his mortal antipathy at the Scotch, I cried to Davies, 'Don't tell where I come from.' However, he said, 'From Scotland.' 'Mr Johnson,' said I, 'indeed I come from Scotland, but I cannot help it.' 'Sir,' replied he, 'that, I find, is what a very great many of your countrymen cannot help.' Mr Johnson is a man of a most dreadful appearance. He is a very big man, is troubled with sore eyes, the palsy and the king's evil. He is very slovenly in his dress and speaks with a most uncouth voice. Yet his great knowledge and strength of expression command vast respect and render him very excellent company. He has great humour and is a worthy man. But his dogmatical roughness of manners is disagreeable. I shall mark what I remember of his conversation.

Journal, 16 May 1763

> *In Boswell's* Life of Johnson *the account of this memorable meeting is elaborately and brilliantly worked up—Davies is described, for instance, as announcing Johnson's approach in the manner of an actor in the part of Horatio addressing Hamlet as his father's ghost approaches—'Look, my lord, it comes.' But what you don't get from the* Life, *and you do get from the Journal, is the disconcerting initial impact of Johnson's appearance.*

In 1764 Boswell set out on his Grand Tour. In Switzerland he introduced himself to Rousseau and had several extended conversations with him:

WE walked out to a gallery pendant upon his wall. BOSWELL: 'In the old days I was a great mimic. I could imitate everyone I saw. But I have left it off.' ROUSSEAU: 'It is a dangerous talent, for it compels one to seize upon all that is small in a character.' BOSWELL: 'True. But I assure you there was a nobleness about my art, I carried mimicry to such a point of perfection. I was a kind of virtuoso. When I espied any singular character I would say, "It must be added to my collection." ' He laughed with all his nerves:

'You are an odd character.' BOSWELL: 'I am a physiognomist, believe me. I have studied that art very attentively, I assure you, and I can rely on my conclusions.' He seemed to agree to this. ROUSSEAU: 'Yet I think the features of the face vary between one nation and another, as do accent and tone of voice; and these signify different feelings among different peoples.' This observation struck me as new and most ingenious. BOSWELL: 'But in time one learns to understand them.'

Journal, December 1764

The following year his travels took him to Corsica, where he formed what was to be a lasting friendship with the Corsican independence leader General Paoli and got to know some of his followers:

THE Corsican peasants and soldiers were quite free and easy with me. Numbers of them used to come and see me of a morning, and just go out and in as they pleased. I did everything in my power to make them fond of the British, and bid them hope for an alliance with us. They asked me a thousand questions about my country, all which I cheerfully answered as well as I could.

One day they would needs hear me play upon my German flute. To have told my honest natural visitants, 'Really, gentlemen, I play very ill,' and put on such airs as we do in our genteel companies, would have been highly ridiculous. I therefore immediately complied with their request. I gave them one or two Italian airs, and then some of our beautiful old Scots tunes: 'Gilderoy', 'The Lass of Patie's Mill', 'Corn rigs are bonny'. The pathetic simplicity and pastoral gaiety of the Scots music will always please those who have the genuine feelings of nature. The Corsicans were charmed with the specimens I gave them, though I may now say that they were very indifferently performed.

My good friends insisted also to have an English song from me. I endeavoured to please them in this too, and was very lucky in that which occurred to me. I sung them 'Hearts of oak are our ships, Hearts of oak are our men.' I translated it into Italian for them, and never did I see men so delighted with a song as the Corsicans were with the *Hearts of Oak*. 'Cuore di quercia,' cried they, 'bravo Inglese!' It was quite a joyous riot. I fancied myself to be a recruiting sea officer. I fancied all my chorus of Corsicans aboard the British fleet.

Journal, October 1765

Boswell's father, Lord Auchinleck, disapproved of his Corsican adventure, and was far from impressed by his friendship with Johnson:

'THERE's nae hope for Jamie, mon. Jamie is gaen clean gyte [mad]. What do you think, mon? He's done wi' Paoli—he's off wi' the land-louping scoundrel of a Corsican; and whose tail do you think he has pinned himself to now, mon? A *dominie*, mon, an auld dominie; he keeped a schule, and cau'd it an acaadamy.'

Walter Scott, notes written for Croker's edition of the *Life of Johnson*, 1831

Scott's probable source was Auchinleck's friend John Ramsay; he may have improved somewhat on Ramsay's recollections.

He obtruded himself every where. Lowe (mentioned by him in his life of Johnson) once gave me a humourous picture of him. Lowe had requested Johnson to write him a letter, which Johnson did, and Boswell came in, while it was writing. His attention was immediately fixed, Lowe took the letter, retired, and was followed by Boswell. 'Nothing,' said Lowe, 'could surprise me more. Till that moment he had so entirely overlooked me, that I did not imagine he knew there was such a creature in existence; and he now accosted me with the most overstrained and insinuating compliments possible.' 'How do you do, Mr Lowe? I hope you are very well, Mr Lowe. Pardon my freedom, Mr Lowe, but I think I saw my dear friend, Dr Johnson, writing a letter for you'—'Yes, Sir'—'I hope you will not think me rude, but if it would not be too great a favor, you would infinitely oblige me, if you would just let me have a sight of it. Every thing from that hand, you know, is so inestimable.'—'Sir, it is on my own private affairs, but'—'I would not pry into a person's affairs, my dear Mr Lowe; by any means. I am sure you would not accuse me of such a thing, only if it were no particular secret'—'Sir, you are welcome to read the letter.'—'I thank you, my dear Mr Lowe, you are very obliging, I take it exceedingly kind.' (having read) 'It is nothing, I believe, Mr Lowe, that you would be ashamed of'—'Certainly not'—'Why then, my dear Sir, if you would do me another favour, you would make the obligation eternal. If you would but step to Peele's coffee-house with me, and just suffer me to take a copy of it, I would do any thing in my power to oblige you.'—'I was overcome,' said Lowe, 'by this sudden familiarity and condescension, accompanied with bows and grimaces. I had no power to refuse; we went to the coffee-house, my letter was presently transcribed, and as soon as he had put his document in his pocket, Mr Boswell walked away, as erect and as proud as he was half an hour before, and I ever afterward was unnoticed. Nay, I am not certain,' added he, sarcastically, 'whether the Scotchman did not leave me, poor as he knew I was, to pay for my own dish of coffee.'

Thomas Holcroft, *Memoirs*, 1816

Mauritius Lowe was an unsuccessful and impoverished painter. Johnson was godfather to his children and left them £100 in his will.

Thomas Jefferson · 1743–1826

While the question of Independence was before Congress, it had its meetings near a livery-stable. The members wore short breeches and silk stockings, and with handkerchief in hand, they were diligently employed in lashing the flies from their legs. So very vexatious was this annoyance, and so great an impatience did it arouse in the sufferers, that it hastened, if it did not aid, in inducing them to promptly affix their signatures to the great document which gave birth to an empire republic.

This anecdote I had from Mr Jefferson in Monticello, who seemed to enjoy it very much, as well as to give great credit to the influence of the flies. He told it with much glee, and seemed to retain a vivid recollection of an attack, from which the only relief was signing the paper and flying from the scene.

Sarah Randolph, *The Domestic Life of Thomas Jefferson*, 1871

Jefferson first became president in 1800. The British minister, Andrew Merry, duly presented himself, and was outraged by the casual manner in which Jefferson was dressed:

I, in my official costume, found myself at the hour of reception he had himself appointed introduced to a man as president of the United States, not merely in an undress, but *actually standing in slippers down at the heels*, and both pantaloons, coat and under-clothes indicative of utter slovenliness and indifference to appearances, and in a state of negligence actually studied. I could not doubt that the whole scene was prepared and intended as an insult, not to me personally, but to the sovereign I represented.

Quoted in James Parton, *Life of Jefferson*, 1874

Richard Brinsley Sheridan · 1751–1816

There was something odd about Sheridan. One day at a dinner he was slightly praising that pert pretender and impostor, Lyttelton (the parliament puppy, still alive, I believe). I took the liberty of differing from him: he turned round upon me, and said, 'Is that your real opinion?' I confirmed it. Then said he, 'Fortified by this concurrence, I beg leave to say that it in fact is also *my* opinion, and that he is a person whom I do absolutely and utterly despise, abhor, and detest.' He then launched out into a description of his despicable qualities, at some length, and with his usual wit, and evidently in earnest (for he hated Lyttelton). His former compliment had been drawn out by some preceding one, just as its reverse was by my hinting that it was unmerited.

One day I saw him take up his own 'Monody on Garrick'. He lighted upon the dedication to the Dowager Lady Spencer: on seeing it he flew into a rage and exclaimed 'that it must be a forgery—that he had never dedicated anything of his to such a d——d canting b——', etc., etc., etc.; and so went on for half an hour abusing his own dedication, or at least the object of it. If all writers were equally sincere, it would be ludicrous.

Lord Byron, 'Detached Thoughts', 1821–2

Joseph Richardson was one of the proprietors of Drury Lane and, in the words of a contemporary, 'one of the gayest spirits about town'. He died at a relatively early age in 1803:

SHERIDAN had for Richardson all the affection that a careless man can have for any thing. He made a point, therefore, of going down to Egham, to see the last offices performed over his remains. Mr Taylor says, they arrived too late by about a quarter of an hour. The clergyman had just retired from the grave. Sheridan was in an agony of grief at this disappointment; but his powerful *name*, properly enforced upon the rector, procured a polite and humane repetition of the close of the service, to enable the tardy orator to say that he had attended the funeral of his friend.

The party dined together at the Inn, and after the cloth was removed, their kindness for the deceased broke forth in *designed* testimonials to his merits. Dr Combe was to choose the kind of stone for his mausoleum, and Sheridan himself undertook to compose a suitable inscription; but no curious stone ever covered his remains, and the promised inscription never was written. Such are the hasty pledges of recent grief, and the performances of indolent genius.

John Boaden, *Memoirs of the Life of John Philip Kemble*, 1825

Sheridan played a leading part in the arraignment of Warren Hastings in 1787. Hastings was acquitted of all the charges against him in 1795. Ten years later he and Sheridan met:

AMONG other persons who came to pay their respects to the Prince during the Autumn of 1805 was Mr Hastings, whom I had never seen before excepting at his trial in Westminster Hall. He and Mrs Hastings came to the Pavilion, and I was present when the Prince introduced Sheridan to him, which was curious, considering that Sheridan's parliamentary fame had been built upon his celebrated speech against Hastings. However, he lost no time in attempting to cajole old Hastings, begging him to believe that any part he had ever taken against him was purely political, and that no one had a greater respect for him than himself, etc, etc, upon which old Hastings said with great gravity that 'it would be a great consolation to him in his declining days if Mr Sheridan would make that sentence more publick'; but Sheridan was obliged to mutter and get out of such engagements as well as he could.

Thomas Creevey (1768–1838), *The Creevey Papers*, 1903

By June 1816 it was clear that Sheridan was dying:

On 4 July Sheridan's former lover Harriet Duncannon, now Lady Bessborough, came to see him. He asked her what she thought of his looks, and she said his eyes were brilliant still. He took her hand and gripped it hard, telling her that he did so as a token that, if he could, he would come to her after death. She became frightened and asked why, having persecuted her all his life, he would want to do so after death. 'Because,' he said, 'I am resolved you should remember me.' Samuel Rogers recalled Sheridan saying on his death-bed, 'Tell Lady Bessborough that my eyes will look up to the coffin-lid as brightly as ever.'

Fintan O'Toole, *A Traitor's Kiss: The Life of Richard Brinsley Sheridan*, 1997

Thomas Chatterton · 1752–1770

Chatterton grew up in Bristol. At the age of 16 he began writing pseudo-medieval poems, which he claimed were authentic fifteenth-century works that he had discovered.

In 1770 he went to London, where he initially lodged in Shoreditch with a relative, Mrs Ballance. A few years after his death she was interviewed by Herbert Croft, who had become fascinated by the poet's career:

Mrs Ballance said he was as proud as Lucifer. He very soon quarrelled with her for calling him 'Cousin *Tommy*,' and asked her if she ever heard of a poet's being called *Tommy*: but she assured him she knew nothing of poets, and only wished he would not set up for a gentleman. Upon her recommending it to him to get into some office, when he had been in town two or three weeks, he stormed about the room like a madman, and frightened her not a little by telling her that he hoped, with the blessing of God, very soon to be sent prisoner to the Tower which would make his fortune. He would often look steadfastly in a person's face, without speaking, or seeming to see the person, for a quarter of an hour or more, till it was quite frightful; during all which time (she supposes, from what she has since heard), his thoughts were gone about something else. He frequently said that he should settle the nation before he had done; but how could she think her poor cousin Tommy was so great a man as she now finds he was? His mother should have written word of his greatness, and then, to be sure, she would have humoured the gentleman accordingly.

Quoted in E. H. W. Meyerstein, *A Life of Thomas Chatterton*, 1930

HE was amusing himself with a friend reading epitaphs in St Pancras Churchyard, and was so deep in thought that he stumbled into a grave just dug. His friend helped him out, observing that he was happy in assisting at the resurrection of genius. Chatterton smiled, and taking him by the arm, replied, 'My dear friend, I feel the sting of a speedy dissolution. I have been at war with the grave for some time, and find it is not so easy to vanquish it as I imagined; we can find an asylum to hide from every creditor but that.' His friend tried to divert his thoughts, but three days later he poisoned himself.

From *The Festival of Wit*, 1783; quoted in Meyerstein, *Life of Thomas Chatterton*

FANNY BURNEY · 1752–1840

One evening in 1783 Fanny Burney went to the opera. She found herself sitting next to an acquaintance, Mr. J—, who was 'affected and dainty, but knew music very well'. He was also very talkative:

'HAVE you read,' he said, 'the new book that has had such a run in France, *Les liaisons dangereuses*?'

'No,' answered I, not much pleased at the name, 'I have not even heard of it.'

'Indeed!—it has made so much noise in France I am quite surprised at that. It is not, indeed, a work that recommends very strict morality; but you, we all know, may look into any work without being hurt by it.'

I felt hurt then, however, and very gravely answered,

'I cannot give myself that praise, as I never look into any books that could hurt me.'

He bowed, and smiled, and said that was 'very right,' and added,

'This book was written by an officer; and he says, there are no characters nor situations in it that he has not himself seen.'

'That, then,' cried I, 'will with me always be a reason to as little desire seeing the officer as his book.'

He looked a little simple at this, but pretended to approve it very much. However, I fancy it will save him the trouble of inquiring into my readings any more. I was really provoked with him, however, and though he was most obsequiously civil to me, I only spoke to him in answer, after this little dialogue . . .

Diary, 11 January 1783

In 1782 Fanny Burney was appointed second keeper of the robes to Queen Charlotte. One of the conversations with Charlotte's husband, George III, which she records, ranged over such topics as Voltaire and Rousseau. Then the king said that 'he found by the newspapers' that the actress Mrs Clive was dead. 'Do you read the newspapers? thought I. Oh, King! you must then have the most unvexing temper in the world, not to run wild.'

The mention of Mrs Clive led on to further discussion first of actors, and after that of plays. The king 'complained of the great want of good modern comedies, and of the extreme immorality of most of the old ones':

'AND they pretend,' cried he, 'to mend them; but it is not possible. Do you think it is?—what?'

'No, sir, not often, I believe;—the fault, commonly, lies in the very foundation.'

'Yes, or they might mend the mere speeches;—but the characters are all bad from the beginning to the end.'

Then he specified several; but I had read none of them, and consequently could say nothing about the matter;—till, at last, he came to Shakespeare.

'Was there ever,' cried he, 'such stuff as great part of Shakespeare? only one must not say so! But what think you?—What?—Is there not sad stuff? What?—what?'

'Yes, indeed, I think so, sir, though mixed with such excellences, that—'

'Oh!' cried he, laughing good-humouredly, 'I know it is not to be said! but it's true. Only it's Shakespeare, and nobody dare abuse him.'

Then he enumerated many of the characters and parts of plays that he objected to; and when he had run them over, finished with again laughing, and exclaiming,

'But one should be stoned for saying so!'

Diary, 19 December 1785

She was in Brussels in the time of the Battle of Waterloo. One of the famous persons she glimpsed there was Caroline Lamb, wife of Lord Melbourne and lover of Byron:

AT Madame de la Tour du Pin's I kept the Fête of Madame de Maurville, with a large and pleasant party; and I just missed meeting the famous Lady C[aroline] L[amb], who had been there at dinner, and whom I saw, however, crossing the Place Royale, from Madame de la Tour du Pin's to the Grand Hotel; dressed, or rather *not* dressed, so as to excite universal attention, and authorise every boldness of staring, from the General to the lowest soldier, among the military groups then constantly parading La Place,—for she had one shoulder, half her back, and all her throat and neck, displayed as if at the call of some statuary for modelling a heathen goddess. A slight scarf hung over the other shoulder, and the rest of the attire was of accordant lightness. As her Ladyship had not then written, and was not, therefore, considered as one apart, from being known as an eccentric authoress, this conduct and demeanour excited something beyond surprise, and in an English lady provoked censure, if not derision, upon the whole English nation . . .

Diary, 23 May 1815

George Crabbe · 1754–1832

As a young man Crabbe was apprenticed to a doctor, but then went to London, determined to make a career as an author. He was eventually taken up by Edmund Burke, but until then, as the journal which he kept makes plain, he lived in great poverty:

It's the vilest thing in the world to have but one coat. My only one has happened with a mischance, and how to manage it is some difficulty. A confounded stove's modish ornament caught its elbow, and rent it halfway. Pinioned to the side it came home, and I ran deploring to my loft. In the dilemma, it occurred to me to turn tailor myself; but how to get materials to work with puzzled me. At last I went running down in a hurry, with three or four sheets of paper in my hand, and begged for a needle, etc., to sew them together. This finished my job, and but that it is somewhat thicker, the elbow is a good one yet.

Quoted in George Crabbe the younger, *The Life of George Crabbe*, 1834

Crabbe subsequently became a clergyman. His first parish was in Leicestershire:

In accordance with the usual habits of the clergy then resident in the vale of Belvoir, he made some efforts to become a sportsman; but he wanted precision of eye and hand to use the gun with success. As to coursing, the cry of the first hare he saw killed, struck him as so like the wail of an infant, that he turned heart-sick from the spot: and, in a word, although Mr Crabbe did, for a season, make his appearance now and then in a garb which none that knew him in his latter days could ever have suspected him of assuming, the velveteen jacket and all its appurtenances were soon laid aside for ever.

George Crabbe the younger, *Life of George Crabbe.*

Crabbe was the target of one of the most widely admired parodies in Rejected Addresses *(1812), by James and Horace Smith:*

John Richard William Alexander Dwyer
Was footman to Justinian Stubbs, Esquire;
But when John Dwyer listed in the Blues,
Emmanuel Jennings polish'd Stubbs's shoes . . .

In a later edition of Rejected Addresses *(1833) James Smith added a note describing his first meeting with Crabbe, some years after the parody was published:*

THE REV. GEORGE CRABBE.—The writer's first interview with this poet, who may be designated Pope in worsted stockings, took place at William Spencer's villa at Petersham, close to what that gentleman called his gold-fish pond, though it was scarcely three feet in diameter, throwing up a *jet d'eau* like a thread. The venerable bard, seizing both the hands of his satirist, exclaimed, with a good-humoured laugh, 'Ah! my old enemy, how do you do?' In the course of conversation, he expressed great astonishment at his popularity in London; adding, 'In my own village they think nothing of me.' The subject happening to be the inroads of time upon beauty, the writer quoted the following lines:—

Six years had pass'd, and forty ere the six,
When Time began to play his usual tricks:
My locks, once comely in a virgin's sight,
Locks of pure brown, now felt th' encroaching white;
Gradual each day I liked my horses less,
My dinner more—I learnt to play at chess.

'That's very good!' cried the bard;—'whose is it?' 'Your own.' 'Indeed! hah! well, I had quite forgotten it.' Was this affectation, or was it not? In sooth, he seemed to push simplicity to puerility.

In his biography of Crabbe, George Crabbe the younger defended his father against the suggestion of affectation: 'If Mr Smith had written as many verses, and lived as long as Mr Crabbe, he would, I fancy, have been incapable of expressing such a suspicion.'

WILLIAM GODWIN · 1756–1836

(political philosopher and novelist; husband of Mary Wollstonecraft)

I AGAIN also occasionally met Godwin. His bald head, singularly wanting in the organ of veneration (for the spot where phrenologists state that 'bump' to be, was on Godwin's head an indentation instead of a protuberance), betokened of itself a remarkable man and individual thinker; and his laugh—with its abrupt, short, monosound—more like a sharp gasp or snort than a laugh—seemed alone sufficient to proclaim the cynical, satirical, hard-judging, deep-sighted, yet strongly-feeling and strangely-imaginative author of 'Political Justice,' 'Caleb Williams,' 'St Leon,' and 'Fleetwood.' His snarling tone of voice exacerbated the effect of his sneering speeches and cutting retorts. On one occasion, meeting Leigh Hunt, who complained of the shortness of his sight and generally wore attached to a black ribbon a small single eye-glass to aid him in descrying objects, Godwin answered his complaints by saying sharply, 'You should wear spectacles.' Leigh Hunt playfully admitted that he hardly liked yet to take to so old-gentlemanly-looking and disfiguring an apparatus; when Godwin retorted, with his snapping laugh, 'Ha! What a coxcomb you must be!'

Charles and Mary Cowden Clarke, *Recollections of Writers*, 1878

William Blake · 1757–1827

At the end of the little garden in Hercules Buildings there was a summer-house. Mr Butts calling one day found Mr and Mrs Blake sitting in this summer-house, freed from 'those troublesome disguises' which have prevailed since the Fall. '*Come in!*' cried Blake; '*it's only Adam and Eve, you know!*' Husband and wife had been reciting passages from *Paradise Lost*, in character, and the garden of Hercules Buildings had to represent the Garden of Eden: a little to the scandal of wondering neighbours, on more than one occasion.

Alexander Gilchrist, *The Life of William Blake*, 1863

The 'Mr Butts' who is quoted as the authority for this anecdote was Blake's friend and patron, Thomas Butts. Many years later Butts's grandson reported that his grandfather had denied that the story was true.

Blake was standing at one of his windows, which looked into Astleys premises (the man who established the theatre still called by his name) and saw a boy hobbling along with a log to his foot such an one as is put on a horse or ass to prevent their straying. Blake called his wife and asked her for what reason the log could be placed upon the boys foot: she answered that it must be for a punishment, for some inadvertency. Blakes blood boiled and his indignation surpassed his forbearance, he sallied forth, and demanded in no very quiescent terms that the boy should be loosed and that no Englishman should be subjected to those miseries, which he thought were inexcusable even towards a slave. After having succeeded in obtaining the boys release in some way or other he returned home. Astley by this time having heard of Blakes interference, came to his house and demanded in an equally peremptory manner, by what authority he dare come athwart his method of jurisdiction; to which Blake replied with such warmth, that blows were very nearly the consequence. The debate lasted long, but like all wise men whose anger is unavoidably raised, they ended in mutual forgiveness and mutual respect. Astley saw that his punishment was too degrading and admired Blake for his humane sensibility and Blake desisted from wrath when Astley was pacified.

Frederick Tatham, 'Life of William Blake', 1830s

'DID you ever see a fairy's funeral, madam?' he once said to a lady, who happened to sit by him in company. 'Never, sir!' was the answer. 'I have,' said Blake, 'but not before last night. I was walking alone in my garden, there was great stillness among the branches and flowers and more than common sweetness in the air; I heard a low and pleasant sound, and I knew not whence it came. At last I saw the broad leaf of a flower move, and underneath I saw a procession of creatures of the size and colour of green and gray grasshoppers, bearing a body laid out on a rose leaf, which they buried with songs, and then disappeared. It was a fairy funeral.'

Allan Cunningham, *Life of William Blake*, 1830

'I KNOW much about Blake—I was his companion for nine years. I have sat beside him from ten at night till three in the morning, sometimes slumbering and sometimes waking, but Blake never slept; he sat with a pencil and paper drawing portraits of those whom I most desired to see. I will show you, Sir, some of these works.' He took out a large book filled with drawings, opened it, and continued, 'Observe the poetic fervour of that face—it is Pindar as he stood a conqueror in the Olympic games. And this lovely creature is Corinna, who conquered in poetry in the same place. That lady is Lais, the courtesan—with the impudence which is part of her profession, she stept in between Blake and Corinna, and he was obliged to paint her to get her away. There! that is a face of a different stamp—can you conjecture who he is?' 'Some scoundrel, I should think, Sir.' 'There now—that is a strong proof of the accuracy of Blake—he is a scoundrel indeed! The very individual task-master whom Moses slew in Egypt. And who is this now—only imagine who this is?' 'Other than a good one, I doubt, Sir.' 'You are right, it is a fiend—he resembles, and this is remarkable, two men who shall be nameless; one is a great lawyer, and the other—I wish I durst name him—is a suborner of false witnesses. This other head now?—this speaks for itself—it is the head of Herod; how like an eminent officer in the army!'

John Varley, as reported in Cunningham, *Life of William Blake*

LEST you should not have heard of the Death of Mr Blake I have Written this to inform you—He died on Sunday Night at 6 o'clock in a most glorious manner. He said He was going to that Country he had all His life wished to see and expressed Himself Happy hoping for Salvation through Jesus Christ—Just before he died His countenance became fair—His eyes Brighten'd and He burst out in Singing of the things he saw in Heaven. In truth He Died like a Saint as a person who was standing by Him Observed—He is to be Buryed on Friday at 12 in morng—Should you like to go to the Funeral—If you should there will be Room in the Coach.

Letter from George Richmond to Samuel Palmer, 15 August 1827

Robert Burns · 1759–1796

Burns's father was liberal in his religious views but strict and severe in matters of conduct. The poet's first breach with him took place when he was already working for him on his farm:

His open rebellion had concerned dancing. He was 'distractedly fond' of it, but his father disapproved and had even forbidden his joining, at his own expense, a country class of the kind where a hired fiddler played for the young people at a penny a time in a barn. Up till then it would seem that absolute obedience had been observed. Now the eldest son went his way 'in absolute defiance.' And although not long afterwards the parental ban was withdrawn, so that younger members of the family were able to join in the dancing without need of defiance, the first to break the circle of obedience felt that he would never be wholly forgiven. Narrating the incident as a crucial one years after his father's death Burns uses some remarkable phrases. 'My father . . .' he says, 'was the sport of strong passions; from that instance of rebellion he took a kind of dislike to me, which I believe was one cause of that dissipation which marked my future years.' In spite of the declaration of repentance that went with this and the explanation that the 'dissipation' could be considered so only by strict Presbyterian standards, the quality of the expressions used and the evident painfulness of the memory may not be disregarded. There must have been unforgettable words between father and son, or a still more cruel silence, or possibly an unwarrantable punishment that failed and so caused humiliation to all concerned.

Catherine Carswell, *Robert Burns*, 1933

After the publication of Poems, Chiefly in the Scottish Dialect *(1786), Burns found himself feted by leading social figures in Edinburgh:*

One of the most hospitable of the literati was Dugald Stewart's predecessor in the chair of Moral Philosophy, Dr Adam Ferguson. He lived at

Sciennes Hill House, then some way out of the city—his friends referred to it jokingly as Kamtschatka, but the bleakness of the surroundings did not keep them away from his weekly conversaziones and to one of these Burns was taken by Stewart. John Home, the author of *Douglas*, was present, and so were James Hutton, the geologist, and Joseph Black, the great chemist and physicist. It is possible that Burns was made uneasy by the very distinction of the company; he seemed at first inclined to hold himself apart, and went round the room looking at the pictures. One print in particular seemed to hold his attention—a sentimental scene showing a soldier lying dead in the snow, a woman with a babe in arms on one side, his dog on the other. The caption was in verse:

> Cold on Canadian hills, or Minden's plain,
> Perhaps that parent wept her soldier slain—
> Bent o'er her babe, her eye dissolved in dew,
> The big drops mingling with the milk he drew . . .

Burns read the lines aloud, but before he could finish his eyes filled with tears. He then asked who the author was, but the cream of the Edinburgh literary establishment was unable to enlighten him. One or two friends of the host's young son were present, however, and after a moment one of them, a pale boy of sixteen with a limp, volunteered that they were the work of one Langhorne and occurred in a poem called 'Justice of Peace'. Burns was impressed. 'You'll be a man yet, sir,' he said. The boy's name was Walter Scott.

Ian McIntyre, *Dirt and Deity: A Life of Robert Burns*, 1995

Burns collected and revised many old songs for the collection The Scots Musical Museum, *and contributed many of his own. In addition, in the words of his biographer Ian McIntyre, 'he was a keen collector of unprintable material, and was in the habit of circulating examples to his friends for their amusement':*

HE enclosed a selection with a short note that he dashed off one evening during the summer to a new friend called William Stewart, who was the factor of the Closeburn estate: 'I go for Ayrshire tomorrow, so cannot have the pleasure of meeting you for some time; but anxious for your "Spiritual welfare & growth in grace," I inclose you the Plenipo.'

This was a piece later included in *The Merry Muses of Caledonia* and is, in effect, an eighteenth-century forerunner of 'The Ball of Kirriemuir'. It was the work of a Captain Morris, an ornament, it seems, of the Carlton House set, and author of *Songs Drinking, Political and Facetious*. The Plenipotentiary in question had been despatched to the Court of St James by the Dey of Algiers, and this 'great-pintled Bashaw' from the Barbary shore was an immediate sensation:

A Duchess whose Duke made her ready to puke,
With fumbling and f— all night, sir,
Being first for the prize, was so pleased with its size,
That she begged for to stroke its big snout, sir.

My stars! cried her Grace, its head's like a mace,
'Tis as high as the Corsican Fairy;
I'll make up, please the pigs, for dry bobs and frigs,
With the great Plenipotentiary.

Although accredited to the Court, the Plenipo was no snob, and made his services freely available at all levels of society:

The next to be tried was an Alderman's Bride,
With a c— that would swallow a turtle,
She had horned the dull brows of her worshipful spouse,
Till they sprouted like Venus's myrtle.

Whores and housemaids, ladies of high breeding, boarding-school mistresses and school marms from France—it was all one to the great Turk. He also carried all before him in the theatre and the opera house, where, with a political correctness well in advance of his time, he exercised no discrimination between the sexes:

The nymphs of the stage did his ramrod engage,
Made him free of their gay seminary;
And Italian Signors opened all their back doors
To the great Plenipotentiary.

With such *samizdat* material did Burns seek to divert his friends.

Ian McIntyre, *Dirt and Deity*

Mary Wollstonecraft · 1759–1797

(author of *A Vindication of the Rights of Woman*)

During the French Revolution Wollstonecraft went to Paris, where she met an American, Gilbert Imlay: they had a daughter, Fanny. Imlay deserted her, and after her return to London she wrote to him announcing that she was going to commit suicide by plunging into the Thames:

For Mary, the way out of a trap was always to fling herself into action, and this is what she now did. In the rainy October afternoon she wrote her note to Imlay and gave it to a servant to be delivered. Fanny—poor Fanny—was hugged and left with Marguerite, who must have known her mistress's state of mind well enough without being able to comfort her;

women intent on suicide have usually convinced themselves they are performing a service for their children and abandon them with almost exalted feelings. Mary set off westwards on foot through the streets towards Battersea Bridge. It was a long walk, but she was a good walker, and there is even a certain numbing comfort in tramping steadily under drizzling skies: she continued to pace about when she reached Battersea. The low, flat, marshy fields made it a dismal place. Men went there to shoot pigeons or fight duels and not much else. But still it turned out to be too public for Mary's purpose, and after a while she decided it would not do.

She had money in her pocket, and approached a boatman. The apparition of a strange damp woman asking for a boat which she proposed to handle herself in the autumn twilight was unusual, but she persuaded him of her need and began to row downstream towards Putney . . .

By now it was raining harder than ever. She beached her boat on the bank under the old wooden bridge and decided to go up on to it, high above the water. Why she did not simply drop into the water from the boat is mysterious, but she may have hoped the fall from the bridge would stun her and make drowning easier.

Putney Bridge had a tollgate at either end with a barrier and a bell which prevented anyone from passing without paying their statutory halfpenny. To make her payment she had therefore to be seen again, but once on the bridge she could conceal herself in the bays constructed all along its length to allow foot passengers to keep out of the way of coaches. It was a busy bridge, but she dodged from bay to bay in the darkness until she felt her clothes were completely soaked in rain. Then she climbed on to the railing, a flimsy structure of two wooden bars, not difficult even for a woman in cumbersome clothes to get over, and jumped.

'All is darkness around her. No prospect, no hope, no consolation—forsaken by him in whom her existence was centred . . . blinded and impelled by the agony which wrings her soul, she plunges into the deep, to end her sufferings in the broad embrace of death.' Goethe's seductive account of suicide, which Mary liked to dwell on, was belied by the reality. There was no broad embrace in the river; she found herself still floating and conscious and struggled to press her wet clothes down around her body. She continued with this effort, gasping and choking, the very pain suffered in the process rousing her to a kind of amazed indignation: if this was the price of death, it was surely too high. But finally she became unconscious.

As it turned out, some watermen had seen her fall. By the time she had floated two hundred yards downstream they reached her and fished her out. They took her to a none too respectable public house called The Duke's Head, on the Fulham side, where a doctor was called and helped to revive her. Nobody knew who she was, and the locals talked about the incident for some time before they learnt the name of the lady who had jumped from the bridge.

Claire Tomalin, *The Life and Death of Mary Wollstonecraft*, 1974

Mary subsequently married the rationalist philosopher William Godwin, but she died of septicaemia shortly after giving birth to their daughter (the future Mary Shelley):

GODWIN's friends sat dishevelled about the house, eager to go on helpful errands, whilst the terrible slow process dragged on. She was no longer coherent in her expressions, but tried to do as she was told, attempting to sleep for instance, though she could not do more than feign the breathing of a sleeping person for a minute or so. She asked her nurses not to bully her, she did not mention religion apart from one exclamation: 'Oh Godwin, I am in heaven', to which he is supposed to have answered anxiously, 'You mean, my dear, that your symptoms are a little easier.'

Tomalin, *Life of Mary Wollstonecraft*

RICHARD PORSON · 1759–1808

(Regius professor of Greek at Cambridge; the most celebrated classical scholar of his time)

THAT Porson drank freely and indiscriminately has never been denied. Horne Tooke said that he would drink ink rather than nothing at all, and Pryse Gordon that the quality of the drink was immaterial so long as he had quantity. But his lack of discrimination has perhaps been exaggerated; we need not believe it when we read that he drank embrocation and eye-water and 'Velno's Vegetable Spirits'. Even the well-known story of his drinking methylated spirits appears somewhat doubtful on inspection. Porson, finding a bottle in the bedroom of his host's wife, drank it up and pronounced it the best gin he had ever tasted; it was the wife who next day told her husband that it was 'spirits of wine for the lamp'.

M. L. Clarke, *Richard Porson*, 1937

William Beckford · 1759–1844

(author of *Vathek*; creator of Fonthill Abbey)

The 'Caliph of Fonthill' was bisexual. In 1785, following a homosexual scandal, he went into temporary exile on the Continent—together with his wife, who died the following year, while they were living in Switzerland. One of the countries where he subsequently stayed was Portugal:

There were no trees around the Lisbon house, indeed no garden is ever mentioned. The house itself was 'tolerably neat and fair to the eye' and 'composed of planks and came ready made from America soon after the earthquake. If destiny impels me to spend many months longer in Portugal I must look out for a more substantial dwelling.' Apparently there was a brothel on the other side of the street, to which Beckford went one night, impelled more by curiosity than lust. It seems to have been a disappointing evening. His entry for that day, Thursday 2 August, is the briefest in the entire *Journal*: 'No paladin who drank at the fountains of Merlin was ever more suddenly disenchanted.' The fountain of Merlin in the magic forest of Ardenna, a favourite theme in Beckford's early writing, was supposed to turn to disgust the passion of love-sick knights who drank from it. This was Beckford's one and only Portuguese experiment in heterosexual intercourse. The next morning he noted that:

> One of the females over the way, who imagines no doubt from the tender compliments she probably received from me last night that I am sighing away my soul for her, had the goodness to let fall a flow of jetty ringlets over a panting bosom, to lean pensively on her arm, and to steal several looks at me full of pity and encouragement. She remained at this sport the whole morning.

It sounds as if he had been drunk the night before, and at least performed convincingly. However, the brothel employed a young lad whom Beckford seems to have preferred to the ladies. He christened him 'the sprite', spotted him in a church the next Sunday, and met him again a week later while strolling before supper in the fountain square near the Necessidades Palace. On that occasion the 'sprite . . . delivered me many kind messages from the signoras'. Beckford wrote wistfully that he 'could have fondled and caressed the sprite' but the severe presence of 'a black pig' (a clergyman, presumably) 'kept me within bounds of the strictest decorum'.

Timothy Mowl, *William Beckford*, 1998

Samuel Rogers · 1763–1855

(poet and banker; celebrated for his breakfast parties)

His wit was perhaps in higher repute than any in his time, except that of Sydney Smith; but whilst Sydney's wit was genial and good-humoured, and even his mockeries gave no offence, that of Rogers was sarcastic and bitter; and the plea which I have heard him advance for its bitterness was, in itself, a satire:—'They tell me I say ill-natured things,' he observed in his slow, quiet, deliberate way; 'I have a very weak voice; if I did not say ill-natured things, no one would hear what I said.'

Henry Taylor, *Autobiography*, 1885

Luttrell was talking of Moore and Rogers—the poetry of the former so licentious, that of the latter so pure; much of its popularity owing to its being so carefully weeded of everything approaching to indelicacy; and the contrast between the *lives* and the *works* of the two men—the former a pattern of conjugal and domestic regularity, the latter of all the men he had ever known the greatest sensualist. He has a passion for little girls and L. said that he cannot walk the streets without being followed by many and he has a police officer in his pay to protect him from impositions and menaces.

Charles Greville, *Memoirs*, entry for 16 December 1835

Mary Lamb · 1764–1847

She had a way of repeating her brother's words assentingly when he spoke to her. He once said (with his peculiar mode of tenderness, beneath blunt, abrupt speech), 'You must die first, Mary.' She nodded, with her little quiet nod and sweet smile, 'Yes, I must die first, Charles.'

Charles and Mary Cowden Clarke, *Recollections of Writers*, 1878

As a young girl, Mary Victoria Novello—the future Mary Cowden Clarke—was taught Latin by Mary Lamb:

On one of these occasions of the Latin lessons in Russell Street, Covent Garden, where Mr and Miss Lamb then lived, Victoria saw a lady come in, who appeared to her strikingly intellectual-looking, and still young; she was surprised, therefore, to hear the lady say, in the course of conversation, 'Oh, as for me, my dear Miss Lamb, I'm nothing now but a stocking-mending old woman.' When the lady's visit came to an end, and she was gone, Mary Lamb took occasion to tell Victoria who she was, and to explain her curious speech. The lady was no other than Miss Kelly; and Mary Lamb, while describing to the young girl the eminent merits of the admirable actress, showed her how a temporary depression of spirits in an artistic nature sometimes takes refuge in a half-playful, half-bitter irony of speech.

Charles and Mary Cowden Clarke, *Recollections*

Maria Edgeworth · 1767–1849

In 1823 Maria Edgeworth undertook a tour of the Highlands in the company of her much younger half-sister and half-brother Sophy and William. At one stage they visited the valley of Glen Roy, north-east of Fort William:

We had a most agreeable guide, not a professed guide, but a Highlander of the Macintosh clan, an enthusiast for the beauties of his own country, and, like the Swiss Chamouni guides, quite a well-informed and, moreover, a fine-looking man, with an air of active, graceful independence; of whom it might be said or sung, '*He's clever in his walking*.' He spoke English correctly, but as a foreign language, with *book* choice of expressions; no colloquial or vulgar phrases. He often seemed to take time to translate his thoughts from the Gaelic into English. He knew Scott's works, *Rob Roy* especially; and gave us accounts of the old family feuds between his own Macintosh clan and the Macdonalds, pointing to places where battles were fought, with a zeal which proved the feudal spirit still lives in its ashes. When he found we were Irish, he turned to me, and all reserve vanishing from his countenance, with brightening eyes he said, as he laid his hand on his breast, 'And you are Irish! Now I know that, I would do ten times as much for you if I could, than when I thought you were Southerns or English. We think the Irish have, like ourselves, more spirit.' He talked of Ossian, and said the English could not give the *force* of the original Gaelic. He sang a Gaelic song for us to a tune like 'St Patrick's Day in the Morning'. He called St Patrick, Phaedrig, by which name I did not recognise him; and our Highlander exclaimed, 'Don't you know your own saint?' Sophy sang the tune for him, with which he was charmed; and when he heard William call her Sophy, he said to himself, 'Sophia Western' [the heroine of *Tom Jones*].

Letter to her aunt, Mrs Ruxton, July 1823

William Wordsworth · 1770–1850

Wordsworth's mother died when he was 8. Long afterwards one of her friends told him that he was the only one of her five children about whose future she had been anxious:

The cause of this was, that I was of a stiff, moody and violent temper; so much so that I remember going once into the attics of my grandfather's house at Penrith, upon some indignity having been put upon me, with an intention of destroying myself with one of the foils which I knew was kept there. I took the foil in hand, but my heart failed. Upon another occasion, while I was at my grandfather's house at Penrith, along with my eldest brother, Richard, we were whipping tops together in the large drawing-room on which the carpet was only laid down upon particular occasions. The walls were hung round with family pictures, and I said to my brother, 'Dare you strike your whip through that old lady's petticoat?' He replied, 'No, I won't.' 'Then,' said I, 'here goes;' and I struck my lash through her hooped petticoat, for which no doubt, though I have forgotten it, I was properly punished. But possibly, from some want of judgement in punishments inflicted, I had become perverse and obstinate in defying chastisement, and rather proud of it than otherwise.

Autobiographical memoranda, 1847

A very interesting day. Rose late; at half-past ten joined Wordsworth in Oxford Road, and we then got into the fields and walked to Hampstead. We talked of Lord Byron. Wordsworth allowed him power, but denied his style to be English. Of his moral qualities we think the same. He adds that there is insanity in Lord Byron's family, and that he believes Lord Byron to be somewhat cracked. I read Wordsworth some of Blake's poems; he was pleased with some of them, and considered Blake as having the elements of poetry a thousand times more than either Byron or Scott; but Scott he thinks superior to Campbell. I was for carrying down the descent to Rogers, but Wordsworth would not allow it. Rogers has an effeminate mind, but he has not the bad, obscure writing of Campbell. Wordsworth says a very large proportion of our noble families are affected by hereditary insanity, as well as the royal families of Europe.

Henry Crabb Robinson, diary, May 1812

Wordsworth spoke in defence of Church establishment, and on the usual grounds said he would shed his blood for it. He declared himself not virtuous enough for a clergyman. Confessed he knew not when he had been in a church at home—'All our ministers are such vile creatures'—and he allowed us to laugh at this droll concession from a staunch advocate for the establishment.

Crabb Robinson, diary, May 1812

SOMEONE having observed that the next Waverley novel was to be 'Rob Roy', Wordsworth took down his volume of Ballads and read to the company 'Rob Roy's Grave'; then, returning it to the shelf, observed, 'I do not know what more Mr Scott can have to say upon the subject.'

Charles and Mary Cowden Clarke, *Recollections of Writers*, 1878

ON my return to London [in 1834] I became more acquainted with Philip Courtenay. I found he was well acquainted with Wordsworth and was his great friend and adviser in matters of investment. He had himself gained considerably by purchasing annuities on the lives of old men—peasants in the remote counties, he ascertaining by the inspection of parish registers that they were of a good stock, and in this way he had also very profitably laid out money for Wordsworth. The Government were thus led to discover the blunder that had been made, inasmuch as though very few live to a great age, say ninety, for instance, yet of those who have already attained eighty a large proportion do, and this fact was overlooked. The law was in consequence altered.

Crabb Robinson, reminiscences, *c.*1850

In 1937 Hugh Kingsmill and Malcolm Muggeridge went to Paris to visit Madame Blanchet, the great-great-granddaughter of Wordsworth and Annette Vallon:

'WE often used to wonder why he left her,' Madame Blanchet said, 'when she loved him so devotedly'; especially as it seems he had 'un sens moral très developée'. We suggested rather diffidently that it was his passionate love of England which made him reluctant to marry a foreigner. 'I think,' Madame Blanchet said gently but firmly, 'that if he had asked her, Annette would have gone over to England with Caroline and made a home there.'

'All the same,' she went on, 'there was no feeling of bitterness on Annette's part or on Caroline's. Caroline was devoted to her father, and often spoke about him.' . . .

Madame Blanchet showed us a number of documents in which Wordsworth's name occurred—Caroline's marriage and birth certificate, a petition to Louis XVIII enumerating all Annette had done for the Royalist cause during Napoleon's reign. They treated Wordsworth's name and habitat in the carefree hit-and-miss French fashion where foreign names are concerned—Mr Williams of Rydalmount near Kindal; W. Wortsworth; Williams Wordsworth, propriétaire, Grasner Kendan, Duchy of Westermorland; and M. Williams.

'It remains in a sense a mystery,' said Madame Blanchet, reverting to Wordsworth's abandonment of Annette, 'but of course he was a poet.' She said this tolerantly; we felt how enigmatic he must appear to a French lady, this Englishman with the wide choice of names, who wrote poetry and had a highly-developed moral sense.

Night and Day magazine, November 1937

James Hogg · 1770–1835

('The Ettrick Shepherd'; promoted as a 'character' by *Blackwood's Magazine*; poet and author of *The Private Memoirs of a Justified Sinner*)

Walter Scott encouraged Hogg's literary efforts while he was still working as a shepherd, and invited him to dinner on one of his visits to Edinburgh:

When Hogg entered the drawing-room, Mrs Scott, being at the time in a delicate state of health, was reclining on a sofa. The Shepherd, after being presented and making his best bow, forthwith took possession of another sofa placed opposite to hers and stretched himself thereupon at all his length; for, as he said afterwards, 'I thought I could never do wrong to copy the lady of the house'. As his dress at this period was precisely that in which any ordinary herdsman attends cattle to the market, and as his hands, moreover, bore most legible marks of a recent sheep-smearing, the lady of the house did not observe with perfect equanimity the novel usage to which her chintz was exposed. The Shepherd, however, remarked nothing of all this—dined heartily and drank freely, and by jest, anecdote, and song afforded plentiful merriment to the more civilised part of the company. As the liquor operated, his familiarity increased and strengthened; from 'Mr Scott' he advanced to 'Shirra', and thence to 'Scott', 'Walter', and 'Wattie'—until, at supper, he fairly convulsed the whole party by addressing Mrs Scott as 'Charlotte'.

J. G. Lockhart, *Life of Scott*, 1837–8

Sir Walter Scott · 1771–1832

At the age of 2 Scott was sent to a farm owned by his grandfather for the sake of his health:

An odd incident is worth recording. It seems my mother had sent a maid to take charge of me that I might be no inconvenience in the family. But the damsel sent on that important mission had left her heart behind her, in the keeping of some wild fellow it is likely, who had done and said more to her than he was like to make good. She became extremely desirous to return to Edinburgh and as my mother made a point of her remaining where she was she contracted a sort of hatred at poor me as the cause of her being detained at Sandyknow. This rose, I suppose, to a sort of delirious affection for she confessed to old Alison Wilson, the house keeper, that she had carried me up to the craigs, meaning under a strong temptation of the Devil to cut my throat with her scissors and bury me in the moss. Alison instantly took possession of my person, and took care that her confidant should not be subject to any farther temptation so far as I was concerned. She was dismissed, of course, and I have heard became afterwards a lunatic.

Memoirs; quoted in J. G. Lockhart, *Life of Scott*, 1837–8

It was in correcting the proof-sheets of *The Antiquary* that Scott first took to equipping his chapters with mottoes of his own fabrication. On one occasion he happened to ask John Ballantyne, who was sitting by him, to hunt for a particular passage in Beaumont and Fletcher. John did as he was bid, but did not succeed in discovering the lines. 'Hang it, Johnnie,' cried Scott, 'I believe I can make a motto sooner than you can find one.' He did so accordingly; and from that hour, whenever memory failed to suggest an appropriate epigraph, he had recourse to the inexhaustible mines of '*old play*' or '*old ballad*', to which we owe some of the most exquisite verses that ever flowed from his pen.

Lockhart, *Life of Scott*

These lines to James Ballantyne [Scott's printer] are without date. They accompanied, no doubt, the last proof-sheet of *Rob Roy*, and were therefore in all probability written about ten days before the 31st of December 1817—on which day the novel was published.

With great joy
I send you Roy.
'Twas a tough job,
But we're done with Rob.

The novel had indeed been 'a tough job'—for lightly and airily as it reads, the author had struggled almost throughout with the pains of cramp or the lassitude of opium. Calling on him one day to dun him for copy, James found him with a clean pen and a blank sheet before him, and uttered some rather solemn exclamation of surprise. 'Ay, ay, Jemmy,' said he, ' 'tis easy for you to bid me get on, but how the deuce can I make Rob Roy's wife speak, with such *curmurring* in my guts?'

Lockhart, *Life of Scott*

THE truth is that Sir Walter had his caprices like other men, and when in bad health he was very cross but I always found his heart in the right place and that he had all the native feelings and generosity of a man of true genius. But he hated all sorts of low vices and blackguardism with a perfect detestation. There was one Sunday when he was riding down Yarrow in his carriage with several attendants on horseback; he being our Sherrif I rode up to him and with a face of the deepest concern stated to him that there was at that instant a cry of *murder* from Broadmeadows wood and that Will Watherston was murdering Davie Brunton. 'Never you mind Hogg' said he with rather a stern air in his face and without a smile on it. 'If Will Watherstone murder Davie Brunton and be hanged for the crime it is the most fortunate thing that can happen to the parish. Peter drive on.'

James Hogg, *Anecdotes of Sir W. Scott*, ed. Douglas Mack, 1983

Scott was a partner in Ballantyne & Co. In 1826 the firm became involved in the bankruptcy of the publisher Constable, and he found himself liable for huge debts:

I HAVE a funeral letter to the burial of the Chevalier Yelin a foreigner of learning and talent who has died at the Royal Hotel. He wished to be introduced to me and was to have read a paper before the Royal Society when this introduction was to have taken place. I was not at the society that evening and the poor gentleman was taken ill in the meeting and unable to proceed. He went to his bed and never arose again—and now his funeral will be the first public place that I shall appear at—he dead and I ruind. This is what you call a meeting.

Journal, 22 January 1826

When Scott found himself facing ruin in 1826, a group of friends offered to help him pay his debts. According to Lord Cockburn (in Memorials of his Time*), 'he paused for a moment, and then, recollecting his powers, said proudly—"No! this right hand shall work it all off!"'*

Overwork helped to kill him. By 1830 he was a sick man, and his publishers were alarmed when he announced a new project, a commentary on current affairs. They tried to talk him out of it; indeed, they hoped that he could be persuaded to give up literary labour completely. And they were not the only ones:

HIS kind and skilful physicians, Doctors Abercrombie and Ross of Edinburgh, had over and over preached the same doctrine, and assured him, that if he persisted in working his brain, nothing could prevent his malady from recurring ere long in redoubled severity. He answered—'As for bidding me not work, Molly might as well put the kettle on the fire and say, "Now, don't boil."'

Lockhart, *Life of Scott*

In 1828 Scott spent six weeks in London. On one occasion while he was there he was entertained by George IV at 'a very private party'. On another, he was the guest of one of the king's sisters-in-law:

MAY 19. Dined by command with the Duchess of Kent. I was very kindly recognised by Prince Leopold—and presented to the little Princess Victoria—I hope they will change her name—the heir-apparent to the crown as things now stand. How strange that so large and fine a family as that of his late Majesty should have died off, or decayed into old age, with so few descendants. This little lady is educating with much care, and watched so closely, that no busy maid has a moment to whisper, 'You are heir of England.' I suspect if we could dissect the little heart, we should find that some pigeon or bird of the air had carried the matter.

Journal; quoted in Lockhart, *Life of Scott*

SYDNEY SMITH · 1771–1845

(one of the founders of the *Edinburgh Review*; wit, advocate of social reform, and canon of St Paul's)

THE other day, as I was changing my neck-cloth which my wig had disfigured, my good landlady knocked at the door of my bedroom, and told me that Mr Smith wished to see me, and was in my room below. Of all names by which men are called there is none which conveys a less determinate idea to the mind than that of Smith. Was he on the circuit? For I do not know half the names of my companions. Was he a special messenger from London? Was he a York attorney coming to be preyed upon, or a beggar coming to prey upon me, a barber to solicit the dressing of my wig, or a collector for the Jews' Society? Down I went, and to my utter amazement beheld the Smith of Smiths, Sydney Smith . . .

T. B. Macaulay, letter to his father, July 1826

In 1828 Smith visited Paris, where his friend Lord Holland was staying:

I DINED with Lord Holland . . . There was at table Barras the Ex Director [member of the Directory which ruled France, 1795–99] in whose countenance I immediately discovered all the signs of blood and cruelty which characterize his conduct. I found out however at the end of the dinner that it was not Barras but a Mr Barante, an historian and man of letters who I believe has never killed anything greater than a flea.

Sydney Smith, letter to his wife, April 1828

AT dinner with the Lyndhursts he defended, for the sake of argument, the Indian custom of suttee. 'But if Lord Lyndhurst were to die, you would be sorry that Lady Lyndhurst should burn herself?' was the sudden and awkward question of one of the guests. 'Lady Lyndhurst,' came the reply, 'would, no doubt, as an affectionate wife, consider it her duty to burn herself, but it would be our duty to put her out; and, as the wife of the Lord Chancellor, Lady Lyndhurst should not be put out like an ordinary widow. It should be a state affair. First, a procession of the judges, then of the lawyers . . .' he paused. 'And the clergy?' insinuated someone. 'All gone to congratulate the new Lord Chancellor,' replied Sydney.

Hesketh Pearson, *The Smith of Smiths*, 1934

DOROTHY WORDSWORTH · 1771–1855

SATURDAY. A divine morning. At breakfast William wrote part of an ode. Mr Olliff sent the dung and Wm. went to work in the garden. We sate all day in the orchard.

The Grasmere Journal, 27 March 1802

The 'part of an ode' which Wordsworth wrote before he began forking the manure was the opening stanza of the Immortality Ode:

There was a time when meadow, grove, and stream,
The earth, and every common sight,
To me did seem
Apparelled in celestial light
The glory and the freshness of a dream . . .

When Compton Mackenzie was living on Capri in 1913, one of his neighbours was a retired member of the Indian Civil Service, aged around 80, called William Wordsworth—a great-nephew of the poet:

WILLIAM WORDSWORTH had been at Rydal Mount when the poet died and as a boy of fourteen had stayed on there with his Aunt 'Durrothy' as he called her and as no doubt the famous Dorothy had been called by her brother.

His Aunt 'Durrothy' liked to sit out in a wheeled chair on the sweep of the gravelled drive up to the house and it was William's job to order away inquisitive visitors who had made their way up the drive to stare at the poet's house.

'On one occasion two middle-aged women had found their way up and when me aunt Durrothy called to me I supposed it was to send them off down the drive. To my surprise me aunt Durrothy told me to bring them to speak to her.

' "Would you like to hear me read to you some of my brother's poetry?" she asked them, and I recall one of the two visitors saying to the other "How pleasant it is to receive attentions from elderly females." I thought it an excessively droll remark at the time.'

And as he said this William Wordsworth chuckled over that memory of over sixty years ago.

'Me aunt began to read the ode on intimations of immortality,' and as he said this William Wordsworth the Second began to declaim the ode in what must have been the exact accents of the poet himself. So today I can brag of being able to read that great ode almost as the poet himself used to declaim it.

'After me aunt Durrothy had been reading for a while she noticed that the two women's glances were wandering. "Go away, you two old cats," me aunt said angrily, "you don't deserve to hear me read to you." And with this she flung the volume at them, and I hastily led them away down the drive.'

Compton Mackenzie, *My Life and Times: Octave V*, 1965

Samuel Taylor Coleridge · 1772–1834

As a young schoolboy Coleridge was a glutton for books, 'my appetite for which was indulged by a singular incident—a stranger, who was struck by my conversation, made me free of a circulating library in King Street, Cheapside':

The incident, indeed, was singular: going down the Strand, in one of his day-dreams, fancying himself swimming across the Hellespont, thrusting his hands before him as in the act of swimming, his hand came in contact with a gentleman's pocket; the gentleman seized his hand, turning round and looking at him with some anger, 'What! so young, and so wicked?' at the same time accused him of an attempt to pick his pocket; the frightened boy sobbed out his denial of the intention, and explained to him how he thought himself Leander, swimming across the Hellespont. The gentleman was so struck and delighted with the novelty of the thing, and with the simplicity and intelligence of the boy, that he subscribed, as before stated, to the library, in consequence of which Coleridge was further enabled to indulge his love of reading.

James Gillman, *The Life of Samuel Taylor Coleridge*, 1838

In his early twenties, crossed in love, Coleridge ran away from Cambridge and joined the 15th Light Dragoons, stationed in Reading. He enrolled as Silas Tomken Cumberbatch or Comberbache, a name spotted on a brass plate in Lincoln's Inn, and proved a hopeless soldier. When the men's carbines were inspected, the officer called out, 'Whose rusty gun is this?' Trooper Cumberbatch: 'Is it *very* rusty, sir?' 'Yes, it *is*.' 'Then, sir, it must be mine.' The manner of confession tickled the officer, and the trooper was spared. He was less lucky with horses, forever falling off one side or the other and bruising himself. (He seems to have stayed in place long enough to acquire boils on his bottom.) He bribed a young soldier to rub down his unruly steed by writing love verses for the youth to send his sweetheart. In the regiment Cumberbatch was considered an amiable idiot.

One day, as he was on sentinel duty, two officers walked past, chatting about Euripides; one of them quoted a couple of lines. Begging their honours' pardon, the sentinel corrected the Greek and observed that the lines actually came from Sophocles. The astonished officers had him transferred to the regimental hospital as an orderly. He was a great success with the patients, who declared that he did them more good than all the doctors. When he told them about the Peloponnesian War and how it lasted for twenty-seven years, 'There must have been famous promotion there,' one poor crock proposed. And another, more dead than alive, asked, 'Can you tell, Silas, how many rose from the ranks?' They had animated discussions, on the nature of the rations in those days, as to whether the famous general, Alexander the Great, could be one of the Cornish Alexanders, and whether the wide Hellespont wasn't the mouth of the Thames, which was very wide indeed.

Before long his friends secured the trooper's discharge by means of a sweetener of around £25 and on a technical doubt concerning his sanity.

D. J. Enright, *Play Resumed*, 1999

IN the summer of 1797, the Author, then in ill health, had retired to a lonely farm-house between Porlock and Linton, on the Exmoor confines of Somerset and Devonshire. In consequence of a slight indisposition, an anodyne had been prescribed, from the effects of which he fell asleep in his chair at the moment that he was reading the following sentence, or words of the same substance, in 'Purchas's Pilgrimage':

Here the Khan Kubla commanded a palace to be built, and a stately garden thereunto. And thus ten miles of fertile ground were inclosed with a wall.

The Author continued for about three hours in a profound sleep, at least of the external senses, during which time he has the most vivid confidence that he could not have composed less than from two to three hundred lines; if that indeed can be called composition in which all the images rose up before him as *things*, with a parallel production of the correspondent expressions, without any sensation or consciousness of effort. On awaking he appeared to himself to have a distinct recollection of the whole, and taking his pen, ink, and paper, instantly and eagerly wrote down the lines that are here preserved. At this moment he was unfortunately called out by a person on business from Porlock, and detained by him above an hour, and on his return to his room, found, to his no small surprise and mortification, that though he still retained some vague and dim recollection of the general purport of the vision, yet, with the exception of some eight or ten scattered lines and images, all the rest had passed away like the images on the surface of a stream into which a stone has been cast, but, alas! without the restoration of the latter!

Note prefixed to 'Kubla Khan'; first published 1816

SAMUEL ROGERS told of Coleridge riding about in a strange shabby dress, with I forget whom at Keswick, and on some company approaching them, Coleridge offered to fall behind and pass for his companion's servant. 'No,' said the other, 'I am proud of you as a friend; but, I must say, I should be ashamed of you as a servant.'

Tom Moore, diary, 1833

ONE day, when dining with some lawyers, he had been more than usually eloquent and full of talk. His perpetual interruptions were resented by one of the guests, who said to his neighbour, 'I'll stop this fellow'; and thereupon addressed the master of the house with 'G—, I've not forgotten my promise to give you the extract from "The Pandects" [a digest of Roman law]. It was the ninth chapter that you were alluding to. It begins: "Ac veteres quidam philosophi".' 'Pardon me; sir,' interposed Coleridge, 'there I think, you are in error. The ninth chapter begins in this way, "Incident saepe causae," etc.' It was in vain to refer to anything on the supposition that the poet was ignorant, for he really had some acquaintance with every subject.

Bryan Procter, *An Autobiographical Fragment*, 1877

COLERIDGE, in his old age, became a characteristic feature in Highgate. He was the terror and amusement of all the little children who bowled their hoops along the poplar avenue. Notwithstanding his fondness for them—he called them 'Kingdom-of-Heaven-ites'—his Cyclopean figure and learned language caused them indescribable alarm. Sometimes he would lay his hand on the shoulders of one of them and walk along discoursing metaphysics to the trembling captive, while the rest fled for refuge and peeped out with laughing faces from behind the trees. 'I never,' he exclaimed one day to the baker's boy—'I never knew a man good because he was religious, but I have known one religious because he was good.'

A. G. L'Estrange, *The Literary Life of the Rev. William Harness*, 1871

ON Wednesday—no Tuesday he saw Mrs Gillman for the last time and took leave of James Gillman. James then saw him raise his head in the air—looking upwards as in prayer—he then fell asleep—from sleep into a state of coma, Torpor, as I understood it, and ceased to breathe at half past six in the morning of Friday. Mr Green was with him that night till he died. In the middle of the day on Thursday he had repeated to Mr Green his formula of the Trinity. His utterance was difficult—but his mind in perfect vigour and clearness—he remarked that his intellect was quite unclouded and he said 'I could even be witty'.

Letter from his daughter Sara to his son Hartley, 5 August 1834

Robert Southey · 1774–1843

While he was still at Oxford, in his most radical phase, Southey wrote a play celebrating Wat Tyler. It was offered to a publisher called Ridgeway, who accepted it but took no steps towards printing it.

Over twenty years later, however, it returned to haunt him. By this time he was Poet Laureate, and an unyielding conservative.

At the beginning of February, 1817, a notable recruit had been added to the vast army of seditious pamphlets already in circulation: the republican drama of Southey's youth, *Wat Tyler*. Its publication at this time, more than twenty years after it was written, was, it need hardly be said, unauthorised. The manuscript had apparently remained in the hands of a dissenting minister of Plymouth named Winterbottom, who had been present when Southey gave it to Ridgeway. Its discovery now was a godsend to the Radicals: here was an opportunity to discredit the Poet Laureate, that black reactionary, to convict him of apostasy out of his own mouth. The poor little drama had an instant *succès de scandale*. It was hawked about the streets of London as a threepenny pamphlet; Radical publishers like Sherwin and Hone issued edition after edition; the author was told first that 30,000, then that 60,000, copies had been sold.

He at once took the only possible counter-action: he attempted to reclaim his property at law and to secure an injunction against the publishers of these unauthorised editions. But here the Spirit of Irony took a hand. The case came before the Lord Chancellor, Eldon, the arch-reactionary of England. He might have been expected to support his fellow-Tory. Instead, he held, quoting good precedent, that 'a person cannot recover in damages for a work which is in its nature calculated to do an injury to the public'; and since Southey had not established—and on this argument could not establish—his right to the property in *Wat Tyler*, the injunction must be refused. So its sale went on unchecked.

Jack Simmons, *Southey*, 1945

The episode was a gift to Southey's enemies, though he himself refused to take it to heart. 'I am no more ashamed of having been a republican,' he wrote, 'than of having been a boy.'

CHARLES LAMB · 1775–1834

As little more than an infant, he was walking through a graveyard with his sister, Mary, ten years his senior, and reading the epitaphs on the universally belauded dead—for he was a precocious reader, who, it is said, 'knew his letters before he could talk'. As he came away, he turned to his sister and asked: 'Mary, where are the naughty people buried?' This, we may be sure, though a joke to the reader, was not uttered as a joke by the small child.

Robert Lynd, 'Charles Lamb', in *The English Wits*, ed. Leonard Russell, 1940

It was at Godwin's that I met him [Lamb] with Holcroft and Coleridge, where they were disputing fiercely which was the best—*Man as he was, or man as he is to be*. 'Give me,' says Lamb, 'man as he is *not* to be.' This saying was the beginning of a friendship between us, which I believe still continues.

William Hazlitt, 'My First Acquaintance with Poets', 1823

Being asked how he knew his own books, one from the other (the choice gleanings of many a studious walk at the book stalls in Barbican), for scarcely any were lettered, and all were to a bibliophilist but a stray set of foundings; 'How does a shepherd know his sheep?' was the answer.

John Mitford, quoted in E. V. Lucas, *The Life of Charles Lamb*, 1905

The Revd John Mitford, a friend of Lamb, was rector of Benhall in Suffolk. Lamb once described him as 'a pleasant Layman spoiled'.

Chatted till eleven with Charles Lamb. He was serious and therefore very interesting. He corrected me not angrily, but as if really pained by the expression 'poor Coleridge,' I accidentally made use of. 'He is a fine fellow, in spite of all his faults and weaknesses. Call him Coleridge—I hate "*poor* Coleridge." I can't bear to hear pity applied to such a one.'

Henry Crabb Robinson, diary, August 1811

Leigh Hunt told me a wonderful story of Charles Lamb and his smile. It appears that a certain Mr Thomas Allsop was talking to Coleridge of the peculiar sweetness of Mr Charles Lamb's smile. 'And,' said he, 'there is still one man living, a stockbroker, who has that smile.' 'And,' added Allsop, 'to those who wish to see the only thing left on earth of Lamb, his best and most beautiful remain—his SMILE—I will indicate its possessor: it is Mr Harman, of Throgmorton Street, City.'

Frederick Locker-Lampson, *My Confidences*, 1896

JANE AUSTEN · 1775–1817

In the autumn of 1815 Jane Austen was in London, helping nurse her brother Henry through a dangerous illness. He was attended by one of the Prince Regent's doctors, who told her 'that the Prince was a great admirer of her novels; that he read them often, and kept a set in every one of his residences; that he himself had thought it right to inform his Royal Highness that Miss Austen was staying in London, and that the Prince had desired Mr Clarke, the librarian of Carlton House, to wait upon her'. The next day Clarke made his appearance and invited her to Carlton House, 'saying that he had the Prince's instructions to show her the library and other apartments'.

During the visit which followed Clarke told her that he had also been commissioned to say that if she had 'any other novel forthcoming she was at liberty to dedicate it to the Prince'. She arranged for a dedication to be prefixed to Emma, *which was about to be printed, but before she went ahead with it she wrote to Clarke asking him whether he could confirm that she was doing the right thing. He assured her that she was, and added an unexpected suggestion of his own:*

ACCEPT my best thanks for the pleasure your volumes have given me. In the perusal of them I felt a great inclination to write and say so. And I also, dear Madam, wished to be allowed to ask you to delineate in some future work the habits of life, and character, and enthusiasm of a clergyman, who should pass his time between the metropolis and the country, who should be something like Beattie's Minstrel—

Silent when glad, affectionate tho' shy,
And in his looks was most demurely sad;
And now he laughed aloud, yet none knew why.

Neither Goldsmith, nor La Fontaine in his 'Tableau de Famille,' have in my mind quite delineated an English clergyman, at least of the present day, fond of and entirely engaged in literature, no man's enemy but his own. Pray, dear Madam, think of these things.

Believe me at all times with sincerity and respect, your faithful and obliged servant,
J. S. CLARKE, Librarian.

Jane Austen replied that she was honoured by his thinking her capable of drawing a clergyman such as the one he had sketched—'but I assure you I am not':

THE comic part of the character I might be equal to, but not the good, the enthusiastic, the literary. Such a man's conversation must at times be on subjects of science and philosophy, of which I know nothing; or at least be occasionally abundant in quotations and allusions which a woman who, like me, knows only her own mother tongue, and has read little in that, would be totally without the power of giving. A classical education, or at any rate a very extensive acquaintance with English literature, ancient and modern, appears to me quite indispensable for the person who would do any justice to your clergyman; and I think I may boast myself to be, with all possible vanity, the most unlearned and uninformed female who ever dared to be an authoress.

Clarke was ready with another proposal, however. He had recently been appointed chaplain and English secretary to Prince Leopold of Saxe-Coburg, who was about to marry Princess Charlotte, and when he wrote to Jane Austen conveying the Prince Regent's thanks for the dedication to Emma, *he added that 'an historical romance illustrative of the august House of Cobourg would just now be very interesting', and might very properly be dedicated to Prince Leopold.*

This time she replied to him with what her nephew, J. E. Austen Leigh, called 'a grave civility':

MY DEAR SIR,—I am honoured by the Prince's thanks and very much obliged to yourself for the kind manner in which you mention the work. I have also to acknowledge a former letter forwarded to me from Hans Place. I assure you I felt very grateful for the friendly tenor of it, and hope my silence will have been considered, as it was truly meant, to proceed only from an unwillingness to tax your time with idle thanks. Under every interesting circumstance which your own talents and literary labours have placed you in, or the favour of the Regent bestowed, you have my best wishes. Your recent appointments I hope are a step to something still better. In my opinion, the service of a court can hardly be too well paid, for immense must be the sacrifice of time and feeling required by it.

You are very kind in your hints as to the sort of composition which might recommend me at present, and I am fully sensible that an historical romance, founded on the House of Saxe Cobourg, might be much more to the purpose of profit or popularity than such pictures of domestic life in country villages as I deal in. But I could no more write a romance than an epic poem. I could not sit seriously down to write a serious romance under any other motive than to save my life; and if it were indispensable for me to keep it up and never relax into laughing at myself or at other people, I am sure I should be hung before I had finished the first chapter. No, I must keep to my own style and go on in my own way; and though I may never succeed again in that, I am convinced that I should totally fail in any other.

I remain, my dear Sir,
Your very much obliged, and sincere friend,
J. AUSTEN.

J. E. Austen Leigh, *A Memoir of Jane Austen*, 1870

SHE supported, during two months, all the varying pain, irksomeness, and tedium, attendant on decaying nature, with more than resignation, with a truly elastic cheerfulness. She retained her faculties, her memory, her fancy, her temper, and her affections, warm, clear and unimpaired, to the last . . . She wrote whilst she could hold a pen, and with a pencil when a pen was become too laborious. The day preceding her death she composed some stanzas replete with fancy and vigour. Her last voluntary speech conveyed thanks to her medical attendant; and to the final question asked of her, purporting to know her wants, she replied, 'I want nothing but death.'

Henry Austen, memoir in the first collected edition of Jane Austen's novels, 1832

The philosopher Gilbert Ryle (1900–1976) was a devoted admirer of Jane Austen:

ONCE, when asked whether he ever read novels, he is said to have replied: 'Oh yes, all six of them, every year.'

P. F. Strawson, in *Dictionary of National Biography 1971–1980*, 1986

WALTER SAVAGE LANDOR · 1775–1864

Landor's most famous lines were inspired by the death of Rose Aylmer:

Ah, what avails the sceptred race!
Ah, what the form divine!
What every virtue, every grace!
Rose Aylmer, all were thine.

Rose Aylmer, whom these wakeful eyes
May weep, but never see,

A night of memories and of sighs
I consecrate to thee.

He had known Rose, though only briefly, before she left for India, where she succumbed to cholera at the age of 20.

One of the poem's most ardent admirers, as Landor learned from Henry Crabb Robinson, was Charles Lamb. In his reply to Robinson, he recalled the circumstances under which it had been composed:

WONDERFUL that Charles Lamb should like the poem of mine which I wrote while cleaning my teeth before going to bed. However the night of sorrow was really devoted to the object.

Letter, November 1831

HE [Tennyson] said that he never met Landor more than once or twice in his life, at the time when he himself was living with James Spedding, under the same roof as John Forster, 58 Lincoln's Inn Fields. Coming home about 10 o'clock one evening he saw Mr Fox, the member for Oldham, standing at the top of the doorsteps of the house. They shook hands, and he went into Forster's, where Landor had been dining. In the meantime Mr Fox had fallen down and broken his arm, and was brought into the dining-room, white from pain, and holding the injured arm with the hand of the other. Old Landor went on eloquently discoursing of Catullus and other Latin poets as if nothing particular had happened, 'which seemed rather hard, but was perhaps better than utter silence.'

Hallam Tennyson, *Alfred Lord Tennyson: A Memoir*, 1897

HE was always losing and overlooking things, and then the tumult that would arise was something too absurd, considering the occasion. He used to stick a letter into a book; then, when he wanted to answer it, it was gone—and some one had taken it—the only letter he wanted to answer—that he would rather have forfeited a thousand pounds than have lost, and so on. Or he used to push his spectacles up over his forehead, and then declare they were lost, lost for ever. He would ramp and rave about the room at such times as these, upsetting everything that came in his way, declaring that he was the most unfortunate man in the world, or the greatest fool, or the most inhumanly persecuted. I would persuade him to sit down and let me look for the lost property; when he would sigh in deep despair, and say there was no use in taking any more trouble about it, it was gone for ever. When I found it, as of course I always did, he would say, 'thank you,' as quietly and naturally as if he had not been raving like a maniac half a minute before.

Eliza Lynn Linton, 'Reminiscences of W. S. Landor', 1870

Matthew Gregory ('Monk') Lewis · 1775–1818

(author of the Gothic novel *The Monk*)

Lord Melbourne told me the other day a queer trait of Lewis. He had a long-standing quarrel with Lushington. Having occasion to go to Naples, he wrote beforehand to him, to say that their quarrel had better be *suspended*, and he went and lived with him and his sister (Lady L.) in perfect cordiality during his stay. When he departed he wrote to Lushington to say that now they should resume their quarrel, and put matters in the 'status quo ante pacem,' [the state they were before their truce] and accordingly he did resume it, with rather more *acharnement* [ferocity] than before.

Charles Greville, *Memoirs*, entry for 29 June 1833

Thomas Campbell · 1777–1844

(poet; best remembered for 'Ye Mariners of England' and other war songs)

I had heard all my life of the vanity of women as a subject of pity to men: but when I went to London, lo! I saw vanity in high places which was never transcended by that of women in their lowlier rank. There was Brougham, wincing under a newspaper criticism, and playing the fool among silly women. There was Jeffrey, flirting with clever women, in long succession. There was Bulwer, on a sofa, sparkling and languishing among a set of female votaries—he and they dizened out, perfumed, and presenting the nearest picture to a seraglio to be seen on British ground—only the indifference or hauteur of the lord of the harem being absent. There was poor Campbell the poet, obtruding his sentimentalities, amidst a quivering apprehension of making himself ridiculous. He darted out of our house, and never came again, because, after warning, he sat down in a room full of people (all authors, as it happened) on a low chair of my old aunt's which went very easily on castors, and which carried him back to the wall and rebounded, of course making everybody laugh. Off went poor Campbell in a huff; and, well as I had long known him, I never saw him again: and I was not very sorry, for his sentimentality was too soft, and his craving for praise too morbid to let him be an agreeable companion.

Harriet Martineau, *Autobiography*, 1877

William Hazlitt · 1778–1830

Henry Crabb Robinson first met Hazlitt in 1798, when he was 20 and Robinson was 23:

The moment I saw him I saw he was an extraordinary man . . . But I was alone of this opinion then. I recollect saying to my sister about this time, 'Whom do you suppose I hold to be the cleverest person I know?'—'Capel Lofft, perhaps?'—'No.'—'Mrs Clarkson?'—'Oh! no.'—'Miss Maling?'—'No.'—'I give it up.'—'William Hazlitt.'—'Oh, you are joking. Why, we all take him to be a fool.' At this time he was excessively shy, and in company the girls always made game of him. He had a horror of the society of ladies, especially of smart and handsome and modest young women. The prettiest girl of our parties about this time was Miss Kitchener. She used to drive him mad by teasing him.

Henry Crabb Robinson, Reminiscences, 1849

Hazlitt got his start in journalism on the Morning Chronicle, *under the editorship of James Perry. His contributions to the paper included some of his finest theatre criticism:*

I have just been reading Hazlitt's *View of the English Stage*—a series of critiques originally printed in different newspapers, particularly the *Chronicle* . . . I was at Tavistock House at the time, and well remember the doleful visage with which Mr Perry used to contemplate the long column of criticism, and how he used to execrate 'the d—d fellow's d—d stuff' for filling up so much of the paper in the very height of the advertisement season. I shall never forget his long face. It was the only time of the day that I ever saw it long or sour. He had not the slightest suspicion that he had a man of genius in his pay—not the most remote perception of the merit of the writing—nor the slightest companionship with the author. He hired him as you hire your footman; and turned him off (with as little or less ceremony than you would use in discharging the aforesaid worthy personage) for a very masterly but damaging critique on Sir Thomas Lawrence, whom Mr P, as one whom he visited and was being painted by, chose to have praised.

Hazlitt's revenge was exceedingly characteristic. Last winter, when his *Characters of Shakespear* and his lectures had brought him into fashion, Mr Perry remembered him as an old acquaintance, and asked him to dinner, and a large party to meet him, to hear him talk, and to show him off as the lion of the day. The lion came—smiled and bowed—handed Miss Bentley to the dining room—asked Miss Perry to take wine—said once 'Yes' and twice 'No'— and never uttered another word the whole evening. The most provoking part of this scene was, that he was gracious and polite past all expression—a perfect pattern of mute elegance—a silent Lord Chesterfield; and his unlucky host had the misfortune to be very thoroughly enraged, without anything to complain of.

Mary Russell Mitford, letter, December 1818

He used to play at rackets for five or six hours at a time; sometimes quarrelling with his adversary, but not bearing malice. He liked a stout antagonist. 'That fellow', said he, speaking of one who showed himself disheartened, 'will never do anything in the world; he never plays well, unless he is successful. If the chances go against him, he always misses the ball: he cries *Craven!*'—'That', said some one, 'is French courage.'—'I don't call it courage at all,' said H., 'and certainly not French courage. The French have fought well; they have endured, too, more than enough—without your present imputation. Did you ever fight a Frenchman?'—'No.'—'Then don't make up your mind yet to your theory: reduce it to practice, and see if it be bullet-proof.'

Bryan Waller Procter, 'My Recollections of the Late William Hazlitt', 1830

Miscalculating his expenses, he once found himself at Stamford reduced almost to his last shilling. He set off to walk to Cambridge, but having a new pair of boots on they gave him acute pain. In this predicament, he tried at twenty different places to exchange them for a pair of shoes or slippers of any sort, but no one would accommodate him. He made this a charge against the English. 'Though they would have got treble the value by exchanging', said he, 'they would not do it, because it would have been useful to me.'—'Perhaps', said some one jestingly, 'they did not know that you came honestly by them.'—'Ah! true,' said H., 'that did not strike me before. That shakes my theory in this respect, if it be true; but then, it corroborates another part of it; so the fact is valuable either way. There is always a want of liberality, either in their thoughts or actions.' (This was merely humour.)

Procter, 'Recollections'.

Thomas Moore · 1779–1852

(Irish poet and satirist; friend of Byron)

In 1806 Francis Jeffrey reviewed Moore's poems in the Edinburgh Review. *He described them as 'a tissue of sick and fantastical conceits', and summed up the author as 'the most licentious of modern versifiers and the most poetical of those who in our time have devoted themselves to the propagation of immorality':*

Moore decided that his only course was to call Jeffrey out. His first difficulty was that Jeffrey was, he believed, in Edinburgh and he could not afford the fare to Scotland. Then, having learnt that Jeffrey was in London, he had some trouble in finding a second. However, eventually his friend, Dr Thomas Hume, agreed to act and Jeffrey secured the services of Francis Horner. It was settled that they should meet next morning at Chalk Farm, but another difficulty arose. Neither Moore nor Jeffrey owned a pistol and the weapons had to be borrowed by Moore from a friend. When they all arrived at Chalk Farm next morning, it was discovered that Horner, Jeffrey's second, was completely ignorant of firearms and the loading of Jeffrey's pistol had to be entrusted to Moore's second, Hume. By the time the two seconds were ready, the principals were engaged in a friendly conversation. Moore had made a conventional remark about the weather, which was quite enough to set Jeffrey off. However, honour demanded that the duel should proceed; they took up their positions and raised their pistols, when a crowd of police-officers jumped out of the neighbouring bushes and arrested them. The lender of the pistols had dined out on the story and, as a result, a Bow Street magistrate had been informed. As they waited at Bow Street for bail to be arranged, Jeffrey lay at full length on a bench and talked about literature.

So far the incident had been ridiculous enough, but worse was to follow. Moore, after he had been released on bail, realised that he had forgotten the pistols. On returning to retrieve them, he found a constable perplexed at the discovery that Moore's pistol had a bullet in it, but Jeffrey's had not. The seconds had been incompetent, but it did not look very well. Moore tried to persuade the seconds to sign an explanation, but Hume decided that he had made a fool enough of himself already. It took Moore a long time to forgive his friend. On top of all that, a newspaper account substituted the word 'pellet' for 'bullet' and the most was made of the misprint, if that is what it was. It was a mistake for Moore to try to save his dignity by writing a letter to *The Times*. But what came out of it all was an enduring friendship between Moore and Jeffrey. Thirty-seven years later Moore wrote in his diary: 'Breakfasted at

Rogers's, to meet Jeffrey and Lord John,—two of the men I like best among my numerous friends. Jeffrey's volubility (which was always superabundant) becomes even more copious, I think, as he grows older. But I am ashamed of myself for finding *any* fault with him. Long may he flourish . . .'

Robert Birley, *Sunk Without Trace*, 1962

In 1841 Moore went back to Ireland for the last time. He was widely fêted, and the send-off he received when he finally returned to England was even warmer than he could have foreseen:

ENCOUNTERED an odd scene on going on board. The packet was full of people coming to see friends off, and among others was a party of ladies who, I should think, had dined on board, and who, on my being made known to them, almost devoured me with kindness, and at length proceeded so far as to insist on each of them *kissing me*. At this time I was beginning to feel the first rudiments of coming *sickness*, and the effort to respond to all this enthusiasm, in such a state of stomach, was not a little awkward and trying. However, I kissed the whole party (about five, I think,) in succession, two or three of them being, for my comfort, young and good-looking, and was most glad to get away from them to my berth, which, through the kindness of the captain (Emerson), was in his own cabin. But I had hardly shut the door, feeling very qualmish, when there came a gentle tap at the door, and an elderly lady made her appearance, who said that having heard of all that had been going on, she could not rest easy without being also kissed as well as the rest. So, in the most respectful manner possible, I complied with the lady's request, and then betook myself with a heaving stomach to my berth.

Thomas Moore, journal, 1841

LEIGH HUNT · 1784–1859

In 1813 Hunt and his brother were sentenced to two years' imprisonment for libelling the Prince Regent in their paper the Examiner*:*

LEIGH HUNT came in sight of the gate and high wall of the prison, and after waiting in the yard 'as long as if it had been the anteroom of a Minister', was taken into the presence of his gaoler—a solemn man with a scarlet face and a white night-cap on, whose first remark was, 'Mister, I'd ha' given a matter of a hundred pounds, that you should not come to this place—a hundred pounds!' This unusual altruist, however, did not propose any immediate softening of the hardship, and Hunt perceived that the sum mentioned was the essential condition.

Edmund Blunden, *Leigh Hunt*, 1930

In 1843 there was quite a comedy between Hunt and Macaulay. Hunt repaid a loan. Macaulay sent back the cheque. Hunt returned it. Macaulay sent it back again. Hunt returned it.

Blunden, *Leigh Hunt*

Hunt was often accused of unscrupulous sponging: this is one of a number of instances Blunden cites which suggest otherwise.

It would be truer to say that he had a gift for attracting generosity—and for squandering the proceeds when he received them. Helping him, according to Byron, was like trying to rescue a drowning man who persisted in throwing himself back into the water.

In one of his essays Max Beerbohm considers the question of how long a young writer should be kept waiting, to achieve maximum impact, when he meets one of his literary heroes for the first time:

I should say, roughly, that in ten minutes the young man would be strung up to the right pitch, and that more than twenty minutes would be too much. It is important that expectancy shall have worked on him to the full, but it is still more important that his mood shall not have been chafed to impatience. The danger of over-long delay is well exemplified in the sad case of young Coventry Patmore. In his old age Patmore wrote to Mr Gosse a description of a visit he had paid, at the age of eighteen, to Leigh Hunt. The circumstances had been most propitious. The eager and sensitive spirit of the young man, his intense admiration for 'The Story of Rimini,' the letter of introduction from his father to the venerable poet and friend of greater bygone poets, the long walk to Hammersmith, the small house in a square there—all was classically in order. The poet was at home. The visitor was shown in. . . . 'I had,' he was destined to tell Mr Gosse, 'waited in the little parlour at least two hours, when the door was opened and a most picturesque gentleman, with hair flowing nearly or quite to his shoulders, a beautiful velvet coat and a Vandyck collar of lace about a foot deep, appeared, rubbing his hands, and smiling ethereally, and saying, without a word of preface or notice of my having waited so long, "This is a beautiful world, Mr Patmore!" ' The young man was so taken aback by these words that they 'eclipsed all memory of what occurred during the remainder of the visit.'

Yet there was nothing wrong about the words themselves. Indeed, to any one with any sense of character and any knowledge of Leigh Hunt, they must seem to have been exactly, exquisitely, inevitably the right words. But they should have been said sooner.

Max Beerbohm, 'A Point to Be Remembered by Very Eminent Men', 1918

Thomas de Quincey · 1785–1859

Henry Crabb Robinson found De Quincey's autobiographical writings entertaining, especially his anecdotes of the Lake Poets, but he deplored what he thought was their unduly personal tone and their betrayal of private confidences:

I was with Wordsworth one day when the advertisement of one of his papers was read. The poet said with great earnestness: 'I beg that no friend of mine will ever tell me a word of the contents of those papers,' and I daresay he was substantially obeyed. It was a year or two afterwards (for these papers went on for a long time and were very amusing) however, that I ventured to say: 'I cannot help telling one thing De Q. says in his last number in these very words—that Mrs W. is a better wife than you deserve.' 'Did he say that?' W. exclaimed in a tone of unusual vehemence, 'Did he say that? That is *so* true that I can forgive him almost anything else he says.' Yet writing of Mrs W. in terms of the most extravagant eulogy, he could not refrain from concluding: '*But she squints.*'

Henry Crabb Robinson, Reminiscences, 1849

When De Quincey was most depressed, there was one talisman I held by which, judiciously used, I could nearly always 'lift' him. This was 'The Baker' in the famous essay on 'Murder Considered as One of the Fine Arts.'

We had somehow gradually established a queer sort of freemasonry about this character. It is difficult to define it. Perhaps I may put it that we had elected to consider him a handy man at a pinch—a man quite free from shilly-shally—always decided in his views, and with a certain ready activity in asserting them.

When the fits of depression came on, and in cold weather they were often long and severe (De Quincey sometimes said to me that he had never been thoroughly warm all his life), I watched my chance.

When I saw that things were at the worst, when some peculiarly moody, morbid observation showed the mental tension and physical misery, I used to remark, rather suddenly and shortly, '*What would the Baker say?*'

The effect was perfectly magical. The drooping head was raised, the pallid face slowly wreathed into a half-amused smile, which seemed to convey: 'Well, that is a good idea. We have not yet considered what can be said and what can be done from that point of view.' It seemed to act as a mental tonic. After a short pause he would start some subject—something often which I saw he expected would make me disputatious. Gradually he warmed to it, and as I kept 'the ball rolling' by a few brisk rejoinders, or some fresh 'feelers' which were not difficult to find, away he went—full speed.

The original subject soon became two; by-and-by it branched and became half a dozen. The torpor and depression seemed to disappear as the active, awakened brain found expression through the tongue, and in two or three hours I would leave him quite a new man.

James Hogg, *De Quincey and his Friends*, 1895

> *The baker in* On Murder Considered as One of the Fine Arts *is a middle-aged German who is 'pursy, unwieldy, half-cataleptic' but who is roused to extraordinary feats of resistance when a would-be killer attacks him.*
>
> *The James Hogg from whose recollections this passage comes was an Edinburgh editor and journalist, not to be confused with the author of* The Private Memoirs of a Justified Sinner.

In 1853 James Payn visited De Quincey at his home a few miles outside Edinburgh:

As I took my leave, after a most enjoyable interview, to meet the coach, I asked him whether he ever came by it into Edinburgh.

'What!' he answered, in a tone of extreme surprise; 'by coach? Certainly not.'

I was not aware of his peculiarities; but the succession of commonplace people and their pointless observations were in fact intolerable to him. They did not bore him in the ordinary sense, but seemed, as it were, to outrage his mind. To me, to whom the study of human nature in any form had become even then attractive, this was unintelligible, and I suppose I showed it in my face, for he proceeded to explain matters. 'Some years ago,' he said, 'I was standing on the pier at Tarbet, on Loch Lomond, waiting for the steamer. A stout old lady joined me; I felt that she would presently address me; and she did. Pointing to the smoke of the steamer, which was making itself seen above the next headland, "There she comes," she said; "La, sir! if you and I had seen that fifty years ago, how wonderful we should have thought it!" Now the same thing,' added my host, with a shiver, 'might happen to me any day, and that is why I always avoid a public conveyance.'

James Payn, *Some Literary Recollections*, 1884

De Quincey had what his biographer Edward Sackville-West calls a 'strange passion for multiplying sets of lodgings':

ONE of his reasons for this extravagant system of living was a desire to escape from the importunities of friends. Another, more important, was his dislike of throwing anything—books, papers, manuscripts—away, combined with an even more intense objection to having his belongings 'tidied'. In this he did not differ from most men of letters; but few even of them can have collected such literary snow-drifts as De Quincey managed to amass during the last years of his life. When tables, chairs, bed and floor were entirely encumbered, and even the narrow path between the door and the fireplace had become silted up, he would simply lock the door of the room and betake himself to another lodging, there to remain until once more driven on by a similar state of affairs. At his death, no less than six sets of lodgings were found in this condition.

Edward Sackville-West, *A Flame in Sunlight*, 1936

Thomas Love Peacock · 1785–1866

Peacock entered the service of the East India Company in 1819. The papers which won him his place there were returned by the examiners with the comment 'Nothing superfluous, nothing wanting'.

One of his colleagues at India House was the Utilitarian philosopher and historian James Mill, a man whom he was never likely to find congenial:

Coulson [a journalist] once asked Peacock: 'When I know Mill well, shall I like him—will he like what I like and hate what I hate?' Peacock replied: 'No, he will hate what you hate, and hate everything you like.'

Edward Strachey, 'Recollections of Peacock', 1891

Richard Whately · 1787–1863

(philosopher and political economist; Archbishop of Dublin)

He was of a gigantic size and a gaunt aspect, with a strange unconsciousness of the body; and, what is perhaps the next best thing to a perfect manner, he had *no* manner. What his legs and arms were about was best known to themselves. His rank placed him by the side of the Lord-Lieutenant's wife when dining at the Castle, and the wife of one of the Lord-Lieutenants has told me that she had occasionally to remove the Archbishop's foot out of her lap.

Henry Taylor, *Autobiography*, 1885

It was Whately who once wrote that 'it is folly to expect men to do all that they may be reasonably expected to do'.

Lord Byron · 1788–1824

Between 1805 and 1807 Byron was an undergraduate at Trinity College, Cambridge.

When he returned to Cambridge in the autumn, he bought a tame bear and lodged him in the small hexagonal tower above his rooms. He enjoyed the sensation he made when he took bruin for walks on a chain like a dog. He announced with pride to Elizabeth Pigot: 'I have got a new friend, the finest in the world, a *tame bear*. When I brought him here, they asked me what I meant to do with him, and my reply was, "he should *sit for a fellowship.*" '

Leslie Marchant, *Byron: A Portrait*, 1971

Drury had some dogs (two, I believe) sent him that had belonged to Lord Byron. One day he was told that two ladies wished to see him, and he found their business was to ask, as a great favour, some relic of Lord Byron. Expecting to be asked for some of his handwriting, or a bit of his hair, he was amused to find that it was a bit of the hair of one of the dogs they wanted. The dog being brought forward the ladies observed a *clot* on his back, which had evidently resisted any efforts at ablution that might have been exerted on the animal, and immediately selected this as the most precious part to be cut off; 'the probability,' they said, 'being that Lord B. might have patted that clot.'

Thomas Moore, journal, June 1827

Somebody possessed Madame de Staël with an opinion of my immorality. I used occasionally to visit her at *Coppet*; and once she invited me to a family-dinner, and I found the room full of strangers, who had come to stare at me as at some outlandish beast in a raree-show. One of the ladies fainted, and the rest looked as if his Satanic Majesty had been among them. Madame de Staël took the liberty to read me a lecture before this crowd; to which I only made her a low bow.

Thomas Medwin, *Conversations of Lord Byron*, 1824

Women, when young, are usually pliant, and readily adapt themselves to any changes. Lady Byron was not of this flexible type: she had made up her mind on all subjects, and reversed the saying of Socrates, that 'all he had learned was, he knew nothing.' She thought she knew everything. She was exacting, capricious, resentful, excessively jealous, suspicious, and credulous. She only lived with him one year out of her long life. Byron was not demonstrative of things appertaining to himself, especially to women, and Lady Byron judged men by her father and the country neighbours, and Byron was so dissimilar to them in all his ways as to bewilder her. She would come into his study when he was in the throes of composition, and finding he took no notice of her, say,

'Am I interrupting you?'

'Yes, most damnably.'

This was to her a dreadful shock; he thought nothing of it; he had received his greater shock in being interrupted.

E. J. Trelawny, *Records of Shelley, Byron, and the Author*, 1878

HE bragged, too, of his prowess in riding, boxing, fencing, and even walking; but to excel in these things feet are as necessary as hands. It was difficult to avoid smiling at his boasting and self-glorification. In the water a fin is better than a foot, and in that element he did well; he was built for floating,—with a flexible body, open chest, broad beam, and round limbs. If the sea was smooth and warm, he would stay in it for hours; but as he seldom indulged in this sport, and when he did, over-exerted himself, he suffered severely; which observing, and knowing how deeply he would be mortified at being beaten, I had the magnanimity when contending with him to give in.

He had a misgiving in his mind that I was trifling with him; and one day as we were on the shore, and the 'Bolivar' at anchor, about three miles off, he insisted on our trying conclusions; we were to swim to the yacht, dine in the sea alongside of her, treading water the while, and then to return to the shore. It was calm and hot, and seeing he would not be fobbed off, we started. I reached the boat a long time before he did; ordered the edibles to be ready, and floated until he arrived. We ate our fare leisurely, from off a grating that floated alongside, drank a bottle of ale, and I smoked a cigar, which he tried to extinguish,—as he never smoked. We then put about, and struck off towards the shore. We had not got a hundred yards on our passage, when he retched violently, and, as that is often followed by cramp, I urged him to put his hand on my shoulder that I might tow him back to the schooner.

'Keep off, you villain, don't touch me. I'll drown ere I give in.'

I answered as Iago did to Roderigo:

'"A fig for drowning! drown cats and blind puppies." I shall go on board and try the effects of a glass of grog to stay my stomach.'

'Come on,' he shouted, 'I am always better after vomiting.' With difficulty I deluded him back; I went on board, and he sat on the steps of the accommodation-ladder, with his feet in the water. I handed him a wine-glass of brandy, and screened him from the burning sun. He was in a sullen mood, but after a time resumed his usual tone. Nothing could induce him to be landed in the schooner's boat, though I protested I had had enough of the water.

'You may do as you like,' he called out, and plumped in, and we swam on shore.

He never afterwards alluded to this event, nor to his prowess in swimming, to me, except in the past tense. He was ill, and kept his bed for two days afterwards.

E. J. Trelawny, *Recollections of the Last Days of Shelley and Byron*, 1858

Teresa, Countess Guiccioli, met Byron in Venice in 1819, when she was 19 and had been married (to a much older man) for little more than a year. She became the poet's 'last attachment', and remained under his spell for the rest of her long life:

In later years Teresa lived much in Paris. Count Guiccioli died in 1840, and after a long courtship the Marquis de Boissy led her to the altar in the chapel of the Luxembourg, a bride of forty-seven. She was still handsome, but the simplicity of her manners, which had pleased Byron, had passed into affectation. Many visitors of later years have reported the absurdity into which she was carried by her Byron-worship. She kept a portrait of her poet lover in her salon, and she would stand before it and exclaim: '*Qu'il était beau! Mon Dieu, qu'il était beau!*' The Marquis, with French complacency, was proud of his wife's liaison with the famous poet, and when asked if she was related to the Countess Guiccioli who had once been connected with Lord Byron, replied with a beaming smile: '*Comment donc, mais c'est elle-même, c'est elle!*' It is also reported that he used to introduce his wife as '*La Marquise de Boissy ma femme, ancienne maîtresse de Byron.*'

After the Marquis's death in 1866, Teresa devoted herself to spiritualism and talked with the spirits of both Byron and her husband. She happily reported: 'They are together now, and are the best of friends.'

Marchant, *Byron*

James Fenimore Cooper · 1789–1851

Cooper died at his home in Cooperstown, NY, the day before his sixty-second birthday:

American literature was still so new that Cooper's was the first death of an American author internationally famous solely as a man of letters. The literary community felt that the unprecedented occasion demanded special forms and observances. Within a few days a meeting was held at City Hall in New York at which Washington Irving presided; a committee was formed which laid plans to set up in New York a colossal statue of the dead novelist . . . The Cooper Monument Association never succeeded in raising enough money, and after years of effort turned over its funds to a group in Cooperstown, which added to them and erected a charming small shaft with a statue of Leather-Stocking, in Lakewood Cemetery outside the village.

James Grossman, *James Fenimore Cooper*, 1950

Leather-Stocking is the hero of Cooper's best-known novels.

Percy Bysshe Shelley · 1792–1822

He had a prejudice against theatres which I took some pains to overcome. I induced him one evening to accompany me to a representation of the *School for Scandal*. When, after the scenes which exhibit Charles Surface in his jollity, the scene returned in the fourth act, to Joseph's library, Shelley said to me—'I see the purpose of this comedy. It is to associate virtue with bottles and glasses, and villainy with books.' I had great difficulty to make him stay to the end. He often talked of 'the withering and perverted spirit of comedy'.

Thomas Love Peacock, *Memoirs of Shelley*, 1858–62

In 1816 Shelley was staying in Switzerland with Mary Shelley, Claire Clairmont, Byron, and the Anglo-Italian physician J. W. Polidori. The members of the party all agreed to try their hand at writing a ghost story. One eventual outcome was Mary Shelley's Frankenstein *(1818), but in his diary Polidori describes a more immediate consequence:*

Began my ghost-story after tea. Twelve o'clock, really began to talk ghostly. Lord Byron repeated some verses of Coleridge's 'Christabel', of the witch's breast; when silence ensued, and Shelley, suddenly shrieking and putting his hands to his head, ran out of the room with a candle. Threw water in his face, and after gave him ether. He was looking at Mrs Shelley, and suddenly thought of a woman he had heard of who had eyes instead of nipples, which, taking hold of his mind, horrified him.

The Diary of Dr John William Polidori Relating to Byron, Shelley, etc., published 1911

When I was at Leghorn with Shelley, I drew him towards the docks, saying:

'As we have a spare hour let's see if we can't put a girdle round about the earth in forty minutes. In these docks are living specimens of all the nationalities of the world; thus we can go round it, and visit and examine any particular nation we like, observing their peculiar habits, manners, dress, language, food, productions, arts, and naval architecture; for see how varied are the shapes, build, rigging, and decoration of the different vessels. There lies an English cutter, a French chasse marée, an American clipper, a Spanish tartan, an Austrian trabacolo, a Genoese felucca, a Sardinian zebeck, a Neapolitan brig, a Sicilian sparanza, a Dutch galleot, a Danish snow, a Russian hermaphrodite, a Turkish sackalever, a Greek bombard. I don't see a Persian dow, an Arab grab, or a Chinese junk; but there are enough for our purpose and to spare. As you are writing a poem, *Hellas*, about the modern Greeks, would it not be as well to take a look at them amidst all the din of the docks? I hear their shrill nasal voices, and should like to know if you can trace in the language or lineaments of these Greeks of the nineteenth century, A.D., the faintest resemblance to the lofty and sublime spirits who lived in the fourth century, B.C. An English merchant who has dealings with them, told me he thought these modern Greeks were, if judged by their actions, a cross between the Jews and gypsies;—but here comes the Capitano Zarita; I know him.'

So dragging Shelley with me I introduced him, and asking to see the vessel, we crossed the plank from the quay and stood on the deck of the 'San Spiridione' in the midst of her chattering irascible crew. They took little heed of the skipper, for in these trading vessels each individual of the crew is part owner, and has some share in the cargo; so they are all interested in the speculation—having no wages. They squatted about the decks in small knots, shrieking, gesticulating, smoking, eating, and gambling like savages.

'Does this realise your idea of Hellenism, Shelley?' I said.

'No! but it does of Hell,' he replied.

The captain insisted on giving us pipes and coffee in his cabin, so I dragged Shelley down. Over the rudder-head facing us, there was a gilt box enshrining a flaming gaudy daub of a saint, with a lamp burning before it; this was Il Padre Santo Spiridione, the ship's godfather. The skipper crossed himself and squatted on the dirty divan. Shelley talked to him about the Greek revolution that was taking place, but from its interrupting trade the captain was opposed to it.

'Come away!' said Shelley. 'There is not a drop of the old Hellenic blood here. These are not the men to rekindle the ancient Greek fire; their souls are extinguished by traffic and superstition. Come away!'—and away we went.

'It is but a step,' I said, 'from these ruins of worn-out Greece to the New World, let's board the American clipper.'

'I had rather not have any more of my hopes and illusions mocked by sad realities,' said Shelley.

'You must allow,' I answered, 'that graceful craft was designed by a man who had a poet's feeling for things beautiful; let's get a model and build a boat like her.'

The idea so pleased the Poet that he followed me on board her. The Americans are a social, free-and-easy people, accustomed to take their own way, and to readily yield the same privilege to all others, so that our coming on board, and examination of the vessel, fore and aft, were not considered as intrusion. The captain was on shore, so I talked to the mate, a smart specimen of a Yankee. When I commended her beauty, he said:

'I do expect, now we have our new copper on, she has a look of the brass sarpent, she has as slick a run, and her bearings are just where they should be.'

I said we wished to build a boat after her model.

'Then I calculate you must go to Baltimore or Boston to get one; there is no one on this side the water can do the job. We have our freight all ready, and are homeward-bound; we have elegant accommodation, and you will be across before your young friend's beard is ripe for a razor. Come down, and take an observation of the state cabin.'

It was about seven and a half feet by five; 'plenty of room to live or die comfortably in,' he observed, and then pressed us to have a chaw of real old Virginian cake, *i.e.* tobacco, and a cool drink of peach brandy. I made some observation to him about the Greek vessel we had visited.

'Crank as an eggshell,' he said; 'too many sticks and top hamper, she looks like a bundle of chips going to hell to be burnt.'

I seduced Shelley into drinking a wine-glass of weak grog, the first and last he ever drank. The Yankee would not let us go until we had drunk, under the star-spangled banner, to the memory of Washington, and the prosperity of the American commonwealth.

'As a warrior and statesman,' said Shelley, 'he was righteous in all he did, unlike all who lived before or since; he never used his power but for the benefit of his fellow-creatures:

"He fought,
For truth and wisdom, foremost of the brave;
Him glory's idle glances dazzled not;
'Twas his ambition, generous and great,
A life to life's great end to consecrate." '

'Stranger,' said the Yankee, 'truer words were never spoken; there is dry rot in all the main timbers of the Old World, and none of you will do any good till you are docked, refitted, and annexed to the New. You must log that song you sang; there ain't many Britishers that will say as much of the man that whipped them; so just set these lines down in the log, or it won't go for nothing.'

Shelley wrote some verses in the book, but not those he had quoted; and so we parted.

E. J. Trelawny, *Recollections of the Last Days of Shelley and Byron*, 1858

BOSCOMBE. Sir Percy and Lady Shelley and *two sisters of Percy Bysshe Shelley*. I sat between them at dinner, having taken in Shelley's favourite sister, whose name is spelt 'Hellen.' She was lively and chatty, and I looked at and listened to her with great interest. She is tall, very slender, and must have been graceful and handsome in her youth. I saw, or fancied, a likeness to Shelley. She was sumptuous in light purple silk, which became her. She looked about fifty-six, but must be much more. Her sister, who seemed rather younger, was much less lively. Tennyson's name occurring in conversation, Miss Hellen Shelley let it plainly appear that neither he nor any modern poet was of the least interest in her eyes.

'After Shelley, Byron, and Scott, you know,' she said to me, 'one cannot care about other poets.'

Somebody had once read to her a poem of Tennyson's, which she liked, but she could not remember what it was. It seemed doubtful that she had ever heard of Browning.

Mr Grantley Berkeley at dinner—a tall strong man over sixty, like a militaire. He lives in this neighbourhood on small means, is a great sportsman, and his talk worth listening to on the habits of animals, etc. . . .

In the drawing-room we found Miss Hellen Shelley stretched on a sofa, with two dainty white satin shoes with rosettes peeping beyond the purple robe, and looking really elegant. Her recollections of Leigh Hunt were not of a friendly sort, so I did not pursue the subject. She always speaks of her brother as 'Bysshe.' A young lady sung an Italian song. I came away about 10. Sir Percy Florence Shelley is a rather short, fair and fattish man of forty-five. The nose, which is like his mother's, projects when seen in profile, but the front face is roundish and smooth, with small eyes, and a bald forehead over which the pale light-brown hair is partly drawn. His voice is very quiet but in a high key (the only point reminding one of his father), his words few, and whole manner placid, and even apathetic. He likes yachting and private theatricals, cares little or nothing for poetry or literature. He has a thinly-humorous, lounging, self-possessed, quietly contemptuous manner of comment and narration. When I mentioned Tennyson's poetry, Sir Percy said fellows had bored him a good deal with it at one time. He never read any of it of his own accord—saw no sense in it.

William Allingham, *Diary*, 1907; entry for 29 October 1864

John Clare · 1793–1864

Clare was the son of a farm labourer; his mother was illiterate.

My father woud sometimes be huming over a song, a wretched composition of those halfpenny ballads, and my boast was that I thought I coud beat it   in a few days afterwards I used to read my composition for his judgment to decide, but their frequent critisisms and laughable remarks drove me to use a process of cunning in the business some time after, for they damp'd me a long time from proceeding. My method on resuming the matter again was to say I had written it out of a borrowd book and that it was not my own   the love of ryhming which I was loath to quit, growing fonder of it every day, drove me to the nessesity of a lie to try the value of their critisisms and by this way I got their remarks unadulterated with prejudice—in this case their expressions woud be, 'Aye, boy, if you coud write so, you woud do.' this got me into the secret at once and without divulging mine   I scribbld on unceasing for 2 or 3 years, reciting them every night as I wrote them when my father returnd home from labour and we was all seated by the fire side   their remarks was very useful to me   at somethings they woud laugh   here I distinguishd Affectation and consiet from nature   some verses they woud desire me to repeat again as they said they coud not understand them here I discovered obscurity from common sense and always benefited by making it as much like the latter as I coud, for I thought if they coud not understand me my taste should be wrong founded and not agreeable to nature, so I always strove to shun it for the future and wrote my pieces according to their critisisms, little thinking when they heard me read them that I was the author

Sketches in the Life of John Clare, 1821

My mother brought me a picturd pocket hankerchief from Deeping may fair as a fairing on which was a picture of Chatterton and his Verses on Resignation   chance had the choice of it   she was mentioning the singular circumstance to me yesterday be asking me wether I remembered it and saying that she little thought I shoud be a poet then as she shoud have felt fearful if she had for Chattertons name was clouded in mellancholly memorys which his extrodinary Genius was scarcly known the common people knew he was a poet and that was all   they know the name of Shakespear as one but the ballad monger who prints and supplys hawkers with their ware are poets with them and they imagine one as great as the other   so much for that envied emenence of common fame

Autobiographical fragments, 1821–8

Clare visited London for the first time in 1820:

On the night we got into London it was announcd in the Play Bills that a song of mine was to be sung at Covent garden by Madam Vestris and we was to have gone but it was too late I felt uncommonly pleasd at the circumstance we took a walk in the town by moonlight and went to westminster bridge to see the river thames I had heard large wonders about its width of water but when I saw it I was dissapointed thinking I shoud have seen a fresh water sea and when I saw it twas less in my eye then Whittlesea Meer I was uncommonly astonished to see so many ladys as I thought them walking about the streets I expressd my suprise and was told they were girls of the town as a modest woman rarely venturd out by her self at nightfall

Autobiographical fragments

In 1837 Clare was admitted to an asylum for the insane near Epping. In 1841 he made his escape from it and set out to walk home to Northamptonshire:

July 20—Reconnitered the rout the Gipsey pointed out and found it a legible one to make a movement and having only honest courage and myself in my army I Led the way and my troops soon followed but being careless in mapping down the rout as the Gipsey told me I missed the lane to Enfield town and was going down Enfield highway till I passed 'The Labour in vain' Public house where A person I knew comeing out of the door told me the way

I walked down the lane gently and was soon in Enfield Town and bye and bye on the great York Road where it was all plain sailing and steering ahead meeting no enemy and fearing none I reached Stevenage where being Night I got over a gate crossed over the corner of a green paddock where seeing a pond or hollow in the corner I forced to stay off a respectable distance to keep from falling into it for my legs were nearly knocked up and began to stagger I scaled some old rotten paleings into the yard and then had higher pailings to clamber over to get into the shed or hovel which I did with difficulty being rather weak and to my good luck I found some trusses of clover piled up about 6 or more feet square which I gladly mounted and slept on there was some trays in the hovel on which I could have reposed had I not found a better bed I slept soundly but had a very uneasy dream I thought my first wife lay on my left arm and somebody took her away from my side which made me wake up rather unhappy I thought as I awoke somebody said 'Mary' but nobody was near—I lay down with my head towards the north to show myself the steering point in the morning

'The Journey from Essex'; notebook, 1841

The 'first wife' Clare refers to was his childhood sweetheart Mary

Joyce. When he went mad he suffered from the delusion that he had been married to her before marrying his actual wife.

John Keats · 1795–1821

Henry Stephens was a fellow-student of Keats at Guy's Hospital. Some thirty-five years later he set down his recollections of the poet at this period:

WHILST attending lectures, he would sit and instead of copying out the lecture, would often scribble some doggerel rhymes among the notes of lecture, particularly if he got hold of another student's Syllabus. In my Syllabus of chemical lectures he scribbled many lines on the paper cover. This cover has been long torn off, except one small piece on which is the following fragment of doggerel rhyme:

Give me women, wine & snuff
Until I cry out, 'hold! Enough'.
You may do so, sans objection
Until the day of resurrection . . .

This is all that remains, and is the only piece of his writing which is now in my possession.

Letter to G. F. Mathew, 1847; quoted in *The Keats Circle*, ed. H. E. Rollins, 1948

Stephens gave up medicine and became a celebrated ink manufacturer. The fragmentary manuscript which he quotes in the letter survives; he omitted the last two lines—

For bless my beard they aye shall be
My beloved Trinity.

WHEN Wordsworth came to Town, I brought Keats to him, by his Wordsworth's desire. Keats expressed to me as we walked to Queen Anne St East the greatest, the purest, the most unalloyed pleasure at the prospect. Wordsworth received him kindly, and after a few minutes asked him what he had been lately doing. *I* said he had just finished an exquisite ode to Pan [the 'Hymn to Pan' in *Endymion*], and as he had not a copy I begged Keats to repeat it—which he did in his usual half chant (most touching), walking up and down the room. When he had done I felt really as if I had heard a young Apollo. Wordsworth drily said

'a very pretty piece of Paganism'—

This was unfeeling & unworthy of his high Genius to a young worshipper like Keats—& Keats felt it *deeply*.

B. R. Haydon, letter to Edward Moxon, 1845

In the spring of 1819 a nightingale had built her nest near my house. Keats felt a tranquil and continual joy in her song; and one morning he took his chair from the breakfast-table to the grass-plot under a plum-tree, where he sat for two or three hours. When he came into the house, I perceived he had some scraps of paper in his hand, and these he was quietly thrusting behind the books. On inquiry, I found those scraps, four or five in number, contained his poetic feeling on the song of our nightingale. The writing was not well legible, and it was difficult to arrange the stanzas on so many scraps. With his assistance I succeeded, and this was his *Ode to a Nightingale*, a poem which has been the delight of every one.

Charles Brown, 'Life of John Keats', written 1836–41

A loose, slack, not well-dressed youth met Mr — and myself in a lane near Highgate. — knew him, and spoke. It was Keats. He was introduced to me and stayed a minute or so. After he had left us a little way, he came back and said: 'Let me carry away the memory, Coleridge, of having pressed your hand!'—'There is death in that hand,' I said to —, when Keats was gone; yet this was, I believe, before the consumption showed itself distinctly.

Samuel Taylor Coleridge, *Table Talk*, 14 August 1832

This meeting took place in April 1819. Coleridge's companion was a member of the staff of Guy's Hospital, Joseph Green.

Keats left a very different account of the same occasion, in the long journal-letter which he sent to his brother and sister-in-law in America the following month: 'Last Sunday I took a Walk towards highgate and in the lane that winds by the side of Lord Mansfield's park I met Mr Green our Demonstrator at Guy's in conversation with Coleridge—I joined them, after enquiring by a look whether it would be agreeable—I walked with him at his alderman-after-dinner pace for nearly two miles I suppose. In those two Miles he broached a thousand things—let me see if I can give you a list—Nightingales, Poetry—on Poetical Sensation—Metaphysics—Different genera and species of Dreams—Nightmare—a dream accompanied by a sense of touch—single and double touch—A dream related—First and second consciousness—the difference between will and Volition—so many metaphysicians from a want of smoking the second consciousness—Monsters—the Kraken—Mermaids—Southey believes in them—Southey's belief too much diluted—A Ghost story—Good morning—I heard his voice as he came towards me—I heard it as he moved away—I had heard it all the interval—if it may be called so.'

ONE night, at eleven o'clock, he came into the house in a state that looked like fierce intoxication. Such a state in him, I knew, was impossible; it therefore was the more fearful. I asked hurriedly, 'What is the matter?—You are fevered?' 'Yes, yes,' he answered, 'I was on the outside of the stage this bitter day till I was severely chilled—but now I don't feel it. Fevered!—of course, a little.' He mildly and instantly yielded—a property in his nature towards any friend—to my request that he should go to bed. I followed with the best immediate remedy in my power. I entered the chamber as he leapt into bed. On entering the cold sheets, before his head was on the pillow, he slightly coughed, and I heard him say, 'That is blood from my mouth.' I went towards him; he was examining a single drop of blood upon the sheet. 'Bring me the candle, Brown, and let me see this blood.' After regarding it steadfastly, he looked up in my face, with a calmness of countenance that I can never forget, and said: 'I know the colour of that blood;—it is arterial blood;—I cannot be deceived in that colour; that drop of blood is my death-warrant—I must die.'

Charles Brown, 'Life of John Keats'

I DREAMT last night of dear Keats. I thought he appeared to me, and said, 'Haydon, you promised to make a drawing of my head before I died, and you did not do it. Paint me now.' I awoke and saw him as distinctly as if it was his spirit. I am convinced such an impression on common minds would have been mistaken for a ghost. I lay awake for hours dwelling on the remembrance of him. Dear Keats, I will paint thee, worthily, poetically.

Benjamin Robert Haydon, journal, 14 November 1831

Haydon failed to make good his vow.

WHILST I was in Rome Mr Severn introduced me to M. and Mme. Valentine de Llanos, a kindly couple. He was a Spaniard, lean, silent, dusky, and literary, the author of *Don Esteban* and *Sandoval*. She was fat, blonde, and lymphatic, and both were elderly. *She was John Keats's sister!* I had a good deal of talk with her, or rather *at* her, for she was not very responsive. I was disappointed, for I remember that my sprightliness made her yawn; she seemed inert and had nothing to tell me of her wizard brother, of whom she spoke as of a mystery—with a vague admiration but a genuine affection. She was simple and natural—I believe she is a very worthy woman.

Frederick Locker-Lampson, *My Confidences*, 1896

Thomas Carlyle · 1795–1881

Mazzini was clever and just in an amusing dispute with 'Thomas' about music. T.C. could see nothing in Beethoven's Sonatas—'It told nothing.' It was like a great quantity of stones tumbled down for a building, and 'it might have been as well left in the quarry'. He insisted on Mazzini telling him what he gained by hearing music, and when Mazzini said inspiration and elevation, Carlyle said something not respectful of Beethoven, and Mazzini ended with: '*Dieu vous pardonne*'.

Emma Darwin, quoted in David Alec Wilson, *Carlyle on Cromwell and Others*, 1925

Carlyle and Macaulay were once fellow guests at one of Samuel Rogers's breakfast parties. Carlyle's friend Monckton Milnes was also among those present:

Macaulay, overflowing with the stores of knowledge which had been accumulating during his sojourn in India, seized the first opportunity that presented itself, and having once obtained the ear of the company, never allowed it to escape even for a moment until the party was at an end. Greatly dissatisfied at the issue of a morning from which he had expected so much (or hoping to hear something worth repeating), Milnes followed Carlyle into the street. 'I am so sorry,' he said, 'that Macaulay would talk so much and prevent our hearing a single word from you.' Carlyle turned round and held up his hands in astonishment. 'What!' he said, 'was that the Right Honourable Tom? I had no idea that it was the Right Honourable Tom. Ah, well, I understand the Right Honourable Tom now.'

T. Wemyss Reid, *Richard Monckton Milnes*, 1890

On a subsequent occasion, when the journalist Francis Espinasse praised Macaulay, Carlyle turned on him and declared: 'Macaulay has never said anything not entirely commonplace.' But then he relented: 'He is a very brilliant fellow. Flow on, thou shining river!'

National Portrait Gallery—Lord Brougham. The Committee wanted to put in Brougham's portrait, the man still living, contrary to rule. C. opposed, and added that when Brougham did die he would speedily be forgotten. Lord Stanhope, Chairman, said with polite surprise, 'Oh, a very remarkable man, surely—great statesman, great orator!' 'No' (C. persisted), 'Brougham had done nothing worth remembering particularly; and at all events the rules of the Gallery, etc.,' and gained his point.

It was on this occasion that C. noticed Dizzy [Disraeli], who was present as a member of the Committee, looking at him in a noticeable way. 'He took no part in the discussion,' C. said, 'but I could see that he was looking at me with a face of brotherly recognition—a wholly sympathetic expression.' C. used often to refer to this brotherly look of Dizzy (which, however, may not have meant very much!) 'I found this look in his face—although I had more than once or twice said hard things of him publicly. I saw he entirely agreed with me as to Brougham.'

It gave C. a little leaning to Dizzy when he thought of it, tho' it did not change his opinion that D.'s success was a scandal and shame for England.

William Allingham, *Diary*, 1907; entry for 10 August 1862

Some of Carlyle's prejudices were decidedly sinister:

He stood still one day, opposite Rothschild's great house at Hyde Park Corner, looked at it a little, and said, 'I do not mean that I want King John back again, but if you ask me which mode of treating these people I hold to have been the nearest to the will of the Almighty about them—to build them palaces like that, or to take the pincers for them, I declare for the pincers.' Then he imagined himself King John, with the Baron on the bench before him. 'Now, sir, the State requires some of those millions you have heaped together with your financing work. "You won't?" very well,' and he gave a twist with his wrist—'Now will you?' and then another twist, until the millions were yielded. I would add, however, that the Jews were not the only victims whose grinders he believed democracy would make free with.

J. A. Froude, *Carlyle: A History of his Life in London*, 1884

Met Carlyle. We had been talking, on some previous day or days, about Stratford on Avon, to which I had paid a visit this May. When I quoted the tombstone lines 'Good Friend, for Jesus sake forbear,' etc., C. wished to correct me to 'Sweet Friend,' and would not be gainsaid: indeed he has used the 'Sweet Friend,' etc., several times in his writings and very frequently in conversation, and would not give it up save on compulsion. Today I brought proof in my pocket in the shape of a photograph of the stone with its inscription clearly legible, and as we sat on a tree-trunk I showed this to him in the quietest possible way—(not the least air of triumph, overt or covert). He looked at the photograph, said nothing or very little ('Ah, well,' perhaps, or the like), and handed it back without any formal retractation, though further argument was plainly impossible; and not long afterwards (I mean a few weeks later) he was using his beloved old formula, 'Sweet Friend,' as if nothing had happened, and so continued.

William Allingham, *Diary*, 1907; entry for 9 June 1873

C. SAID, 'I am reading Shakespeare again. I read *Othello* yesterday all through, and it quite distressed me. O what a fellow that is—honest Iago! I was once at this Play at Drury Lane (it would be in Macready's time—but *he* did not do me any good in it), and when Emilia said—

> O the more angel she
> And you the blacker devil!

a murmur swelled up from the whole audience into a passionate burst of approval, the voices of the men rising—in your imagination—like a red mountain, with the women's voices floating round it like blue vapour, you might say. I never heard the like of it.' (I thought this a curious remark—the interpretation of sound by colour in it.)

I out in St John's Wood, and call on George Eliot. She was looking well in a high cap and black silk dress. I told her of C. and Othello—'the red mountain and blue vapour.' 'Like an imaginative child's description,' she said.

Allingham, *Diary*; entry for 19 April 1880

I WAS walking with him one Sunday afternoon in Battersea Park. In the open circle among the trees was a blind man and his daughter, she singing hymns, he accompanying her on some instrument. We stood listening. She sang Faber's 'Pilgrims of the Night'. The words were trivial, but the air, though simple, had something weird and unearthly about it. 'Take me away!' he said after a few minutes, 'I shall cry if I stay longer.'

Froude, *Carlyle: His Life in London*

MARY SHELLEY · 1797–1851

Matthew Arnold recounts a story he heard from a woman who knew Mary Shelley:

MRS SHELLEY was choosing a school for her son, and asked the advice of this lady, who gave for advice—to use her own words to me—'just the sort of banality, you know, one does come out with: Oh, send him somewhere where they will teach him to think for himself!' I have had far too long a training as a school inspector to presume to call an utterance of this kind a *banality*; however, it is not on this advice that I now wish to lay stress, but upon Mrs Shelley's reply to it. Mrs Shelley answered: 'Teach him to think for himself? Oh, my God, teach him rather to think like other people!'

'Shelley', 1888, reprinted in Arnold's *Essays in Criticism: Second Series*

Thomas Hood · 1799–1845

In 1843 Hood published his poem 'The Song of the Shirt' in Punch. *It was inspired by an article on inhuman conditions in the cheap clothing trade which had appeared in the same magazine:*

He was certainly astonished, and a little amused at its wonderful popularity, although my mother had said to him, when she was folding up the packet ready for the press: 'Now mind, Hood, mark my words, this will tell wonderfully! It is one of the best things you ever did!' This turned out a true prophecy. It was translated into French and German; and even I believe into Italian. My father used often to laugh and wonder how they rendered the peculiar burthen, 'Stitch, stitch, stitch!', and also 'Seam and gusset and band!' It was printed on cotton pocket handkerchiefs for sale, and has met with the usual fate of all popular poems, having been parodied times without number. But what delighted, and yet touched my father most deeply was that the poor creatures, to whose sorrows and sufferings he had given such eloquent voice, seemed to adopt its words as their own, by singing them about the streets to a rude air of their own adaptation.

Tom Hood (the author's son), *Memorials of Thomas Hood*, 1860

Thomas Babington Macaulay · 1800–1859

An incident from Macaulay's early life—he was about 4 years old at the time:

About this period his father took him on a visit to Lady Waldegrave at Strawberry Hill, and was much pleased to exhibit to his old friend the fair bright boy, dressed in a green coat with red collar and cuffs, a frill at the throat and white trousers. After some time had been spent among the wonders of the Orford Collection, of which he ever after carried a catalogue in his head, a servant who was waiting upon the company in the gallery spilt some hot coffee over his legs. The hostess was all kindness and compassion, and when, after a while, she asked how he was feeling, the little fellow looked up in her face and replied, 'Thank you, madam, the agony is abated.'

George Otto Trevelyan, *The Life of Lord Macaulay*, 1876

He was always willing to accept a friendly challenge to a feat of memory. One day in the Board-room of the British Museum, Sir David Dundas saw him hand to Lord Aberdeen a sheet of foolscap, covered with writing arranged in three parallel columns down each of the four pages. This document, of which the ink was still wet, proved to be a full list of the Senior Wranglers at Cambridge, with their dates and colleges, for the hundred years during which the names of Senior Wranglers had been recorded in the University Calendar. On another occasion Sir David asked: 'Macaulay, do you know your Popes?' 'No,' was the answer, 'I always get wrong among the Innocents.' 'But you can say your Archbishops of Canterbury?' 'Any fool,' said Macaulay, 'could say his Archbishops of Canterbury backwards'; and thereupon he went off at score, drawing breath only once to remark about the oddity of there having been both an Archbishop Sancroft and an Archbishop Bancroft, until Sir David stopped him at Cranmer.

Trevelyan, *Life of Lord Macaulay*

John Henry Newman · 1801–1890

As a young boy, Newman began writing down his thoughts in a manuscript volume called Memoranda*:*

A PERSISTENT element in his character produced one strange, even frightening, entry: it shows him when he was eleven standing outside himself, or inside himself, looking at himself convolutedly, or as what we would say nowadays in a highly introverted manner. He wrote: "*John Newman wrote this just before he was going up to Greek* [at his boarding school] *on Tuesday, June 10, 1812, when it only wanted three days to his going home, thinking of the time (at home) when, looking at this, he shall recollect when he did it.*' It is an entry that one reads many times. 'I am thinking this, thinking what I shall think when I read it again and think what I was thinking when I was thinking it.'

Sean O'Faolain, *Newman's Way*, 1952

The Reverend L. R. Phelps was Provost of Oriel—Newman's old Oxford college—in the 1920s. He had already been a member of the Oriel senior common room back in 1879, when Newman—then aged 78—was made a cardinal:

IT was not, I think, the Provost himself who told me how, as a very junior fellow of the college, he was despatched with a group of more senior Anglican clergy having the delicate task of congratulating a former fellow on becoming a prince of the Holy Roman Catholic and Apostolic Church. Young Phelps broke the ice by advancing upon the new Cardinal of St George in Velabro with outstretched hand and the words 'Well done, Newman, well done!'

J. I. M. Stewart, *Myself and Michael Innes*, 1987

Jane Welsh Carlyle · 1801–1866

(married Thomas Carlyle in 1826; author of brilliant letters and journals)

In 1855 Jane Carlyle went to the Income Tax Office in Chelsea to appeal on her husband's behalf against his tax assessment. While she waited in the outer office a number of men and women joined her—'the men seemed as worried as the women, though they put a better face on it, even carrying on a sort of sickly laughing and bantering with one another'. Then she was summoned to face the Commissioners themselves:

'*First-come lady*,' called the clerk, opening a small side-door, and I stept forward into a grand *peut-être*. There was an instant of darkness while the one door was shut behind and the other opened in front; and there I stood in a dim room where three men sat round a large table spread with papers. One held a pen ready over an open ledger; another was taking snuff, and had *taken* still worse in his time, to judge by his shaky, clayed appearance. The third, who was plainly the cock of that dungheap, was *sitting for Rhadamanthus*—a Rhadamanthus *without the justice*. 'Name,' said the horned-owl-looking individual holding the pen. 'Carlyle.' 'What?' 'Carlyle.' Seeing he still looked dubious, I spelt it for him. 'Ha!' cried Rhadamanthus, a big, bloodless-faced, insolent-looking fellow. 'What is this? why is Mr Carlyle not come himself? Didn't he get a letter ordering him to appear? Mr Carlyle wrote *some nonsense* about being exempted from coming, and I desired an answer to be sent that he must come, must do as other people.' 'Then, sir,' I said, 'your desire has been neglected, it would seem, my husband having received no such letter; and I was told by one of your fellow Commissioners that Mr Carlyle's personal appearance was not indispensable.' '*Huffgh! Huffgh!* what does Mr Carlyle mean by saying he has no income from his writings, when he himself fixed it in the beginning at a hundred and fifty?' 'It means, sir, that, in ceasing to write, one ceases to be paid for writing, and Mr Carlyle has published nothing for several years.' 'Huffgh! Huffgh! I understand nothing about that.' 'I do,' whispered the snuff-taking Commissioner at my ear. 'I *quite* understand a literary man does not always make money. *I would take it all off*, for *my* share, but (sinking his voice still lower) I am only one voice here, and not the most important.' 'There,' said I, handing to Rhadamanthus Chapman and Hall's account, 'that will prove Mr Carlyle's statement.' 'What am I to make of that? Huffgh! we should have Mr Carlyle here to swear to this before we believe it.' 'If a gentleman's word of honour written at the bottom of that paper is not enough, you can put me on my oath: *I* am ready to swear to it!' '*You!* you, indeed! No, no! we can do nothing with *your* oath!' 'But, sir, I understand my husband's affairs fully, better than he does himself.' 'That I can *well* believe; but we can make nothing of this,' flinging my document contemptuously on the table. The horned owl picked it up, glanced over it while Rhadamanthus was tossing papers about, and grumbling about 'people that wouldn't conform to rules;' then handed it back to him, saying deprecatingly: 'But, sir, this is a very plain statement.' 'Then what has Mr Carlyle to live upon? You don't mean to tell me he lives on that?' pointing to the document. 'Heaven forbid, sir! but I am not here to explain what Mr Carlyle has *to live on*, only to declare his income from Literature during the last three years.' 'True! true!' mumbled the not-most-important voice at my elbow, 'Mr Carlyle, I believe, has landed income.' 'Of which,' said I haughtily, for my spirit was up, 'I have fortunately no account to render in this kingdom and to this board.' 'Take off fifty pounds, say a hundred—take off a hundred pounds,' said Rhadamanthus to the horned owl. 'If we write Mr Carlyle down a *hundred and fifty* he has no reason to complain, I think. There, you may go. Mr Carlyle has no reason to complain.'

Second-come woman was already introduced, and I was motioned to the door; but I could not depart without saying that 'at all events there was no use in complaining, since they had the power to enforce their decision.' On stepping out, my first thought was, what a mercy Carlyle didn't come himself! For the rest, though it might have gone better, I was thankful that it had not gone worse. When one has been threatened with a great injustice, one accepts a smaller as a favour.

Journal, 21 November 1855

A 'grand peut-être' *is a joking allusion to the last words of Rabelais—'Je m'en vais chercher un grand peut-être' (I am going to seek a great perhaps).*

Harriet Martineau · 1802–1876

(social reformer, journalist, and Positivist; author of *Society in America*)

Harriet Martineau suffered from deafness:

It was about this time, I think, that, chancing to be in London, she consulted Mr Toynbee, the aurist, upon her ailment. He did her little or no good, but was very kind and gracious to her, which made a great impression upon her. She was so pleased indeed with the interest he had taken in her case, that she resolved to leave him, by testamentary bequest, her ears. She announced this intention in the presence of Mr Shepherd, who, to my infinite amazement, observed, 'But, my dear madam, you can't do that: it will make your other legacy worthless.' The fact was, in the interests of science, Miss Martineau had already left her head to the Phrenological Society. I asked the doctor how he came to know that. 'Oh,' he said, 'she told me so herself; she has left ten pounds in her codicil to me for cutting it off.'

There was nothing of course improper in such a bequest, but it was certainly very unusual; and I never afterwards felt quite comfortable, even at cribbage—in the society of the testatrix and her doctor. I don't think I *could* play cribbage with a lady upon whom I had undertaken to perform such an operation, but then I am neither a philosopher nor a man of science. As it happened, the doctor died before his patient, who subsequently altered her intentions altogether. I never, at least, heard of them being carried out.

James Payn, *Some Literary Recollections*, 1885

Ralph Waldo Emerson · 1803–1882

The Quaker poet John Greenleaf Whittier once asked Emerson a large general question:

'What does thee pray for, friend Emerson?'

'Well,' said Mr Emerson, 'when I first open my eyes upon the morning meadows, and look out upon the beautiful world, I thank God that I am alive, and that I live so near Boston.'

Mary Claflin, *Personal Recollections of John Greenleaf Whittier*, 1893

He questioned me about what I had seen of Concord, and whom besides Hawthorne I had met, and when I told him only Thoreau, he asked if I knew the poems of Mr William Henry Channing. I have known them since, and felt their quality, which I gladly owned a genuine and original poetry; but I answered then truly that I knew them only from Poe's criticisms: cruel and spiteful things which I should be ashamed of enjoying as I once did.

'Whose criticisms?' asked Emerson.

'Poe's,' I said again.

'Oh,' he cried out, after a moment, as if he had returned from a far search for my meaning, '*you mean the jingle-man!*'

William Dean Howells, *Literary Friends and Acquaintances*, 1901

In 1874 an American magazine published an interview with Emerson in the course of which he was quoted as describing Swinburne as 'a perfect leper and a mere sodomite'—a criticism, the paper said, which recalled 'Carlyle's scathing description of that poet—as a man standing up to his neck in a cesspool and adding to its contents'. It is possible that the interviewer misrepresented Emerson, but he never published a disavowal.

A friend in America sent Swinburne a copy of the interview. In reply he composed 'a few sentences for you to make such use of as you please'. The most memorable of these observations, which the friend passed on to the New York Daily Tribune, *was the following:*

A FOUL mouth is so ill-matched with a white beard that I would gladly believe the newspaper scribes alone responsible for the bestial utterances which they declare to have dropped from a teacher whom such disciples as these exhibit to our disgust and compassion as performing on their obscene platform the last tricks of tongue now possible to a gap-toothed and hoary-headed ape, carried at first into notice on the shoulder of Carlyle, and who now in his dotage spits and chatters from a dirtier perch of his own finding and fouling; Coryphaeus or choragus of his Bulgarian tribe of autocoprophagous baboons who make the filth they feed on.

New York Daily Tribune, February 1875

'Coryphaeus' and 'choragus' mean leader of a chorus; 'Bulgarian' in this context is a reference to buggery.

In his Study of Shakespeare *(1880) Swinburne described Emerson as 'an impudent and foul-mouthed Yankee philosophaster', although in a private letter he conceded that some of the American's poems were 'exceptionally beautiful and powerful'.*

Henry Wadsworth Longfellow, who was four years younger than Emerson, died in his home in Cambridge, the Craigie House, in March 1882:

Two days later a funeral service was held at the Craigie House, which was attended only by the family and a few close friends, and the body was then carried, 'under the gently falling snow,' to Mount Auburn Cemetery, where it was buried. One of the few friends present was Emerson, who had himself only a few weeks more to live, and whose hold on the factual had almost entirely failed him. Howells, who was also present, tells us that, after the services were over, Emerson turned to his daughter Ellen and said: 'The gentleman we have just been burying was a sweet and beautiful soul; but I forget his name.'

Newton Arvin, *Longfellow*, 1962

Benjamin Disraeli, Earl of Beaconsfield
1804–1881

Disraeli's first novel, Vivian Grey *(1826), was savaged by the critics. The review which upset him most was in* Blackwood's Magazine*; five years later he gave an account, in fictionalized form, of his feelings on reading it:*

With what horror, with what blank despair, with what supreme appalling astonishment did I find myself for the first time in my life the subject of the most reckless, the most malignant and the most adroit ridicule. I was sacrificed, I was scalped . . . The criticism fell from my hand. A film floated over my vision, my knees trembled. I felt that sickness of heart that we experience in our first scrape. I was ridiculous. It was time to die.

Disraeli, *Contarini Fleming*, 1832

Lord Beaconsfield's flattery was sometimes misplaced. An instance recurs to my recollection. He was staying in a country house where the whole party was Conservative with the exception of one rather plain elderly lady, who belonged to a great Whig family. The Tory leader was holding forth on politics to an admiring circle when the Whig lady came into the room. Pausing in his conversation, Lord Beaconsfield exclaimed, in his most histrionic manner, 'But hush! We must not continue these Tory heresies until those pretty little ears have been covered up with those pretty little hands'—a strange remark under any circumstances, and stranger still if, as his friends believed, it was honestly intended as an acceptable compliment.

G. W. E. Russell, *Collections and Recollections*, 1903

Along with the portraits painted by James MacNeill Whistler, there is an intriguing might-have-been:

Another selected sitter who failed to appreciate the honour paid to him had been Disraeli. Whistler had long wished to paint that remarkable man, whose bizarre appearance appealed strongly to him as a subject, and he had tried through many channels to attain his desire, but in vain.

One day he had come upon the longed-for model sitting alone in St James's Park, apparently absorbed in thought. Even Whistler experienced an unusual sensation which he recognised as shyness in the strange and sinister presence, but plucking up his courage, he plunged boldly in, endeavouring to recall himself to the mystic Prime Minister and finally making his request. The Sphinx remained silent throughout; then, after an icy pause, gazed at him with lack-lustre eyes and murmured, 'Go away, go away, little man.'

Whistler went, and with him the Great Poseur's chance of immortality on canvas. He shortly afterwards graciously assented to sit to Millais, who produced—nothing in particular to everybody's entire satisfaction.

W. Graham Robertson, *Time Was*, 1931

Nathaniel Hawthorne · 1804–1864

Hawthorne was notorious for his silences and lack of sociability. Henry James Sr., who saw him dining in a club, compared his manner to that of a rogue in the company of detectives ('How he buried his eyes in a plate, and ate with such a voracity that no person should dare to ask him a question!'), and Rebecca Harding Davis thought that even in his own home he was like 'Banquo's ghost among the thanes at the banquet':

Generally, however, he was much easier when he was in control of the situation.

I love Mr Hawthorne very much [wrote Ada Shepard to her fiancé, while she was staying with the Hawthornes in Europe], and do not understand why people believe him cold. He is certainly extremely reserved, but he is noble and true and good, and is full of kindly feeling. . . . I admire him exceedingly, and do not feel in the least afraid of him as I had imagined I should be.

Yet it is interesting that she had expected to be. 'Why do they treat me so?' Hawthorne once asked a friend. 'Why, they're afraid of you' was the reply. 'But I tremble at *them*,' said Hawthorne. 'They think,' she explained, 'that you're imagining all sorts of terrible things.' 'Heavens,' he exclaimed; 'if they only knew what I *do* think about.'

Edward Wagenknecht, *Nathaniel Hawthorne: Man and Writer*, 1961

From 1853 to 1857 Hawthorne served as American consul in Liverpool. While there, he frequently helped compatriots who were in trouble out of his own pocket:

Among the objects of Hawthorne's benevolence in England, his countrywoman Delia Bacon, the mother of the Baconian theory, received by far the greatest attention. He admired *The Philosophy of the Plays of Shakespeare Expounded* (1857), oddly enough, not because he shared Miss Bacon's contempt for the 'Stratford Player' but because he did not; her appreciation of the greatness of the plays, despite her heresy concerning their authorship, was so penetrating, he believed, that her book would show Shakespeare an even greater writer than he had ever appeared before. He arranged for the publication of the volume, therefore, on both sides of the Atlantic, and risked—and lost—$1000 on the printing of it, and it was not all for the glory of Shakespeare; much of it was pure, unselfish pity for a brilliant but unstable woman who was rapidly approaching a final crack-up. He admitted he 'would rather that Providence had employed some other instrument,' but since it had not, and since Miss Bacon 'must be kept alive,' it seemed to him there was only one thing to do. 'You say nothing about the state of your funds,' he writes in one letter to her. 'Pardon me for alluding to the subject; but you promised to apply to me in case of need. I am ready.' When she broke at last he made himself responsible for her care and kept in touch with her until he left England; at one time he had even arranged for her return to America. Of course she turned against him in spite of all his kindness; indeed she nearly refused to permit the book to be published after it had been printed, so incensed was she over his failure to avow himself a Baconian and her disciple in the Preface he wrote for her. Disgustedly he vowed that 'this shall be the last of my benevolent follies, and I will never be kind to anybody again as long as I live.'

Wagenknecht, *Nathaniel Hawthorne*

Despite this last outburst, Hawthorne's benefactions continued, both in Britain and after his return to America.

Frederick Lehmann, who had met Hawthorne in Liverpool, saw him again when he visited America in 1862:

As usual, he hardly ever spoke, and I only remember his breaking his apparent vow of silence when appealed to by a Mr Bradford. This gentleman, after a fiery denunciation of the South, having come to the end of his peroration, passionately turned to his silent listener with the words, 'Don't you agree with me?' Then Hawthorne astonished him by uttering the monosyllable 'No,' after which he again relapsed into silence.

Quoted in R. C. Lehmann, *Memories of Half a Century*, 1906

He began somehow to speak of women, and said he had never seen a woman whom he thought quite beautiful. In the same way he spoke of the New England temperament, and suggested that the apparent coldness in it was also real, and that the suppression of emotions for generations would extinguish it at last.

William Dean Howells, *Literary Friends and Acquaintances*, 1901

Francis Sylvester Mahony · 1804–1866

(Irish poet and journalist who wrote under the pseudonym Father Prout)

A SUCCESSFUL form of mystification was invented by Father Prout. This was to translate a well-known poem into some foreign language, and then to pass off the translation as a much earlier work and the undoubted original. In his *Rogueries of Tom Moore* Prout gravely charges that Moore's song 'Go Where Glory Waits Thee' is but 'a literal and servile translation of an old French ditty which is among my papers, and which I believe to have been composed by that beautiful and interesting lady Francoise de Foix, Comtesse de Chateaubriand, born in 1491'; that 'Lesbia hath a Beaming Eye' was stolen from 'an old Latin song of my own, which I made when a boy, smitten with the charms of an Irish milkmaid'; and so on through half a dozen of Moore's best-known poems.

William Walsh, *Handy-book of Literary Curiosities*, 1894

John Stuart Mill · 1806–1873

In 1865 Mill stood as parliamentary candidate for Westminster. One of the meetings he addressed was for working people who didn't have the vote:

MILL was laboriously expounding his political faith, when suddenly there came an interruption. A bill-board was brought in, bearing the deadly words from his *Thoughts on Parliamentary Reform*:

'THE LOWER CLASSES,
THOUGH MOSTLY HABITUAL LIARS,
ARE ASHAMED OF LYING'

They asked him, had he written that? For a second he paused, but he never wavered. 'I did.' There was another pause. Then, instead of the stony silence, the discontented mutterings he expected, the whole of the stolid audience rose to greet him. They clapped, they whistled; they cheered, and stamped their feet. Their leader, George Odger, stood up beaming and announced that 'the working class had no desire not to be told of their faults; they wanted friends, not flatterers.'

Michael St John Packe, *The Life of John Stuart Mill*, 1954

Mill was elected, and served as an independent MP from 1865 to 1868.

In the autumn of 1870 Mill stayed with Lord and Lady Amberley (soon to become Bertrand Russell's parents) in their new home:

WEDNESDAY SEPTEMBER 28. After dinner Mr Mill read us Shelley's Ode to Liberty and he got quite excited and moved over it rocking backwards and forwards and nearly choking with emotion; he said himself: 'it is almost too much for me.'

The Amberley Papers, ed. Bertrand and Patricia Russell, 1937

HENRY WADSWORTH LONGFELLOW · 1807–1882

By the time he was middle-aged Longfellow enjoyed enormous fame, and his home in Cambridge, Mass., the Craigie House, attracted a constant stream of visitors, both fellow countrymen and callers from abroad. Many of them were celebrated figures in their own right:

PERHAPS the most unlikely visitor, from our point of view, was the Russian anarchist Mikhail Bakunin, who had escaped from Siberia a few months earlier and, having made his way eastward across the Pacific, en route to Europe, had reached the northern United States, and came to call at the Craigie House. He stayed so long, Ernest Longfellow [the poet's son] tells us, that he had to be invited to lunch; 'Yiss,' he answered, 'and I will dine with you too'—as he did. He may have proved a somewhat fatiguing guest—his vehemence was notorious—but Longfellow seems to have been charmed by him, and describes him in his journal as 'a giant of a man, with a most ardent, seething temperament.'

Newton Arvin, *Longfellow*, 1962

EDGAR ALLAN POE · 1809–1849

As a boy, Poe suffered from night fears:

THE superstitious sceptic, who could be terrified by his own imagination, later confessed to the editor George Graham that 'he disliked the dark, and was rarely out at night. On one occasion he said to me, "I believe that demons take advantage of the night to mislead the unwary—although, you know," he added, "I don't believe in them." '

Jeffrey Meyers, *Edgar Allan Poe: His Life and Legacy*, 1992

Poe reviewed several of Dickens's early novels. In his review of the serial version of Barnaby Rudge,

HE correctly predicted, from the opening chapters, 'that Barnaby, the idiot, is the murderer's own son.' Poe later boasted to friends that he had been completely right in his predictions about the plot and that Dickens had sent him a letter of flattering acknowledgment, asking if his prophecies had been inspired by dealings with the devil. In fact, only the first of his five predictions about the novel was correct, and there is no evidence that Dickens ever sent an admiring letter. When reviewing the completed novel, Poe dismissed his own errors as insignificant and disingenuously attributed them to Dickens' inconsistency: 'if we did not rightly prophesy, yet, at least, our prophecy *should have been* right.'

Meyers, *Edgar Allan Poe*

In one of Poe's most memorable stories, 'A Descent into the Maelström', a sailor describes how he is shipwrecked and sucked into a whirlpool:

IT was extremely ironic that the author of the article on 'Whirlpool' in the ninth edition of the *Encyclopedia Britannica* gave Poe credit for information that Poe had lifted from an earlier edition of the same *Encyclopedia*, and then quoted as facts the parts of the story that Poe himself had invented.

Meyers, *Edgar Allan Poe*

Shortly after writing 'The Raven', Poe met the poet William Ross Wallace on the streets of New York:

'WALLACE,' said Poe, 'I have just written the greatest poem that ever was written.'

'Have you?' said Wallace. 'That is a fine achievement.'

'Would you like to hear it?' said Poe.

'Most certainly,' said Wallace.

Thereupon Poe began to read the soon-to-be-famous verses in his best way—which . . . was always an impressive and captivating way. When he had finished it he turned to Wallace for his approval of them—when Wallace said:

'Poe—they are fine; uncommonly fine.'

'Fine?' said Poe, contemptuously. 'Is that all you can say for this poem? I tell you it's the greatest poem that was ever written.'

Joel Benton, quoted in Meyers, *Edgar Allan Poe*

In 1836 Poe married his 13-year-old cousin Virginia Clemm. She died of tuberculosis at the age of 24:

HER death had a tragic effect on Poe, yet he managed to summon strength enough to support him to the graveyard of the Fordham Dutch

Reformed Church, where she was buried. Even after death, however, she was not permitted to rest. As though she were indeed the symbol of all his dying heroines and must continue her performance in one of his fantastic, gruesome tales, in 1875, when the cemetery in which she lay was destroyed, her bones were tossed aside. Poe's early biographer, William F. Gill, reverently gathered them together and placed them in a box which he kept under his bed and opened to those guests who wished to fondle the bones of the great man's beloved. Finally, they were again buried, this time beside the remains of Poe himself in Baltimore.

Philip Lindsay, *The Haunted Man*, 1953

Alfred, Lord Tennyson · 1809–1892

FROM very early years he was puzzled by the problem of personality, and would sit upon the damp moss of Holywell Glen saying 'Alfred, Alfred' to himself, and again 'Alfred' . . .

Harold Nicolson, *Tennyson*, 1923

TENNYSON told us that often on going to bed after being engaged on composition he had dreamed long passages of poetry ('You, I suppose', turning to me, 'dream photographs?') which he liked very much at the time, but forgot entirely when he woke. One was an enormously long one on fairies, where the lines from being very long at first gradually got shorter and shorter, till it ended with fifty or sixty lines of two syllables each! The only bit he ever remembered enough to write down was one he dreamed at ten years old, which you may like to possess as a genuine unpublished fragment of the Laureate, though I think you will agree with me that it gives very little indication of his future poetic powers:

May a cock-sparrow
Write to a barrow?
I hope you'll excuse
My infantine muse.

C. L. Dodgson (Lewis Carroll), letter, 1859

WE spoke of Byron. T. greatly admired him in boyhood, but does not now.

'When I heard of his death (it was at Somersby, my Father's rectory) I went out to the back of the house and cut on a wall with my knife, "Lord Byron is dead." '

'Parts of *Don Juan* are good, but other parts badly done. I like some of his small things.'

A.—'Any of his Tales, or Mysteries, or Plays?'

T.—'No.'

A.—'He was the one English writer who disparaged Shakespeare. He was a Lord, and talked about, and he wrote vulgarly, therefore he was popular.'

T.—'Why am I popular? I don't write very vulgarly.'

A.—'I have often wondered that you are, and Browning wonders.'

T.—'I believe it's because I'm Poet-Laureate. It's something like being a lord.'

William Allingham, *Diary*, 1907; entry for 18 May 1866

HE would pretend to look upon his bottle of port as a sort of counsellor to be heard sometimes before finally making up his mind upon moot-points, and after the varying moods of the day about them. For instance, he told me, 'The night before I was asked to take the Laureateship, which was offered to me through Prince Albert's liking for my *In Memoriam*, I dreamed that he came to me and kissed me on the cheek. I said, in my dream, "Very kind, but very German." In the morning the letter about the Laureateship was brought to me and laid upon my bed. I thought about it through the day, but could not make up my mind whether to take it or refuse it, and at the last I wrote two letters, one accepting and one declining, and threw them on the table, and settled to decide which I would send after my dinner and bottle of port.'

James Knowles, 'A Personal Reminiscence', 1893

DINED with Sidney Colvin. He told me he once heard Tennyson read *The Revenge* in his deep chant—a sort of intoning with little variety of manner or expression, and he ended 'To be lost evermore in the main!' adding immediately in exactly the same voice and attitude without any pause 'And the scoundrels only gave me £300 for that! It was worth £500!' I don't like the story, but record it as first-hand and oddly characteristic of one side of Tennyson. If he had said it was worth £3,000 it would have been less absurd.

John Bailey, *Letters and Diaries*, 1935

ONE very characteristic incident I remember connected with lunch at Aldworth: the incident of the fungi. As I say, he was a great naturalist and he'd been out walking one morning and he came back with the great wideawake hat full of the most terrible-looking fungi, which he brought into the drawing-room where I happened to be with my grandmother. He showed her his hat full of these objects and said: 'Emily, will you please have these cooked for luncheon?' My grandmother was absolutely horrified: 'My dear Ally'—she always called him Ally—'you couldn't possibly eat those. I'm sure they're most unsafe and poisonous.' He said: 'Emily, I know quite well what they are. They're very good to eat and I should like to have them cooked for luncheon.' I think my grandmother, although she was said to influence his poetry unduly, always knew when she was beaten, so she rang the bell and gave the hat full of mushrooms to the butler, who carried them off and had them cooked. At luncheon they appeared on a large dish, and they were handed all round the table, and everybody refused them until they got to him—he was, of course, last on the circuit—and rather aggressively he took the whole contents of the dish and ate them all with everybody glaring anxiously at him, thinking that he would probably fall down dead.

Sir Charles Tennyson, 'Memories of my Grandfather', 1969

I WONDER whether I have anywhere put down a walk with Bradley and Tennyson. [*The writer is E. W. Benson, Archbishop of Canterbury; Bradley was Dean of Westminster.*] Bradley had been reading *A Grammarian's Funeral*, and he said, 'We'll ask Tennyson whether Browning's writing at large is poetry or no.' Tennyson's answer was, 'I'll think about it.' In a walk a week later apropos of nothing he observed, 'I have thought, and it is.' We had no idea for a moment as to what he spoke of.

A. C. Benson, *The Life of Edward White Benson*, 1899

Archbishop Benson features in another story about Tennyson, recounted by his son E. F. Benson:

A PLEASANT link between the author of so much noble verse and the lover of less exalted rhymes was his affection for the form known as the 'Limerick.' He liked its terseness, he also, it is idle to deny, took a sort of school-boy pleasure in the hectic situations which it sometimes disclosed. Little tales of the same sort pleased him: he could tell them himself with considerable gusto. In this connection I cannot forbear to recount a story which, though I will not vouch for its authenticity, I give on the authority of Sir Edmund Gosse. He and my father were talking about Tennyson: they were contrasting him with Dickens; Dickens, they agreed, was not very markedly Puritanical in his life, whereas Tennyson was Galahad. But Dickens abhorred any sort of coarseness in conversation, whereas Tennyson had no great objection to it. Then said my father:

'Yes, that's quite true. I went out for a walk with him the last time I ever saw him, and he suddenly said to me, "Shall I tell you a bawdy story?" Of course I said, "No, certainly not." '

Their talk went on for a little, till there came a pause. Gosse broke it with a touch of that impish humour of his.

'I feel sure Your Grace heard that story!' he said.
My father was a little off his guard.
'Well, it wasn't so very bad after all,' he replied.

E. F. Benson, *As We Were*, 1930

Edward FitzGerald · 1809–1883

(translator of *The Rubaiyat of Omar Khayyam*)

In 1860 FitzGerald moved to lodgings in Woodbridge, in Suffolk:

For a long time his attendance at church had been little more than a polite observance of social custom, but now he ceased going almost completely. The rector of Woodbridge, the Revd Thomas Mellor, called on him and said, 'I am sorry, Mr FitzGerald, that I never see you at church.' FitzGerald replied, 'Sir, you might have conceived that a man has not come to my years without thinking much on these things. I believe I may say that I have reflected on them fully. You need not repeat this visit.'

Robert Bernard Martin, *With Friends Possessed: A Life of Edward FitzGerald*, 1985

Abraham Lincoln · 1809–1865

Personal ridicule belonged to Lincoln's armory throughout his career, and was usually offered with the favorite guileless air. He used it as an habitual form of reply to admonitory speeches made to him by pretentious citizens during the war. 'Why, Mr Harvey, what tremendous great calves you have!' he exclaimed at the end of one of these. He took a bottle from a shelf and gave it to another gentleman who had long outstayed his time, a bald-headed man, and told him it would grow hair on a pumpkin. Lincoln contrived many jokes and stories about pumpkins and pumpkin-heads, and applied the rude metaphor when Seward and Chase were finally induced to resign. 'Now I can ride, for I have a pumpkin in each bag.'

Lincoln belonged indeed to a hardy and contentious school of humor, even though his manner could become elaborately gentle, as in his well-known ridicule of Douglas. 'I had understood before that Mr Douglas had been bound out to learn the cabinet-making business, which is all well enough, but I was not aware until now that his father was a cooper. I have no doubt, however, that he was one, and I am certain also that he was a very good one, for'—and here Lincoln bowed gravely to Douglas—'he has made one of the best whiskey casks I have ever seen.'

Often Lincoln's stories were drawn from a homely backwoods experience, as in the story of the little boy at a backwoods school who blundered over reading the names of Shadrach, Meshach, and Abednego, and later set up a wail as he saw his turn approaching again. 'Look there, marster—there comes them same damn three fellers again!' As Lincoln told the story he stood at a window overlooking Pennsylvania Avenue. As he finished he pointed to three men on their way to the White House. They were Sumner, Stevens, and Wilson. The episode became a metaphor; and the three figures, after Lincoln's slow reminiscence, took on rather more than human energy and size.

In Lincoln two of the larger strains of American comedy seemed to meet. He showed the western ebullience, even in brief fragments. He was likely to call a bowie-knife a scythe. He told of a fight in which a man fought himself out of one coat and into another. But his economy of speech and his laconic turn seemed derived from the Yankee strain that belonged to his ancestry, and no doubt was strengthened by many encounters with Yankees in the West. In a debate against the Mexican War he mentioned an Illinois farmer who declared, 'I ain't greedy about land. I only want what jines mine.' The narrow phrasing was Yankee; the concealed inflation belonged to the West.

Constance Rourke, *American Humor*, 1931

Oliver Wendell Holmes · 1809–1894

(poet, physician, author of *The Autocrat of the Breakfast Table*)

I REMEMBER the delight Henry James, the father of the novelist, had in reporting to me the frankness of the doctor, when he had said to him, 'Holmes, you are intellectually the most alive man I ever knew.' 'I am, I am,' said the doctor. 'From the crown of my head to the sole of my foot, I'm alive, I'm alive!'

William Dean Howells, *Literary Friends and Acquaintances*, 1902

Elizabeth Gaskell · 1810–1865

The heroine of Ms Gaskell's novel Ruth *(1853) is an unmarried mother—something which provoked shock and outrage when the book first appeared:*

ALL over the country *Ruth* was debated in drawing-rooms, clubs, churches, chapels—even Oxford colleges. Josephine Butler, later the bravest of all opponents of the double standard in the campaign to repeal the Contagious Diseases Act, was a young wife in Oxford in 1853 and bitterly remembered the dons' pious insistence that no pure woman should know of such things. She heard one young man saying 'he would not allow' his *mother* to read *Ruth*.

Jenny Uglow, *Elizabeth Gaskell: A Habit of Stories*, 1993

MARGARET FULLER · 1810–1850

(author, editor, feminist)

Emerson enormously admired Margaret Fuller, though not quite as much as she admired herself:

HER confidence in herself was boundless, and was frankly expressed. She told Samuel Ward that she had seen all the people worth seeing in America, and was satisfied that there was no intellect comparable to her own.

Emerson, Journal, 1850

> *There is a story, probably apocryphal, that when Emerson and Margaret Fuller went to see a performance by Fanny Elssler, the dancer, he exclaimed, 'Margaret, this is Poetry!' to which she replied, 'Waldo, that is Religion!'*

There is one anecdote about Margaret Fuller which is almost too famous. It is the only thing which many people know about her:

'I ACCEPT the universe' is reported to have been a favorite utterance of our New England transcendentalist, Margaret Fuller; and when someone repeated this phrase to Thomas Carlyle, his sardonic comment is said to have been: 'Gad! she'd better!'

William James, *The Varieties of Religious Experience*, 1902

In 1846 Margaret Fuller moved to Italy, where she married an Italian nobleman, the Marquis Ossoli. In 1850 she and her husband and their small son Nino set out for America on a sailing ship (because a steamer was too expensive). They were just short of their destination, off Fire Island, New York, when the ship was wrecked in a great storm:

ABOUT three o'clock the ship began to break up. The cabin had been swept away, and now the forecastle was flooded and the last remaining mast was beginning to loosen, prying the deck up with it. The eight people on board gathered around it, and Bates [the steward] made a last desperate effort to persuade Margaret to part with Nino. Even as he succeeded Ossoli was washed overboard, but Margaret, intent on her child, did not see him go. A moment later a last, mountainous wave broke over the vessel carrying off the mast and everyone remaining on board. The cook and the carpenter, thrown clear, saw Ossoli and Celeste [a fellow passenger] cling for a moment to the rigging, then disappear. There was no sign of Margaret. The bodies of Nino and the steward were washed up on the beach a few minutes later.

Paula Blanchard, *Margaret Fuller*, 1978

William Makepeace Thackeray · 1811–1863

His habit of observation began very early. His mother told me that once, when only three or four years old, and while sitting on her knee at the evening hour, she observed him gazing upwards and lost in admiration. 'Ecco!' he exclaimed, pointing to the evening star which was shining, like a diamond, over the crescent moon. This struck her the more as she had herself noticed the same beautiful combination on the night of his birth.

Jane Pryme and Alycia Bayne, *Memorials of the Thackeray Family*, 1879

At the age of 10 Thackeray was sent to Charterhouse, a school where life was characterized both by brutal punishments and by lack of supervision:

What the boys did outside school hours was largely ignored. Extra-curricular activities consequently ranged from bringing in pornographic books and planning excursions to watch public executions at nearby Newgate, to wandering around Holywell Street, where the local prostitutes stood soliciting custom . . .

The effect of all this on a diffident and sensitive boy like Thackeray must have been deeply shocking. Many years later he told the *Punch* table that the first words spoken to him by an older boy were 'Come and frig me.'

D. J. Taylor, *Thackeray*, 1999

In 1844 Thackeray undertook a tour of the Near East, reporting on it in a series of articles for Punch *entitled 'Wanderings of our Fat Contributor'. Eventually his journey brought him to Egypt:*

Here, having taken himself off to the pyramids, he perpetrated what must have been the most audacious piece of advertising in *Punch*'s three-year history:

The 19th of October was *Punch's Coronation*; I officiated at the august ceremony . . . ON THE 19TH OF OCTOBER 1844, I PASTED THE GREAT PLACARD OF PUNCH ON THE PYRAMID OF CHEOPS. I did it, the Fat Contributor did it. If I die, it could not be undone. If I perish, I have not lived in vain . . .

With the help of bemused Arab factotums—Thackeray's own illustration shows three native assistants manhandling an enormously fat, moustachoied man in a sun-hat—the placard was pushed into place as the clock of the great Cairo minaret reached nineteen minutes past seven. 'My heart throbbed when the deed was done . . .' Thackeray told his readers. 'There was *Punch*—familiar old *Punch*—his back to the desert, his beaming face turned to watch the Nile.' It is impossible not to read something symbolic into this episode: the shimmering sands, the Cairo minaret visible in the distance, the puzzled onlookers, the burly Englishman come 2,000 miles, whose idea of a joke is to deck a pyramid with a poster advertising a comic magazine.

Taylor, *Thackeray*

WE all remember Thackeray's observation, 'When I say I know women I mean that I know I don't know them'. One thing is certain, however; he hungered after their admiration, for he openly confessed this on several occasions in my hearing, and he was, moreover, childishly vain when he succeeded in securing it. It may be bad taste to mention the circumstance, but more than once I received from him drawings on wood for his Christmas books, wrapped up in notes from his feminine correspondents, who at times allowed their admiration to wander somewhat indiscreetly beyond the range of his books. These communications could scarcely have been so numerous, I fancy, as to have been brought under my notice by mere accident on Mr Thackeray's part. He rather wished, I think, to publish abroad that he was overburthened with this sort of idolatry.

Henry Vizetelly, *Glimpses Back through Seventy Years*, 1893

Vizetelly published Thackeray's work in his magazine Pictorial Times.

THE first time I saw Thackeray was when I called upon him to ask if he would come to dinner to meet the author of *Jane Eyre*, who was staying with my mother. Charlotte Brontë was devoured with curiosity to meet Thackeray, to whom she had dedicated the second edition of her book. I told Thackeray there would be no one with us excepting Sir John Forbes, and explained that Miss Brontë was incognita in London, and begged him not to say a word to indicate his knowledge of her identity as the authoress of *Jane Eyre*. He replied in his large way, 'I see! It will be all right: you are speaking to a man of the world.'

But unhappily it was not all right. When the ladies had left the dining-room I offered Thackeray a cigar. The custom of smoking after dinner was not common then, but I had been told he liked a cigar, and so provided for his tastes. To my dismay, when we rejoined the ladies in the drawing-room, he approached Miss Brontë and quoted a familiar and much-criticised passage from *Jane Eyre*. It was that in which she describes 'the warning fragrance' which told of the approach of Mr Rochester.

The quotation, in one sense, was happy enough, and it did credit to Thackeray's memory of *Jane Eyre*; but not to his memory of his agreement with me. Miss Brontë's face showed her discomposure, and in a chilly fashion she turned off the allusion. But I was almost as much discomposed as Miss Brontë by this sudden assault on what she was so anxious to guard—her identity as the authoress of *Jane Eyre*. She cast an accusing look at me.

Thackeray, however, had no sense of either awkwardness or guilt. From my house he went to the smoking-room of the Garrick Club and said, 'Boys! I have been dining with "Jane Eyre"!' To have her identity expounded in the smoking-room of the Garrick Club was the last experience which the morbidly shy and sensitive little lady would have chosen.

George Smith, quoted in Leonard Huxley, *The House of Smith, Elder*, 1923

ON expressing my regret to Thackeray that the jackals that followed their heels had been able to separate him and Dickens, I found him inflexible. 'It is a quarrel, I wish it to be a quarrel, and it always will be a quarrel', he said with great warmth.

George Russell, in Constance Russell, *Swallowfield and its Owners*, 1901

HARRIET BEECHER STOWE · 1811–1896

Mrs Stowe said that she had written Uncle Tom's Cabin *'with my heart's blood'*:

THE story took its own way, and she followed where it led, regardless of money payment or her own strength. She had contracted with *The National Era* for a short serial, to run about three months. *Uncle Tom's Cabin* ran ten months, and she received only the $300 agreed upon. This did not trouble her much; neither did she heed the cries of the prospective book publisher that a double-decker antislavery novel would be a commercial impossibility. So it might very well turn out to be, but how did that concern her? 'Your Annie reproached me for letting Eva die,' she told her friend Mrs Howard. 'Why! I could not help it! . . . it affected me so deeply that I could not write a word for two weeks after her death.'

Edward Wagenknecht, *Harriet Beecher Stowe*, 1965

LOWELL told me that when Mrs Stowe was invited to dine with the Atlantic Club, she refused to drink wine, and it was banished for that day. But Lowell said, 'Mrs Stowe, you took wine with the Duke of Argyle when you visited him?' She acknowledged that she did. 'And now do you mean to treat us as if we were not as good as he?' 'No,' she said. 'Bring some champagne,' cried Lowell, and Mrs Stowe and the company drank. 'And how did you know,' I asked, 'that she did take wine at the Duke's?'—'Oh, I divined that,' he said, 'Of course she did.'

R. W. Emerson, Journal, April 1864

CHARLES DICKENS · 1812–1870

In 1866 Dickens visited Portsmouth in the course of a reading tour. Before the reading, he and his tour manager, George Dolby, decided to visit Southsea—in the hope, as Dolby later recalled, 'that the sea breezes might have the effect of relieving Mr Dickens of the cold from which he was still suffering':

ON the morning after our arrival we set out for a walk, and turning the corner of a street suddenly found ourselves in Landport Terrace. The name of the street catching Mr Dickens's eye, he exclaimed, 'By Jove! here is the place where I was born'; and, acting on his suggestion, we walked up and down the terrace for some time, speculating as to which of the houses had the right to call itself his cradle. Beyond a recollection that there was a small front garden to the house, he had no idea of the place, for he was only two years old when his father was removed to London from Portsmouth. As the houses were nearly all alike, and each had a small front garden, we were not much helped in our quest by Mr Dickens's recollections, and great was the laughter at his humorous conjectures. He must have lived in one house because 'it looked so like his father'; another one looked like his home because it looked like the birth-place of a man who had deserted it; a third was very like the cradle of a puny, weak youngster such as he had been; and so on, through the row. According to his own account, Southsea had not contributed much to his physical strength, neither indeed had Chatham . . . But as none of the houses in Landport Terrace could cry out and say, as he recounted these facts, 'That boy was born here!' the mystery remained unsolved, and we passed on.

George Dolby, *Charles Dickens as I Knew Him*, 1912

Dickens was actually born in Mile End Terrace, about a mile away. His family moved to Wish Street, a continuation of Landport Terrace, shortly before his second birthday, and stayed there for around a year.

Wish Street—the name was later changed to Kings Road—has

other literary connections, as Michael Allen points out in The Childhood of Charles Dickens *(1988). H. G. Wells served an apprenticeship in a drapery shop there; Arthur Conan Doyle practised medicine there from 1882 to 1890.*

On his visit to America in 1842 Dickens was entertained by the leading lights of Boston society, including an eminent judge:

In the course of the entertainment a discussion arose among the gentlemen as to which was the more beautiful woman, the Duchess of Sutherland or Mrs Caroline Norton. 'Well, I don't know,' said Dickens expanding himself in his green velvet waistcoat: 'Mrs Norton perhaps is the more beautiful; but the duchess, to my mind, is the more kissable person.' Had a bombshell dropped upon Judge Prescott's dinner table, it could hardly have startled the company more than this remark.

Elizabeth Wormeley Latimer, 'A Girl's Recollections of Dickens', *Lippincott's Magazine*, 1893

Once—tremendous moment—my mother was asked to a neighbour's house to meet Charles Dickens, but—it really distresses me to record it—she did not like him. That is to say, she did not like his waistcoat which was of spun glass and shone like all the rainbows of the heavens reflected in all the diamonds of Golconda. It dazzled her; she could not 'beyond it find the Man'; there seemed to be nothing but flaming, scintillating waistcoat. A veil of spun glass was between her and the great and beloved creator of half our best friends, and she could not break through it.

To atone for this insult to his blessed memory I must set down an unrecorded remark of Dickens, overheard by a friend. A lady was showing him some new and many-coloured chair-covers and begging his opinion thereon. Said Dickens, after grave consideration, 'They look as if they had been sat upon by a damp Harlequin.'

W. Graham Robertson, *Time Was*, 1931

He was a strict disciplinarian when it came to matters of public morals, an amusing instance of which is cited by Dickens himself when, quite unconscious of any irony, he declared in *Household Words* that he had felt compelled to take action against those who used bad language in public places. 'The writer has himself obtained a conviction by a police magistrate . . . for this shameful and demoralising offence—which is as common and as public as the mud in the streets. He obtained it with difficulty, the charge not being within the experience of anyone concerned; but he insisted on the law, and it was clear (wonderful to relate!) and was enforced.' We can see Dickens hauling in an offender; insistent, peremptory, in the face of what was no doubt the incredulity of the authorities.

Peter Ackroyd, *Dickens*, 1990

In 1867–8, in the course of his American reading tour, Dickens again found himself in Boston. He was accompanied by George Dolby, who acted as his manager.

AFTER dinner the other night, Mr Dickens thought he would take a warm bath; but, the water being drawn, he began playing the clown in pantomime on the edge of the bath (with his clothes on) for the amusement of Dolby and Osgood; in a moment and before he knew where he was, he had tumbled in head over heels, clothes and all.

Diary of Annie Fields (the wife of Dickens's American publisher), 1868

Thackeray's friends the Revd W. H. Brookfield, and his wife, were also friends of Dickens. In his memoirs, their son Charles—who appears in a less amiable light on page 198—recalls an example of Dickens's solicitude, and of his remarkable memory:

WHEN my father was given the living of Somerby, near Grantham, both my mother and he rather dreaded the monotony of life in a small country village. Dickens did his best to cheer my mother on the subject. 'Are there *no* old friends living anywhere in the neighbourhood of Somerby?' he inquired. 'Surely there must be *somebody* you know within ten miles or so?' 'No,' replied my mother mournfully, 'not a single soul. Oh! I think there *is* one acquaintance of my husband's,' she suddenly recollected. 'A Mr Maddison, I fancy the name is. But he is not an intimate friend. William knows him only very slightly.' 'Ah, but that's all right!' exclaimed Dickens, his whole face brightening. 'You'll find Maddison a delightful resource. You'll discover there's a lot more in Maddison than you ever dreamed there was. Maddison will become a very important factor in your life. Yes, I'm glad you've got Maddison.' And wringing her heartily by the hand, he went his way.

It so happened that my mother did not meet Dickens again for three or four years, till one evening at a crowded party she caught his eye at the other end of the room. His face immediately lit up with a humorous expression, and he picked his way through the crush until he reached her side. 'Well,' he enquired, in an eager undertone, 'and *how's Maddison*?'

Charles Brookfield, *Random Reminiscences*, 1911

DICKENS's death came as a great shock to us. He lunched with us just before we went abroad and was telling us a story of President Lincoln having told the Council on the day he was shot, that something remarkable would happen, because he had just dreamt for the third time a dream which twice before had preceded events momentous to the nation. The dream was, that he was in a boat on a great river all alone—and he ended with the words 'I drift—I drift—I drift.'

Dickens told this very finely. I thought him looking dreadfully shattered then. It is probable that he never recovered from the effect of the terrible railway accident.

George Eliot, letter to Sara Hennell, June 1870

Robert Browning · 1812–1889
and
Elizabeth Barrett Browning · 1806–1861

Elizabeth Barrett's childhood home was Hope End in Herefordshire, where the family lived between 1809 and 1832:

In my sixth year for some lines on virtue which I had penned with great care I received from Papa a ten shilling note enclosed in a letter which was addressed to *the Poet Laureate of Hope End*; I mention this because I received much more pleasure from the word *Poet* than from the ten shilling note—I did not understand the meaning of the word Laureate, but it being explained to me by my dearest Mama, the idea first presented itself to me of celebrating our birthdays by my verse. '*Poet Laureate of Hope End*' was too great a title to lose.

'Glimpses into my own Literary Character', 1820–1

Elizabeth was actually 9 at the time of the incident she describes.

At the age of 8 Robert Browning was sent to school as a part-time boarder:

His attendance at Miss Ready's school only kept him from home from Monday till Saturday of every week; but when called upon to confront his first five days of banishment he felt sure that he would not survive them. A leaden cistern belonging to the school had in, or outside it, the raised image of a face. He chose the cistern for his place of burial, and converted the face into his epitaph by passing his hand over and over it to a continuous chant of: 'In memory of unhappy Browning'—the ceremony being renewed in his spare moments, till the acute stage of the feeling had passed away.

Mrs Sutherland Orr, *Life and Letters of Robert Browning*, 1891

Robert and Elizabeth married in 1846 and went to live in Italy. One of their friends there was Elizabeth Kinney, the wife of the American chargé d'affaires in Turin:

MRS KINNEY's horror at hearing both Brownings proclaim George Sand 'a great woman' reflects perfectly the Victorian outlook which they so frequently outraged, for they admitted that she had a series of lovers. Lust, Elizabeth said, was no worse than intemperance or gluttony. George Sand's mind was 'godlike,' and she was kind and charitable. But, said Mrs Kinney, 'lascivious,' with her unlawful loves.

'Love,' exclaimed husband and wife together; 'she never loved anyone but herself.'

Maisie Ward, *Robert Browning and his World: The Private Face*, 1967

A COMFORT is that Robert is considered here to be looking better than he ever was known to look. And this notwithstanding the greyness of his beard, which indeed is, in my own mind, very becoming to him, the argentine touch giving a character of elevation and thought to the whole physiognomy. This greyness was suddenly developed; let me tell you how. He was in a state of bilious irritability on the morning of his arrival in Rome from exposure to the sun or some such cause, and in a fit of suicidal impatience shaved away his whole beard, whiskers and all! I *cried* when I saw him, I was so horror-struck. I might have gone into hysterics and still been reasonable; for no human being was ever so disfigured by so simple an act. Of course I said, when I recovered breath and voice, that everything was at an end between me and him if he didn't let it all grow again directly, and (upon the further advice of his looking-glass) he yielded the point, and the beard grew. But it grew *white*, which was the just punishment of the gods—our sins leave their traces.

Elizabeth Barrett Browning, letter to Browning's sister Sarianna, 1854

AT Pisa an English couple had been spreading unkind gossip about Elizabeth: she gave herself airs, had been too proud to return their call. Browning visited them and talked blandly of gossip he had heard, repeating their own words to them as of unnamed malicious folk while he watched them writhe.

Ward, *Robert Browning*

For a time Mrs Browning fell under the influence of Daniel Dunglas Home, the American medium. Browning loathed Home and drew a devastating portrait of him in his poem 'Mr Sludge, "The Medium" ', *though he didn't publish it until 1864, after Elizabeth's death. By this time he was back living in London:*

To Warwick Crescent to lunch with Browning by invitation. Pen [Browning's son] plays 'Chopin.' I say to R. B., 'Did you ever play as well as that?' to which he replied, 'A thousand times as well!' We spoke of Tennyson. T. told B. he thought 'Sludge' too long. B. answered, 'I hope *he* thought it too long!'—that is, Sludge, when the confession was forced from him. Sludge is Home, the Medium, of whom Browning told me today a great deal that was very amusing. Having witnessed a séance of Home's, at the house of a friend of B.'s, Browning was openly called upon to give his frank opinion on what had passed, in presence of Home and the company, upon which he declared with emphasis that so impudent a piece of imposture he never saw before in all his life, and so took his leave. Next day Browning's servant came into his room with a visitor's card, and close behind followed the visitor himself—no other than Mr Home, who advanced with a cordial smile and right hand outstretched in amity. He bore no ill-will—not he! Browning looked sternly at him (as he is very capable of doing) and pointing to the open door, not far from which is rather a steep staircase, said—'If you are not out of that door in half a minute I'll fling you down the stairs.' Home attempted some expostulation, but B. moved towards him, and the Medium disappeared with as much grace as he could manage. 'And now comes the best of it all,' said B.—'What do you suppose he says of me?—You'd never guess. He says to everybody, "How Browning hates me!—and how I love him!" ' He further explains B.'s animosity as arising out of a séance at Florence, where a 'spirit-wreath' was placed on Mrs Browning's head, and none on her husband's.

William Allingham, *Diary*, 1907; entry for 30 June 1864

ONE night Wilkie Collins, William Black, Millais, Browning and I were dining all together at the Reform Club. Browning began telling a story from an old Florentine poem. It took him between twenty minutes and half an hour, and we sat open-mouthed, like children, listening to the wonderful rhythm of the words and entranced by the marvellous power of the speaker. It was all impromptu, but some time afterwards Black referring to it said, 'Do you know, that might have been taken down verbatim, and it would have stood as splendid literature without a single alteration of a word!'

But there was another side to Browning, which came out at the same dinner. We were talking about the disappearance of the commercial or advertising poet whose verses were used to proclaim the superiority of his employer's wares. 'How funny those were,' said Browning, and he quoted a most absurd verse in laudation of Somebody's Trousers, as glibly as if he were the author. We were even more surprised than ever. Millais said, 'How on earth can you remember such beastly things?'

'Because I don't forget them,' replied Browning. 'You know we go through a wood and gather burrs and thousands of dead leaves and all kinds of rubbish, and find them sticking to our clothes, but when we come to look we find we have lost our *watch*!'

Interview with the painter George Henry Boughton, *Strand Magazine*, 1900

Browning published his poem Red Cotton Night-Cap Country *in 1873. There was an allusion to it in a prank played by students when he was honoured by Oxford nine years later:*

IN June 1882, while he sat in the Sheldonian Theatre, attired in a flame-colored gown and awaiting an honorary D.C.L. from Oxford, an immense cartoon of himself descended from a thronged upper gallery. Lowered jerkily on a string, a red cotton night cap collapsed on the head of a Professor of Divinity. As if aware of a sublime error, it hopped away, paused, and alighted at last on Robert's white curls.

Authorities threatened terrible reprisal until Browning worked wonders: 'Am I, or am I not, a member of your University?' he demanded of the vice chancellor.

'Certainly you are one,' came the deferential reply.

'Then let that poor boy off!'—whereupon an irreverent student was entirely pardoned.

William Irvine and Park Honan, *The Book, the Ring and the Poet*, 1975

BROWNING looked at a photograph of himself on my chimney-piece and said, 'There I am—and I don't recollect when or where it was done, or anything about it. I find gaps in my memory. The other day I came by chance on an old letter of my own, telling how I had seen Ristori in Camma—if that was the word, and I could not and cannot recollect in the very least what Camma is, or what I refer to: yet there it was in my own handwriting—a judgment on me for my opinion of my Grandfather, when I asked him if he had seen Garrick in *Richard the Third* and he replied 'I *suppose* I have,' and I thought 'Bless my soul! shall *I* ever come to this.'

William Allingham, *Diary*, 1907; entry for 6 April 1876

EDWARD LEAR · 1812–1888

One of Lear's expeditions took him into Calabria, a region then notorious for bandits:

THE most dangerous characters to be met with in Calabria were fugitives from justice. Hardly less dangerous were members of the local Mafia . . .

Yet it was two Englishmen at the Hotel Giordano in Reggio who probably did Lear more harm than any of these. He overheard the following fragment of their conversation at breakfast:

1ST MAN. I say, Dick, do you know who that fellow is who we were just talking to last night?
2ND MAN. No?
1ST MAN. Why, he's nothing but a dirty landscape painter.

Lear called himself a Dirty Landscape Painter ever after.

Susan Chitty, *That Singular Person Called Lear*, 1988

In 1845 and 1846 Lear gave drawing lessons to Queen Victoria. The two got on well:

ON one occasion 'the Queen was showing him some of the priceless treasures in the cabinets at Buckingham Palace . . . Mr Lear, entirely carried away, exclaimed, "Oh! how *did* you get all these beautiful things?" The reply was swift and sharp, "I inherited them, Mr Lear." '

Lady Strachey, Introduction to *Letters of Edward Lear*, 1907, quoted in Chitty, *That Singular Person*

In 1860 Lear was in Rome during the pre-Lent carnival:

THERE were ugly incidents in the streets and Lear saw two men stabbed at Tivoli. Giorgio [Lear's manservant] was instructed to take a basket with him when he went shopping 'to put your head in if it happens to be cut off'. 'No, sir,' was Giorgio's ready reply, 'I take soup tureen—hold him better.'

Chitty, *That Singular Person*

ANTHONY TROLLOPE · 1815–1882

In his early days working at the General Post Office, Trollope was frequently in trouble with his superior, Colonel Maberly:

I WAS always on the eve of being dismissed, and yet was always striving to show how good a public servant I could become, if only a chance were given me. But the chances went the wrong way. On one occasion, in the performance of my duty, I had put a private letter containing bank-notes on the secretary's table,—which letter I had duly opened, as it was not marked private. This letter was seen by the Colonel, but had not been moved by him when he left his room. On his return it was gone. In the meantime I had returned to the room, again in the performance of some duty. When the letter was missed I was sent for, and there I found the Colonel much moved about his letter, and a certain chief clerk, who, with a long face, was making suggestions as to the probable fate of the money. 'The letter has been taken,' said the Colonel, turning to me angrily, 'and by G—! there has been nobody in the room but you and I.' As he spoke, he thundered his fist down upon the table. 'Then,' said I, 'by G—! you have taken it.' And I also thundered my fist down;—but, accidentally, not upon the table. There was there a standing movable desk, at which, I presume, it was the Colonel's habit to write, and on this movable desk was a large bottle full of ink. My fist unfortunately came on the desk, and the ink at once flew up, covering the Colonel's face and shirt-front. Then it was a sight to see that senior clerk, as he seized a quire of blotting-paper, and rushed to the aid of his superior officer, striving to mop up the ink; and a sight also to see the Colonel, in his agony, hit right out through the blotting-paper at that senior clerk's unoffending stomach. At that moment there came in the Colonel's private secretary, with the letter and the money, and I was desired to go back to my own room. This was an incident not much in my favour, though I do not know that it did me special harm.

An Autobiography, 1883

Some ten years after Trollope's death, one of his former Post Office colleagues, A. M. Cunynghame, put the record straight in the course of an interview (quoted in Trollope: Interviews and Recollections, *ed. R. C. Terry, 1987): 'You remember the story about his upsetting a bottle of ink on Colonel Maberly's waistcoat? Sir Arthur Blackwood told me one day, after he had heard Trollope tell the story, that there was no truth in it. The fact was, Trollope had told it so often that he came to believe it himself, just as George IV believed he had been at Waterloo, but he was a delightful companion all the same.'*

In The Last Chronicle of Barset *(1866–7), Trollope bade farewell to one of his most famous characters:*

It was with many misgivings that I killed my old friend Mrs Proudie. I could not, I think, have done it, but for a resolution taken and declared under circumstances of great momentary pressure.

It was thus that it came about. I was sitting one morning at work upon the novel at the end of the long drawing-room of the Athenaeum Club,—as was then my wont when I had slept the previous night in London. As I was there, two clergymen, each with a magazine in his hand, seated themselves, one on one side of the fire and one on the other, close to me. They soon began to abuse what they were reading, and each was reading some part of some novel of mine. The gravamen of their complaint lay in the fact that I reintroduced the same characters so often!

'Here,' said one, 'is that archdeacon whom we have had in every novel he has ever written.' 'And here,' said the other, 'is the old duke whom he has talked about till everybody is tired of him. If I could not invent new characters, I would not write novels at all.' Then one of them fell foul of Mrs Proudie. It was impossible for me not to hear their words, and almost impossible to hear them and be quiet. I got up, and standing between them, I acknowledged myself to be the culprit. 'As to Mrs Proudie,' I said, 'I will go home and kill her before the week is over.' And so I did. The two gentlemen were utterly confounded, and one of them begged me to forget his frivolous observations.

I have sometimes regretted the deed, so great was my delight in writing about Mrs Proudie, so thorough was my knowledge of all the little shades of her character. It was not only that she was a tyrant, a bully, a would-be priestess, a very vulgar woman, and one who would send headlong to the nethermost pit all who disagreed with her; but that at the same time she was conscientious, by no means a hypocrite, really believing in the brimstone which she threatened, and anxious to save the souls around her from its horrors. And as her tyranny increased so did the bitterness of the moments of her repentance increase, in that she knew herself to be a tyrant,—till that bitterness killed her. Since her time others have grown up equally dear to me,—Lady Glencora and her husband, for instance; but I have never dissevered myself from Mrs Proudie, and still live much in company with her ghost.

An Autobiography

TOWARDS freshness or presumption he was unmerciful. . . . There was a lady once who ventured an impertinence. Sitting next Trollope at dinner she noticed that he partook largely of every dish offered to him. 'You seem to have a very good appetite, Mr Trollope,' she observed. 'None at all, madam,' he replied, 'but, thank God, I am very greedy.'

Michael Sadleir, *Trollope: A Commentary*, 1927

DURING a visit to London in December Hardy attended a Conference on the Eastern Question at St James's Hall, and heard speak Mr Gladstone, Lord Shaftesbury, Hon. E. Ashley, Anthony Trollope, and the Duke of Westminster. 'Trollope outran the five or seven minutes allowed for each speech, and the Duke, who was chairman, after various soundings of the bell, and other hints that he must stop, tugged at Trollope's coat-tails in desperation. Trollope turned round, exclaimed parenthetically, "Please leave my coat alone," and went on speaking.'

Florence Emily Hardy, *The Early Life of Thomas Hardy*, 1928

The Brontës

(see also separate entries under Charlotte Brontë and Emily Brontë)

Fond of talking of the Brontës is an old lady of eighty-seven who lived in Haworth the first half of her life, and, after the manner of the old, it is to Haworth, the place of her youth as it was in the days of her youth when the Brontës lived there, that her thoughts turn now, where her memory lingers.

'Eh, dear, when I think about them I can see them as plain to my mind's eye as if they were here. They wore light-coloured dresses all print, and they were all dressed alike until they gate into young women. I don't know that I ever saw them in owt but print—I've heard it said they were pinched—but it was nice print: plain with long sleeves and high neck and tippets down to the waist. The tippets were marrow to their dresses and they'd light-coloured hats on. They looked grand.'

If my memory serves me correctly, I believe the Miss Brontës' dresses have been criticised by others as being somewhat quaint and prim and old-fashioned and indeed anything but 'grand', but then these critics had not lived in Haworth all their lives and brought up a family on twelve shillings a week hardly earned in a mill, as had my old lady.

C. Holmes Cautley, 'Old Haworth Folk Who knew the Brontës', *Cornhill Magazine*, 1910

In August 1847 the Brontë sisters' fortunes were in the ascendant. Charlotte, with the encouragement of its future publisher, was completing Jane Eyre, *Emily and Anne were correcting the proof sheets of* Wuthering Heights *and* Agnes Grey*:*

Ellen Nussey tells of a curious, seemingly supernatural but in their altered circumstances wholly appropriate occurrence which she witnessed during her visit to Haworth that summer. Ellen Nussey told Mary Duclaux of it, and it first appeared in her *Memoir of Emily Brontë.*

Once, at this time, when they were walking on the moors together a sudden change of light came into the sky. 'Look!' said Charlotte; and the four girls looked up and saw three suns shining clearly overhead. They stood a little while gazing at the beautiful parhelion; Charlotte, her friend, and Anne clustered together, Emily a little higher, standing on a heathery knoll. 'That is you,' said Ellen at last, 'you are the three suns.' 'Hush!' cried Charlotte, indignant at the too shrewd nonsense of her friend; but as Ellen, her suspicions confirmed by Charlotte's violence, lowered her eyes to the earth again, she looked a moment at Emily. She was still standing on her knoll, quiet, satisfied; and round her lips there hovered a very soft and happy smile.

Winifred Gérin, *Emily Brontë*, 1971

A parhelion is defined by the Concise Oxford Dictionary *as 'a bright spot on the solar halo'.*

Charlotte Brontë · 1816–1855

WHILE her imagination received powerful impressions, her excellent understanding had full power to rectify them before her fancies became realities. On a scrap of paper, she has written down the following relation:—

'*June* 22, 1830, *6 o'clock* P.M.
Haworth, near Bradford.

The following strange occurrence happened on the 22nd of June, 1830:—At the time papa was very ill, confined to his bed, and so weak that he could not rise without assistance. Tabby and I were alone in the kitchen, about half-past nine antemeridian. Suddenly we heard a knock at the door; Tabby rose and opened it. An old man appeared, standing without, who accosted her thus:—

OLD MAN. Does the parson live here?
TABBY. Yes.
OLD MAN. I wish to see him.
TABBY. He is poorly in bed.
OLD MAN. I have a message for him.
TABBY. Who from?
OLD MAN. From the Lord.
TABBY. *Who?*
OLD MAN. The Lord. He desires me to say that the bridegroom is coming, and that we must prepare to meet him; that the cords are about to be loosed, and the golden bowl broken; the pitcher broken at the fountain.

Here he concluded his discourse, and abruptly went his way. As Tabby closed the door, I asked her if she knew him. Her reply was, that she had never seen him before, nor any one like him. Though I am fully persuaded that he was some fanatical enthusiast, well meaning, perhaps, but utterly ignorant of true piety; yet I could not forbear weeping at his words, spoken so unexpectedly at that particular period.'

Elizabeth Gaskell, *The Life of Charlotte Brontë*, 1857

Charlotte was 14 at the time this incident took place. 'Tabby' was Tabitha Aykroyd, the family servant.

I WAS once speaking to her about *Agnes Grey*—the novel in which her sister Anne pretty literally describes her own experience as a governess—and alluding more particularly to the account of the stoning of the little nestlings in the presence of the parent birds. She said that none but those who had been in the position of a governess could ever realise the dark side of 'respectable' human nature; under no great temptation to crime, but daily giving way to selfishness and ill-temper, till its conduct towards those dependent on it sometimes amounts to a tyranny of which one would rather be the victim than the inflicter. We can only trust in such cases that the employers err rather from a density of perception and an absence of sympathy, than from any natural cruelty of disposition. Among several things of the same kind, which I well remember, she told me what had once occurred to herself. She had been entrusted with the care of a little boy, three or four years old, during the absence of his parents on a day's excursion, and particularly enjoined to keep him out of the stable-yard. His elder brother, a lad of eight or nine, and not a pupil of Miss Brontë's, tempted the little fellow into the forbidden place. She followed, and tried to induce him to come away; but, instigated by his brother, he began throwing stones at her, and one of them hit her so severe a blow on the temple that the lads were alarmed into obedience. The next day, in full family conclave, the mother asked Miss Brontë what occasioned the mark on her forehead. She simply replied, 'An accident, ma'am,' and no further inquiry was made; but the children (both brothers and sisters) had been present, and honoured her for not 'telling tales.' From that time, she began to gain influence over all, more or less, according to their different characters; and as she insensibly gained their affection, her own interest in them was increasing. But one day, at the children's dinner, the small truant of the stable-yard, in a little demonstrative gush, said, putting his hand in hers, 'I love 'ou, Miss Brontë.' Whereupon, the mother exclaimed, before all the children, 'Love the *governess*, my dear!'

Gaskell, *Life of Charlotte Brontë*

On one of Charlotte's visits to London Thackeray gave a party in her honour. The evening was not a success:

MRS BROOKFIELD, who was perfectly at home in any society, said that Charlotte Brontë was the most difficult woman to talk to she had ever met. That evening at Thackeray's house she tried hard to enter into conversation with her. Mrs Brookfield used to relate with some humour what she called 'my conversation with Charlotte Brontë'. She said, 'I opened it by saying I hoped she liked London; to which Charlotte Brontë replied curtly, "I do and I don't." ' Naturally Mrs Brookfield's audience used to wait for more, but, said Mrs Brookfield, 'that is all'.

George Smith, 'Charlotte Brontë', *Cornhill Magazine*, 1900

Henry David Thoreau · 1817–1862

My Aunt Maria asked me to read the life of Dr Chalmers [the Scottish theologian], which, however, I did not promise to do. Yesterday, Sunday, she was heard through the partition shouting to my Aunt Jane, who is deaf, 'Think of it! He stood half an hour today to hear the frogs croak, and he wouldn't read the life of Chalmers.'

Journal, 28 March 1853

He noted what repeatedly befell him, that, after receiving from a distance a rare plant, he would presently find the same in his own haunts. And those pieces of luck which happen only to good players happened to him. One day, walking with a stranger, who inquired where Indian arrowheads could be found, he replied, 'Everywhere,' and, stooping forward, picked one on the instant from the ground.

Ralph Waldo Emerson, 'Thoreau', 1863

Our kitten Min, two-thirds grown, was playing with Sophia's broom this morning, as she was sweeping the parlour, when she suddenly went into a fit, dashed round the room, and, the door being opened, rushed up two flights of stairs and leaped from the attic window to the ice and snow by the side of the doorstep—a descent of little more than twenty feet—passed round the house and was lost. But she made her appearance again about noon, at the window, quite well and sound in every point, even playful and frisky.

Journal, 1 February 1856

Thoreau had his squeamish side. As Joseph Wood Krutch observed, 'he wanted no earthiness where sex was concerned':

At twenty-two he had expressed the opinion that to be shocked at vice was to reveal a lingering sympathy for it, and much later in life, when he met Whitman and read *Leaves of Grass*, he was to attempt to apologize for the book on somewhat similar grounds. But the truth seems to be that he was sometimes shocked in a way hardly becoming to a man who, sometimes at least, wished to accept all nature. When, at thirty-nine, he saw for the first time the rather startling fungus accurately denominated in the catalogues *Phallus impudicus*, he was not entertained as the scientist who named it obviously was, but genuinely shocked. 'Pray, what was nature thinking of when she made this? She almost put herself on the level with those who draw in privies.'

Joseph Wood Krutch, *Henry David Thoreau*, 1949

LAST evening one of our neighbors, who has just completed a costly house and front yard, the most showy in the village, illuminated in honor of the Atlantic telegraph. I read in great letters before the house the sentence 'Glory to God in the highest'. But it seemed to me that that was not a sentiment to be illuminated, but to keep dark about. A simple and genuine sentiment of reverence would not emblazon these words as on a signboard in the streets. They were exploding countless crackers beneath it, and gay company, passing in and out, made it a kind of housewarming. I felt a kind of shame for it, and was inclined to pass quickly by, the ideas of indecent exposure and cant being suggested. What is religion? That which is never spoken.

Journal, 18 August 1858

During the last year or two of Thoreau's life he found a new hero—Captain John Brown of the raid on Harper's Ferry:

TALKING with Walcott and Staples today, they declared that John Brown did wrong. When I said that I thought he was right, they agreed in asserting that he did wrong because he threw his life away, and that no man had a right to undertake anything which he knew would cost him his life. I inquired if Christ did not foresee that he would be crucified if he preached such doctrines as he did, but they both, as though it was their only escape, asserted that they did not believe that he did. Upon which a third party threw in, 'You do not think that he had so much foresight as Brown.' Of course, they as good as said that, if Christ *had* foreseen that he would be crucified, he would have 'backed out'. Such are the principles and the logic of the mass of men.

Journal, 3 December 1860

FREDERICK DOUGLASS · 1817–1895

Douglass, the most distinguished American black leader of the nineteenth century, was born a slave in Maryland. In 1838 he made his escape to Massachusetts, where he initially lived in the town of New Bedford and lodged with a remarkable black couple, Nathan and Mary Johnson:

ONCE initiated into the new life of freedom, and assured by Mr Johnson that New Bedford was a safe place, the comparatively unimportant matter, as to what should be my name, came up for consideration. It was necessary to have a name in my new relations. The name given me by my beloved mother was no less pretentious than 'Frederick Augustus Washington Bailey'. I had, however, before leaving Maryland, dispensed with the *Augustus Washington* and retained the name *Frederick Bailey.*

Between Baltimore and New Bedford, however, I had several different names, the better to avoid being overhauled by the hunters, which I had good reason to believe would be put on my track. Among honest men an honest man may well be content with one name, and to acknowledge it at all times and in all places; but towards fugitives, Americans are not honest. When I arrived at New Bedford, my name was Johnson, and finding that the Johnson family in New Bedford were already quite numerous—sufficiently so to produce some confusion in attempts to distinguish one from another—there was the more reason for making another change in my name. In fact, 'Johnson' had been assumed by nearly every slave who had arrived in New Bedford from Maryland, and this much to the annoyance of the original 'Johnsons' (of whom there were many) in that place. Mine host, unwilling to have another of his own name added to the community in this unauthorized way, after I spent a night and a day at his house, gave me my present name. He had been reading *The Lady of the Lake*, and was pleased to regard me as a suitable person to bear this, one of Scotland's many famous names. Considering the noble hospitality and manly character of Nathan Johnson, I have felt that he, better than I, illustrated the virtues of the great Scottish chief. Sure am I, that had any slave-catcher entered his domicile, with a view to molest any of his household, he would have shown himself like him of the 'stalwart hand'.

My Bondage and my Freedom, 1855

The father of the heroine of Walter Scott's poem The Lady of the Lake *(1810) is the wrongfully outlawed Lord James of Douglas.*

Benjamin Jowett · 1817–1893

(classical scholar; Master of Balliol College, Oxford)

Jowett's style, in his official dealings with dons and undergraduates, was marked by what E. F. Benson called 'a rather arid incisiveness'—'when he delivered his terse ultimatums there was no more to be said':

He dealt in this way with my friend Dr David Hogarth, who, as a junior don at Magdalen, was in charge of the production of one of Aristophanes' comedies, which was to be performed by the undergraduates. Dr Hogarth had cut out of the play certain witty lines which bore on the Athenian code of ethics with regard to boys—he just struck them out. The Master heard that this had been done and requested Hogarth to call on him. 'I hear you have been making cuts in the Greek play,' he said. 'Aristophanes wrote it. Who are you?'

E. F. Benson, *As We Were*, 1930

JOWETT asked Swinburne [who was staying in the Master's Lodgings] to look at his translation of Plato's *Symposium* and when the poet suggested a sentence could be construed differently Jowett's eyes widened: 'Of course that is the meaning. You would be a good scholar if you were to study.' Swinburne was set down in an adjoining room to continue the good work, and a friend talking to Jowett was interrupted by a cackle from next door. 'Another howler, Master.' 'Thank you, dear Algernon,' said Jowett as he shut the door.

Noel Annan, *The Dons*, 1999

EMILY BRONTË · 1818–1848

THE helplessness of an animal was its passport to Charlotte's heart; the fierce, wild, intractability of its nature was what often recommended it to Emily. Speaking of her dead sister, the former told me that from her many traits in Shirley's character were taken; her way of sitting on the rug reading, with her arm round her rough bull-dog's neck; her calling to a strange dog, running past with hanging head and lolling tongue, to give it a merciful draught of water, its maddened snap at her, her nobly stern presence of mind, going right into the kitchen, and taking up one of Tabby's red-hot Italian irons to sear the bitten place, and telling no one, till the danger was well-nigh over, for fear of the terrors that might beset their weaker minds. All this, looked upon as a well-invented fiction in *Shirley*, was written down by Charlotte with streaming eyes; it was the literal true account of what Emily had done.

Elizabeth Gaskell, *The Life of Charlotte Brontë*, 1857

IN the hurry of the fresh departures after the Christmas holidays—Anne and Branwell to Thorp Green and Charlotte to Brussels on 27 January 1843, the onus of investing their aunt's legacies fell, ironically enough, on Emily, who had never given money a thought. In the event, she proved herself a very able business-woman, as Charlotte was the first to acknowledge later. She took shares for her sisters and herself in the York and North Midland Railway Company which had been started in 1839 by the enterprising George Hudson. It may well be that the decision to take Hudson Shares was made after consultation with Anne, for Anne was in a position to have first-hand information on the subject. Hudson's railway was a York enterprise (he was a local man, twice mayor of the city) and she could hear the views of the Robinsons and their circle on the advisability of buying shares in his booming company. At that time, before the shadow of failure fell across Hudson's multiple enterprises, the Misses Brontë might consider themselves lucky to be allotted shares then continually soaring with the rising railway mania. Emily and Anne were very content with their successful incursion into high finance, and would hear nothing of Charlotte's subsequent doubts of George Hudson's honesty when he multiplied his activities at the expense of his railway stock, and they resolutely joined the subscribers to the testimonial raised by his grateful share-holders, with a guinea apiece, the record of which still stands on the company's books. When, in 1846, Hudson's fortunes began to fluctuate, and there was a rush by shareholders to sell out, Emily and Anne stuck to their guns and would not be persuaded by the prudent Charlotte to follow the trend.

Winifred Gérin, *Emily Brontë*, 1971

John Ruskin · 1819–1900

My mother had, as she afterwards told me, solemnly 'devoted me to God' before I was born; in imitation of Hannah [the mother of the prophet Samuel] . . .

'Devoting me to God' meant, as far as my mother knew herself what she meant, that she would try to send me to college, and make a clergyman of me: and I was accordingly bred for 'the Church'. My father, who—rest be to his soul—had the exceedingly bad habit of yielding to my mother in large things and taking his own way in small ones, allowed me, without saying a word, to be thus withdrawn from the sherry trade [the family business] as an unclean thing; not without some pardonable participation in my mother's ultimate views for me. For, many and a year afterwards, I remember, while he was speaking to one of our artist friends, who admired Raphael, and greatly regretted my endeavours to interfere with that popular taste,—while my father and he were condoling with each other on my having been impudent enough to think I could tell the public about Turner and Raphael,—instead of contenting myself, as I ought, with explaining the way of their souls' salvation to them—and what an amiable clergyman was lost in me,—'Yes,' said my father, with tears in his eyes (true and tender tears, as ever father shed,) 'he would have been a Bishop.'

Praeterita, 1885–9

I was still in the bonds of my old Evangelical faith; and, in 1858, it was with me, Protestantism or nothing: the crisis of the whole turn of my thoughts being one Sunday morning, at Turin, when, from before Veronese's Queen of Sheba, and under quite overwhelmed sense of his God-given power, I went away to a Waldensian chapel, where a little squeaking idiot was preaching to an audience of seventeen old women and three louts, that they were the only children of God in Turin; and that all the people in the world out of sight of Monte Viso, would be damned. I came out of the chapel, in sum of twenty years of thought, a conclusively *un*-converted man.

Fors Clavigera, April 1877, quoted in Tim Hilton, *Ruskin: The Early Years*, 1985

IN 1871, in one of my walks at Abingdon [where Ruskin was living in an inn, while preparing his lectures as Slade Professor at Oxford], I saw some ragged children playing by the roadside on the bank of a ditch, and gathering what buttercups they could find. Watching them a little while, I at last asked them what they were doing. 'This is my garden,' answered a little girl about nine years old. 'Well, but gardens ought to be of use; this is only full of buttercups. Why don't you plant some strawberries in it?' 'I have none to plant.' 'If you had a little garden of your own, and some to plant, would you take care of them?' 'That I would.' Thereupon I told her to come and ask for me at the Crown and Thistle, and with my good landlady Mrs Wonnacott's help, rented a tiny piece of ground for her. Her father and mother have since died; and her brothers and sisters (four, in all) are in the Union [the workhouse] in Abingdon. I did not like this child to go there too, so I've sent her to learn shepherding at a kindly shepherd's, close to Arundel . . . this ten pounds is for her board etc., till she can be made useful.

Fors Clavigera, July 1876; quoted in Tim Hilton, *Ruskin: The Later Years*, 2000

It was at the home of his friends the Aclands in Oxford that Ruskin met Julia Margaret Cameron. The Aclands' daughter Angie describes what happened:

DURING the time that Mr Ruskin was with us Mrs Cameron, a very well-known artistic portrait photographer of those days was also with us on a visit and the two had frequent skirmishes about photography. I was lying on my couch in the drawing room one day when Mrs Cameron insisted on showing Mr Ruskin some of the wonderful heads of well-known people which she had taken. He got more and more impatient until they came to one of Sir John Herschel in which his hair all stood up like a halo of fireworks. Mr Ruskin banged to the portfolio upon which Mrs Cameron thumped his poor frail back exclaiming 'John Ruskin you are not worthy of photographs!' They then left the room. Mrs Cameron wore a red bonnet with strings and when she got very excited she pushed it back and it hung down her back by the strings. Apparently they went out but arrived back to luncheon with bonnet on and peace signed.

Sarah Angelina Acland, 'Memories in my 81st Year', quoted in Hilton, *Ruskin: The Later Years*

HERMAN MELVILLE · 1819–1891

MRS HAWTHORNE used to tell of one evening when he [Melville] came in, and presently began to relate the story of a fight which he had seen on an island in the Pacific, between some savages, and of the prodigies of valor one of them had performed with a heavy club. The narrative was extremely graphic; and when Melville had gone, and Mr and Mrs Hawthorne were talking over his visit, the latter said, 'Where is that club with which Mr Melville was laying about him so?' Mr Hawthorne thought he must have taken it with him; Mrs Hawthorne thought he had put it in a corner; but it was not to be found. The next time Melville came, they asked him about it; whereupon it appeared the club was still in the Pacific island, if it were anywhere.

Julian Hawthorne, *Nathaniel Hawthorne and his Wife*, 1885

In 1851, while he was at work on Moby-Dick, *Melville received a request from his friend Evert Duyckinck for a daguerreotype—a photograph—from which an engraving could be made for a new magazine which Duyckinck was about to edit. He was unable to oblige:*

As for the Daguerreotype (I spell the word right from your sheet) that's what I can not send you, because I have none. And if I had, I would not send it for such a purpose, even to you.—Pshaw! you cry—and so cry I.—'This is intensified vanity, and not true modesty or anything of that sort!'—Again, I say so too. But if it be so, how can I help it. The fact is, almost everybody is having his 'mug' engraved nowadays; so that this test of distinction is getting reversed; and therefore, to see one's 'mug' in a magazine is presumptive evidence that he's a nobody. So being as vain a man as ever lived; and believing that my illustrious name is famous throughout the world—I respectfully decline being *oblivionated* by a Daguerreotype (what a devil of an unspellable word!)

Letter to Duyckinck, 12 February 1851

On 7 July 1851, Melville wrote a note in his copy of Robert Burton's Anatomy of Melancholy, *recording a discovery which his brother Allan had made in the book—a faint signature, 'A. Melville':*

'I BOUGHT this book more than four years ago at Gowan's store in New York. Today, Allan, looking at it, first detected the above pencil signature of my father's; who—as it now appears—must have had the book, with many others, sold at auction, at least twenty-five years ago.—Strange!'

Quoted in Hershel Parker, *Herman Melville*, 1996

The Anatomy of Melancholy *was a favourite of Melville's. In*

Moby-Dick, *in the words of Hershel Parker, 'it served as his sonorous textbook on morbid psychology'.*

GEORGE ELIOT (born Mary Anne Evans) · 1819–1880

HER gravity at the age of nine or ten is illustrated by an authentic anecdote recalled by Mrs Shaw, who at a children's party noticed Mary Anne sitting alone. Going up to her, Mrs Shaw said,

'My dear, you do not seem happy; are you enjoying yourself?'

'No, I am not,' said Mary Anne. 'I don't like to play with children. I like to talk to grown-up people.'

Gordon S. Haight, *George Eliot*, 1968

George Eliot lived with George Henry Lewes from 1854 until his death in 1878:

IN the winter of 1866 my wife and family were at Pau, while I was alone in London. George Eliot was a very fair pianist, not gifted, but enthusiastic, and extremely painstaking. During a great part of that winter I used to go to her every Monday evening at her house in North Bank, Regent's Park, always taking my violin with me. We played together every piano and violin sonata of Mozart and Beethoven. I knew the traditions of the best players, and was able to give her some hints, which she always received eagerly and thankfully. Our audience consisted of George Lewes only, and he used to groan with delight whenever we were rather successful in playing some beautiful passage.

Frederick Lehmann in R. C. Lehmann, *Memories of Half a Century*, 1908

When Middlemarch *was first published it was very much the book of the hour:*

JUDGE FITZGERALD reported that 'at the opening of the Dublin Exhibition he was struck with the attention of the Archbishop to the interior of his hat, which at first he took for devout listening to the speeches, but on close examination saw he was reading something, and as this was so intent he was prompted to look also into the hat, and found the Archbishop had *Middlemarch* there laid open—what a much better way of listening to "opening speeches"!'

Haight, *George Eliot*

THE ever-present sense of her moral responsibility as a leader of thought was a religion to her. In *Daniel Deronda* she quoted a line or two from

Walt Whitman as a heading to one of her chapters, but when the book had gone to press, she regretted her imprudence, and tried to get it cancelled, fearing that, since in these headings she quoted no poet except Walt Whitman, her readers might mistakenly think that he was her favourite bard. Similarly, when *Theophrastus Such* was published seven months after G. H. Lewes's death, she required her publisher to insert a slip saying that it was written before her bereavement; the public must not think that she had spent the early months of her widowhood in writing. Mrs Gaskell sent her a very enthusiastic letter about *Scenes from Clerical Life*, and she forwarded this to a friend 'because it did honour to Mrs Gaskell. . . . If there is any truth in me that the world wants, nothing will prevent the world from drinking what it is athirst for.'

E. F. Benson, *Final Edition*, 1940

I REMEMBER Burne-Jones telling me of a day spent at 'The Heights' with George Eliot, and of his departure thence on a pitch-black autumn evening. The lady, who, in spite of her genius, was hopelessly vague in mundane affairs, bade him farewell at the door, and saying—'If you turn to the right you will get to the station'—shut him out into the darkness. He stumbled blindly down the drive and into the lane where, hearing the distant approach of the train, he turned to the right as directed (incidentally scrambling over a fence), and—sure enough—got to the station, but upside-down, much torn by brambles and considerably bruised, after having fallen and rolled down a fairly perpendicular bank about thirty feet high. This rather inconvenient vagueness of the great lady was probably fostered by the exaggerated care taken of her by G. H. Lewes, of which another of Burne-Jones's stories gives instance.

He came across her standing monumentally alone at Waterloo Station, and, as he talked with her, they walked for a short distance along the platform. Suddenly Lewes rushed up to them, panic pale and breathlessly exclaiming—'My God! You are HERE!' George Eliot gravely admitted it. 'But,' stammered Lewes, 'I left you THERE!' That his precious charge should have walked by herself, without proper escort and chaperonage, for over ten yards was a portent almost beyond possibility.

Yet, in spite of the incense and high ritual that surrounded her, George Eliot seems to have remained a very simple and kindly woman. Once, during an illness of Mrs Allingham in London, she arrived to take the children for a drive, and their nurse, in telling me of it, said—'When I got into the carriage I thought she was the ugliest woman I had ever seen, but when she had been talking for awhile, I couldn't see that she was ugly at all.'

W. Graham Robertson, *Time Was*, 1931

Walt Whitman · 1819–1892

The first edition of Whitman's Leaves of Grass *was published in 1855—printed by Whitman himself, and distributed by Fowler and Wells, a firm which specialized in promoting phrenology. Whitman had already been in touch with them for a number of years:*

As early as 1846 he had become mildly interested in the books on phrenology which he reviewed in the [Brooklyn] *Eagle*, and in the summer of 1849 he began visiting the Fowlers' Phrenological Cabinet at 131 Nassau Street in New York City, where charts and physiological exhibits were on display to advertise this pseudo-science. In July Lorenzo Fowler examined Whitman's cranium and drew up a very flattering 'chart of bumps' for the young journalist. He was found to be amply endowed in all the desirable categories on the phrenological chart, and ranked at the very top of the scale in 'Amativeness' (sexual love), 'Philoprogenitiveness' (love of mankind), and 'Adhesiveness' (male friendship). The first paragraph of Fowler's analysis contained some rather shrewd guesses (or maybe he knew Whitman so well by this time that they were not guesses):

This man has a grand physical constitution, and power to live to a good old age. He is undoubtedly descended from the soundest and hardiest stock. Size of head large. Leading traits of character appear to be Friendship, Sympathy, Sublimity, and Self-Esteem, and markedly among his combinations the dangerous faults of Indolence, a tendency to the pleasure of Voluptuousness and Alimentiveness and a certain reckless swing of animal will, too unmindful, probably, of the conviction of others.

Gay Wilson Allen, *The Solitary Singer*, 1955

The great American naturalist John Burroughs grew up on a farm in the Catskills. As a young man, in 1863, he went to work as a government clerk in Washington. He was drawn to the city by the presence there of Whitman, who was tending Civil War casualties in army hospitals, and the two men became friends:

When Whitman wrote his great poem in memory of President Lincoln ['When lilacs last in the dooryard bloom'd'] it was Burroughs who suggested the 'shy and hidden bird'. The lilacs were in their April bloom on the day that Lincoln died—they were always to bring back to Whitman a memory of the moment—and, as it happened, in the early spring just before the assassination the great star Venus in the West seemed exceptionally brilliant. Restlessly haunting the Potomac, he had watched it, far off, aloof and somehow moody as himself. The star and the lilacs connected themselves in his mind with Lincoln, and then Burroughs described to him the hermit thrush he had known as a boy, a bird that Audubon apparently had never discovered. Burroughs had occasionally heard its song, a quarter of a mile away rising over a chorus of wrens and warblers, resembling no other sound that he recalled in nature, a beatitude that was religious, pure and serene. This was the bird that appeared in Whitman's poem.

Van Wyck Brooks, *The Times of Melville and Whitman*, 1947

Some of the most interesting of the pilgrims who sought Whitman out in his later years in Camden, New Jersey, came from England:

OSCAR WILDE, wearing his brown velvet suit, crossed over to Camden with J. M. Stoddard, the publisher. They were admitted to the Whitman home on Stevens Street by Walt's sister-in-law, who offered them elderberry wine. Wilde drank it off as if it 'were the nectar of the gods,' and confided to Stoddard later that, 'If it had been vinegar, I would have drunk it all the same, for I have an admiration for that man which I can hardly express.' The two poets got along splendidly together. Walt called him 'Oscar,' and the younger man sat at his feet on a low stool, with his hand on the poet's knee. Next day to a Philadelphia *Press* reporter Whitman stated for publication that he thought Wilde 'was glad to get away from lecturing, and fashionable society, and spend a time with an "old rough." We had a very happy time together. I think him genuine, honest, and manly.'

Allen, *The Solitary Singer*

HERBERT SPENCER · 1820–1903

(philosopher)

THE late Mr Herbert Spencer once sat at table next to a connection of my own for three consecutive days. He sat in deep silence. Upon the fourth day he took from his ears two little pads of cotton-wool. He exhibited them to the lady and remarking, 'I stop my ears with these when I perceive there is no one at the table likely to afford rational conversation,' he put them back again.

Ford Madox Ford, *Ancient Lights*, 1911

Matthew Arnold · 1822–1888

Arnold was an undergraduate at Oxford from 1841 to 1844:

Matthew's formal achievements were unimpressive, but his clothes, laughter, antics, and minor feats were remarkable. People recalled his leap over Wadham's railings. [He jumped over a 5 foot 3 inch spiked railing outside Wadham College for a bet.] They even remembered him naked. Capering on a riverbank one day, he made such a show of himself that a clergyman 'came up to remonstrate', according to G. H. Lewes's diary. 'Is it possible,' Matthew replied while waving a towel, 'that you see anything indelicate in the human form divine?'

Park Honan, *Matthew Arnold*, 1981

He worked as an inspector of schools for thirty-five years:

Most teachers were as glad to see him perhaps as Reverend Dymond was at Edmonton one day. Surprised by his 'loud voice' and a 'moppy abundance' of hair parted in the middle, Dymond noted: 'a good half hour behind the appointed time he burst into the school.' Arnold apologized for his want of punctuality 'by some joking reference.' He gave an amusing lecture to Dymond, five minutes long, 'on the functions of a "foot-scraper," ' while pupils sat on their hands. Coaxed into a classroom, the inspector with a booming voice promptly 'frightened a little girl into a crying fit.'

Arnold called the little girl to his knee: 'His patience with the children,' says Dymond, 'was wonderful.' Either then or at another time, he put his face next to a girl with a bandaged head and ascertained she had an earache: 'Ah,' boomed Arnold, 'I know what that is! I used to have bad ears when I was a little boy. I know how they hurt me. Go home and take that to your mother'—slipping the girl a shilling—'and tell her to tie your head up in hot flannel, and don't come back to school until you are quite better.'

Quite evidently his questions for toddlers were delightfully simple, if he reserved hard meaningless queries for older boys. 'Well, my little man,' Arnold might begin, 'and how do you spell dog?' 'Please sir, d-o-g.' 'Capital, very good indeed. I couldn't do it better myself. And now let us go a little further, and see if we can spell cat.' (Chorus excitedly,) 'C-A-T.' 'Now, this is really excellent.'

Dymond however noticed that when he left the Edmonton four- and five-year-olds, he was 'riled' by an older smart aleck—until that boy volunteered that Shakespeare's knowledge was not so much 'learnt' as 'picked up.' 'Now,' Arnold stated, 'I must give you credit for that.'

Honan, *Matthew Arnold*

Logan Pearsall Smith met Arnold while staying in Dresden as a young man, and was disappointed that the poet seemed cheerful and worldly, and less preoccupied with literature than with the favourable reception he had received at the Saxon Court:

I SPECIALLY remember how shocked I was when, after sitting in ecstatic reverence at a splendid performance of the *Valkyrie*, I ventured to ask him, as we walked back together to the hotel, what impression the music had made upon him. 'Oh, I had to go,' he said in his offhand manner, 'but I only went because my wife and daughters would have scoffed at me if I hadn't. But if you ask me what I thought of it—well, it seemed to me—like—what shall I say?—it seemed to me the sort of thing I should have composed myself if I happened to try my hand at composing music.' 'Oh, Matthew Arnold,' I murmured to myself, 'is this the way you strive for a many-sided perfection? Is it thus that you listen with particular heed to those voices of foreign culture which are especially likely to escape us in our provincial Anglo-Saxon darkness?'

Logan Pearsall Smith, *Unforgotten Years*, 1938

In 1883–4 he undertook a lecture tour of North America. One of the regular topics on which he spoke was Emerson:

ON a memorable day, in late December 1883, Arnold looked out over a sea of hats, at last, belonging to members of the Jersey City Aesthetic Society. Their President, Mrs Smith, was an honorable white member of the Tuscarora Indian Tribe. He had survived a luncheon with her. And now, even before she introduced him as the age's leading aesthetician, there was trouble: peculiarly he had a view of only *half* of her church. Rustling the papers of 'Emerson,' he looked towards Erminnie Smith in despair. Erminnie led him to a 'music stand,' and repositioned him. But instead of sitting down, she 'extended to the Society the holiday greeting,' as a reporter noticed, 'and quoted some appropriate lines from Mrs Robert Browning and Margaret Fuller' (two authors whom Matthew rather disliked) 'which drew from Mr Arnold a smile, and a look of appreciation.' Certainly he might now begin his talk? As he looked up, a quartet known as the Meigs Sisters stood up and sang 'God Save the King.' Feeling that he was pretty well introduced, Arnold looked apprehensively round the church. Mr Courtland Palmer rose with a 'few remarks laudatory' of the Aesthetic Society of Jersey City. Arnold listened. Was he being *deliberately* tortured? Did they want him to speak or not? Who were these people? Would an ecclesiastical sign be given to tell when he might open his mouth? Miss Henrietta Markstein now stood up, walked to a piano, and played a 'solo, "Old Black Joe," with variations.' After applause for Miss Markstein died down, Arnold opened his mouth. He began reciting

'Emerson,' as a reporter felt, in a wavering, indistinct voice as if 'reading prayers,' and finally, just as his British voice ended, Mrs Clementine Lassar Studwell stood up and sang 'The Star Spangled Banner.' Arnold had trouble even in sitting down. After the national anthem, there was a new outburst of Aesthetic Society energy. An Aesthetician complimented him, whereupon Mrs Studwell stood up again to sing 'Within a Mile of Edinburgh Town.' Arnold's eyes studied exit doors. He might break his way out rudely, get through a cluster of ladies at the side exit if something distracted them, or, of course, he could run to the door while smiling normally. He settled on a smile and a brisk walk. Just as all four Meigs sisters stood up to sing 'Little Jack Horner,' as the reporter noticed, 'Mr Arnold took his leave.'

Honan, *Matthew Arnold*

Wilkie Collins · 1824–1889

In his autobiography the popular novelist Hall Caine recalled a conversation he had had with Collins about opium addiction:

The two men had been discussing legal matters for some hours when Collins, complaining that his brain was not very clear, opened a cupboard in the corner of the room and took out a wineglass and a bottle, from which he poured out a full glass of what looked like port.

'I am going to show you the secrets of my prison-house' he said. 'Do you see that? It's laudanum', and he drank the whole glass-full.

'Good heavens, Wilkie Collins! how long have you taken that drug?' asked Hall Caine.

'Twenty years.'

'More than once a day?'

'Oh yes, much more. Don't be alarmed. Remember that De Quincey used to drink laudanum out of a jug'. Wilkie Collins then related a long story of how a servant of his had killed himself by taking less than half of one of Collins's opium doses. There is no corroboration of this story, which seems to have been an opium fantasy, perhaps originating with Fergusson's dinner-table remark about Collins's doses being enough to kill a whole party of normal men.

'Why do you take it?' Hall Caine asked him.

'To stimulate the brain and steady the nerves'.

'And you think it does that?'

'Undoubtedly' replied Wilkie Collins, and turned back to the legal matter they had been discussing, saying that he would see it more clearly now, after his laudanum dose. But Hall Caine persisted. Did laudanum have the same stimulating effect on other people as on Collins?

'It had on Bulwer Lytton. He told me so himself'.

Hall Caine, claiming that he himself suffered severely from nervous exhaustion, asked whether Collins advised him to use the drug. Collins, he records, 'paused, changed colour slightly, and then said quietly "No" '.

Alethea Hayter, *Opium and the Romantic Imagination*, 1968, quoting from Hall Caine, *My Story*, 1908

William Stubbs · 1825–1901

(historian; Bishop of Oxford)

The great Bishop Stubbs, in company with four strapping sons on a walking-tour, slept the night at an inn where Gosse was staying in some remote part of France. Next morning the landlady came to Gosse with an air of concern. 'Pardon monsieur—that gentleman who was here last night—those four young men—is it true that they are his sons?' Gosse told her they were. 'Oh monsieur!' cried the devout old thing, 'un évêque! quel cynisme!'

Edward Marsh, *A Number of People*, 1939

Introducing this story, Marsh recalled that 'Wilfred Blunt used to say that you could put ten per cent on to any story by making its leading figure a Bishop'.

William McGonagall · 1825?–1902

(much-derided popular versifier: 'The Great McGonagall')

Mr William Power in his book *My Scotland* tells how he attended one of McGonagall's performances in the Albion Halls in Glasgow many years ago. 'He was an old man, but, with his athletic though slightly stooping figure and his dark hair, he did not look more than forty-five; and he appeared to have been shaved the night before. He wore a Highland dress of Rob Roy tartan and boy's size. After reciting some of his own poems, to an accompaniment of whistles and cat-calls, the Bard armed himself with a most dangerous-looking broadsword, and strode up and down the platform, declaiming "Clarence's Dream" and "Give me another horse—Bind up my wounds". His voice rose to a howl. He thrust and slashed at imaginary foes. A shower of apples and oranges fell on the platform. Almost before they touched it, they were met by the fell edge of McGonagall's claymore and cut to pieces. The Bard was beaded with perspiration and orange juice. The audience yelled with delight;

McGonagall yelled louder still, with a fury which I fancy was not wholly feigned. It was like a squalid travesty of the wildest scenes of *Don Quixote* and *Orlando Furioso*. I left the hall early, saddened and disgusted.'

Hugh MacDiarmid, *Scottish Eccentrics*, 1936

Walter Bagehot · 1826–1877

(writer on literature and politics; editor of *The Economist*; author of *The English Constitution*)

In 1874 the Bagehots decided to buy a house in London, and settled on 8 Queen's Gate Place, which they gave into the hands of William Morris's firm to furnish and decorate, De Morgan tiles, of course, being a feature of the decoration.

Walter wrote to me that 'Wardle is doing most of the house, but the great man himself, William Morris, is composing the drawing-room, as he would an ode.' Walter would at times meet William Morris at the Bloomsbury depot when choosing papers and tiles, and the two would talk poetry as well as furniture. Walter's fancy was tickled at the quaint combination, and at William Morris's autocratic attitude towards all questions of taste. However amusing the culture of aesthetics might be they could not wean Walter entirely. He always had a great fondness for children. Amidst the choice designs of an inner hall, which the Morris firm had treated as a special feature in the new house, stood a fine large rocking horse, crude in colour and carving as such things are, my sister's gift to my boy. As we were passing it one day Walter spurted out suddenly, as he used to do when he enunciated something that was *really* true, '*That's* the best thing in the house.'

Mrs Russell Barrington, *The Works and Life of Walter Bagehot*, 1915

Mrs Barrington was Bagehot's sister-in-law.

Dante Gabriel Rossetti · 1828–1882

Mr Allingham took me for a walk, and as he displayed the enchanting countryside, I lured him to speaking of the old days and of Rossetti . . . I cannot recall much of that talk, but remember a quaint description of Rossetti's carefully explaining to him the points of his favourite model, Fanny Cornforth, in that lady's presence and with almost embarrassing minuteness.

'Her lips, you see'—following their curve with an indicating finger—'are just the red a woman's lips should always be—not really red at all, but with the bluish pink bloom that you find in a rose petal'—Miss Cornforth the while spreading her ample charms upon a couch and throwing in an occasional giggle or 'Oh, go along, Rissetty!'

W. Graham Robertson, *Time Was*, 1931

In the 1860s, when Rossetti lived in Cheyne Walk, 'he collected almost anything that attracted his attention, particularly china, furniture and animals':

OF the last he had at one time and another a Pomeranian puppy called Punch, an Irish wolfhound called Wolf, two brown owls called Jenny and Bobby, some rabbits, dormice, hedgehogs, white mice, squirrels, a mole, a chameleon, some salamanders, a deer, a wallaby, some kangaroos, two wombats, a Canadian marmot, a woodchuck, an armadillo, a racoon, a Brahmin Bull, a jackass, and numerous birds including peacocks, Chinese horned owls, talking grey parrots, a raven, and a grass parakeet. These lived a life of conflict and depredation in and about the house and gardens and those of his neighbours. The armadillo disappeared for several weeks, and suddenly appeared through the floor of a basement kitchen some distance away, to the great alarm of the cook, 'who opined that if it was not the devil, there was no knowing what it was'; the deer stamped out all the tail feathers of the peacock, who in turn made so much noise that a clause was in future introduced into all the leases on the Cadogan Estate forbidding them to be kept in the neighbourhood.

It does not appear that Rossetti lavished any personal affection upon his various pets, except perhaps upon the first of the wombats; he met their frequent deaths and disappearances with fortitude; some indeed died or disappeared almost the moment they were acquired, and some, such as the Brahmin Bull, which Rossetti bought for twenty pounds at Cremorne Gardens because it had eyes that reminded him of Janey Morris, proved quite unmanageable. But he liked to have them about the place, and he particularly delighted in visits to Jamrach's shop, where in an acrid atmosphere, beasts from all countries chattered and rattled against their bars.

Evelyn Waugh, *Rossetti: His Life and Works*, 1928

ROSSETTI came often into Yeats's talk, nowhere more memorably than in his account of an incident told him by his father, the painter John Butler Yeats. The painter was a close friend of Rossetti. One day, when they were walking together, a chaffinch by the roadside showed signs of agitation, and fluttered along beside them from bush to bush as they walked. Rossetti stopped, and nodded towards it. 'That is my wife's soul,' he said sadly—and immediately the chaffinch came and perched on his shoulder.

L. A. G. Strong, *Green Memory*, 1961

George Meredith · 1828–1909

In his old age Meredith enjoyed being visited by younger writers at his home in the country, Box Hill. One author who made the pilgrimage was G. K. Chesterton:

I went through the garden and saw an old man sitting by a table, looking smallish in his big chair. His hair and beard were both white, not like snow, but like something feathery, or even fierce. I came up quite close to him; he looked at me as he put out his frail hand, and I saw of a sudden that his eyes were startlingly young. He was deaf and he talked like a torrent—not about the books he had written—he was far too much alive for that. He talked about the books he had not written. He asked me to write one of the stories for him, as he would have asked the milkman, if he had been talking to the milkman. It was a splendid and frantic story, a sort of astronomical farce, all about a man who was rushing up to the Royal Society with the only possible way of avoiding an earth-destroying comet; and it showed how even on this huge errand the man was tripped up by his own weakness and vanities; how he lost a train by trifling or was put in gaol for brawling. That is only one of them. I went out of that garden with a blurred sensation of the million possibilities of creative literature. I really had the feeling that I had seen the creative quality; which is supernatural.

Chesterton, quoted in Siegfried Sassoon, *Meredith*, 1948

Meredith had been contemplating the plot which Chesterton describes for many years. He subsequently decided that H. G. Wells would be the right man for the job, but failed to persuade him.

Christina Rossetti · 1830–1894

Christina Rossetti's happiest hours as a young child were spent visiting her maternal grandparents in Buckinghamshire, though she had one nasty experience there which always haunted her:

It was the small creatures of the countryside which fascinated her, birds, rabbits, squirrels, frogs, toads, mice. She would pick up and fearlessly handle beetles, caterpillars and worms which even country-bred children might find repulsive. She enjoyed playing at funerals and on one unforgettable occasion she buried a dead mouse in a moss-lined grave, planning to dig it up again a few days later. When she did so, expecting to find the little furry body as whole and beautiful as ever, she saw a loathsome black insect emerging from the decaying corpse and fled in horror from the sight. It was her first, never to be forgotten, experience of corruption.

Georgina Battiscombe, *Christina Rossetti*, 1981

IN the winter of 1874, I was asked to secure some influential signatures to a petition against the destruction of a part of the New Forest. Mr Swinburne promised me his, if I could induce Miss Christina Rossetti to give hers, suggesting as he did so, that the feat might not be an easy one. In fact, I found that no little palaver was necessary; but at last she was so far persuaded of the innocence of the protest that she wrote *Chr*; she then stopped, dropped the pen and said very earnestly, 'Are you sure that they do not propose to build churches on the land?' After a long time I succeeded in convincing her that such a scheme was not thought of, and she proceeded to write *istina G Ros*, and stopped again. 'Nor schoolhouses?', fluctuating with tremulous scruple. At length she finished the signature, and I carried the parchment off to claim the fulfilment of Mr Swinburne's promise.

Edmund Gosse, *Critical Kit-Kats*, 1896

EMILY DICKINSON · 1830–1886

Emily Dickinson could be an elusive friend. Emily Fowler, who was on close terms with her when they were in their early twenties, was a frequent visitor to the Dickinson house, but the main point of the poet's letters to Fowler (or those which survive) is to explain that a reciprocal visit is impossible:

THE most interesting of these notes must be reproduced in its entirety:

Thursday morn

Dear Emily,

I cant come in this morning, because I am so cold, but you will know I am here—ringing the big front door bell, and leaving a note for you.

Oh I *want* to come in, I have a great mind *now* to follow little Jane into your warm sitting room; are you there, dear Emily?

No, I resist temptation, and run away from the door just as fast as my feet will carry me, lest if I once come in, I shall grow so happy, *happy*, that I shall stay there *always*, and never go home at all! You will have read this quite, by the time I reach the office, and you cant think how fast I run!

Aff[ectionately]
Emily

P.S. I have just shot past the corner, and now all the wayside houses, and the little gate flies open to see me coming home!

In this fantastically ingenious concoction, Dickinson describes herself as present within the message, and then as running home while the recipient reads it, finally entering the gate as the postscript is read. Fleet-footed Emily professes a wish to stay, but the speed with which she heads north past the intersection of Main and West Streets reveals her true desire. And then her gate flies open of its own accord to welcome her.

The note was written in ink on a minuscule piece of paper that had been scissored and torn down to size, then folded to make four sides or pages, one of which was reserved for the recipient's name. That the postscript neatly fills the last bit of open space on the third written page shows how perfectly the apparent spontaneity had been worked out in advance.

Alfred Habegger, *My Ways Are Laid Away in Books: The Life of Emily Dickinson*, 2002

In 1862 Emily Dickinson sent some of her poems to the writer and editor Thomas Wentworth Higginson, asking him for his opinion. It marked the beginning of a long correspondence between them, although it was not until 1870 that Higginson paid a visit to her home in Amherst and met her for the first time:

In the entry hall he heard a 'step like a pattering child's and in glided a little plain woman with two smooth bands of reddish hair . . . in a very plain and exquisitely clean white pique and a blue net worsted shawl.' He was looking for what his wife would notice. Twice he used the word 'childlike.' His hostess presented him with two day lilies as her 'introduction,' then, asking him to 'forgive me if I am frightened; I never see strangers and hardly know what I say,' she began talking. She talked 'continuously' but 'deferentially—sometimes stopping to ask me to talk instead of her'—and then resuming. Comparing her to other seemingly uninhibited naifs, such as Louisa May Alcott's often fatuous father, he judged her to be 'thoroughly ingenuous and simple.' Although he doubted his wife would care for her, he considered much of what she said 'wise.' Her parting speech—'Gratitude is the only secret that cannot reveal itself'—tells us she hadn't been able to express what she felt she owed him for having 'saved my Life.' As he walked away, he carried the photograph she had given him of Barrett Browning's grave, a gift that probably meant more to the hostess than to the visitor . . .

Only after the train had carried him into Vermont and New Hampshire did Higginson record his relief. 'I never was with any one who drained my nerve power so much. Without touching her, she drew from me. I am glad not to live near her.'

Habegger, *My Ways Are Laid Away*

Elizabeth Barrett Browning was one of Emily Dickinson's great heroes. When one of her friends was visiting Florence, she wrote asking him to make a pilgrimage to Mrs Browning's grave and 'put one hand on the Head, for me—the unmentioned Mourner.'

A FEW glimpses of Emily Dickinson's ordinary life remain from the last years. Cooking activities of a limited sort engaged her energies. Mme Bianchi [Martha Dickinson Bianchi, her niece] remembered that her aunt was rather 'précieuse' in the kitchen, that she chose to stir with a silver spoon and to measure with a glass. A kind of 'imaginary line' or taboo separated her cooking utensils from those used by Maggie [the family servant] and Lavinia [Emily's sister]. Her niece's memory is that Aunt Emily's craftsmanship was delicate and precise in such feats as sliding the wine-jelly uninjured from its mould. In making even such delicacies as the one she called Homestead Charlotte Russe, she rigorously curbed the temptation to imaginative improvisation and stuck closely to the rules, lest, as her niece remembers her to have said on one occasion, a 'quarter of a teaspoon of Eternity' should get in by mistake.

Richard Chase, *Emily Dickinson*, 1952

LEWIS CARROLL · 1832–1898

(pen-name of Charles Lutwidge Dodgson)

HIS desire for anonymity carried him to strange lengths. 'If I had written them,' he once told an earnest enquirer who asked him if he were really the author of the *Alice* books, 'I should answer NO, No.'

Claude Blagden, *Well Remembered*, 1953

DODGSON was overcome by the beauty of Cologne Cathedral. I found him leaning against the rails of the Choir and sobbing like a child. When the verger came to show us over the chapels behind the Choir, he got out of the way: he said that he could not bear the harsh voice of the man in the presence of so much beauty.

Henry Parry Liddon, *The Russian Journal: A Record of a Tour Taken with C. L. Dodgson in the Summer of 1867*, ed. Morton N. Cohen, 1979

MR DODGSON was very fond of little girls, and especially of child actresses, or children who loved plays. At a matinée in Brighton, he once sat in the stalls beside a little girl of about four, and their mutual enjoyment made them quickly friends. After the theatre, he tracked her to her home, and then found out who lived in the house. Though, as I have said, he never appeared very proud of having written *Alice in Wonderland*, he quite appreciated the value of being the author of that book, when he wanted to make a fresh 'child friend'. He now wrote to the mother of this little girl, saying who he was, and inviting the child to tea. He received a curt and crushing reply. The lady wrote:

'The young lady whom you speak of as my "little girl" is not so very childish after all, and she is not my daughter, but my niece. If she were my own child, I should certainly ask you your intentions before allowing her to accept your invitation, and I must do the same now.'

Mr Dodgson replied that his intentions were honourable, 'though one does not usually have specific "intentions" with regard to a child of four or five'.

By some mistake, the letter had reached the wrong lady, and one who, oddly enough, had been at the same matinée with a niece of nineteen. The episode hurt Mr Dodgson's feelings very much, and he told me that he thought the name of Lewis Carroll might have been allowed to guarantee the safety of a young girl of any age whatever.

Edith Olivier, *Without Knowing Mr Walkley*, 1938

Louisa May Alcott · 1832–1888

She was tremendously moved, just as other girls were then, by *Goethe's Correspondence with a Child*, which she had discovered while browsing in Emerson's library. This was published in 1835, and tells of the romantic passion a young girl, Bettina von Arnim, conceived for the poet when he was nearly sixty years old. Louisa immediately imagined herself the Bettina of the letters, and replaced Goethe, whom she had always adored, with her father's friend, Mr Emerson.

She wrote passionate letters to Ralph Waldo Emerson, but never sent them. She sat in the tall walnut tree in front of his house, at midnight, singing to the moon—until an owl scared her back to bed. She left wild flowers at the door of her 'master's' study and sang songs under his window in very bad German.

Of course, Emerson was totally unaware of this devotion from the nice child who ran in and out of his house as freely as his own daughter, Ellen.

Marjorie Worthington, *Miss Alcott of Concord*, 1958

William Morris · 1834–1896

Morris first met Edward Burne-Jones when they were undergraduates at Oxford. (It was Burne-Jones who bestowed on him the nickname 'Topsy'.) Later, after coming down, they lived for two years in Red Lion Square,

Holborn, in a house in which Rossetti and a minor Pre-Raphaelite, Walter Deverell, had previously shared a studio:

WHEN the second wave of the aesthetic movement broke with such a decrease of strength and with so much foam of affectation and decadence, biographers found it expedient to emphasise, in rather a tiresome way, the tremendous heartiness of its pioneers. Anecdote after anecdote of brutish horseplay is invoked to show the gulf that separated Red Lion Square from Reading Gaol. It is recorded with the utmost relish how 'Topsy' threw a small plum-pudding at the housemaid; how he flew into fits of ungovernable rage, and would throw the furniture about the room, tear at his infrangible hair and beard, and champ up spoons and forks with his teeth; how he roared downstairs, 'Mary, those six eggs were bad. I've eaten them, but don't let it happen again'; how in 1859 they all joined the Artists' Rifle Corps, and paraded weekly in grey and silver uniforms; how they tied Morris's hair into knots while he was sitting for a drawing; how he kept an owl in the house—cruelly, one cannot help thinking—and how he would himself imitate an eagle, 'climbing on to a chair and, after a sullen pause, coming down with a heavy flop.'

Evelyn Waugh, *Rossetti: His Life and Works*, 1928

OF Dickens his knowledge and appreciation were both complete. It is not without value as an illustration of his curiously compounded personality that in the moods when he was not dreaming of himself as Tristram or Sigurd, he identified himself very closely with two creations of a quite different mould, Joe Gargery and Mr Boffin. Both of those amiable characters he more or less consciously copied, if it be not truer to say more or less naturally resembled, and knew that he resembled. The 'Morning, morning!' of the latter, and the 'Wot larks!' of the former he adopted as his own favourite methods of salutation. And one of the phrases that were most constantly on his lips, which he used indiscriminately to indicate his disapproval of anything from Parliamentary institutions to the architecture of St Paul's Cathedral, was, as all his friends will remember, the last recorded saying of Mr F.'s Aunt, 'Bring him forard and I'll chuck him out o' winder.'

J. W. Mackail, *The Life of William Morris*, 1899

In 1885 a street-corner meeting of the Socialist League in Limehouse was broken up by the police, and a number of men were arrested:

WHEN the prisoners were brought up at the Thames Police Court next morning, there was the usual amount of confused and contradictory evidence given as to the amount of obstruction that had really happened, and the degree of violence used by or against the police. Finally, after some rather irrelevant remarks about the nationality of the prisoners and the contents of the bills announcing the meeting, Mr Saunders, the sitting magistrate, sentenced one of them to two months' hard labour and imposed fines all round on the rest. What is known as a scene in court followed; there were loud hisses and cries of 'Shame!' In these Morris, who was in court with other members of the League, joined: there was some hustling before order was restored, and he was arrested and charged on the spot with disorderly conduct and striking a policeman. To this charge he gave a direct negative. No evidence was called on either side, but the following curious dialogue ensued.

MR SAUNDERS. What are you?
PRISONER. I am an artist and a literary man, pretty well known, I think, throughout Europe.
MR SAUNDERS. I suppose you did not intend to do this?
PRISONER. I never struck him at all.
MR SAUNDERS. Well, I will let you go.
PRISONER. But I have not done anything.
MR SAUNDERS. Well, you can stay if you like.
PRISONER. I don't want to stay.

He was accordingly discharged, and left the court. It was the one instance in which he was stung into asserting his own reputation in public, and the incautious words were long remembered against him.

Mackail, *The Life of William Morris*

The episode represented a victory for Morris and the League, however. There were widespread protests against the police action, as an infringement of free speech, culminating in a protest march in which many thousands took part. 'All goes well,' Morris wrote. 'We Socialists have suddenly become popular, and your humble servant could hardly have received more sympathy if he had been racked by Mr Saunders.'

Samuel Butler · 1835–1902

(author of *Erewhon* and *The Way of All Flesh*)

When I came over from Calais last December after spending a few days at Boulogne according to my custom, it was rough, and I had a cold upon me, so I went down into the second-class cabin. Several people of all ages and sexes were on the sofas, and they soon began to be sea-sick. There was no steward, so I got them each a basin and placed it for them as well as I could; then I sat down at a table in the middle and went on with my translation, or rather analysis, of the *Iliad*, while they were sick all round me. I had to get the *Iliad* well in my head before I began my lecture on *The Humour of Homer*, and I could not afford to throw away a couple of hours, but I doubt whether Homer was ever before translated under such circumstances.

Butler, notebooks, February 1892

Mark Twain · 1835–1910

(pen-name of Samuel Clemens)

HOWELLS said that Mark Twain usually makes a good speech. But once he heard him fail. In his speech he was telling a story of an occasion when he was in some western city, and found that some impostors personating Longfellow, Emerson, and others had been there. Mark began to describe these impostors, and while doing it found that Longfellow, Emerson, etc., were present, listening, and, from a titter or two, found also that his satirical description of the impostors was becoming regarded as an oblique satirical description of the originals. He was overspread by a sudden cold chill, and struggled to a lame ending. He was so convinced that he had given offence that he wrote to Emerson and Longfellow, apologizing. Emerson could not understand the letter, his memory of the incident having failed him, and wrote to Mark asking what it meant. Then Mark had to tell him what he wished he had never uttered; and altogether the fiasco was complete.

Thomas Hardy in Florence Emily Hardy, *The Early Life of Thomas Hardy*, 1928

There is a much fuller account of this episode in Justin Kaplan's biography Mr Clemens and Mark Twain. *The occasion was a dinner in Boston in honour of John Greenleaf Whittier's seventieth birthday. The story Twain told described his supposed stopover in a miner's cabin in Nevada:*

THE miner said Twain was 'the fourth literary man that has been here in twenty-four hours,' and told him a story about three boozy and rough-looking tramps—'Confound the lot!'—who had stopped off the evening before and said they were Emerson ('a seedy little bit of a chap'), Holmes ('fat as a balloon'), and Longfellow ('built like a prize-fighter'). They took over the cabin, gorged themselves on the miner's bacon, beans and whisky, played cards with a greasy deck and cheated, and at seven the next morning left with the miner's only pair of boots. 'I'm going to move,' the miner says to Mr Twain. 'I ain't suited to a littery atmosphere.'

Although Twain did subsequently write a formal letter of apology to Emerson, Longfellow and Holmes, according to Justin Kaplan both he and Howells 'persisted in exaggerating the dimensions of the scandal. In actuality the speech had been greeted with a fair amount of laughter; Emerson, it is true, had been in a trance but Whittier, Longfellow and Holmes had shown some polite amusement.'

Throughout his life Twain had a number of what seemed to him psychic experiences. Perhaps the most striking of them was a dream which he had in 1858 concerning his younger brother Henry:

HE saw his brother, dead, lying in a metallic casket, supported by two chairs. On his breast was a bouquet of white flowers with a single crimson bloom in the centre; the dream was so vivid that he woke up the next morning believing his brother to be dead, and it was not until after he had dressed and got out into the street he realised the truth. In June Henry was blown up with the *Pennsylvania* [a steamboat disaster]. After the body had been prepared for burial Sam found his brother in a leaden casket, exactly like the one he had seen in his dream, and whilst he stood rapt in the wonder of it, an elderly lady entered the room, bringing a floral offering. The flowers were pure white, and there was a single red rose in the centre.

Many years later, in one of his sceptical moods, Mark Twain denied the reality of all psychic manifestations. When Paine [Albert Bigelow Paine, his biographer] reminded him of this experience, he replied, 'I ask nobody to believe that it ever happened. To me it is true; but it has no logical right to be true, and I do not expect belief in it.'

Edward Wagenknecht, *Mark Twain: The Man and his Work*, 1961

An evening in Hartford described by Twain's servant Katy Leary:

I HEARD about one night when there was a company at the Warners' and Mr Clemens was there, and it was a perfectly lovely night and there was a full moon outside and no lights in the house. They was just settin' there in the music room, looking out at the moonlight. And suddenly Mr Clemens got right up without any warning and begun to sing one of them negro Spirituals. A lady that was there told me he just stood up with both his eyes shut and begun to sing kind of soft like—a faint sound, just as if there was wind in the trees, she said; and he kept right on singin' kind o' low and sweet, and it was beautiful and made your heart ache somehow. And he kept on singin' and singin' and became kind of lost in it, and he was all lit up—his face was. 'Twas somethin' from another world, she said, and when he got through, he put his two hands up to his head, just as though all the sorrow of the negroes was upon him; and then he begun to sing, 'Nobody Knows the Trouble I Got, Nobody Knows but

Jesus.' That was one of them negro spirituals songs, and when he come to the end, to the Glory Halleluiah, he gave a great shout—just like the negroes do—he shouted out the Glory, Glory, Halleluiah! They said it was wonderful and none of them would forget it as long as they lived.

Mary Lawton, *A Lifetime with Mark Twain: The Memories of Katy Leary*, 1925

One of the great passions of Mark Twain's later years was billiards. The game was also the occasion for some of his alarming displays of anger:

HE was not an even-tempered player. When his game was going badly his language sometimes became violent and he was likely to become critical of his opponent. Then reaction would set in, and remorse. He would become gentle and kindly, hurrying the length of the table to set up the balls as I knocked them into the pockets, as if to show in every way except by actual confession in words that he was sorry for what no doubt seemed to him an unworthy display of temper.

Once, when luck seemed to have quite deserted him and he was unable to make any of his favorite shots, the air became fairly charged, the lightning fierce and picturesque. Finally with a regular thunder blast he seized the cue with both hands and literally mowed the balls across the table, landing some of them on the floor. I do not recall his remarks during that performance—I was chiefly concerned in getting out of the way. Then I gathered up the balls and we went on playing as if nothing had happened, only he was very gentle and sweet, like a sunny meadow after a storm had passed by. After a little he said:

'This is a most—amusing game. When you play—badly, it—amuses *me*. And when I play badly, and lose my temper, it certainly *must*—amuse—*you*.'

Albert Bigelow Paine, *Mark Twain: A Biography*, 1912

ALFRED AUSTIN · 1835–1913

(Poet Laureate)

GOSSE handed down from Robert Browning's lips an incident of another dinner-party. The guests were assembled around the fire at the end of the room, most of which was occupied by an unusually large table. The butler threw open the door to announce *Mr Alfred Austin*. 'And I give you my word of honour,' said Browning, '*nothing whatever* came into the room.' A moment later the tiny form of the future Poet Laureate was seen to be trotting round the edge of the table, which was just on a level with the top of his head.

Edward Marsh, *A Number of People*, 1939

Austin's elevation to the Laureateship was a political rather than a literary appointment. His most notorious poem was his celebration of the Jameson Raid, the armed incursion into the Transvaal which preceded the Boer War:

So we forded and galloped forward,
As hard as our beasts could pelt,
First eastward, then trending norward,
Right over the rolling veldt . . .

Sir W. S. Gilbert · 1836–1911

A BARBER cutting Gilbert's hair once bent over his ear to murmur, 'When are we to expect anything further, Mr Gilbert, from your fluent pen?'

'What do you mean, sir, by fluent pen?' snapped Gilbert. 'There is no such thing as a fluent pen. A pen is an insensible object. And, at any rate, I don't presume to enquire into your private affairs; you will please observe the same reticence in regard to mine.'

Anyone who could thus snub a barber out of his one privilege, would strike a child . . . though, as a matter of fact, Gilbert wouldn't. He was friendly and companionable with children, just as he was an excellent host and a generous supporter of charitable things. He kept his quarrels for his own world, and for the law courts, where he lived in litigation. . . . 'The judge,' he said, in writing of one of his lost actions, 'summed up like a drunken monkey. He's in the last stage of senile decay.' After Sir Edward Carson won a case against him, Gilbert made a point of cutting him dead.

As a result, Gilbert's life was filled with bitter quarrels. There were some people he wouldn't speak to for ten years; others were on the twenty-year list. As his old age drew on, a strange repentance seized him, especially as the former friends, put on the silent list, began to pass into a silence longer still. As each died, Gilbert was all contrition, with flowers sent to hospitals, looking for old ties to rebind, the egotism all paled out of him. He could have made a wonderful *Ballad* out of it—*The Contrite Playwright*.

Stephen Leacock, *The Boy I Left Behind Me*, 1947

'*A wonderful* Ballad'—*the reference is to* The Bab Ballads, *Gilbert's most successful work before the Savoy Operas.*

Algernon Charles Swinburne · 1837–1909

Mr Arthur Severn has related how on one occasion Swinburne was leaving a club and looked for his hat in the hall. He only found four tall top-hats belonging to other members of the club. He tried on the hats one after another, and as they did not fit his large head, threw them, in turn, on the floor. When the hall porter, hearing a noise, appeared, he found Swinburne executing a war dance on the hats. The infuriated poet went for the hall porter, demanding, with that sanguinary power of invective which was his peculiar gift, where his hat was. The man replied that he believed Mr Swinburne had no hat when he entered the club that evening.

S. M. Ellis, *A Mid-Victorian Pepys*, 1926

For science he had no taste whatever, and his lack of musical ear was a byword among his acquaintances. I once witnessed a practical joke played upon him, which made me indignant at the time, but which now seems innocent enough, and not without interest. A lady, having taken the rest of the company into her confidence, told Swinburne that she would render on the piano a very ancient Florentine ritornello which had just been discovered. She then played 'Three Blind Mice', and Swinburne was enchanted. He found that it reflected to perfection the cruel beauty of the Medicis—which perhaps it does.

Edmund Gosse, *Portraits and Sketches*, 1912

William Dean Howells · 1837–1920

(novelist, critic, and editor; known in his later years as 'the dean of American letters')

His dislike of assassination was instinctive. He once stood at a reception listening while a female humorist destroyed the arts of Thomas Hardy, George Moore and Henry James and suddenly he began to tell anecdote after anecdote of his alarmed provincialism when he first came from Boston to New York. At the twentieth recital of his tremors and bewilderments, the lady bulkily withdrew her humours into another room. Her public greatness had been subtly rebuked, without a word addressed to her.

Thomas Beer, *The Mauve Decade*, 1926

WALTER PATER · 1839–1894

PATER went imperturbably on . . . Life became, increasingly, a system of aesthetics. 'But why should we be good, Mr Pater?' an undergraduate is supposed to have asked.

'Because it is so beautiful,' was the reply.

William Gaunt, *The Aesthetic Adventure*, 1945

In his series of satirical dialogues The New Republic *(1877) W. H. Mallock lampooned Pater under the guise of 'Mr Rose':*

WHAT, Mr Rose asks, does successful life consist in? 'Simply,' he answers in Paterian strain, 'in the consciousness of exquisite living.' The warring of endless doubts was wearisome to him. He took 'a profounder and more exquisite pleasure in the colour of a crocus, the pulsations of a chord of music, or a picture of Botticelli's.' Mr Rose, the author of *The New Republic* conveys, is more than a little odd. He is made to show undue interest in certain books of a curious character, including the *Cultes Secrets des Dames Romaines*, which occupy a locked compartment of his host's bookcase. There is a faint suggestion that his languid enthusiasms are not only sickly but even a bit dubious in morality.

Pater, as always impervious to the opinions of others, did not object to, even enjoyed the portrait of Mr Rose 'the Pre-Raphaelite'. 'I am pleased,' he said, 'to be called Mr Rose—the rose being the queen of flowers.'

Gaunt, *The Aesthetic Adventure*

JOHN PENTLAND MAHAFFY · 1839–1919

(classical scholar, Provost of Trinity College, Dublin; celebrated snob)

A CERTAIN visit to Windsor Castle always gave Mahaffy great satisfaction. King Edward had summoned him to deal as a buffer with the Kaiser whom he could talk down in his own language. On this occasion he met Queen Ena of Spain for the first time and entertained her with the famous division of proper uses between European languages—'French to address a friend, Italian to make love to a mistress, Spanish to speak to God, and German to give orders to a dog!'

The Queen laughed heartily whereat the Kaiser rushed across the room to learn the joke. As he was more or less the subject of the pleasantry, Mahaffy saved the situation by saying: 'Your Majesty, I have only had the honour of the Queen's acquaintance for twenty minutes and we already share a secret.'

Shane Leslie, quoted in W. B. Stanford and R. S. McDowell, *Mahaffy*, 1971

The remark about the appropriate use of languages is attributed to the Emperor Charles V.

THOMAS HARDY · 1840–1928

Between the ages of 16 and 21 Hardy was articled to a local architect, John Hicks:

AN unusual incident occurred during his pupillage at Hicks's which, though it had nothing to do with his own life, was dramatic enough to have mention. One summer morning at Bockhampton, just before he sat down to breakfast, he remembered that a man was to be hanged at eight o'clock at Dorchester. He took up the big brass telescope that had been handed on in the family, and hastened to a hill on the heath a quarter of a mile from the house, whence he looked towards the town. The sun behind his back shone straight on the white stone façade of the gaol, the gallows upon it, and the form of the murderer in white fustian, the executioner and officials in dark clothing and the crowd below being invisible at this distance of nearly three miles. At the moment of his placing the glass to his eye the white figure dropped downwards, and the faint note of the town clock struck eight.

The whole thing had been so sudden that the glass nearly fell from Hardy's hands. He seemed alone on the heath with the hanged man, and crept homeward wishing he had not been so curious. It was the second and last execution he witnessed, the first having been that of a woman two or three years earlier, when he stood close to the gallows.

Florence Emily Hardy, *The Early Life of Thomas Hardy*, 1928

The two volumes of biography published under his wife's name after his death were in fact largely written by Hardy himself.

JANUARY 8. To the City. Omnibus horses, Ludgate Hill. The greasy state of the streets caused constant slipping. The poor creatures struggled and struggled but could not start the omnibus. A man next me said: 'It must take all heart and hope out of them! I shall get out.' He did; but the whole remaining selfish twenty-five of us sat on. The horses despairingly got us up the hill at last. I *ought* to have taken off my hat to him and said: 'Sir, though I was not stirred by your humane impulse I will profit by your good example'; and have followed him. I should like to know that man; but we shall never meet again!

Diary, 1889; in Hardy, *Early Life*

In the 1890s Hardy became friendly with Lord Pembroke, 'a fellow Wessex man':

HE [Pembroke] was now ill at a nursing home in London, and an amusing incident occurred while his visitor was sitting by his bedside one afternoon, thinking what havoc of good material it was that such a fine and handsome man should be prostrated. He whispered to Hardy that there was a 'Tess' in the establishment, who always came if he rang at that time of the day, and that he would do so then that Hardy might see her. He accordingly rang, whereupon Tess's chronicler was much disappointed at the result; but endeavoured to discern beauty in the very indifferent figure who responded, and at last persuaded himself that he could do so. When she had gone the patient apologized, saying that for the first time since he had lain there a stranger had attended to his summons.

Florence Emily Hardy, *The Later Years of Thomas Hardy*, 1930

In 1896 Hardy and his wife visited Warwick, where they were shown over the castle and the church:

A STRANGE reminder of the transitoriness of life was given to Hardy in the church, where, looking through a slit by chance, he saw the coffin of the then recent Lord Warwick, who, a most kindly man, some while before, on meeting him in London, had invited him to Warwick Castle, an invitation which he had been unable to accept at the time, though he had promised to do so later. 'Here I am at last', he said to the coffin as he looked; 'and here are you to receive me!'

Hardy, *Later Years*

HE went on to talk about days of the week and colours and associations. Monday was colourless, and Tuesday a little less colourless, and Wednesday was blue—'this sort of blue' pointing to an imitation Sèvres plate—and Thursday is darker blue, and Friday is dark blue, and Saturday is yellow, and Sunday is always red . . .

Elliott Felkin, 'Days with Thomas Hardy', *Encounter*, 1962 (recalling a conversation in 1919)

In July 1922 E. M. Forster reported to his mother that he had had 'simple, almost dull tea at the Hardys':

T. H. showed me the graves of his pets, all overgrown with ivy, their names on the head stones. Such a dolorous muddle. 'This is Snowbell—

she was run over by a train. . . . this is Pella, the same thing happened to her. . . . this is Kitkin, she was cut clean in two, clean in two—' 'How is it that so many of your cats have been run over, Mr Hardy? Is the railway near?'—'Not at all near, not at all near—I don't know how it is. But of course we have only buried here those pets whose bodies were recovered. Many were never seen again.' I could scarcely keep grave—it was so like a caricature of his own novels or poems.

Selected Letters of E. M. Forster, vol. ii, 1985

In 1923 Hardy was interviewed by the American novelist Hamlin Garland:

IN speaking of the Lowells, I mentioned Lawrence Lowell, President of Harvard, and was astounded to have Hardy hesitatingly inquire, 'Is that a girls' school?'

Whilst I laboriously explained the relative positions of Harvard and Yale, he listened politely but without deep interest. That he could be ignorant of this great university was astounding. Perhaps it should be set down as a weakness due to his advancing years. . . .

Hamlin Garland, *Afternoon Neighbours*, 1934

Garland's account of his visit is quoted by James Gibson in Thomas Hardy: Interviews and Recollections *(1999). Gibson adds: 'This is a revealing interview because it shows how Hardy could behave in the presence of someone who was boring him and wasting his time. The give-away is his question about Harvard, "Is that a girls' school?" As in 1919 he had turned down an invitation to give a lecture at Yale University, he could no more have been ignorant of Harvard than one could be ignorant of Oxford if one knew Cambridge.'*

WILLIAM JAMES · 1842–1910

(American philosopher; brother of Henry)

HE had gone, he told me, by tram that afternoon to Boston; and as he sat and meditated in the Cambridge horse-car two strains of thought had occupied his mind. One of these was the notion, which Mrs James had recently derived from the perusal of Kipling's writings, that our civil order, that all the graces and amenities of our social life, had for their ultimate sanction nothing but force, however much we might disguise it—the naked fist, in fact, the blow of the sword, the crack of the pistol, or the smoke and roar of guns. Superimposed upon this meditation began to recur, with greater and greater persistence, the memory of certain remarks of his brother Henry, who, on a recent visit to America had indignantly protested against the outrageous pertness of the American child and the meek pusillanimity with which the older generation suffered the behaviour of their children without protest.

It was not long, William James said, before he became aware of what had aroused this second line of thought; it was the droning sound which filled the horse-car—the voice, in fact, of an American child, who was squeaking over and over again an endless, shrill, monotonous singsong. Growing more and more irritated by this squeaking, William James resolved that he at least would not suffer it without protest; so, addressing the mother of the vocal infant, he said politely, 'I think, madam, you can hardly be aware that your child's song is a cause of annoyance to the rest of us in this car.' The lady thus addressed paid no attention; but a gallant American, who had heard it, turned on him and said with great indignation, 'How dare you, sir, address a lady in this ungentlemanly fashion!' At this insult William James, recalling the doctrine of naked force which his wife had impressed upon him, replied with manly promptness, 'Sir, if you repeat that remark, I shall slap your face.' The remark, to his consternation, was repeated, and the professor was compelled to make good his word. The slap was conscientiously administered; the occupants of the horse-car arose in indignation, pressing their cards upon the victim of the assault, and protesting their willingness to be witnesses at any legal proceedings which might ensue. Then they all sat down; and as the car clattered along through the dust towards Boston, with the child still shrilly singing, the grave burden of the public disapproval which William James had encountered became almost more, he said, than he could bear.

He looked from hostile face to hostile face, longing for some sign of sympathy and comprehension, and fixed at last all his hopes on a lady who had taken no part in the uproar, and whose appearance suggested foreign travel perhaps, or at any rate a wider point of view. He felt that she at least understood the motive of his action; and so great was his longing for sympathy that when at last the car reached Boston and they all got out he committed the error of trying to make sure of her approbation. 'You, madam,' he said, addressing her, 'you, I feel sure, will understand . . .' Thereupon the lady drew back from him and exclaimed, 'You brute!'

Logan Pearsall Smith, *Unforgotten Years*, 1938

AMBROSE BIERCE · 1842–?1914

(American journalist and short-story writer; his best-known collection of stories was *In the Midst of Life*)

WHEN he first came to London, he sold a collection of newspaper articles to John Camden Hotten, who took over Swinburne's 'Poems and Ballads' when it was withdrawn by J. Bertram Payne, of Moxon's, who shrank from the storm created by John Morley's anonymous attack in the *Saturday Review*. Hotten paid Bierce the sum of twenty pounds for the book rights of the articles; and, as Bierce had no banking account in London, his friend Henry Sampson, the founder and editor of the *Referee*, gave him cash for the draft which was returned unpaid. When Bierce was informed of this he got in a furious rage and rushed to Hotten's premises in Piccadilly, and demanded to see him at once. On being told that Hotten had not been to business for some days he asked where he was to be found. The clerk reluctantly gave him his master's address, 4, Maitland Park Villas, Haverstock Hill, to which Bierce lost no time in going, for he was determined, as he put it, to have Hotten's blood.

When he arrived, the door was opened by a little maidservant.

'Where's Mr. Hotten?' asked Bierce.

'Come this way, sir,' replied the girl, 'and I'll take you to him.'

Bierce followed the maid, who opened the door of a dark room where Hotten was lying in bed. 'What the hell's the meaning of this, Hotten?' shouted Bierce as he waved the dishonoured cheque in his hand; but when he drew nearer the bed, he started back in horror.

John Camden Hotten was dead, and the maid had mistaken Bierce for the undertaker.

Eveleigh Nash, *I Liked the Life I Lived*, 1941

HENRY JAMES · 1843–1916

E. S. Nadal, who was Second Secretary of the American Legation in London, got to know James in 1877, the year after the novelist had moved into lodgings in Bolton Street, off Piccadilly:

I WOULD often go to see him. There was a slender, tall, dark, rather pretty girl who usually came to the door when I called. She was not a servant but a relation of the landlady. James, with his quick sympathy and the keen interest he had lately acquired in English habits, said: 'She's an English character. She is what they call in England a "person". She isn't a lady and she isn't a woman; she's a person.'

His personal relations with English society were very much in his mind . . . Some lady of the English middle class whom he had lately visited in the country had said to him, 'That is true of the aristocracy, but in one's own class it is different,' meaning, said James, 'her class and mine'. He did not wish to be confounded with the mass of English people and to be adjudged a place in English society in accordance with English standards.

E. S. Nadal, 'Personal Recollections of Henry James', *Scribner's Magazine*, 1920

In 1883 James went back to America for a visit of several months. He was not to return there for over twenty years:

IT was a little later than this that that somewhat acidulated patriot Colonel Higginson, in reply to someone who said that Henry James was a cosmopolitan, remarked, 'Hardly! for a cosmopolitan is at home even in his own country!'

Edmund Gosse, *Aspects and Impressions*, 1922

Thomas Wentworth Higginson: man of letters, Abolitionist, commander of the first black regiment in the American Civil War. Today he is best remembered as the advisor and editor of Emily Dickinson *(see p. 170).*

I MET him at a dinner party once, shortly before the production of a play of his, and his hostess asked him if he did not find rehearsals a great strain. To which he replied: 'I have been sipping the—er—cup of Detachment.' No phrase could be a more perfect description of the state of mind to which most dramatists find themselves reduced at a certain stage of rehearsals.

F. Anstey, *A Long Retrospect*, 1936

H.J. was complaining to us that Ellen Terry had asked him to write a play for her, and now that he had done so, and read it to her, had refused it. My wife, desiring to placate, asked: 'Perhaps she did not think the part suited to her?' H.J. turned upon us both, and with resonance and uplifting voice replied: 'Think? *Think?* How should the poor, toothless, chattering hag THINK?' The sudden outpouring of improvised epithets had a most extraordinary effect. A crescendo on 'toothless' and then on 'chattering' and then on 'hag'—and 'think' delivered with the trumpet of an elephant.

Edmund Gosse, letter to John Bailey in *John Bailey 1864–1931: Letters and Diaries*, 1935

THAT he spoke French to perfection was of course quickly evident to anyone who had even a slight acquaintance with him. M. Bourget once gave me a wonderful illustration of it. He said that Mr James was staying with himself and Madame Bourget at their villa at Hyères, not long after the appearance of Kipling's *Seven Seas*. M. Bourget, who by that time read and spoke English fluently, complained of Mr Kipling's technicalities, and declared that he could not make head or tail of McAndrew's Hymn. Whereupon Mr James took up the book, and standing by the fire, fronting his hosts, there and then put McAndrew's Hymn into vigorous idiomatic French—an extraordinary feat, as it seemed to M. Bourget.

Mrs Humphry Ward, *A Writer's Recollections*, 1918

The technicalities of which Paul Bourget complained include such terms as 'coupler-flange' and 'crosshead-gibs'. It is hard to believe that James translated the entire poem on this occasion: it runs to over 200 lines.

I HAVE been staying at Rye with Henry James. He was telling me that some young actresses, staying at Winchelsea, had expressed a desire to see him, and had come over to tea. I asked, 'Were they pretty?' He replied, 'Pretty! Good Heavens!!' and then, with the air of one who will be scrupulously just, he added: 'One of the poor wantons had a certain cadaverous grace.'

Edmund Gosse, letter to Maurice Baring, 1899

I REMEMBER once saying to Henry James, in reference to a novel of the type that used euphemistically to be called 'unpleasant': 'You know, I was rather disappointed; that book wasn't nearly as bad as I expected;' to which he replied with his incomparable twinkle: 'Ah, my dear, the abysses are all so shallow.'

Edith Wharton, *A Backward Glance*, 1934

George du Maurier and his wife were opposed to their son Gerald becoming an actor, and wondered how they could dissuade him:

ONE afternoon they were discussing the position with Henry James, who said that if Gerald really wanted to go on the stage he didn't see how they could prevent it. 'That's all very well, James; but what would you say if you had a son who wanted to go into the Church?' Lifting both hands in horror Henry James replied, 'My dear du Maurier, a father's curse!'

G. C. Hoyer Millar, *George du Maurier and Others*, 1937

HE would occasionally say he was a hermit, and speak as if he lived a life remote from the world. I once heard him say this during a brilliant party at Stafford House, where he was the guest of Millicent, Duchess of Sutherland.

Marie Belloc Lowndes, *Diaries and Letters*, 1971

I TOLD him I was going on a first visit to Paris, and he warned me against a possible disappointment. . . . 'Do not,' he said, 'allow yourself to be "put off" by the superficial and external aspect of Paris; or rather (for the *true* superficial and external aspect of Paris has a considerable fascination) by what I may call the superficial and external aspect *of* the superficial and external aspect of Paris.' This was surely carrying lucidity to dazzling-point; I did my best to profit by it, but I couldn't be sure that I was exercising exactly the right discrimination, and in the end I surrendered to the charm of Paris without too much circumspection.

Edward Marsh, *A Number of People*, 1939

The novelist Ada Leverson had a naturally low voice:

SHE told me, some years after I first met her—and it proves, I think, that she had always been inclined to speak in this manner—that on the first occasion she had sat next to Henry James at dinner, she had not been able to resist putting to him certain questions about his books, for she had been a lifelong admirer of him, and that, at last, after he had answered some of these murmured enquiries, he had turned his melancholy gaze upon her, and had said to her, 'Can it be—it must be—that you are that embodiment of the incorporeal, that elusive yet ineluctable being to whom through the generations novelists have so unavailingly made invocation; in short, the *Gentle Reader*?'

Osbert Sitwell, *Noble Essences*, 1950

POOR old Godkin had had a stroke. At breakfast H.J. made some ordinary remark—'Pass me the butter', perhaps. Godkin thought it a joke and laughed aloud. H.J. at first was puzzled; then (and it was one of the nicest things I ever saw) began to smile as if hesitating to laugh at his own wit, and finally joined in Godkin's hearty laugh. It made a great impression on me.

Henry Dwight Sedgwick, quoted in Simon Nowell-Smith, *The Legend of the Master*, 1947

GERARD MANLEY HOPKINS · 1844–1889

Hopkins entered the Society of Jesus in 1868. Having completed his noviciate, he was sent to the seminary at Stonyhurst:

THE Jesuits had the civilized habit of betraying little curiosity about the eccentricities of others, but Hopkins could hardly help attracting some attention when he hung over a frozen pond to observe the pattern of trapped bubbles or, instead of drinking the chocolate provided as mild refreshment from the austerities of the Lenten diet, put his face down to the cup to study the 'grey and grained look' of the film on its surface. Some thirty years after his death one old lay brother remembered how he would sprint out of the Seminary building after a shower to stoop down on a garden path and study the glitter of crushed quartz before the water could evaporate. 'Ay, a strange yoong man,' said the brother, 'crouching down that gate to stare at some wet sand. A fair natural 'e seemed to us, that Mr 'Opkins.'

Robert Bernard Martin, *Gerard Manley Hopkins*, 1991

In 1873 Hopkins recorded a fearful dream and its aftermath:

'I THOUGHT something or someone leapt onto me and held me quite fast: this I think woke me, so that after this I shall have had the use of reason.' He felt 'a loss of muscular control reaching more or less deep; this one to the chest and not further, so that I could not speak, whispering at first, then louder.' He lay for a time thinking that if he could move a finger, then he could move his arm and so the whole body. 'The feeling is terrible: the body no longer swayed as a piece' and the 'nervous and muscular instress seemed to fall like a dead weight on the chest. I cried on the holy name and by degrees recovered myself as I thought to do.'

The whole terrifying nightmare reads like a medieval description of the visitation of a succubus (or, for that matter, an incubus), with its vaguely sexual suggestion of sweat and terror as the invading presence leaps on to his supine body, initially inhibiting his ability to cry out for help, then disappearing at the invocation of God's name: 'It made me think that this was how the souls in hell would be imprisoned in their bodies as in prisons and of what St Theresa says of the "little press in the wall" where she felt herself to be in her vision.'

Martin, *Gerard Manley Hopkins*

Between 1874 and 1877 Hopkins was a 'Theologian'—theology student—at St Beuno's in north Wales. Towards the end of his time there he was ordered to preach an evening sermon in the dining hall, and chose as his subject the miracle of the loaves and fishes:

WITH all the detailed curiosity at his command, Hopkins examined each minute aspect of the story of the miracle, until the modern reader (and presumably the Theologians in his audience) becomes unclear about the point of the sermon. Yet the curious mixture of the learned and the homely in this discourse is closely related to the unexpected combination of orders of experience that makes his best poetry witty.

What else may have contributed to the mirth of the Theologians is not clear, but his intensity must have seemed amusing to them, presumably because it was very much what they already knew of Hopkins. At last, in one paragraph he said five times the words of Christ, 'Make the men sit down.' It was too much for his auditors. As Hopkins himself wrote, 'People laughed at it prodigiously, I saw some of them roll on their chairs with laughter. This made me lose the thread, so that I did not deliver the last two paragraphs right but mixed things up. The last paragraph, in which *Make the men sit down* is often repeated, far from having a good effect, made them roll more than ever.' A blue pencil mark on the sermon indicates the spot at which he had to stop speaking.

Martin, *Gerard Manley Hopkins*

In his final years, when he taught at University College, Dublin, Hopkins was often deeply unhappy and displayed many oddities of behaviour:

AT one house he was left alone for a few minutes before his hostess appeared, and when she walked into the drawing room he was seated before the fire with his coat off, sewing up a rent in his waistcoat. At the College his behaviour became increasingly odd: once he was discovered blowing pepper through a keyhole to interrupt a meeting within the room by making the occupants sneeze. Even on his deathbed he wrote to Bridges about a joke that had gone wrong: 'I have it now down in my tablets that a man may joke and joke and be offensive; I have had several warnings lately leading me to make the entry, tho' goodness knows the joke that gave most offence was harmless enough and even kind.'

Martin, *Gerard Manley Hopkins*

The source for the story about the pepper is one of Hopkins's colleagues at University College, Fr Joseph Darlington, whose reliability as a witness has been called in question.

W. A. SPOONER · 1844–1930

(Warden of New College, Oxford)

Spooner gave his name to the spoonerism—'Kindly sew these ladies into their sheets' is a famous example. But according to his colleague Sir Ernest Barker, he was 'seldom guilty of metathesis, or transposition of sounds. What he transposed was ideas':

SIR ERNEST himself, in the course of one conversation, heard Spooner say Athenaeus when he meant Aulus Gellius, and Grotius when he meant Grocyn. And there is the well-known story of the sermon which referred throughout to Aristotle, in rather surprising contexts, at the end of which, after a brief pause, Spooner is supposed to have said 'In the sermon I have just preached, whenever I said Aristotle, I meant St Paul'. But the matter is generally more complex than this. There is the well-authenticated story of Spooner walking with a friend in North Oxford and meeting a lady dressed in black, to whom he lifted his hat. When she had passed 'Poor soul', he said, 'very sad; her late husband, you know, a very sad death—eaten by missionaries—poor soul!'

William Hayter, *Spooner*, 1977

Some of his spoonerisms were physical rather than verbal. The most famous is described by A. J. Toynbee:

THE acted spoonerism was witnessed by my mother's old friend Eleanor Jourdain. At a dinner party in Oxford, she saw Dr Spooner upset a salt-cellar and then reach for a decanter of claret. He then poured claret on the salt, drop by drop, till he had produced the little purple mound which would have been the end-product if he had spilled claret on the table-cloth and had then cast a heap of salt on the pool to absorb it.

Hayter, *Spooner*. The quotation is from Arnold Toynbee, *Acquaintances*

SIR EDMUND GOSSE · 1849–1928

(man of letters)

JUST after the explosion created by Churton Collins's attack on Edmund Gosse [a slashing review of Gosse's book *From Shakespeare to Pope*], a friend of mine was at a performance of the Hellas Society at St James's Hall. There Robert Browning told him that very morning the servants after family prayers in the Gosse household had announced through the cook that they had entered the service of Mr Gosse (as he was then) under the impression that he was an eminent man of letters but that they now read in the newspapers that he was a literary charlatan and must therefore give notice . . . This is a charming legend; but the real truth of the matter was that the cook on giving notice and being asked to give some reason for it, said that she did not like seeing Mr Gosse's name so much in the newspapers. This well illustrates the growth of a myth and is also creditable to the Victorian attitude (even of the lower orders) towards publicity.

E. S. P. Haynes, *The Lawyer*, 1950

Robert Louis Stevenson · 1850–1894

A friend recalls a dinner party given by Stevenson's parents at their home in Edinburgh. Stevenson's father was a celebrated engineer; he had hoped that his son would follow him in his profession:

Our end of the table was, to me, almost uncomfortably brilliant. Mr Stevenson had taken me in, and Louis Stevenson was on my other side. Father and son both talked, taking diametrically opposite points of view on all things under the sun. Mr Stevenson seemed to me, on that evening, to be the type of the kindly, orthodox Edinburgh father. We chatted of nice, concrete, comfortable things, such as the Scottish Highlands in autumn; and in a moment of Scottish fervour he quoted—I believe *sotto voce*—a bit of a versified psalm. But Louis Stevenson, on my other side, was that evening in one of his most recklessly brilliant moods. His talk was almost incessant. I felt quite dazed at the mount of intellection he expended on each subject, however trivial in itself, that we touched upon. He worried it as a dog might worry a rat, and then threw it off lightly, as some chance word or allusion set him thinking, and talking, of something else. The father's face at certain moments was a study; an indescribable mixture of vexation, fatherly pride and admiration, and sheer bewilderment at his son's brilliant flippancies and the quick young thrusts of his wit and criticism.

Our talk turned on realism as a duty of the novelist. Louis Stevenson had been reading Balzac. He was fascinated by Balzac; steeped in Balzac. It was as if he had left Balzac and all his books locked up in some room upstairs—had turned the key on him, with a 'Stay there, my dear fellow, and I'll come back as soon as I can get away from this dinner!'

I knew nothing about Balzac, and I believe I said so. I remember feeling sorry and rather ashamed that I did not know; and Louis Stevenson began telling me about Balzac, and about his style and vocabulary; and I felt grateful to the father for at least appearing to know as little about Balzac as I did, and to care even less. It may have been Balzac's vocabulary that set us talking about the English language; the father and son debated, with some heat, the subject of word-coinage and the use of modern slang. Mr Stevenson upheld the doctrine of a 'well of English undefiled', which of course made Louis Stevenson rattle off with extraordinary ingenuity whole sentences composed of words of foreign origin taken into our language from all parts of the world—words of the East, of classical Europe, of the West Indies, and modern American slang. By a string of sentences he proved the absurdity of such a doctrine, and indeed its practical impossibility. It was a real feat in the handling of language, and I can see to this day his look of pale triumph. The father was silenced;

but for a moment he had been almost tearfully in earnest. One could see it was not a matter of mere vocabulary with him.

Flora Masson in *I Can Remember Robert Louis Stevenson*, ed. Rosalie Masson, 1922

HIS endurance in illness and in work we have seen: no pain was too great to bear, no malady too long: he never murmured until it was over. No task was too irksome, no revision too exacting—laboriously, and like an eager apprentice he went through with it to the end.

But on the other hand, when impatience came to the surface, it blazed up like the anger of a man who had never known a check. It was generally caused by some breach of faith or act of dishonesty or unjustifiable delay. The only time I know of its being displayed in public was in a Paris restaurant, where Stevenson had ordered a change of wine, and the very bottle he had rejected was brought back to him with a different label. There was a sudden explosion of wrath; the bottle was violently broken; in an instant the restaurant was emptied, and—so much for long-suffering—the proprietor and his staff were devoting the whole of their attention and art to appease and reconcile the angry man.

Graham Balfour, *The Life of Robert Louis Stevenson*, 1901

Henry Adams got to know Stevenson when he visited Samoa during his travels in the Pacific:

WE like him, but he would be, I think an impossible companion. His face has a certain beauty, especially the eyes, but it is the beauty of disease. He is a strange compound of callousness and susceptibility, and his susceptibility is sometimes more amusing than his callousness. We were highly delighted with one trait which he showed in absolute unconsciousness of its simplicity. The standard of domestic morality here is not what is commonly regarded as rigid. Most of the traders and residents have native wives, to whom they are married after the native custom: that is, during pleasure. A clerk in the employ of an American trader named Moors was discovered in too close relation with the native wife of a lawyer named Carruthers. The offence was condoned once, and this lenity seemed very proper to Stevenson, who declared that he had no difficulty in forgiving his wife once, but not a second time. Recently the scandal was renewed, and caused great tribulation. Stevenson was deeply outraged, and declared that he would no longer dine with Moors for fear of meeting the clerk. Moors, who has had various wives to say nothing of incidental feminine resources, was also scandalized, and dismissed the clerk, though the clerk was indispensable to his business. . . . The unfortunate clerk is the victim of outraged Samoan morality, and is to be sent back to San Francisco where the standard is, I presume, less exalted.

This part of Stevenson's talk was altogether the most humorous, and as grotesque as the New Arabian Nights; but Stevenson was not in the least conscious of our entertainment.

Letter to Elizabeth Cameron, November 1890

George Moore · 1852–1933

(Anglo-Irish novelist)

George Moore and Edward Martyn [the Irish dramatist] were inseparable friends, because their friendship was based on mutual contempt. Yeats once said to Edward, 'You know, Edward, Moore has some good points.'

'Yeats,' he answered solemnly, 'I have known him longer than you have, and he has no good points.'

Then, one day, not long afterwards, Moore came to Yeats and said, 'You know, Yeats, Edward is the most selfish of men. He believes I am damned, and he doesn't care!'

After the trilogy [Moore's autobiographical sequence *Hail and Farewell*, in which Martyn was caricatured], Moore called on Edward Martyn. 'I didn't think you'd receive me,' he said, when he was shown up.

'Why should I be angry with you?' said Edward. 'You have betrayed me, but I always knew you would betray me. You have betrayed all your friends. The worst thing you ever did was to betray Zola, for he was very kind to you. If you were not ridiculous, Moore, you would be despicable.'

Moore said it was very wittily put.

L. A. G. Strong, *Green Memory*, 1961

Then he talked of Héloïse's letters to Abelard. He had just read them; 'Last night, I dined with Mrs Craigie, and I talked about these letters; no woman has ever written *me* such letters, I said; could they be genuine?'

William Rothenstein, *Men and Memories 1872–1900*, 1931

A relative of the Somervilles told me that his aunt had the unpleasant duty of announcing to George Moore that his friend Violet Martin, the 'Martin Ross' of 'Somerville and Ross' fame, was dead. As she entered Moore's study to break the sad news to him, Moore looked up from his writing. 'I have sad news for you, Mr Moore,' she said. 'I regret to inform you that your friend Martin Ross is dead.' Moore clasped his head. 'How sad,' he said, 'how very sad.' He arose and paced his study agitatedly. 'How sad,' he repeated. 'Here am I in the midst of this,' and he waved his hand dramatically at the books around him, 'alive, and my friend, my dear friend, Edmund Gosse, dead.' The lady interrupted gently, 'I beg your pardon, Mr Moore,' she said, 'it is Martin Ross who is dead, not Edmund Gosse.' Moore drew himself up and looked at her in an indignant fashion: 'My dear woman,' he said, 'surely you don't expect me to go through all that again?'

Roger McHugh, in *Irish Literary Portraits*, edited by W. R. Rodgers, 1972

Sir Hall Caine · 1853–1931

(author of *The Manxman*, *The Christian*, *The Eternal City*, and other best-selling novels)

Caine was of Manx descent, and eventually settled in the Isle of Man. The young Compton Mackenzie was once summoned to his home there, Greeba Castle. Mackenzie, who came from a theatrical family, was being considered for a part in a play Caine had written:

Hall Caine himself met me at the quay with his car; although I could not help finding him a little ridiculous, I could not help liking him more and more as we drove to Greeba Castle. The Castle, which I had supposed would have some signs of Gothic grandeur, turned out to be a medium-sized red brick villa. In the small dining-room, which opened on a small conservatory full of brown and yellow calceolarias, was an engraving of *The Blessed Damozel* in the frame of which was stuck a card, 'From D. G. Rossetti to Hall Caine 1881', a souvenir of the days when Hall Caine had attended the poet during his last days at Birchington-on-Sea.

The garden at the back ran up in a fairly steep slope to level ground on which Hall Caine had built himself a granite study, furnished inside with massive and severe furniture which included a bare table as large as a four-post bed.

'It's all so simple,' Hall Caine commented, in a dreamy, slightly sepulchral voice. 'So simple, so utterly in keeping with the simple life of this little island, and if I may say so with the books I write here in complete seclusion.'

Remembering the music-halls and dancing palaces of Douglas, I did not fancy that life was quite so simple in the Isle of Man as Hall Caine suggested, but I felt I ought to play up to his mood.

'Yes, indeed,' I said. 'One can imagine Aeschylus writing his plays in surroundings like this.'

'Thank you,' Hall Caine almost intoned, 'thank you, Mr Compton, that is one of the nicest things ever said to me.' (I had dropped 'Mackenzie' for the family stage-name.) 'I shall cherish that observation of yours. Yes, that is one of the nicest things ever said to me. And so true!'

Compton Mackenzie, *My Life and Times: Octave Four*, 1965

Oscar Wilde · 1856–1900

By the 1880s the rivalry between Wilde and James McNeill Whistler was one of the legends of literary and artistic London. There was the social gathering they both attended in 1883, for instance, at which Wilde was quoted in Punch *as having made an elaborate comparison between the American actress Mary Anderson and Sarah Bernhardt:*

According to *Punch*, he said, 'Sarah Bernhardt is all moonlight and sunlight combined, exceedingly terrible, magnificently glorious. Miss Anderson is pure and fearless as a mountain daisy. Full of change as a river. Tender, fresh, sparkling, brilliant, superb, placid.' On reading this, Wilde telegraphed to Whistler, '*Punch* too ridiculous. When you and I are together we never talk about anything except ourselves.' To this came the reply, also by wire, 'No, no, Oscar, you forget. When you and I are together, we never talk about anything except me.' The telegrams were published by mutual consent in *The World*. A third one is said to have contained Wilde's reply: 'It is true, Jimmy, we were talking about you, but I was thinking of myself.'

Richard Ellmann, *Oscar Wilde*, 1987

Early in his literary career Arthur Conan Doyle was invited to dinner in London by the agent for the American magazine Lippincott's. *One of his fellow guests was Wilde:*

His conversation left an indelible impression upon my mind. He towered above us all, and yet had the art of seeming to be interested in all that we could say. He had delicacy of feeling and tact, for the monologue man, however clever, can never be a gentleman at heart. He took as well as gave, but what he gave was unique. He had a curious precision of statement, a delicate flavour of humour and a trick of small gestures to illustrate his meaning, which were peculiar to himself. The effect cannot be reproduced, but I remember how in discussing the wars of the future he said: 'A chemist on each side will approach the frontier with a bottle'—his upraised hand and precise face conjuring up a vivid and grotesque picture.

His anecdotes, too, were happy and curious. We were discussing the cynical maxim that the good fortune of our friends made us discontented. 'The devil,' said Wilde, 'was once crossing the Libyan Desert, and he came upon a spot where a number of small fiends were tormenting a holy hermit. The sainted man easily shook off their evil suggestions. The devil watched their failure and then he stepped forward to give them a lesson. "What you do is too crude," said he. "Permit me for one moment." With that he whispered to the holy man, "Your brother has just been made Bishop of Alexandria." A scowl of malignant jealousy at once clouded the serene face of the hermit. "That," said the devil to his imps, "is the sort of thing which I should recommend".'

Arthur Conan Doyle, *Memories and Adventures*, 1924

After a misunderstanding with Edmond de Goncourt, Wilde wrote apologizing to him for his imperfect French:

ON peut adorer une langue sans bien la parler, comme on peut aimer une femme sans la connaître. Français de sympathie, je suis Irlandais de race, et les Anglais m'ont condamné à parler le langage de Shakespeare.

Letter to Edmond de Goncourt, December 1891

ONE evening, at a party, I met the Wildes. He and I had much to say to each other. Mrs Oscar approached us, looking exquisite in a dress the fashion of which just suited her. We both gazed at her admiringly. As she passed by, Oscar gave a deep sigh, and murmured half to himself and half to me:

'If only I could be jealous of her!'

Louise Jopling, *Twenty Years of my Life*, 1925

IN addition to the steadies, like Robert Ross, and the fly-by-night Cockney lovers like Charlie Parker and Alfred Wood, there were a number of young men whose relationships with Wilde are not recorded in any known letters, like Ben Horniman, the brother of Roy Horniman the novelist. Oscar told him, and he proudly repeated the story fifty years later, that he had the most beautiful feet in Europe.

Rupert Croft-Cooke, *The Unrecorded Life of Oscar Wilde*, 1972

As an illustration of Wilde's imperturbability at the beginning of his terrible debacle, Max repeated a story told him many years before by Lewis Waller, a matinée idol of the time. Waller was walking down Piccadilly with Allan Aynesworth, another accomplished actor. Waller was playing Sir Robert Chiltern in *An Ideal Husband* and Aynesworth Algernon in *The Importance of Being Earnest*. The Wilde scandal looked like closing both plays. The two actors were deep in talk about the source of their imminent unemployment when, to their horror, they were hailed cheerily by their disemployer, riding blithely down Piccadilly in a hansom cab. They returned his greeting pallidly, hoping Wilde would ride on, but he didn't. He got out and came up to them. 'Have you heard,' he inquired, 'what that swine Queensberry has had the effrontery to say?' Writhing with embarrassment, they both protested that no rumour of the Marquess's allegation had reached their chaste ears. 'Since you haven't heard it, I'll tell you,' said Wilde, with the eagerness of a tutor avid to fill in a gap in folklore. 'He actually had the effrontery to say'—and he fixed his eye on Waller—'that *The Importance of Being Earnest* was a better-acted play than *An Ideal Husband*!' He smiled radiantly, waved, got back into his hansom, and rode off down Piccadilly, leaving his victims gasping.

S. N. Behrman, *Conversations with Max*, 1960

Charles Brookfield was an actor—he appeared in the original production of An Ideal Husband—*who subsequently became examiner of plays for the Lord Chamberlain:*

When the scandal—the Queensberry scandal—broke out, Brookfield went about London, wherever he could go, organizing an opposition to Wilde. As he knew a vast number of people, and had a very persuasive speech, and a superb talent for ridicule, it is quite probable that he did considerably injure Wilde's cause.

I once heard Robert Ross complaining before Wilde, with much indignation, of Brookfield's activities. 'How absurd of Brookfield!' said Oscar. That was all.

Vincent O'Sullivan, *Aspects of Wilde*, 1936

As a child, Wilde's younger son Vyvyan could only guess at the circumstances which had led to his father disappearing from his life:

Up to the age of eighteen, whenever I tried to broach the subject to my mother's family, or even to my brother, my inquiries were always side-tracked. But one day in Lausanne I put the matter bluntly to my aunt, and she, being a simple woman, not gifted with overmuch tact, gave me an equally blunt answer. The full import of this information did not immediately strike me, and my first feeling was one of great relief. The reticence of my mother's family through the years had led me to conjure up all kinds of pictures of what my father might have done. My imagination showed him to me alternately as an embezzler or a burglar. Sometimes I thought that he might have committed bigamy in marrying my mother, and that Cyril and I were illegitimate; indeed, that was my most frequent fear. And when I say I was relieved, it was because I discovered that we were legitimate after all, and that whatever my father had done had not brought distress to anyone but his own immediate family.

Vyvyan Holland, *Son of Oscar Wilde*, 1954

George Bernard Shaw · 1856–1950

The first moral lesson I can remember as a tiny child was the lesson of teetotalism, instilled by my father, a futile person you would have thought him. One night when I was still about as tall as his boots, he took me out for a walk. In the course of it I conceived a monstrous, incredible suspicion. When I got home I stole to my mother and in an awestruck whisper said to her, 'Mamma: I think papa's drunk.' She turned away with impatient disgust and said, 'When is he ever anything else?' I have never believed in anything since: then the scoffer began.

Letter to Ellen Terry, 1897

'The word Shavian,' Shaw told me, 'began when William Morris found in a medieval MS by one Shaw the marginal comment "Sic Shavius, sed inepte [Thus Shaw, but absurdly]." It provided a much-needed adjective; for Shawian is obviously impossible and unbearable.'

Hesketh Pearson, *Bernard Shaw*, 1942

The first performance [of *Arms and the Man*] was boisterous. The author took a curtain call, and was received with cheers. When they had subsided, and before G.B.S. could utter a syllable, a solitary hiss was heard in the gallery. It was made by R. Golding Bright, who was afterwards a very successful literary agent, and it was made, as he told me, under a misapprehension. He thought that G.B.S., in his satire on florid Balkan soldiers, was reflecting on the British Army. G.B.S. bowed to him, and remarked, 'I quite agree with you, sir, but what can two do against so many?'

St John Ervine, *Bernard Shaw*, 1956

W. B. Yeats, who was present, commented: 'And from that moment Bernard Shaw became the most formidable man in modern letters, and even the most drunken of medical students knew it.'

Shaw and Bertrand Russell first met when they were on holiday with Beatrice and Sidney Webb in Monmouth in 1895:

At this time he and I were involved in a bicycle accident, which I feared for a moment might have brought his career to a premature close. He was only just learning to ride a bicycle, and he ran into my machine with such force that he was hurled through the air and landed on his back twenty feet from the place of the collision. However, he got up completely unhurt and continued his ride. Whereas my bicycle was smashed, and I had to return by train. It was a very slow train, and at every station Shaw with his bicycle appeared on the platform, put his head into the carriage and jeered. I suspect that he regarded the whole incident as proof of the virtues of vegetarianism.

Bertrand Russell, *Portraits from Memory*, 1956

Shaw's mother died in 1913:

HE chose Granville Barker to accompany him as sole other mourner at the cremation. He had a horror of earth burial, knowing too much of it from behind the scenes of Mount Jerome, Dublin's great extramural Protestant cemetery, of which his uncle-in-law was resident secretary and manager. The service was Church of England, not because his mother had ever had any relations with that institution but for two reasons: (1) Shaw felt that as between one professional man and another he could not decently do the chaplain out of his fee. (2) He wanted to test the service by its effect on himself. Accordingly he and Granville Barker sat it out, they two and the chaplain being the only persons present.

The effect was not satisfactory. When later on the Reverend Dick Sheppard, who ranked Shaw as a considerable religious influence, asked him to revise the Prayer Book, he condemned the burial service very strongly as morbid and macabre. But when he went behind the scenes and saw the coffin pushed into what seemed a chamber radiant with sunshine, and bursting into twirling ribbons of soaring garnet-coloured flame, he was transported by the wonderful æsthetic effect, and became more ardent than ever in his advocacy of cremation, which he carried to the length of declaring that earth burial should be made a criminal offence.

When the furnace closed he went for a walk with Granville Barker. Before they returned the cremation was finished. They found the calcined remains of Mrs Carr Shaw strewn on a stone table at which two men in white caps and overalls, looking exactly like cooks, were busily picking out and separating the scraps of molten metal and wood ash, so as to leave nothing on the table but the authentic relics of the deceased lady. Shaw's sense of humour at once extinguished his sense of propriety. He felt that his mother was looking over his shoulder and sharing his amusement. He was recalled to the decencies of the occasion by Granville Barker's amazed comment: 'You certainly are a merry soul, Shaw.'

Pearson, *Bernard Shaw*

SHAW once came across one of his books in a secondhand shop, inscribed *To — with esteem, George Bernard Shaw.* He bought the book and returned it to —, adding the line, *With renewed esteem, George Bernard Shaw.*

Anne Fadiman, *Ex Libris*, 1999

In 1934 Shaw sat for the sculptor Jacob Epstein:

ONE day Robert Flaherty [the documentary film-maker] brought along the Aran boatman, Tiger King, who was the chief character in the film, *Man of Aran*, written about fishermen. In the studio, when Tiger King was introduced, Shaw immediately started talking to him on how to sail a boat, what happened in storms, and generally instructed him in sea-lore.

Jacob Epstein, *Epstein: An Autobiography*, 1955

GABRIEL PASCAL told me on one occasion that when he heard that Mrs Shaw was dying he came back by plane—the plane was delayed so he didn't arrive in time for the funeral. He came to Ayot St Lawrence and met Shaw and Shaw was full of high spirits. Shaw began to do dance steps in front of the house and Pascal said to him, 'Really, really, it's rather surprising after your wife's death.' And Shaw said, 'You don't know what it's been like, Pascal. It's as though all your life you've been carrying a beautiful silver casket on your shoulders and it was too heavy for you to bear and at last you leave it down and you just want to dance and sing the whole day, that's how I feel after it.'

Frank O'Connor, in *Irish Literary Portraits*, ed. W. R. Rodgers, 1972

MAX [Beerbohm], whose life at Rapallo was a long evocation, in memory, of the people he had known, of their foibles and mistakes and their enchantment when they were at their best, found less understandable than anything else about Shaw his remark when he was asked whether he missed any of his contemporaries who had died. 'No,' said Shaw, 'I miss only the man I was.' Max's comment on this was, 'When I think of the gay and delightful people he knew . . .' He shook his head in bewilderment.

S. N. Behrman, *Conversations with Max*, 1960

WILLIAM ARCHER · 1856–1924

(theatre critic and translator of Ibsen)

'DID you know that Archer, who always wished to demonstrate that, though a drama critic, he could write a play, had one night of triumph when he felt that he had achieved a beautiful play? He told me this himself. One night, between sleeping and waking, it seemed to him that he had evolved a perfect plot, saw the whole thing from beginning to end. He saw that it only remained to write it—like that!' Max snapped his fingers. 'Then he fell into a blissful sleep. When he wakened, he went over the whole plot again in his mind. He had a disillusioning, a frightful revelation. What he had dreamt was *Hedda Gabler*.'

Max Beerbohm in S. N. Behrman, *Conversations with Max*, 1960

In 1886 the Shelley Society gave a private performance of Shelley's play The Cenci *at the Court Theatre:*

THE critic William Archer slept very soundly, then fell forward flat on his face with a tremendous noise, leaving a dent in the floor which may still be seen by curious visitors.

Bernard Shaw, article in the *Star*, 1890

FRANK HARRIS · 1856–1931

(journalist and biographer; his books include a notoriously unreliable memoir, *My Life and Loves*, and *The Man Shakespeare*)

To the awe inspired in Harris by Shakespeare a famous incident at the Café Royal testifies. There, during a lull in conversation at one of his luncheon parties, the conversation shifted to homosexuality. A great hush descended upon the room at the mention of a subject that, in those days, was taboo. Harris, however, thundered on in his powerful basso: 'Homosexuality? No, I know nothing of the joys of homosexuality. My friend Oscar can no doubt tell you all about that.' Further silence, even more profound. Harris continued: 'But I must say that if *Shakespeare* asked me, I would have to submit.'

S. Schoenbaum, *Shakespeare's Lives*, 1991

JOSEPH CONRAD · 1857–1924

In 1881 Conrad signed on as second mate aboard the Palestine, *a barque bound for Bangkok. His adventures on the voyage are recalled in his short story 'Youth' (1898), although the story isn't entirely the 'record of experience' which he said it was:*

THE crew Conrad extolled in 'Youth' was recruited from 'Liverpool hard cases' who not only could work with impressive self-discipline in critical moments, but also display surprising understanding for the beauty inherent in good sailsmanship: 'It was something in them, something inborn and subtle and everlasting. I don't say positively that the crew of a French or German merchantman wouldn't have done it, but I doubt whether it would have been done in the same way. There was a completeness in it, something solid like a principle, and masterful like an instinct—a discourse of something secret—of that hidden something, that gift of good or evil that makes racial difference, that shapes the fate of nations.' But in fact there was not a single Liverpudlian on the *Palestine*. Five men came from Cornwall, one from Ireland, and the remainder were foreigners—an Australian, a Negro from the Antilles, a Dutchman and a Norwegian.

Zdzisław Najder, *Joseph Conrad: A Chronicle*, 1983

There is a similar discrepancy between the composition of the crew of the ship in The Nigger of the 'Narcissus' *and that of the actual vessel on which it was based. 'In retrospect,' Zdzisław Najder writes, Conrad 'obviously wanted to present his service at sea as unequivocally English in character.'*

GREAT quickness of eye was one of Conrad's gifts. I remember while sitting one evening with him in the Café Royal I asked him, after a painted lady had brushed haughtily past our table, what he had specially noticed about her. 'The dirt in her nostril,' he replied instantly.

Edward Garnett, article in *Century Magazine*, 1928

WHEN we had finally decided on collaborating on *Romance*, he insisted on driving the seven miles that separated the Pent from Spade House in order to break the news to Mr H. G. Wells. I suppose he regarded Mr Wells as the doyen of the younger school of writers. Certainly Mr Wells had written of *Almayer's Folly* with extraordinary generosity. Anyhow, to my discomfort we drove in state in a hired fly from the Pent to pay a call on Mr Wells at Sandgate. There was a curious incident. As we stood on the door-step of Mr Wells's villa, in the hesitant mind of those paying a state call, behold, the electric bell-push, all of itself, went in and the bell sounded. . . . Conrad exclaimed, '*Tiens!* . . . The Invisible Man!' and burst into incredible and incredulous laughter. In the midst of it the door opened before grave faces.

Ford Madox Ford, *Joseph Conrad: A Personal Remembrance*, 1924

H. G. Wells wrote a letter to the Manchester Guardian *in 1924 denying that the incident had taken place.*

WHEN Conrad first met Shaw in my house, Shaw talked with customary freedom. 'You know, my dear fellow, your books won't *do*'—for some Shavian reason I have forgotten—and so forth.

I went out of the room and suddenly found Conrad on my heels, swift and white-faced. 'Does that man want to *insult* me?' he demanded.

The provocation to say 'Yes' and assist at the subsequent duel was very great, but I overcame it. 'It's humour,' I said, and took Conrad out into the garden to cool. One could always baffle Conrad by saying 'humour'. It was one of our damned English tricks he had never learnt to tackle.

H. G. Wells, *Experiment in Autobiography*, 1934

He had been persuaded to write about books occasionally for the *Daily Mail*, and would, of course, have given of his heart's blood to the work, as he gave it to everything he wrote. It would have been setting a razor to cut a grindstone in any case, and perhaps it was as well for his sake that it came to an end when it did.

On the Saturday before Cowes Week the news came through of the arrest of Crippen, the murderer, on his arrival in Canada. Marlowe [the editor of the *Daily Mail*] had chartered a small yacht and called in at the office on his way to Southampton to join her. He found Kennedy Jones [right-hand man of Northcliffe, the paper's proprietor] there, excited by the news. More cablegrams were coming through, and one of them contained a list of the books Crippen had read on his voyage across. Presently K.J. said, 'That list of books—there might be something in that. I wonder if anybody could be got to write an article about Crippen's sea library.' One of them thought of trying Conrad. Their practice was always to try everything, and he could only say no. The telegram was sent and Marlowe left for his yacht. Conrad might light his pipe with it, or he might reply declining the proposal. Or their luck might be in, and they would get an interesting article.

What happened was that poor dear Conrad exploded in epistolary fury at being asked to do such a thing and severed his connection with our journal.

Archibald Marshall, *Out and About*, 1933

Once, when we were in town together, I was told off to secure rooms in the hotel where we usually stayed. Conrad, as he had some business, arranged to join me later. (I remember vividly his comic disgust while relating what had happened to him, in the interval.) His business over, he had walked rapidly into another hotel and curtly requested the waiter to 'tell my wife I am here.' The waiter's very natural question, 'What name, sir?' had exasperated him, and he had answered sharply, 'Mrs Conrad, of course.' When the man returned after a short absence with the information that there was no one of that name in the hotel, Conrad called for the manager, and now, greatly irate, turned on him tensely with the command, 'Produce my wife!' It was with difficulty he was persuaded that he was in the wrong hotel.

Jessie Conrad, *Joseph Conrad as I Knew Him*, 1926

Jacob Epstein worked on his bust of Conrad at the novelist's home in Kent:

A SCULPTOR had previously made a bust of him which represented him as an open-necked, romantic, out-of-door type of person. In appearance Conrad was the very opposite. His clothes were immaculately conventional, and his collar enclosed his neck like an Iron Maiden's vice or garrotter's grip. He was worried if his hair and beard were not trim and neat as became a sea captain. There was nothing shaggy or Bohemian about him. His glance was keen despite the drooping of one eyelid. He was the sea captain, the officer, and in our talks he emphasised the word 'responsibility'. Responsibility weighed on him and weighed him down. He used the word again and again and one immediately thought of *Lord Jim*—the conscience suffering at the evasion of duty. It may have been because of my meeting him late in life that Conrad gave me a feeling of defeat; but defeat met with courage.

He was crippled with rheumatism, crotchety, nervous, and ill. He said to me, 'I am finished'. There was pathos in his pulling out of a drawer his last manuscript to show me that he was still at work. There was no triumph in his manner, however, and he said that he did not know whether he would ever finish it. 'I am played out,' he said, 'played out.'

We talked after the sittings, mostly in the afternoons when we had tea together and Conrad was full of reminiscences about himself. We were usually alone. There, in this country house, he seemed to live alone although the house was filled with servants. A few visitors came at the weekends, but he appeared a lonely, brooding man, with none too pleasant thoughts . . .

I looked at Conrad's bookshelf. He had not many books. In no sense a library. A complete edition of Turgeniev in English. We talked of books and, expecting him to be interested in Melville's *Moby Dick*, I mentioned it, and Conrad burst into a furious denunciation of it. 'He knows nothing of the sea. Fantastic, ridiculous,' he said. When I mentioned that the work was symbolical and mystical: 'Mystical my eye! My old boots are mystical.' 'Meredith? His characters are ten feet high.' D. H. Lawrence had started well, but had gone wrong. 'Filth. Nothing but obscenities.' For Henry James he had unqualified admiration.

Jacob Epstein, *Epstein: An Autobiography*, 1955

George Gissing · 1857–1903

SOMETIMES I added the labour of a porter to my fasting endured for the sake of books. At the little shop near Portland Road Station I came upon a first edition of Gibbon, the price an absurdity—I think it was a shilling a volume. To possess those clean-paged quartos I would have sold my coat. As it happened, I had not money enough with me, but sufficient at home. I was living at Islington. Having spoken with the bookseller, I walked home, took the cash, walked back again, and—carried the tomes from the west end of Euston Road to a street in Islington far beyond the *Angel*. I did it in two journeys—this being the only time in my life when I thought of Gibbon in avoirdupois. Twice—three times, reckoning the walk for the money—did I descend Euston Road and climb Pentonville on that occasion. Of the season and the weather I have no recollection; my joy in the purchase I had made drove out every other thought. Except, indeed, of the weight. I had infinite energy, but not much muscular strength, and the end of the last journey saw me upon a chair, perspiring, flaccid, aching—exultant!

The well-to-do person would hear this story with astonishment. Why did I not get the bookseller to send me the volumes? Or, if I could not wait, was there no omnibus along that London highway? How could I make the well-to-do person understand that I did not feel able to afford, that day, one penny more than I had spent on the book? No, no, such labour-saving expenditure did not come within my scope; whatever I enjoyed I earned it, literally, by the sweat of my brow. In those days I hardly knew what it was to travel by omnibus. I have walked London streets for twelve and fifteen hours together without ever a thought of saving my legs, or my time, by paying for waftage. Being poor as poor can be, there were certain things I had to renounce, and this was one of them.

Years after, I sold my first edition of Gibbon for even less than it cost me; it went with a great many other fine books in folio and quarto, which I could not drag about with me in my constant removals; the man who bought them spoke of them as 'tomb-stones.' Why has Gibbon no market value? Often has my heart ached with regret for those quartos. The joy of reading the *Decline and Fall* in that fine type! The page was appropriate to the dignity of the subject; the mere sight of it tuned one's mind. I suppose I could easily get another copy now; but it would not be to me what that other was, with its memory of dust and toil.

Gissing, *The Private Papers of Henry Ryecroft*, 1902

The Private Papers *is ostensibly a work of fiction but essentially autobiographical. The story about buying the edition of Gibbon, which also appears in Gissing's novel* The Unclassed, *draws directly on his own experience.*

Sir Arthur Conan Doyle · 1859–1930

I LOVE that solid, precise way he has of talking, like Sherlock Holmes. He was telling me once that when he was in America, he saw an advertisement in a paper: CONAN DOYLE'S SCHOOL OF WRITING. LET THE CONAN

DOYLE SCHOOL OF WRITING TEACH YOU HOW TO SELL—or something to that effect. In other words, some blighter was using his name to swindle the public. Well, what most people in his place would have said would have been, 'Hullo! This looks fishy.' The way he put it when telling me the story was, 'I said to myself, "Ha! There is villainy afoot." '

P. G. Wodehouse, *Performing Flea*, 1953

Doyle's later years were dominated by his passionate belief in spiritualism:

EVERY lecturing record was broken by Doyle when he toured North America, but it is difficult to say whether this was due to the general interest in Sherlock Holmes or the next world. True he told his interviewers that they would all find themselves in Paradise after death, but being pressmen they felt dubious on the point. This is the sort of thing to which they subjected him:

'Well now, Mr Doyle, say! Do they have golf in the next world?'
'No. I have no reason to say that.'
'You never heard them speak of golf?'
'No, I never have.'
'Well, you said they had amusements.'
'Yes, they say they have more than we.'
'Well, maybe golf is among them.'
'I never heard them say so.'

Next morning a newspaper headline ran: 'Doyle says they play golf in Heaven.'

Hesketh Pearson, *Conan Doyle: His Life and Art*, 1943

A. E. HOUSMAN · 1859–1936

A Shropshire Lad *was originally published, at the poet's own expense, in February 1896, without great success. Grant Richards, who was just setting up as a publisher on his own account, wrote to Housman offering to take over future editions; Housman initially replied with a letter which neither rejected his proposal, nor accepted it.*

IT must have been more than a year later that, sitting in Henrietta Street, I was surprised and elated at having brought to me a card bearing the name of A. E. Housman.

'Show him in.' Of course I was elated: he could only have come about one thing.

And I was right. Yes, I might have *A Shropshire Lad*; the first edition was at last exhausted.

'And the terms? What royalty shall I pay? What business arrangements are we to have?'

'Royalties? I want no royalties. You may produce the book—that's all.'

'But the profit? The book will become better and better known. It won't take over two years to sell the second edition. There is bound to be profit.'

'Well, if there is, then apply it to a reduction in the price of the book. I am not a poet by trade; I am a Professor of Latin. I do not wish to make profit out of my poetry. It is not my business. The Americans send me cheques. I return them.'

'But there is no separate edition of the book, is there, no "pirated" edition?'

'No, not as far as I know, but there's a magazine—*McClure's*—which every now and then fills up one of its pages with a poem from my book. I suppose I couldn't prevent it even if I wanted to. There's a man on the staff who seems to like it. It's he who is responsible for such appearances as I make there.'

'And they send you cheques and you send them back?'

'Yes, and I shall no doubt continue to do so; by and by they'll no doubt learn to save themselves the trouble.'

Grant Richards, *Author Hunting*, 1934

Housman eventually arranged to receive royalties for his work, but not until 1926.

He had written six of the poems before he set foot in Shropshire, but having decided on the title he felt he should pay the county a visit—'to gain local colour', he added with a laugh and a look of derision.

Percy Withers, *A Buried Life*, 1940

Housman's friend Percy Withers once made the mistake of playing him recordings of some musical settings of his poems:

Of music he knew nothing, and confessed it meant nothing to him. I thought one evening in the library to quiet a reaction so tumultuous, following the gramophone records of Vaughan Williams' setting of four of his lyrics, that my wife, who sat near him, was momentarily expecting him to spring from his chair and rush headlong out of the room; and the torment was still on his suffused and angry visage when the records were finished, and I first realized the havoc my mistaken choice had caused. I thought to soothe him by playing some record of his own choosing. He looked rather lost when I asked him to name one, but presently suggested the Fifth Symphony, for the curious reason that he remembered to have heard it well spoken of. At the end he made a non-committal and quite colourless comment on the slow movement; the others he ignored. It was not the result one could have wished, nor did it suggest the desirability of continuing the music; for us at least it was enough that the turbulence was quieted.

Withers, *A Buried Life*

Sir Sidney Lee · 1859–1926

(literary scholar)

Lee was on the editorial staff of the Dictionary of National Biography *from the start, and became editor-in-chief in 1891:*

It was Sir Sidney's idea that the Prince [of Wales—the future Edward VII] ought to give a dinner to those responsible for the completion of this monumental work. The monumental work had escaped the Prince's attention, don't you know, and Sir Sidney had painfully to explain to him what it was. The Prince, you know, was not an omnivorous reader. Sir Sidney managed to obtain his grudging consent. 'How many?' asked the Prince. 'Forty,' said Sir Sidney. The Prince was appalled. 'For-r-ty!' he gasped. 'For-r-ty wr-ri-ter-rs! I can't have for-r-ty wr-ri-ter-rs in Marlborough House! Giff me the list!' Sir Sidney gave it to him, and the Prince, with a heavy black pencil, started slashing off names. Sir Sidney's heart sank when he saw that the first name the Prince had slashed was that of Sir Leslie Stephen. He conveyed, as tactfully as he could, that this was a bad cut, since Stephen was the animating genius of the whole enterprise. Reluctantly, the Prince allowed Sir Leslie to come. Eventually, Sir Sidney put over his entire list. The dinner took place. Among the contributors present was Canon Ainger, a distinguished cleric whose passion was Charles Lamb, on whom he was considered a very great authority indeed. He had written the articles on Charles and Mary Lamb for the *Dictionary*. Sir Sidney sat at the Prince's right and found it heavy weather, don't you know. The Prince must have found it heavy going also; to be having dinner with forty writers was not his idea of a cultivated way to spend an evening. His eye roamed the table morosely, in self-objurgation for having let himself in for a thing like this. Finally, his eye settled on Canon Ainger. 'Who's the little parson?' he asked Lee. 'Vy is *he* here? He's not a wr-ri-ter!' 'He is a very great authority,' said Lee, apologetically, 'on Lamb.' This was too much for the Prince. He put down his knife and fork in stupefaction; a pained outcry of protest heaved from him: 'On *lamb*!'

Max Beerbohm in S. N. Behrman, *Conversations with Max*, 1960

Sir James Barrie · 1860–1937

During the rehearsals of *Peter Pan* (and it is evidence in my favour that I was admitted to them) a depressed man in overalls, carrying a mug of tea or a paint-pot, used often to appear by my side in the shadowy stalls and say to me, 'The gallery boys won't stand it.' He then mysteriously faded away as if he were the theatre ghost. This hopelessness of his is what all dramatists are said to feel at such times, so perhaps he was the author.

Dedication (1928) to *Peter Pan*

Frederick Rolfe · 1860–1913

(writer and fantasist also known as Baron Corvo; author of *Hadrian the Seventh*)

Corvo professed to have a horror of reptiles. He told me that he had once fallen into a trance after stumbling over a lizard, and had very nearly been buried alive. . . .

I thought this was another of his 'tall' stories, but later I was persuaded there was some truth in it. One Sunday afternoon we had taken a walk down to the river, and when we got back we found the house empty, it being church time. I climbed over the yard door and got through the kitchen window, then I opened the house door for Corvo and went upstairs. Suddenly I heard a blood-curdling shriek, and on rushing downstairs I found him in the kitchen, his face as white as chalk, his mouth twitching. He was staring fixedly at something I did not at first see. I followed his gaze, and under the table I saw a little toad. I spoke to him, shouted to him, but he did not answer. I got a chair and pushed him into it, and he sat there for more than an hour quite motionless except for the working of his mouth. When he had recovered enough to stand and walk, I accompanied him to the studio and laid him on his bed. He fell at once into a deep sleep, and when I went round early the next morning to see how he was, I found him still asleep. I didn't wake him, and he slept on till eleven without stirring once. When I questioned him later, he told me he remembered nothing after first seeing the toad.

John Holden, quoted in A. J. A. Symons, *The Quest for Corvo*, 1934

Rabindranath Tagore · 1861–1941

(Bengali poet and man of letters; first Asian to win the Nobel Prize for Literature)

Before Tagore left for India, Yeats and I arranged a small dinner in his honour. After dinner we asked Tagore to sing *Bande Mataram*, the nationalist song. He hummed the tune but after the first words broke down; he could not remember the rest. Then Yeats began the Irish anthem—and his memory, again, was at fault; and Ernest Rhys could not for the life of him recollect the words of the Welsh national anthem. 'What a crew!' I said, when I too stumbled over *God save the King*.

William Rothenstein, *Men and Memories 1900–1922*, 1932

Edith Wharton · 1862–1937

Edith Wharton's ambition to be a novelist of manners manifested itself at an early age:

My first attempt (at the age of eleven) was a novel which began: ' "Oh, how do you do, Mrs Brown?" said Mrs Tompkins. "If only I had known you were going to call I should have tidied up the drawing-room".' Timorously I submitted this to my mother, and never shall I forget the sudden drop of my creative frenzy when she returned it with the icy comment: 'Drawing-rooms are always tidy.'

Edith Wharton, *A Backward Glance*, 1934

I remember one day at Qu'acre when Howard Sturgis, turning the pages of her latest story (it was *Ethan Frome*) read out a passing remark of her fictitious narrator's—'I had been sent by my employers', and how Henry [James] caught at the words, with his great round stare of drollery and malice at the suggested image—of Edith *sent*, and by *employers*!—what a power of invention it implied in her to think of that!

Percy Lubbock, *Portrait of Edith Wharton*, 1947

Rudyard kipling · 1865–1936

Until the age of 6 Kipling lived with his parents in Bombay. His ayah, *or nurse, came from Goa:*

There were far-going Arab dhows on the pearly waters, and gaily dressed Parsees wading out to worship the sunset. Of their creed I knew nothing, nor did I know that near our little house on the Bombay Esplanade were the Towers of Silence, where their Dead are exposed to the waiting vultures on the rim of the towers, who scuffle and spread wings when they see the bearers of the Dead below. I did not understand my Mother's distress when she found 'a child's hand' in our garden, and said I was not to ask questions about it. I wanted to see that child's hand. But my *ayah* told me.

Something of Myself, 1937

Willie [Somerset] Maugham who dined with me and Avilde tonight in Monte Carlo talked of Rudyard Kipling 'not being quite a gent'. Kipling once dined with Willie in the Villa Mauresque at Cap Ferrat and the name of a mutual friend was mentioned. 'He's a white man,' exclaimed Kipling. Willie thought, 'This is characteristic. How I wish, in order to fulfil my preconceptions of him, he would say he was a pukka sahib.' 'He's a pukka sahib all right,' continued Kipling.

James Lees-Milne, *A Mingled Measure: Diaries 1953–1972*, 1994

During the heyday of the A.E.F. [American Expeditionary Force], Kipling, momentarily placated by our having sent two million soldiers to France, gave *Stars and Stripes* the privilege of being the first to publish one of his poems. In acknowledgment, we sent a courier, accompanied by a blushing young orderly, to deliver the first copy off the press. Kipling received them and it at Brown's Hotel. The courier acquitted himself as instructed and the incident was about to close when the private, whose name I've forgotten and who was breathing heavily and obviously bursting with excitement, suddenly stepped forward, shook the gifted hand and said, 'My, Mr Kipling, it will be a great day when my folks in Georgia hear that I actually met the man who wrote the *Rubaiyat of Omar Khayyam*.'

Alexander Woollcott, letter to Edmund Wilson, 1941

Kipling, though no doubt he loved his fame, hated its public effects. Carrie [his wife] had suffered its worst excesses in New York in 1899 [when the Kiplings' young daughter died]; now she was determined to use all the powers that money provided them to hold the inquisitive and the impertinent at bay. Kipling maintained an extraordinary politeness in his rebuffs but, with her help and after initial perusal of the day's mail, rebuff he did, sometimes with a humour that must have given them great pleasure. As when, in 1925, he wrote to a lady in Leamington: 'Dear Madam, I have to thank you for your letter of June 10th. I don't remember ever having been in Leamington except once when I only passed through in a motor. I would, therefore, have been quite unable to have had the pleasure of meeting you; and the rumour that a poem was written by me with you as its subject is quite unfounded, With all good wishes. Yours sincerely.'

Angus Wilson, *The Strange Ride of Rudyard Kipling*, 1977

W. B. Yeats · 1865–1939

When I came to know her I used to question Katharine Tynan about W.B.'s youth.

'What was he like? Was he as picturesque as the Sargent drawing? Were you in love with him?' I once asked her.

'I can't imagine any woman being in love with the young Willie Yeats.'

She proceeded to describe a moist-handed, shy youth, quite incapable of inspiring passion. When A.E. came to tea with me in Swanage a year or two before his death, he told me, among other recollections of their joint boyhood, the story of W.B.'s proposal to Katie. His father remarked to him one day, 'Willie, you've been seeing a lot of that girl. It is time that you proposed.' So Willie dutifully made his way out to the Tynans' farm near Tallaght and offered his hand and heart to Katie. It was refused. Whereupon, his manner indicating some slight relief, Katharine Tynan asked him, 'But why did you do this?' 'Well, my father thought—' and the whole story came out.

Monk Gibbon, *The Masterpiece and the Man: Yeats as I Knew Him*, 1959

Yeats recalls life as a young man in London:

Sometimes I told myself very adventurous love-stories with myself for hero, and at other times I planned out a life of lonely austerity, and at other times mixed the ideals and planned a life of lonely austerity mitigated by periodical lapses. I had still the ambition, formed in Sligo in my teens, of living in imitation of Thoreau on Innisfree, a little island in Lough Gill, and when walking through Fleet Street very homesick I heard a little tinkle of water and saw a fountain in a shop-window which balanced a little ball upon its jet, and began to remember lake-water. From the sudden remembrance came my poem *Innisfree*, my first lyric with anything in its rhythm of my own music.

The Trembling of the Veil, 1922

In after-life I came across several Seers, Witches and Warlocks, but none had his little flock in better order than the poet, W. B. Yeats. He seemed to have a way with Ghosts and Spirits, and under his kindly sway they dropped many of their ill-bred tricks and showed (occasionally) quite ordinary intelligence.

He was telling me once the true history of one of the often recurrent Catholic wonders, a picture belonging to a village priest which shed miraculous blood-drops.

'But how did you find out?' I asked. 'Did you go to —' (a distant place in France).

'No. I sent a Spirit to look into the whole thing,' said Yeats, as simply as though he had said, 'I sent a boy messenger.' And certainly, under Yeats's control, the Spirit brought back as direct and fair a report as could be wished.

'The man is perfectly genuine,' said the Spirit, 'but there has been no Miracle. It is merely a case of self-deception.' Then it described the means whereby the effect had been produced. 'The next development,' went on the Spirit, 'will be the appearance of the Stigmata upon the person of the enthusiast,' and the Spirit was quite right.

Now here was sound information given in straightforward terms. It really seemed as though the Spirit, gratified at being selected as confidant by a charming and distinguished man, had pulled itself together and minded its manners.

W. Graham Robertson, *Time Was*, 1931

One day we were talking about music, and Yeats told me that some people said he didn't know one tune from another. When I asked if that was true he hummed and hawed a bit, he was a little grieved about this rumour, as anyone would be.

I comforted him the best I could by asserting that, to my very own knowledge, he knew two tunes perfectly. Yeats was curious about everything that was about himself, and he would listen to anybody's opinion about him till the cows came home: so, in a little time, he asked what were the two tunes that he knew, because he couldn't just remember what they were.

I replied, honourably and honestly, that to my certain knowledge he knew the tune of 'God Save The King'; and that he also immediately recognized the tune of 'God Save The Queen,' and I insisted that he never mistook these tunes for 'The Night Before Larry Was Stretched,' or 'The Wearing of the Green.'

He laughed a bit about this and we both took it for a joke, but he revenged himself a month later when I was saying a couple of verses of my own—I am inclined to sing-song when the poem permits it—'Stephens,' he said gravely, 'has a very original talent, he has discovered

Gregorian Chaunt.' I'll bet it took him three weeks to work that one out.

James Stephens, 'Yeats and Music', 1947; in *James, Seumas & Jacques: Unpublished Writings*, 1964

Arthur Hannah was the proprietor of a well-known bookshop in Dublin:

I CAN remember Yeats well, he came into our shop quite a lot. As a matter of fact, all he bought from us were detective novels. On one occasion he came into me, reprimanded me, said I had sold him a detective novel in which there was far too much detection. Well, then I sold him an Edgar Wallace and he went out very happy.

Arthur Hannah, in *Irish Literary Portraits*, edited by W. R. Rodgers, 1972

YEATS was very critical of musical settings of his own words, with the criterion that one note should represent one syllable . . . Shaking with laughter, he complained of hearing a lullaby sung by three men with stentorian voices, and of a composer who said to him, 'I wish you could have heard my setting of *Innisfree*, sung in the open by two thousand boy scouts.'

He laughed again, and quoted, 'And I shall have some peace there.'

L. A. G. Strong, *Green Memory*, 1961

H. G. WELLS · 1866–1946

I LIKE Wells. An odd bird, though. The first time I met him, we had barely finished the initial pip-pippings when he said, apropos of nothing, 'My Father was a professional cricketer.' If there's a good answer to that, you tell me. I thought of saying, 'Mine had a white moustache,' but finally settled for, 'Oh, ah,' and we went on to speak of other things.

P. G. Wodehouse, *Performing Flea*, 1953

Wells's father played for Kent.

The 'Gip' who figures in the following incident was the elder of Wells's two sons, G. P. Wells:

IN the evenings, when other visitors had gone, we played bridge. On one occasion, after some gross overbidding by H.G. and myself, Gip threw down his hand and shouted 'Bastard' at his father. After a shocked silence, H.G. replied in his squeaky voice, 'In the old days, God would have thought nothing of striking you dead for less than that.'

Julian Huxley, *Memories*, 1972

Walter Allen was greatly impressed by his friend V. S. Pritchett's 'wonderful ability to evoke rapidly in speech the manner and mannerisms of others':

THUS, I remember, though I did not hear it from him till years later, the story of an encounter on the one occasion with both Wells and Yeats, whom he had met when as a young man he had worked as a correspondent in Ireland for the *Christian Science Monitor*. As a relatively new member, he had gone into his club early one lunchtime, found the dining room still almost empty and sat down alone half-way along a long table. Then Wells, whom he knew slightly, came in and joined him. They had just begun to eat when Yeats appeared, hovered in the doorway and peered round him myopically. Recognising Pritchett, he came and took the place beside him, so that V. S. was now sandwiched between the two great men. Wells craned round and said: 'Yeats? It is Yeats, ain't it? I ain't seen you since that weekend at Lady Warwick's in 1913.'

Wells's high-pitched slightly Cockney voice was admirably suggested, as was Yeats's sonorous gravity. 'It was indeed a long time ago, Wells,' he concurred. Wells was now in spate. 'D'you remember that beautiful girl who was there that weekend at Lady Warwick's, Lady —, wasn't her name?'

'She was indeed strikingly beautiful,' said Yeats.

'Well, Yeats, you should see her now. I ran into her yesterday. 'Orrible, Yeats, 'Orrible.' He drew his hand down his left arm and clutched it to his side, so indicating paralysis, and twisted his mouth askew. ''Orrible, Yeats,' he said again, with relish.

Walter Allen, *As I Walked Down New Grub Street*, 1981

GILBERT MURRAY · 1866–1957

(classical scholar)

HE told stories in a quiet, unassuming way and you never quite knew what to expect. An example of his art is this, 'I knew a learned Turk. He knew all about Cicero, and had read everything about Cicero. No one has ever known so much about Cicero . . . He hated Cicero.'

C. M. Bowra, *Memories*, 1966

AMONG professional scholars he had detractors. When Henry Jackson, Regius Professor of Greek at Cambridge, first saw in the Preface of Murray's *Ancient Greek Literature* the words, 'To read and re-read the scanty remains now left to us of the literature of Ancient Greece, is a pleasant and not a laborious task', he scrawled in the margin, 'Insolent puppy!'

Bowra, *Memories*

Ernest Dowson · 1867–1900

(*fin de siècle* poet; member of the Rhymers Club)

A Rhymer had seen Dowson at some café in Dieppe with a particularly common harlot, and as he passed, Dowson, who was half drunk, caught him by the sleeve and whispered, 'She writes poetry—it is like Browning and Mrs Browning'.

W. B. Yeats, *The Trembling of the Veil*, 1922

Arnold Bennett · 1867–1931

Bennett wrote The Old Wives' Tale *while living in Paris. A fellow novelist, also living there, whom he saw from time to time was Somerset Maugham:*

One evening [Maugham records] after we had been dining together and were sitting amid the Empire furniture of his apartment, he said:

'Look here, I have a proposal to make to you.'

'Oh?'

'I have a mistress with whom I spend two nights a week. She has another gentleman with whom she spends two other nights. She likes to have her Sundays to herself and she's looking for someone who'll take the two nights she has free. I've told her about you. She likes writers. I'd like to see her nicely fixed up and I thought it would be a good plan if you took the two nights that she has vacant.'

The suggestion startled me.

'It sounds rather cold-blooded to me,' I said.

'She's not an ignorant woman, you know,' Arnold insisted. 'Not by any manner of means. She reads a great deal, Madame de Sévigné and all that, and she can talk very intelligently.'

But even that didn't tempt me.

Somerset Maugham, *In Vagrant Mood*, 1952

Bennett rejoiced in his fame and success:

His tufted forelock had become a true *panache*: 'it took men's eyes,' wrote Gerald Gould in the *Observer*. You could pick him out by it at once in the crowded foyer at a fashionable first night. It was conspicuous in the throng at the Royal Academy private view. 'There's Arnold Bennett—!'

Or, as an artist whom he did not know very well shouted to him across the pavement of Sloane Street one morning: 'Why, if it isn't the big pot from the Potteries!' Apparently the obvious joke had not reached Bennett's ears before. He was amused and 'laffed like anything', he said.

Reginald Pound, *Arnold Bennett*, 1952

Charlotte Mew · 1869–1928

(poet; the only collection of her work published in her lifetime was *The Farmer's Bride*)

In 1914 a friend noted in her diary that 'Charlotte has been bothering and annoying May'—the novelist May Sinclair, whose literary encouragement Charlotte Mew had misinterpreted as something more romantic:

It seems rather unlucky—but Charlotte was hardly ever lucky—that this incident, like Shelley's first wedding and Swinburne's decline, has only been recorded in terms of farce. Rebecca West sent to May Sinclair's biographer, Dr Theophilus Boll, a copy of a letter from the novelist G. B. Stern ('Peter'). The letter recalled, at a distance of time, how May had told both of them 'in her neat, precise little voice' that 'a lesbian poetess, Charlotte M., had chased her upstairs into the bedroom—"And I assure you, Peter, and I assure you, Rebecca, I had to leap the bed five times!"' And Dr Boll, a most painstaking American academic, was left to calculate, as he tells us, whether May, at the age of fifty-one, would really have been able to do all this leaping, and if she did, how she could have managed after the fifth leap, which would have trapped her against the wall. I am not sure how Dr Boll could tell whether, in the summer of 1914, May's bed was against the wall or not. What is certain is that there was an uncontrolled physical confession of furious longing, desiring and touching which terrified May, and perhaps also terrified Miss Lotti [Charlotte Mew herself].

Penelope Fitzgerald, *Charlotte Mew and her Friends*, 1984

Since Charlotte Mew is still not as well known as she should be, it is perhaps worth adding that she was an exceptionally fine poet.

Lord Alfred Douglas · 1870–1945

In a review reprinted in his collection Girls will be Girls, *Arthur Marshall discusses the memoirs of Christabel Lady Aberconway and her encounters with a variety of figures, most of them well known:*

SHUFFLING, with Osbert Sitwell, late into a theatre, 'I was given a fearful pinch on my left buttock. It was a savage pinch.' The culprit? Lord Alfred Douglas. Then a porter at Calais selected the same plump portion for a manly nip, and later on Thomas Hardy forgot himself before luncheon: 'He gave me a surprisingly strong, virile pinch, again on my left buttock: all three pinches have been on that side: I wonder why?' Of the three pinches, recollected in tranquillity, Lord Alfred's comes out as the sharpest. Blood will tell.

Arthur Marshall, *Girls will be Girls*, 1974

The writer Hugh Kingsmill first met Lord Alfred Douglas in Douglas's old age, when he was living in Hove:

THE first thing that struck me about Douglas was his looks. He is decidedly plain. I cannot imagine that even in his prime his nose can have meant much to connoisseurs. It has a curious cleft at the base, odd rather than pleasing. His eyes, hair, etc., have all lost their glow, and he is too restless and irritable to have acquired any of the dignity of age. In short, not at all impressive, and owing to a stoop he looks hardly more than low middle height—say five foot six—I suppose you would call five foot nine low middle . . .

The thing that appealed most to my imagination during the afternoon was our walk along the front. A bitter east wind; Douglas wizened and bowed; his nose jutting out from beneath his soft hat. If anyone had been told by God (he would not have accepted it from lesser authority) that one of these two men had been the handsomest man in England in his youth, he must have picked me out. We struggled along, left the promenade, and made for a bun shop to get some cakes for tea. I thought of the world-wide hurricane that had raged over Douglas, and here he was lamenting in the most ordinary tones that Wilde 'never could get any work done after he left Naples . . . You know he really did all his best work with me, all his comedies. Why, even *De Profundis* was written to me. By Jove, that never occurred to me before!' he laughed, 'when he wasn't with me he couldn't work except in the form of a letter to me. By Jove, I never thought of that before! He either had to have me with him, or if I wasn't there he couldn't do any work except . . .'

Best touch of all, which much endeared him to me, was as we neared the bun shop. I said something about [Frank] Harris having made out that Wilde was heartless. 'He was the kindest chap', said Douglas, 'the kindest chap'.

Hesketh Pearson and Malcolm Muggeridge, *About Kingsmill*, 1951

Hilaire Belloc · 1870–1953

Belloc and G. K. Chesterton were for many years inseparable literary companions. Bernard Shaw nicknamed them 'the Chesterbelloc':

At the great Requiem which was offered for Chesterton's soul in Westminster Cathedral, it was inevitably to Belloc that the newspaper cameras and reporters turned. In the course of the mass he managed to sell his exclusive obituary of Chesterton to no less than four different editors.

A. N. Wilson, *Hilaire Belloc*, 1984

Stephen Crane · 1871–1900

In 1897, while Crane was in Florida, rumours of his death reached his friend, the self-promoting journalist Elbert Hubbard:

Hubbard reported that Crane had drowned. '*He died trying to save others,*' said *The Philistine* [Hubbard's magazine] for February, 1897. In flamboyant sentiment Hubbard wrote: 'How he faced death the records do not say; but I know, for I knew the soul of the lad. Within the breast of that pale youth there dwelt a lion's heart. He held his life and reputation lightly. He sided with the weak, the ignorant, the unfortunate, and his strength and influence were ever given lavishly to those in need . . . So here's to you, Steve Crane, wherever you may be! You were not so very good, but you were as good as I am—better, in many ways—our faults were different, that's all. I don't know where you are, Stevie, and when I die I hope I will face Death as manfully as you did; and I hope, too, that I shall then go where you are now. And so, Stevie, good-bye and good-bye!'

When he had stayed with the Hubbards in December 1895, some woman—probably Hubbard's wife—had remarked: 'Stevie is not quite at home here—he'll not remain so very long.' But when Hubbard's *Philistine* announced Crane drowned, he was on dry land or wading the swamps of Florida. It was Hubbard himself who went to the bottom of the sea when the *Lusitania* sank on May 6, 1915. He went down manfully with his wife Alice, their arms linked when last seen by a survivor.

R. W. Stallman, *Stephen Crane*, 1968

Crane was living in England during the early stages of the Boer War:

Crane was critical of English smugness, their 'colossal serenity'. At Henry James's tea-party he also remarked upon the Boer situation: 'People tell me a couple of Guard regiments could whip them in a week.

When a Yankee says such things he is bragging, but I guess an Englishman is just lugging the truth out from some dark cave.'

Stallman, *Stephen Crane*

Theodore Dreiser · 1871–1945

Bennett Cerf recalls some dealings between Dreiser and his publisher Horace Liveright:

HORACE said, 'I'll make a deal with you, Dreiser. The first fifty thousand dollars I get for your book in Hollywood, you get complete. After that, we go fifty-fifty.'

Dreiser said, 'You won't get a dollar for it. Nobody will make that picture, Horace.'

Horace said, 'Watch me!'

So they shook hands. In those days fifty thousand dollars was a lot of money for movie rights. But Horace sold *American Tragedy* for eighty-five thousand dollars! When he came back, of course, Horace had to boast about his triumphs, and I was a very good person to tell, because I was always appreciative. So he called me up and said, 'What do you think I got for *American Tragedy*? Eighty-five thousand dollars! Wait till I tell Dreiser!'

I said, 'Gee, I'd like to be there.'

He said, 'I'm taking him to lunch next Thursday at the Ritz, and I'd like you to come and watch Dreiser when I tell him.'

So the three of us went to the Ritz. The main dining room had a balcony all the way around it, a few steps above the main part of the restaurant, and we had a table on the balcony right next to the railing.

Dreiser said, 'What do you want with me, Liveright?'

Horace was very coy. He said, 'Now, now, we'll have our lunch.'

Dreiser was getting grumpier. 'What have you got to tell me?'

Finally after we had finished our meal, before the coffee came, Horace said, 'Dreiser, I sold *American Tragedy*.'

Dreiser said, 'Oh, come on.'

Horace said, 'I did.'

Finally Dreiser said, 'Well, what did you get for it?'

Horace said, 'Eighty-five thousand dollars.'

It took a few moments for this to sink in, and then Dreiser let out a cry of triumph. He exulted, 'What I'm going to do with that money!' He took a pencil out of his pocket and began writing on the tablecloth. He said, 'I'm going to pay off the mortgage on my place up in Croton and I'm going to get an automobile,' and so on.

Horace listened for a minute, then reminded Dreiser, 'You know, you're not getting the whole eighty-five thousand. Remember our deal? You get fifty and then we split the thirty-five. You're going to get sixty-seven thousand, five hundred.'

Dreiser put down his pencil and looked at Liveright. He said, 'Do you mean to tell me you're going to take seventeen thousand, five hundred dollars of *my* money?'

Horace said, 'Dreiser, that was the deal we made. You didn't think I'd sell your book at all.'

Just at this moment the waiter brought the coffee in. Suddenly Dreiser seized his cup and threw the steaming coffee in Liveright's face. It was shocking. Horace jumped up, coffee streaming down his shirt front. Luckily it didn't hit him in the eyes. Dreiser got up from the table without a word and marched out of the restaurant. Horace, always the showman, always gallant, stood there mopping himself up, and retained enough of his equilibrium to say, 'Bennett, let this be a lesson to you. Every author is a son of a bitch.'

Bennett Cerf, *At Random*, 1977

J. M. Synge · 1871–1909

As a young man Synge lived in Paris, working intermittently as a freelance journalist. His closest friend there was his fellow Irishman Stephen MacKenna, the translator of Plotinus:

Both Synge and MacKenna were distressingly hard up. 'How do those two young men live?' said an inquisitive person. 'Oh, Synge lives on what MacKenna lends him, and MacKenna lives on what Synge pays him back.'

E. R. Dodds, preface to *Journal and Letters of Stephen MacKenna*, 1936

I remember asking him what sensations an author had when his play was being performed for the first time. 'I sit still in my box,' he said, 'and curse the actors.'

John Masefield, *Synge: A Few Personal Recollections*, 1915

When Synge's masterpiece, The Playboy of the Western World, *was first presented by the Abbey Theatre in Dublin in 1907, it aroused fierce controversy. Nationalist critics condemned it as immoral and unpatriotic; there were riots in the theatre and angry exchanges in the press. Subsequently the Abbey took it on tour in America. Here, too, there were violent demonstrations:*

But the determination of the Abbey directors in continuing to present the play eventually succeeded. The quality of the play was slowly recognised, and by now none of the objections once so loudly proclaimed seem valid. Indeed, no one seemed to find it either surprising or even amusing that when the Abbey company, in 1968, had a special audience with the Pope, they presented him with a rare edition, bound in white leather, of the play which once caused riots: *The Playboy of the Western World.*

James Kilroy, *The 'Playboy' Riots*, 1971

Sir Max Beerbohm · 1872–1956

One of the earliest anecdotes about Beerbohm to become widely known featured his brother, the famous actor Herbert Beerbohm Tree (who was some twenty years his senior). Interviewed by a fashionable magazine when he was only 22, Max was asked what work he was engaged on at the time, and replied that he was writing a set of psychological sketches of the brothers of great men. 'You are a brother of Mr Beerbohm Tree, I believe,' observed the interviewer. 'Yes,' said Max, 'he is coming into the series.'

The joke shouldn't give anyone the wrong idea. Beerbohm admired his brother enormously, and cherished his idiosyncrasies:

Of his shrewdness wrapped in vagueness I can give an example that befell me one day while I was staying with him in Hampstead. He asked meditatively what I intended to *be*. I reminded him that I was going to the Bar. 'Ah . . . the Bar . . . You at the Bar . . . I should have thought you'd better be a—a sort of writer, and then, perhaps' he added, 'drift into Diplomacy.' This was merely his way of saying what the average man would have said thus: 'You haven't a single one of the qualities that make for success at the Bar. But I fancy you might do well in journalism.' Or more likely the average man would have advised me to cultivate the acquaintance of solicitors, and would *not* (as I hadn't ever attempted to write anything) have guessed that I had a bent for writing. The delightful touch about 'drifting' into the Diplomatic Service was added merely to please himself and me.

'From A Brother's Viewpoint', in *Herbert Beerbohm Tree*, by Max Beerbohm and others, 1920

In 1909 Beerbohm attended a memorial service for George Meredith in Westminster Abbey:

As he came out of the Abbey a girl approached him. 'Oh, Mr Barrie,' she said, 'can I have your autograph?' 'I felt a devil rising in me that I could not resist,' related Max. 'I took her book and wrote in it, "Aye, lassie, it's a sad day the noo, J. M. B." '

David Cecil, *Max*, 1964

Compton Mackenzie visited Beerbohm in Rapallo in 1913:

Max Beerbohm's own exquisite aquatints in prose of the visits he had paid to various great men might induce in the most confident writer a sense of presumption in venturing to record a visit to him. I remember with a qualm of self-reproach that on this very visit Max told me that his last hours would be haunted by the fancy of the good story that would be fathered on him by the paragraph gossips on the morning of his obituary notice. 'Mr Max Beerbohm, whose regrettable demise is chronicled this morning, will perhaps always be best remembered for the following story . . .' he antequoted with an urbane shudder. And then would be set down, for ever indisputable, some horribly pointless anecdote for which the wretched author was never responsible and never could have been responsible, or some base coin of wit he would have scorned to pass. And I, who have now lived long enough as a speck of dust in the public eye to read such anecdotes about myself, can appreciate that macabre anticipation in which Max indulged fifty-one years ago. Shall all my labours end in finding myself best remembered for a bad pun I never made?

Compton Mackenzie, *My Life and Times: Octave Four*, 1965

In 1936 Beerbohm and his wife spent two months living in rented rooms in Bloomsbury. He disliked many of the intellectual attitudes which had come to be associated with the area; even though he hadn't greatly enjoyed his time at Charterhouse, he was particularly irritated by Bloomsbury's automatic hostility to 'the Old School Tie':

It had never occurred to me to exercise my right to wear such a tie. But now, here, in the heart of Bloomsbury, I felt that I would belatedly do so, and I went to my hosier and ordered two Old Carthusian ties. Do you know the colours? They are three: bright crimson, salmon pink, and royal blue. They are dangerous to the appearance of even a quite young man. To that of an old man they are utterly disastrous. Nevertheless, I, without faltering, wore one of my pair until my sojourn in Bloomsbury came to its end.

'From Bloomsbury to Bayswater', 1942 (in *Mainly on the Air*)

Bertrand Russell · 1872–1970

One evening, when he was only 17, Russell found himself left tête-à-tête *with Mr Gladstone:*

He came to stay at Pembroke Lodge, and nobody was asked to meet him. As I was the only male in the household, he and I were left alone together at the dining-table after the ladies had retired. He made only one remark: 'This is very good port they have given me, but why have they given it me in a claret glass?' I did not know the answer, and wished the earth would swallow me up. Since then I have never again felt the full agony of terror.

Bertrand Russell, *Autobiography*, vol. i, 1967

In 1910 Russell and Alfred North Whitehead completed Principia Mathematica*:*

IT was not, of course, the sort of manuscript that could be typed, or even copied. When we finally took it to the University Press, it was so large that we had to hire an old four-wheeler for the purpose. Even then our difficulties were not at an end. The University Press estimated that there would be a loss of £600 on the book, and while the syndics were willing to bear a loss of £300 they did not feel they could go above this figure. The Royal Society very generously contributed £200, and the remaining £100 we had to find ourselves. We thus earned minus £50 each by ten years' work. This beats the record of *Paradise Lost*.

Russell, *Autobiography*, vol. i

HE seemed always on the prowl when attractive and vivacious young women were around, and he assumed that my interest in extracurricular matrimonial activity was as keen as his own. On occasions I was rendered speechless by his unsolicited advice on how to 'make' a girl and what to do after one made her. 'Hook,' he once advised, 'if you ever take a girl to a hotel and the reception clerk seems suspicious, when he gives you the price of the room have her complain loudly, "It's *much* too expensive!" He's sure to assume she is your wife . . .'

Sidney Hook, *Out of Step*, 1987

LEAST of all to Russell's taste [among the work of younger British philosophers] was the fashion which J. L. Austin spread at Oxford, in the late 1940s and throughout the 1950s, of treating philosophy as the meticulous investigation of ordinary linguistic usage . . . Russell was quite incapable of seeing any merit in 'ordinary language philosophy' and did not even try to take it seriously. Thus in a paper on the subject which he read to the Metalogical Society he pointed out that when a charwoman says 'I ain't never done no harm to nobody', she does not mean 'There is at least one moment at which I was injuring the entire human race.'

A. J. Ayer, *More of my Life*, 1984

Ford Madox Ford · 1873–1939

Ford looks back at his time as editor of the English Review *from 1908 to 1910. (The Miss Thomas to whom he refers was his secretary; 'Ezra' was Ezra Pound.)*

To some extent that undertaking had justified its existence for me. It had got together, at any rate between its covers, a great number—the majority—of the distinguished writers of imaginative literature in England of that day and a great many foreign writers of distinction. It had been quite impossible to get the distinguished to come together in person. The attractions of their hilltops and attendant worshippers were too overpowering. Conrad came and stayed for several days with me on several occasions, but he always managed to be out at tea-time, in case anyone literary should come in. James always rang up on the telephone before coming to see me, so as to make sure of meeting no writers—and so it went down the list. I think that only one contributor to my first two numbers did not tell me that the *Review* was ruined by the inclusion of all the other contributors. James said: 'Poor old Meredith, he writes these mysterious nonsenses and heaven alone knows what they all mean.' Meredith had contributed merely a very short account of his dislike for Rossetti's breakfast manners. It was quite as comprehensible as a seedsman's catalogue.

Meredith said on looking at James's *Jolly Corner* which led off the prose of the review:

'Poor old James. He sets down on paper these mysterious rumblings in his bowels—but who could be expected to understand them?' So they went on.

With the younger writers it was different. They crowded my office drawing-room, they quarrelled, they shouted. They attended on me like body-guards when I took my walks abroad. I remember only one dull moment.

Most beautifully and incredibly wealthy ladies who liked to look up to those spirited young creatures and ask them to their dances used to crowd my office. It was rather a handsome large drawing-room in an old house. There were pictures by Pre-Raphaelites, old furniture, a rather wonderful carpet. The room was lit from both ends and L-shaped so that if you wanted a moment's private conversation with anyone you could go round the corner. Miss Thomas, large, very blonde and invariably good-tempered, presided over the tea-table. Ezra looked after the cakes.

On the dull occasion nothing would go. I had a red-purple velvet divan. It was the gift of my mother, so I had to display it. But it was a startling object. On it sat three young men as dumb as mile-stones.

Thomas Hardy remained for the whole afternoon round the corner of that L talking in low tones to the wife of the Bishop of Edinburgh.

The rest of the room was occupied by beautiful creatures who had come specially to hear Thomas Hardy and those young men. The young men sat side by side on that egregious divan. Their legs were stretched out, their ankles were clothed, as to the one pair in emerald green socks, as to the next in vermilion and as to the next in electric blue. Merely to look in the direction of that divan was to have a pain in the eyes. The young men kept their hands deep in their trouser-pockets and appeared to meditate suicide. Ezra did not even eat any cakes.

He had the tooth-ache. Next to him was Gilbert Cannan: he had just been served with papers in a disagreeable action. Next to Cannan was Mr Hugh Walpole. He had just published a particularly admirable novel called *Mr Perrin and Mr Traill.* But he was suffering agonies of fear lest his charming mother, who was the wife of the Bishop of Edinburgh and hidden round the corner, might hear something that should shock her. I think myself that humorous lady, taking a swallow's flight into Bohemia, would have liked to be a little shocked.

Return to Yesterday, 1931

G. K. Chesterton · 1874–1936

One of Chesterton's publishers was The Bodley Head:

Chesterton's appearance one evening, after office hours, at Vigo Street with some corrected proofs rapidly became an office legend. Greeted at the door, after much unbolting, by the sole remaining member of the staff (an accountant, no doubt under stress) Chesterton, still on the steps, produced from his Gladstone bag not only his proofs but a bottle of port and a glass, only to be told that the accountant was a teetotaller. 'Good heavens,' Chesterton is reported to have said in a dismayed falsetto, 'give me back my proofs!'

J. W. Lambert and Michael Ratcliffe, *The Bodley Head*, 1987

In 1921 Chesterton visited America for the first time:

The lights on Broadway evoked from him the exclamation: 'What a glorious garden of wonders this would be for anyone who was lucky enough to be unable to read.'

Maisie Ward, *Chesterton*, 1944

Gertrude Stein · 1874–1946

When the First World War broke out Gertrude Stein and her companion Alice B. Toklas were staying in Cambridge (England) with the philosopher Alfred North Whitehead and his wife Evelyn. The Whiteheads supported the war, and their son North enlisted almost at once.

One of the many visitors who came to see them at this time was Bertrand Russell:

He was a pacifist and argumentative and although they were very old friends Doctor and Mrs Whitehead did not think they could bear hearing his views just then. He came and Gertrude Stein, to divert everybody's mind from the burning question of war or peace, introduced the subject of education. This caught Russell and he explained all the weaknesses of the american system of education, particularly their neglect of the study of greek. Gertrude Stein replied that of course England which was an island needed Greece which was or might have been an island. At any rate greek was essentially an island culture, while America needed essentially the culture of a continent which was of necessity latin. This argument fussed Mr Russell, he became very eloquent. Gertrude Stein then became very earnest and gave a long discourse on the value of greek to the english, aside from its being an island, and the lack of value of greek culture for the americans based upon the psychology of americans as different from the psychology of the english. She grew very eloquent on the disembodied abstract quality of the american character and cited examples, mingling automobiles with Emerson, and all proving that they did not need greek, in a way that fussed Russell more and more and kept everybody occupied until everybody went to bed.

Gertrude Stein, *The Autobiography of Alice B. Toklas*, 1933

Gertrude Stein's final illness reached a stage at which the doctors no longer felt that surgery was advisable, on account of her weakened condition:

A young surgeon was called in, and Gertrude told him bluntly, 'I order you to operate. I was not made to suffer.' It was the choice she made.

The operation was scheduled for the afternoon of July 27. Alice [her companion, Alice B. Toklas] waited anxiously beside Gertrude's bed—Gertrude was already under heavy sedation. She turned to Alice and murmured, 'What is the answer?' Alice, unable to answer, remained silent. Gertrude said, 'In that case, what is the question?' The afternoon, Alice remembered, was 'troubled, confused, and very uncertain.' Then the orderlies arrived and Gertrude was wheeled down the long corridor.

In the course of the operation, what was suspected proved to be true;

Gertrude had inoperable cancer. At about 5.30 in the evening, she lapsed into a coma. Doctors worked on her for an hour. At 6.30, she was pronounced dead.

Knowledge had been her province. During the long years of the German occupation, she had drawn a valuable lesson from life. 'You have to learn to do everything,' she observed, 'even to die.'

James R. Mellow, *Charmed Circle: Gertrude Stein & Company*, 1974

Sir Winston Churchill · 1874–1965

FINDING that he liked poetry I quoted to him from one of my own favourite poets, Blake. He listened avidly, repeating some lines to himself with varying emphases and stresses, then added meditatively: 'I never knew that that old Admiral had found the time to write so much good poetry.'

Violet Bonham Carter, *Winston Churchill as I Knew Him*, 1965

Violet Bonham Carter took it for granted that her readers would recognize that the admiral with whom Churchill had confused the poet was Robert Blake, hero of the first of the seventeenth-century wars between England and the Dutch.

In 1910 Churchill was about to become Home Secretary. One of his concerns was that inmates in prisons should be provided with plenty of reading matter:

I ASKED what books he thought they would enjoy and he trotted out several old favourites from his first days of self-education at Bangalore headed by Gibbon and Macaulay. I expressed some doubts about the popularity of his list. 'If you had just committed murder would you feel inclined to read Gibbon?' 'Well, the stern and speedy process of the Law might place a noose around my neck and string me up before I had time to launch myself on that broad stream. But for robbery with violence, arson, rape . . .' Here followed a long inventory of crimes well fitted to whet the appetite of their authors for Gibbon. I said that I would rather be hanged than endure a life-sentence. He vehemently disagreed. 'Never abandon life. There is a way out of everything—except death.' He was obviously confident of finding his way out of a life-sentence and I daresay he was right. I quoted Dickens, 'Life is given us on the understanding that we defend it to the last.' He liked that and repeated it to himself. ' "Defend it to the last"—I'd do it. So would you. What is it you once called yourself—"red in tooth and claw"? I like to see you plunge your claws—those delicate and rosy claws—into the vitals of a foe.' 'It wasn't my phrase, it was Tennyson's.' 'Never read him. Should I like his books?' 'Not much I think, nor would the criminals.'

Bonham Carter, *Winston Churchill as I Knew Him*

Robert Frost · 1874–1963

In 1935 Frost visited Santa Fe, where the poet Witter Binner gave a large lunch for him at his home:

Frost arrived late, annoying Binner from the outset. A tense discussion soon followed over a recent book of poetry by Horatio Colony, one of Binner's Harvard classmates. The book was full of thinly veiled celebrations of homosexuality—a subject that Frost found distasteful. Binner praised the book as one of the best things he had read since first encountering A. E. Housman (another poet whose work had a vivid strain of homoeroticism). This comment insulted Frost, and in his impish vein he pretended that he, too, was a great admirer of Colony's book; indeed, he asked to read one of his favourite poems aloud. Binner was briefly deceived and passed the book to Frost, who read an obviously charged passage in which the implications of the poem were clear. Frost then teased Binner by saying that he was 'too young and innocent to understand such verse'. Seeing that he had been had, Binner exploded, pouring a whole mug of beer over Frost's snowy head. Far from recoiling, Frost actually enjoyed Binner's outburst and remained calm and smiling; he had made his point and provoked a scene. As a friend later remarked, 'Robert took great pleasure in setting the cat among the pigeons . . .'

Jay Parini, *Robert Frost*, 1998

interviewer. But when you read Stevens, for example, do you find anything that is familiar to you from your own poetry?

frost. Wallace Stevens? He was years after me.

interviewer. I mean in your reading of him, whether or not you felt any—

frost. Any affinity, you mean? Oh, you couldn't say that. No. Once he said to me, 'You write on subjects.' And I said, 'You write on bric-a-brac.' And when he sent me his next book he'd written 'S'more bric-a-brac' in it. Just took it good-naturedly. No, I had no affinity with him. We were friends.

Writers at Work: The Paris Review *Interviews*, second series, 1963

In 1957, while visiting Britain, Frost gave an address at the University of London:

NOTICING that T. S. Eliot was sitting in the third row, Frost made a witty remark about poets who give up their citizenship. 'I can understand how someone of another nationality might wish to become an American,' he said, 'but I could never see how an American chose to become, for instance—a Canadian.' This produced laughter all around, even from Eliot. The long-running rivalry between Eliot and Frost had mellowed considerably over the years, largely because Eliot consistently refused to notice it. 'Eliot was peculiarly without interest in this sort of battle,' recalled Stephen Spender. 'He quite admired Frost, although he considered him so very American, especially in his competitiveness.'

Parini, *Robert Frost*

In December 1960 Frost agreed to read a poem at the inauguration of John F. Kennedy as president:

KENNEDY telephoned Frost in Cambridge to discuss what he might read at the ceremony, gingerly suggesting that he write a poem especially for the occasion. The poet quickly dismissed the president-elect's notion: 'Oh, that could never happen,' he said. Kennedy followed with another suggestion: How about his reading 'The Gift Outright,' changing the last line from 'such as she would become' to 'such as she will become,' making it a bit more optimistic and emphatic. 'I suppose so,' Frost responded, hesitantly. Even a president-elect should not tamper with his work . . .

In the event Frost did write a new poem, 'Dedication', which was meant to serve as a preamble to 'The Gift Outright', and on the day of the ceremony, 20 January 1960, he was called forward just ahead of Kennedy's swearing in:

HE ambled slowly to the podium, then fumbled for a while with his manuscript; at last, haltingly, he began to read his 'Dedication' but the light struck the page in such a way that he could not see, and he said, 'I'm having trouble with this.' The new vice president [Lyndon B. Johnson] tried to help by shielding the page with his top hat, but Frost brushed him aside with a joke. He then delighted the audience by launching into 'The Gift Outright', which he declaimed by heart. He ended magnificently, dragging out the last line: 'Such as she was, such as she *would* become, *has* become, and I—and for this occasion let me change that to—what she *will* become.'

Parini, *Robert Frost*

W. Somerset Maugham · 1874–1965

On Maugham's eightieth birthday he was given a dinner in his honour by the Garrick Club, in the course of which he addressed the assembled guests:

He spoke the customary salutations, paused for a moment and said, 'There are many . . . virtues in . . . growing old.' He paused, he swallowed, he wet his lips, he looked about. The pause stretched out, he looked dumbstruck. The pause became too long—far too long. He looked down, studying the tabletop. A terrible tremor of nervousness went through the room. Was he ill? Would he ever be able to get on with it? Finally he looked up and said, 'I'm just . . . trying . . . to think what they are!'

Garson Kanin, *Remembering Mr Maugham*, 1966

For many years Maugham was on notoriously bad terms with his daughter Liza, Lady Glendevon:

A story about WSM and Liza and her husband made the rounds some years ago. I heard it a dozen times from different people, each time in a slightly different mutation.

This is how he himself told it to us:

'Liza came down here with John a while ago. They had an idea—rather brilliant, actually—of how to avoid excessive . . . death duties. I like John. He's not only intelligent, but wise. The scheme involved . . . turning over much of my estate now. I would retain use of it, you see, but legal provision would have been made for its . . . transfer. I declined. And when Liza asked, "But why won't you, Pa?" I said, "Because, my dear, I have . . . read *King Lear*." We all had a good laugh over that.'

Kanin, *Remembering Mr Maugham*

When Kanin's book appeared it carried an erratum slip which was pasted in alongside this story—a quotation from a letter which he had received from Lady Glendevon: 'This episode is entirely without foundation: the reported conversation never took place. When I learned that my father was telling this story I remonstrated with him. He admitted to me that it was an invention with the words, "Never mind dear it makes a good story." '

Willa Cather · 1876–1947

(novelist; her books include *My Ántonia* and *Death Comes for the Archbishop*)

After graduating from the University of Nebraska, in the city of Lincoln, Willa Cather described herself as 'dead tired, body and brain'. She had combined her studies with working as a columnist and theatre critic for the local paper, the Nebraska State Journal*:*

After her day at the University she would spend the evening at the theatre, then go over to the *Journal* office and write her review of the play, getting home at one or two o'clock in the morning. Her first meeting with Stephen Crane took place on one of these occasions. He was on his way to the Coast, and dropped into the *Journal* office one night about midnight. He was fascinated by the sight of a young girl—Willa Cather—standing *fast asleep*. He said it was the only time he had ever seen anyone asleep on their feet like that.

Edith Lewis, *Willa Cather Living*, 1953

Edith Lewis, who records this incident, was Willa Cather's close companion for many years. Oddly enough Cather herself makes no mention of it in her vivid account of her conversations with Crane while he was in Lincoln, 'When I Knew Stephen Crane' (1900).

John Masefield · 1878–1967

Masefield was Poet Laureate for thirty-seven years, from 1930 until his death. During this period he wrote innumerable poems marking royal occasions or significant public events, all of them designed to appear in The Times *on the day in question:*

J.M. did not take publication for granted. After his death *The Times* revealed that with each manuscript he sent a stamped addressed envelope so that it could be returned if not acceptable.

Constance Babington-Smith, *John Masefield*, 1978

E. M. Forster · 1879–1970

In 1908 Forster went on holiday to Italy with a young Cambridge don, Victor Woolley. In Mantua they ran into another Cambridge friend, the musicologist E. J. Dent, who was sitting at a café table with two Italian officers:

They joined the party, and Forster made efforts at conversation, in Italian, which went as follows:

FORSTER. Lei è stato in Inghilterra? [Have you ever been to England?]
LIEUTENANT. Mai. Ma l'anno prossimo vengo—scusa! ecco una donna bellissima che passa . . . [Never. But I am coming next year—excuse me! there's the most beautiful woman just going by . . .]
MAJOR. Una donna francese, credo. [She's French, I think.]
LIEUTENANT. Francese—Italiana—Tedesca—a me lo stesso. [French—Italian—German—it's all the same to me.]
WOOLLEY. What's he saying?
DENT. He has seen a beautiful lady.
WOOLLEY. Oh, I see.
LIEUTENANT (to Forster). Ma scusa tanto! Cosa diceva? [I do beg your pardon. What were you saying?]
FORSTER. Lei non è stato in Inghil . . . [You have never been to Eng . . .]
LIEUTENANT (grasping him affectionately by the wrist). Ecco un'altra! Non mi piace tanto. È un' po borghese. [There's another! But I don't like her so much. Too middle-class.]
WOOLLEY (to Dent). Had not your Italian friend better change places with me? Then he will be able to see the passers-by without turning round in his seat. It is a pity I should have such a good position when I do not value it.

Dent passed the suggestion on; there were cries, protests and clankings of spurs, and everyone rose to their feet; then they all sat down again in the same places.

P. N. Furbank, *E. M. Forster: A Life*, vol. i, 1977

Forster joined forces with Virginia Woolf to protest against the legal suppression of Radclyffe Hall's lesbian novel The Well of Loneliness*:*

At about this time, he went down for a weekend with the Woolfs in Sussex, and, prompted by the *Well* affair, the conversation turned to male and female homosexuality. Forster told the Woolfs that a certain Doctor Head claimed to be able to 'convert' homosexuals. 'And would you like to be converted?' asked Leonard. 'No,' said Forster, without hesitation. From this they got on to lesbianism. He and Virginia were both a little tipsy, and with a queer burst of frankness he told her he found it disgusting—partly out of conventionality, and partly because he 'disliked the idea of women being independent of men'. Virginia was not outraged. Indeed, this weekend, they were unusually in harmony, and to her diary she confided that he was 'timid, touchy, infinitely charming'.

P. N. Furbank, *E. M. Forster: A Life*, vol. ii, 1978

Forster turned down a knighthood, telling his friends that 'it wasn't good enough for him', but in 1952 he accepted the offer of a Companionship of Honour:

THE award was announced in the New Year's Honours for 1953, and he went to Buckingham Palace for the investiture the following month. It was quite a lengthy audience, in the course of which the Queen said how sad it was he had published no book for so long—upon which he politely corrected her. As he left, he brandished the insignia to an equerry, exclaiming brightly 'Well, I got my little toy,' and was received with freezing glances. They failed to chill him, and he returned to Cambridge in a glow of loyalty, declaring that if the Queen had been a boy he would have fallen in love with her.

Furbank, *Forster: A Life*, vol. ii

SHORT sight was a difficulty, and he is said to have bowed gravely to a wedding cake when his friend Lord Harewood, the Queen's cousin, married, under the impression that it was Queen Mary. But then it was a natural mistake.

George Watson, 'Forever Forster', *Hudson Review*, 2003

In the 1950s Forster began to enjoy what his biographer calls 'a period of idolization':

HIS friends were not all so reverent. Lord Kennet reported an exchange between Forster and Percy Lubbock in 1955.

LUBBOCK. It's too funny your becoming the holy man of letters. You're really a spiteful old thing. Why haven't people found you out, and run you down?
FORSTER (cheerfully): They're beginning.

Furbank, *Forster: A Life*, vol. ii

Wallace Stevens · 1879–1955

Stevens worked for an insurance company in Hartford, Connecticut, eventually becoming vice-president. Not everyone there was fond of him—his assistant Walter Downs, for instance:

He worked for Wallace for many years. Stevens had a lot of respect for Downs, but he didn't like him and he mistreated him badly—let's say salary and things like that. He was tough on him, and Walter Downs hated him with a passion. In fact, he made remark that he could think of nothing he'd rather do than go to his funeral.

E. A. Cowie in Peter Brazeau, *Parts of a World: Wallace Stevens Remembered*, 1983

My father-in-law [the late Ivan Daugherty, who worked under Stevens as a bond lawyer for twenty-five years] said once that he was not a friend of Stevens because Stevens didn't have any friends. But he called himself an intimate: he was as close to him as Stevens was to anybody. And I think he rather enjoyed that.

Stevens would confide in my father-in-law. Stevens and his wife had a terrible row once. She was so angry that she threw something at him. Stevens came into work and said, 'Doc, I just don't understand women. I don't know what to do. What do you think I should do?' My father-in-law told him, 'Why don't you go home, put down your briefcase, put your arms around her, and tell her you love her? Buy her a bunch of roses and send them to her.' 'What the hell for?' He was puzzled, but he said, 'All right, I'll do it.' Apparently it did the trick, because he came into work afterward and said, 'Gee, I don't understand that, but it worked.' That story sticks because I remember thinking at the time, Here's this tremendously sensitive man, and the idea of showing his wife a little appreciation or affection comes as 'Gee, how come it worked? How come she was happy about these flowers?'

Lilian Daugherty in Brazeau, *Parts of a World*

Stevens was very conscientious about coming up for the Visiting Committee meetings [at Harvard] though in the questioning of the department he never said anything. He was one of the appointed members; we always had some writers and scholars. On one occasion, after dinner and after the speeches and questions at the Harvard Club, we adjourned to the rathskeller. A relatively small group, two or three people in the department and Stevens. He was really very glad to have a stiff drink or two. I have the impression that because of his shyness, he sometimes relied on this to break the ice. At any rate, he then began to talk, and he told us one or two smoking-car stories. They wouldn't be considered anything today, but in those days they might have been considered slightly risqué. My colleague Walter Jackson Bate was there. He'd always had a very good sense of humor, but with each joke he grew grimmer. Stevens finally said, 'I'm afraid I'm not amusing you, Mr Bate.' And Bate, who was then very much the *enfant terrible* of the department, said, 'You'll have to be funnier than that to make me laugh, Stevens!' Poor Stevens was quite humiliated, got very red, and stopped talking.

Harry Levin in Brazeau, *Parts of a World*

Walter Jackson Bate's books included an outstanding biography of Dr Johnson.

Frieda Lawrence · 1879–1956

In 1932, two years after D. H. Lawrence's death, Frieda, who was visiting London, was invited to lunch by Bernard Shaw and his wife:

FROM their spacious apartment you could see through the big windows the boats and barges going past on the Thames. For lunch there were several people: Lady S., a feminist, and a famous bookseller and another man, I think a general. We had chicken for lunch, but Shaw, who sat beside me, only had vegetables. A footman waited on us, we had wine, but Shaw did not. On the way to the lunch in the taxi I had said to myself: 'Now look out and don't make a fool of yourself for Lawrence's sake. Shaw is too clever for you.'

Lawrence and Shaw were such worlds apart. Shaw and Lady S. talked about a Welsh miner who had just written a book. 'Do they put Lawrence on the same level with this man?' I thought. Then Lady S. asked me: 'Don't you think we all like to belong to a class, Mrs Lawrence?' Class? after all I had married a miner's son. 'No,' I told her, 'I would like to be a Hottentot.' 'I think you are an aristocrat,' said Shaw to me.

Suddenly Shaw turned to me: 'Is it true that you broke a plate over your husband's head?'

'Yes, it is true.'

'What did you do that for?'

'Lawrence had said to me women had no souls and couldn't love. So I broke a plate over his head.'

This Shaw thought over. Such a quick, violent response was alien to his make-up.

Then he asked about the ranch in New Mexico. I told them about the cabins high up among the pines, we only had horses and a buggy, and how Lawrence milked the cow Susan and looked after the chickens and split the wood for the stove and the big fireplace that he had built with the help of the Indians. How we had no civilised comforts and how wild and far away from everything the place was and how we loved it. He listened and said: 'And that man wrote.' I wanted to say: 'Yes, but not like you,' but didn't. Then they both said: 'We will visit you at the ranch.' But that never happened.

After lunch I told Mrs Shaw: 'I am so glad to meet you.'

She opened her eyes wide: 'Me, they always want to meet Shaw.'

I laughed: 'I also have been a writer's wife, I know.'

There was such a wonderfully free atmosphere about, you were sure that nothing you said or did would shock or surprise them. If you had suddenly turned a somersault they would have taken it along with the rest. Because of this freedom Shaw and Lawrence might have liked each other, I am sorry they never met.

I am glad I had lunch with the Shaws.

Frieda Lawrence: The Memoirs and Correspondence, ed. E. W. Tedlock, 1961

Lytton Strachey · 1880–1932

A major Bloomsbury royalty at that time was Lytton Strachey; I knew him but slightly. He made the impression on me of the benevolent demons in the Russian ballet *Children's Tales*—a demon with a long beard of gardener's bass, and a head which existed only in profile. He seemed to have been cut out of rather thin cardboard. He wasted no words. A young and robustious friend of ours, meeting him at a party, said 'you don't remember me, Mr Strachey. We met four years ago.' 'Quite a nice interval, I think, don't you?' Mr Strachey remarked, pleasantly, and passed on.

Edith Sitwell in *Coming to London*, ed. John Lehmann, 1957

Strachey's sister Pippa helped to look after him during his last illness:

He thought about literature, not so much about people: He talked of Shelley's youth; and with deep satisfaction, he would recite lines of poetry:

Lorsque le grand Byron avait quitté Ravenne . . .

It was the music of such lines, a river of sound, that soothed him. He also tried to compose poems of his own. 'But it's so difficult,' he sighed. 'Poetry is so very difficult.'

'Don't think about poetry,' Pippa advised him, 'it's too tiring. Think of nice simple solid things—think about teapots and chairs.'

'But I don't *know* anything about teapots and chairs.'

'Well,' replied Pippa, 'think of people playing croquet, moving quietly about on a summer lawn.'

Lytton seemed pleased. 'Ah yes, that's nice.' Then a pause. 'But I don't remember *any* reference to croquet in French literature.'

Michael Holroyd, *Lytton Strachey*, 1994

H. L. Mencken · 1880–1956

(journalist and controversialist; author of *The American Language*)

Charles Angoff describes office life with Mencken:

The office telephone rang and I answered it. 'Miss Edna Ferber calling,' I said.

Mencken spat into the brass spittoon, wiped his mouth, and picked up the telephone on his own desk. 'The great critic, H. L. Mencken, talking. Sure, good idea [he always pronounced this word with the accent on the first syllable]. Certainly. Be glad to honor your house with my presence. White tie or black? Say, Edna, do you mind if I bring along some of my colored relatives? Well, you know, in the South, it's like in Hollywood, everybody is related. Are you still as pretty as you used to be? I'll never forget the Jewish meal we had . . . oh, pardon, I guess I mixed you up. Well, anyway, it was a good Jewish meal I once had. Lovely, lovely. I'll take a bath, too, and I'll bring along my store teeth. Goodbye, and much obliged.'

He turned to the bottles again, spat into the spittoon, unwrapped another bottle, and continued: 'Now, look at this, Highland Scot. No telling what these bootleggers will bring next. I asked for some Scotch and they give me this. Isn't it lovely? Angoff, what looks better, President Abbott Lawrence Lowell of Harvard or this beautiful bottle?'

'The bottle, by far.'

'Remind me to give you an honorary LL.D.'

Charles Angoff, *H. L. Mencken: A Portrait from Memory*, 1956

Angoff, who was a Harvard graduate—hence the crack about Abbott Lawrence Lowell—served under Mencken as assistant editor of the American Mercury. *He initially hero-worshipped him, but later came to resent him: the 'portrait from memory' which he published after Mencken's death is unmistakably hostile, but probably closer to the truth than Mencken's admirers would like to admit.*

On another occasion Mencken tried to persuade Angoff that when a 'Babbitt' gave money to a hospital or medical foundation, the spirit of Babbittry invariably crept in:

'Why, we could have had syphilis licked ages ago if it weren't for this

Babbitt money. The Babbitts don't want syphilis licked. They want people to suffer for their so-called sins.'

'But don't Babbitts sin themselves?' I asked.

'Sure, they do. But always with a crying conscience, and so their sinning has no pleasure. Ever been to bed with a minister's wife?'

'No.'

'Then you don't know what conscience can do to mess up a bed.'

'Did you ever go to bed with a minister's wife?' I asked.

'Hell, no. Think I'm crazy?'

Angoff, *H. L. Mencken*

Clive Bell · 1881–1964

(author of *Civilization* and other books; husband of Vanessa Bell, brother-in-law of Virginia Woolf)

As a 16-year-old Richard Kennedy worked for Leonard and Virginia Woolf at the Hogarth Press, and got to know other members of the Bloomsbury group. On one occasion he played in a cricket match in which several of them took part:

David Garnett gave us a very agreeable welcome and fed us beer and sandwiches. We went to the pavilion where Clive Bell was holding forth about cricket being like a ballet . . . He approached the crease rather like Serge Lifar. He made a ridiculous sort of cow shot at the first ball, was lucky to connect and scored a boundary, but when he was stumped he started to argue with the umpire in the most unsportsmanlike manner, making all sorts of allusions to Japanese literature.

Richard Kennedy, *A Boy at the Hogarth Press*, 1972

P. G. Wodehouse · 1881–1975

The first distinguished writer I remember meeting after Swinburne was P. G. Wodehouse, a friend of my brother Perceval, whom he later gently caricatured as 'Ukridge'. Wodehouse was then in his early twenties, on the staff of *The Globe* and writing school stories for *The Captain* magazine. He gave me a penny, advising me to get marshmallows with it. Though too shy to express my gratitude at the time, I have never since permitted myself to be critical about his work.

Robert Graves, *Goodbye to All That*, 1929

I FIND it curious, now that I have written so much about him, to recall how softly and undramatically Jeeves entered my little world . . . On that occasion, he spoke just two lines.

The first was:

'Mrs Gregson to see you, sir.'

The second:

'Very good, sir, which suit will you wear?'

That was in a story in a volume entitled *The Man with Two Left Feet* [1917]. It was only some time later, when I was going into the strange affair which is related under the title of 'The Artistic Career of Corky', that the man's qualities dawned upon me. I still blush to think of the off-hand way I treated him at our first encounter.

Wodehouse, introduction to *The World of Jeeves*, 1967

In his book Over Seventy *Wodehouse defended himself at some length against a correspondent who had written to the press under the pen-name 'Indignant', claiming that his writings were badly overrated:*

I DO not wish to labour this point, but I must draw Indignant's attention to a letter in *The Times* from Mr Verrier Elwin, who lives at Patangarth, Mandla District, India. Mr Elwin speaks of a cow which came into his bungalow one day and ate his copy of *Carry On, Jeeves*, 'selecting it from a shelf which contained, among other works, books by Galsworthy, Jane Austen and T. S. Eliot'. Surely a rather striking tribute.

Over Seventy, 1957

JAMES JOYCE · 1882–1941

Joyce and his brother Stanislaus shared a good deal of their early reading:

HE held style, good or bad, to be the most intimate revelation of character, and slovenly writing invariably provoked his angry contempt. When I had read W. H. Mallock's *Is Life Worth Living?*, that forerunner of many modern conversions to Anglo-Catholicism, some remarks on it in my diary induced Jim to begin reading it. After ploughing through about a third of the book, he threw it aside with a contemptuous question: 'Is prose of that kind worth writing?'

Stanislaus Joyce, *My Brother's Keeper*, 1958

Joyce told the following story to his friends Frank Budgen and Paul Suter when they met one evening in the Pfauen, a restaurant in Zurich:

'A GERMAN lady called to see me to-day. She is a writer and wanted me to give an opinion on her work, but she told me she had already shown it to the porter of the hotel where she stays. So I said to her: "What did your hotel porter think of your work?" She said: "He objected to a scene in my novel where my hero goes out into the forest, finds a locket of the girl he loves, picks it up and kisses it passionately." "But," I said, "that seems to me to be a very pleasing and touching incident. What did your hotel porter find wrong with it?" And then she tells me he said: "It's all right for the hero to find the locket and to pick it up and kiss it, but before he kissed it you should have made him wipe the dirt off it with his coat sleeve."'

'And what did you tell her?' said Paul and I together.

'I told her,' said Joyce '(and I meant it too) to go back to that hotel porter and always to take his advice. "That man," I said, "is a critical genius. There is nothing I can tell you that he can't tell you." '

Frank Budgen, *James Joyce and the Making of Ulysses*, 1934

ONE evening in the Pfauen the conversation turned on types of feminine beauty, and I said that I had read somewhere of a king of some cannibal island or other who lined the women folk of the tribe, naked backs against a long horizontal pole. With his royal eye he enfiladed the exposed posteriors, and the possessor of that of greatest prominence he chose for his royal consort. Joyce listened till I had finished the description, then said without a ghost of a smile:

'I sincerely hope that when Bolshevism finally sweeps the world it will spare that enlightened potentate.'

Budgen, *James Joyce*

AS for Joyce, he treated people invariably as his equals, whether they were writers, children, waiters, princesses, or charladies. What anybody had to say interested him; he told me that he had never met a bore. Sometimes I would find him waiting for me at the bookshop, listening attentively to a long tale my concierge was telling him. If he arrived in a taxi, he wouldn't get out until the driver had finished what he was saying. Joyce himself fascinated everybody; no one could resist his charm.

Sylvia Beach, *Shakespeare and Company*, 1960

AN eye operation must be a dreadful ordeal, particularly for someone as sensitive as Joyce. Conscious, he watched it going on, and, as he told me, the instrument looming up in front of his eye appeared like a great axe.

When he was recovering from his operation, he lay with bandaged eyes, hour after hour, never in the least impatient. He had no time to be bored; so many ideas came into his head.

Indeed, how could anyone as inexhaustibly creative as Joyce be bored?

Besides, there were his memory exercises. He had kept them up since his early youth, and this accounted for a memory that retained everything he had ever heard. Everything stuck in it, he said.

'Will you please bring "The Lady of the Lake",' he asked me one day. The next time I went to see him, I had the 'Lady' with me. 'Open it,' he said, 'and read me a line.' I did so, from a page chosen at random. After the first line, I stopped, and he recited the whole page and the next without a single mistake. I'm convinced that he knew by heart, not only 'The Lady of the Lake', but a whole library of poetry and prose. He probably read everything before he was twenty, and thenceforth he could find what he needed without taking the trouble of opening a book.

Beach, *Shakespeare and Company*

I WALKED to James Joyce's flat in the Rue Galilée. It is a little furnished flat as stuffy and prim as a hotel bedroom. The door was opened by the son. A strange accent he had, half-German, half-Italian—an accent of Trieste. We sat down on little hard chairs and I tried to make polite conversation to the son. Then Joyce glided in. It was evident that he had just been shaving. He was very spruce and nervous and chatty. Great rings upon little twitching fingers. Huge concave spectacles which flicked reflections of the lights as he moved his head like a bird, turning it with that definite insistence to the speaker as blind people do who turn to the sound of a voice. Joyce was wearing large bedroom slippers in check, but except for that, one had the strange impression that he had put on his best suit. He was very courteous, as shy people are. His beautiful voice trilled on slowly like Anna Livia Plurabelle. He has the most lovely voice I know—liquid and soft with undercurrents of gurgle.

He told me how the ban had been removed from *Ulysses* ('Oolissays', as he calls it) in America. He had hopes of having it removed in London, and was in negotiation with John Lane . . .

He told me that a man had taken Oolissays to the Vatican and had hidden it in a prayer-book, and that it had been blessed by the Pope. He was half-amused by this and half-impressed. He saw that I would think it funny, and at the same time he did not think it wholly funny himself.

Harold Nicolson, diary, 4 February 1934

In 1929 the American expatriates Harry and Caresse Crosby, who lived in Paris, published Tales Told of Shem and Shaun—*extracts from the work that was to become* Finnegans Wake. *As a frontispiece they reproduced a portrait of Joyce which they had commissioned from Constantin Brancusi. They rejected his original sketch, asking for something more abstract, and the artist duly complied:*

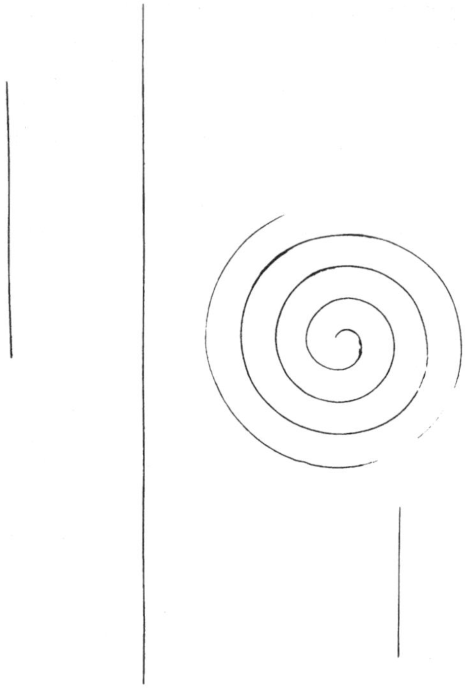

A copy of the book was sent to Joyce's father in Dublin. According to Joyce, in a letter to Harriet Shaw Weaver, the old man looked for a long time at the portrait and finally remarked: 'Jim has changed more than I thought.'

HIS attitude toward political groups and personalities was strikingly revealed during a Saint Patrick's Day celebration at the home of Paul Léon in Paris the evening before I was to leave for the United States. At that time the political sky in Europe seemed to be growing steadily darker, and so the discussion touched, of course, on National Socialist Germany, whereupon fears, suspicions, and curses were voiced by several of those present. James Joyce had assumed a calm, pensive attitude, but suddenly he began to talk and declared in his objective and cool manner that Hitler was surely a historical phenomenon of colossal force that wouldn't be easy to cope with. The detached and emotionless way he spoke, as though referring to a personal adversary, particularly bothered the women present. Nora Joyce, who had listened to him intently, now suddenly jumped up, and, while Joyce continued his calm, interested analysis of Hitler's personality from the point of view of its immense force and drive, she grabbed her knife, which she had just then been using on a *poulet de bresse*, rushed toward him and shouted, 'Jim, another calm word about that devil and I will murder you!' Her response had a strange mixture of genuine anger and burlesque acting, and such a beautiful élan that I suddenly wished I could see this high-spirited Irish woman, who was now standing at the head of the table with her drawn knife, confronting Hitler not Joyce, like an armed and fearless Charlotte Corday. The poet seemed to accept her outburst, just as he always admired the natural behavior of his wife and listened in fascination when she intuitively and spontaneously decided matters that he had scrutinized carefully from every angle, *sine ira et studio* [without either anger or zeal].

Carola Giedion-Welcker, 'Meetings with Joyce', in Willard Potts (ed.), *Portraits of the Artist in Exile*, 1979

WHEN a young man came up to him in Zurich, and said, 'May I kiss the hand that wrote *Ulysses*?' Joyce replied, somewhat like King Lear, 'No, it did lots of other things too.'

Richard Ellmann, *James Joyce*, 1959

WYNDHAM LEWIS · 1882–1957

At one period Lewis was sought out by Lady Cunard, a hostess who liked taking risks:

As I have said, she welcomed danger; but seldom had it confronted her in a more dramatic form than when she decided, during the nineteen-thirties, that the impressionable Heir to the Throne really ought to meet some famous writers, and invited the author of *The Apes of God* to a royal luncheon party in Grosvenor Square. Wyndham Lewis accepted the invitation, contrary to his usual practice; but he was taciturn and pensive and self-absorbed, and, as soon as they had sat down to luncheon, produced from his pocket a small pearl-handled revolver, which he placed beside his wine-glasses. Did he mean to assassinate the Prince? Was it his intention to commit suicide? At all events, a crisis threatened; and, disengaging herself from the guest of honour, she turned her attention at the first opportunity to Mr Wyndham Lewis' 'pretty little pistol', admiring its workmanship and the elegance of the design, handling it as if it had been a Fabergé Easter Egg or an enamelled Georgian snuff-box, at length with an absent-minded smile dropping the weapon into the bag she carried; after which she turned back to the Prince and resumed her social duties.

Peter Quennell, *The Sign of the Fish*, 1960

IN general his paranoia was redeemed by the exaggerative humour with which it was expressed. His world was peopled with enemies (and some of them were real), but his ways of discomfiting them were so grotesque that it was difficult to believe he took the feuds seriously on a personal level—on the level of art he took everything seriously. I remember his description of how a well-known critic, regarded by Lewis as an enemy, was brought up to him at the Leicester Galleries.

'I wasn't paying much attention you see, Symons, and then Eddie Phillips came up to me and said "Here's Mr —, he'd like to meet you", and I put out my hand and something got hold of it, something slimy, and I looked down and, Symons, it was a marine growth, a marine growth had got hold of my hand. No no, I said, no no, and I tried to pull my hand away but the growth had my hand, Symons, it had my hand and it wouldn't let go. I tell you I was really frightened, I had to pull hard to get my hand away from its suckers and I was very relieved to be able to manage it.'

All his conversation was touched with this sort of humour; sometimes he would mimic people, in a manner so ludicrously unlike them that it was in itself comic, sometimes his suppositions about them would run so far outside the course of possibility that they were wildly funny. It was not only acknowledged or imagined enemies who received this treatment: friends and admirers came in for it too, and I have no doubt that my own way of speech and thought were parodied.

Julian Symons, *Critical Occasions*, 1966

Virginia Woolf · 1882–1941

Virginia Woolf's sister Vanessa recalls an incident from childhood:

I REMEMBER one evening, as we were jumping about naked, she and I, in the bathroom, she suddenly asked me which I liked best, my father or mother. Such a question seemed to me rather terrible; surely one ought not to ask it. I felt certain Thoby [their brother] would have snubbed the questioner. However, being asked, one had to reply, and I found I had little doubt as to my answer. 'Mother,' I said, and she went on to explain why she, on the whole, preferred my father. I don't think, however, her preference was quite as sure and simple as mine. She had considered both critically and had more or less analysed her feelings for them which I, at any rate consciously, had never attempted. This seemed to begin an age of much freer speech between us. If one could criticise one's parents, what or whom could one not criticise? Dimly some freedom of thought and speech seemed born, created by her question.

Vanessa Bell, 'Notes on Virginia's Childhood', 1940s (published 1974)

David Cecil recalls an occasion when he dined with the Woolfs:

THE other guest at that time was a lady novelist. After dinner, about 10 o'clock, this lady's husband came in to fetch her. He was an unromantic figure, a philistine man with a toothbrush moustache and a square face. But he wanted to do his best; so he said, 'Are you writing anything now?' and she replied, 'I don't suppose you're very interested in writing,' with her ironical smile. He took that rather well. Then the conversation went on, and about a quarter of an hour later he said, 'I think we must go. I will have to go and wind up my car.' She said, 'What kind of car have you got?' and he said, 'I don't suppose you're very interested in cars.' I thought he won that interchange. But she took it with a smile.

David Cecil, in Joan Russell Noble (ed.), *Recollections of Virginia Woolf*, 1979

A young boy in Sussex is allowed to accompany two older boys from the village, Reg and Perce, while they go fishing for a pike which has made its home in a pond that runs off the local river. At first nothing much happens:

IT was rather boring, I thought, and I was quite pleased when a lady came slowly walking across the field. She was tall and thin with a long woolly, and fairish hair which looked rather wispy as if she had just washed it. She was carrying a walking stick and a bunch of wild flowers. When she saw us she stopped and shaded her eyes with her hand to see us better against the white light of the river. Reg looked up very grumpily at her and went on fishing. Perce just hunched his shoulders up and didn't move, which was very rude because she was smiling a little and looked quite kind.

'Fishing?' she said in a silly way. Because what else could they be doing? Reg just looked at her and nodded his head, and Perce didn't do anything. She looked vaguely round her and said: 'I think I'm lost, I can't find the bridge.'

Reg swung his rod into the air and looked sullen. 'Up behind you, on the road,' he said gruffly, and re-cast his line so that I heard the bait plop into the still morning water.

'Thank you,' said the lady and then she held up the bunch of flowers for us all to see. No one said anything, so she turned and started walking back the way she had come, towards the bridge, stepping carefully over the mole hills and tussocks. She didn't look back and I was glad, because we had been very rude, but she hadn't spoken to me so I didn't feel quite to blame, and I didn't dare speak or move because of the pike and Perce's face, which was very red and cross.

'Bloomin' nuisance her. She's always about when I get here. Always up and down the river she is, like a bloomin' witch.' He reeled in his line and told me to give him another grasshopper because the one he had was drowned and not jerking any longer. While he baited his hook again we all watched her scramble up the bank to the road and then walk across the bridge swinging the stick in her hand; she was smelling her bunch of flowers and didn't look back at us again.

Dirk Bogarde, *A Postillion Struck by Lightning*, 1977

The lady, though the author doesn't name her in this passage, was Virginia Woolf; the river was the one in which she subsequently drowned herself.

William Carlos Williams · 1883–1963

Williams was a doctor; by his own admission, he was also a man who wanted to make love to every woman he met. The writer Brendan Gill sometimes accompanied him on visits to his patients:

Williams and I would pull up in his car in front of some not very savory-looking bungalow, and Williams would slap my knee and say, 'Wait till you get a look at this one!' We would ring the bell, and the door would be opened by some slatternly woman in her late twenties or early thirties, wearing a soiled rayon dressing gown and with her dyed hair done up in a dozen or so pink plastic curlers. She would have an infant in her arms, purple-faced from screaming and with diapers unpleasantly tapestried, and the odds were that however sick the infant was, the mother was suffering from something equally unpleasant—at the very least, so I seem to remember, a severe case of post-nasal drip. Williams wouldn't be daunted. He would examine the baby, write out a prescription, and then spend five or ten minutes in happy banter with the dull, distracted, and wholly undesirable mother. Back in the car, he would be breathing hard and radiant. 'What a girl!'

Brendan Gill, *Here at the New Yorker*, 1975

After Williams visited the girls' college at Bennington in Vermont, his friend the critic Kenneth Burke was full of stories about his absent-mindedness:

Addressing the Bennington girls with a speech he'd already delivered to aspiring writers at Yale and Harvard, without making the change in gender necessary for his audience, Dr Williams had squeaked at the girls, his voice high with passionate conviction (and Kenneth's rising even higher in imitation of it), 'If you want to write poetry, you've got to be men! You've got to be men!' The young women, first puzzled, then resentful, slid deeper and deeper into their seats. 'Why are they all so sullen?' Williams, who was used to having women of all ages find him attractive, asked Kenneth afterward.

Eileen Simpson, *Poets in their Youth*, 1982

Maxwell Perkins · 1884–1947

(celebrated publisher's editor; the authors who benefited from his advice included Hemingway, Faulkner, and Thomas Wolfe)

It seems that Hemingway's novel, in its serial form, had to be expurgated for the readers of *Scribner's Magazine*. And when Maxwell Perkins came to go through the manuscript, he found three words which he was doubtful about printing even in the book. The words were *balls, shit,* and *cocksucker*. So he had a solemn conference on the subject with old Mr Charles Scribner. The first two words were discussed, and it was decided to suppress them, but when Perkins came to the third—which he thought Mr Scribner had probably never heard—he couldn't get it out, and wrote it down on a piece of paper. Old Mr Scribner put on his pince-nez and considered it with serious attention—then said, 'Perkins, do you think that Hemingway would respect you, if he knew that you were unable to say that word, but had to write it out?' Perkins was so flustered by the incident that he forgot and left the memorandum pad with *cocksucker* on it on a bracket in his office, where it was just on the level of the eyes of anybody who came in. He didn't discover it until just before he left in the afternoon—by which time it had thrown the whole Scribner's office into a state of acute embarrassment, deep mental and moral distress, and troubling mystification.

Edmund Wilson, letter to Burton Rascoe, 1929, in *Letters on Literature and Politics*, 1977

Sir Hugh Walpole · 1884–1941

(novelist)

In 1913 Walpole and Edmund Gosse helped to organize the seventieth birthday celebrations of Henry James:

James had accepted the homage of his friends, together with a golden bowl, and had graciously agreed to sit to Sargent for his portrait. This work, now completed, was to be shown privately to subscribers in Sargent's studio in Tite Street on three days in December. Printed letters of invitation were prepared and were to be sent out over the names of Gosse and Hugh. James took great interest in the arrangements and was consulted by Hugh on all points. The letters were sent off, and a day or two later Hugh dined with Maurice Hewlett. 'I knew, dear Hugh,' said he with his usual sardonic charm, 'that you were fond of me but, frankly, I had not supposed that Gosse cared for me very greatly. This letter has reassured me.' Hugh's heart sank: something terrible had happened. Hewlett showed him the letter on which, as on all its fellows, Hugh had forgotten to add the name of the recipient, so that they all began: 'Dear,' *tout court*, and ended: 'We are, Dear, Yours sincerely, Edmund Gosse, Hugh Walpole.'

Rupert Hart-Davis, *Hugh Walpole*, 1952

Ivy Compton-Burnett · 1884–1969

I WROTE to her, saying that I had been asked to write an essay for *Writers and their Work*, for the British Council and Longmans Press, on her novels. In reply, she sent me a postcard, in her pellucid handwriting, inviting me to dinner. I gladly accepted.

The point here, if I may make excuses, is that I am by nature pathologically punctual. At seven-thirty, I was outside her flat, in Cornwall Mansions, in a freezing Sherlock Holmes fog: to the best of my belief, half an hour early. This, I thought, simply wouldn't do. I was, I believed, expected at eight. So I went for a perfectly horrible walk, round and round that Gothic square, and at last, at five to eight, presented myself. Miss Compton-Burnett's maid greeted me, if greeting it could be called. She said: 'Madam has been at dinner this past half-hour.'

I had mistaken the time.

I was led over what seemed like acres of parquet into a big, lofty-ceilinged room. At a table in the corner were Miss Compton-Burnett, her friend Miss Margaret Jourdain, both small, and a lady who seemed to me equally small—though this may have been the result of my trauma in the fog—whose name I did not catch. I made my apologies as best I could.

Miss Compton-Burnett, ivorine, sharp-featured, with eyes green as peeled grapes, interrogated me. Was her handwriting illegible? No, I replied, but in fact when I received the card I had been in the midst of a domestic crisis, and had misread it. The questioning continued. Yes. No. I'm awfully sorry. No. But. How—?

At last I was permitted to sit. I do not think the dinner could have been utterly spoiled since the main course was corned beef. And during the next three-quarters of an hour, nobody spoke a word to me. There was a good deal of gossip about displeasing creatures the three of them met, in some place or another. I was silent: though not as a result of rebuke. In fact, I was furious. She did address one sentence to me. This was: 'Do you know a *person* called Cyril Connolly? I call him a person.' (In some way, he must have affronted her.)

At last we rose, and went into another Gothic room, very cold, where someone had set light to a fire of little twigs. No smoking, of course: no appropriate apparatus.

At first, whenever I attempted, at some decent hour, to take my departure, a tiny but firm hand—my hostess's, put me down. As I eventually fought my way to the hall door, I was accompanied by Miss Jourdain. She said to me kindly, 'You mustn't mind. Ivy isn't at her best tonight.' Outside, I sat on the steps of Cornwall Mansions—still in the fog—and smoked and smoked. I was thoroughly unnerved.

Pamela Hansford Johnson, *Important to Me*, 1974

Despite this incident, Pamela Hansford Johnson continued to admire Ivy Compton-Burnett's work, to use her own word, 'inordinately'.

Sinclair Lewis · 1885–1951

In 1920, when H. L. Mencken and George Jean Nathan were editing the American Mercury, *a colleague called T. R. Smith invited them over to his apartment. Nathan takes up the story:*

When we got there, we found with Smith a tall, skinny, paprika-headed stranger to whom we were introduced as one Lewis. . . .

Barely had we taken off our hats and coats . . . when the tall, skinny, paprika-headed stranger simultaneously coiled one long arm around Mencken's neck and the other around mine, well nigh strangling us and putting resistance out of the question, and—yelling at the top of his lungs—began: 'So you guys are critics, are you? Well, let me tell you something. I'm the best writer in this here gottdamn country and if you, Georgie, and you, Hank, don't know it now, you'll know it gottdamn soon. Say, I've just finished a book that'll be published in a week or two and it's the gottdamn best book of its kind that this here gottdamn country has had and don't you guys forget it! I worked a year on the gottdamn thing and it's the goods, I'm atelling you! Listen, when it comes to writing a novel, I'm so far ahead of most of the men you two think are good that I'll be gottdamned if it doesn't make me sick to think of it! Just wait till you read the gottdamn thing. You've got a treat coming, Georgie and Hank, and don't you boys make no mistake about *that!*'

Projected from Smith's flat by the self-endorsing uproar—it kept up for fully half an hour longer—Mencken and I jumped into a taxicab, directed the driver to speed us posthaste to a tavern where we might in some peace recover our equilibrium and our ear-drums, and looked at each other. 'Of all the idiots I've ever laid eyes on, that fellow is the worst!' groaned Mencken, gasping for breath. Regaining my own breath some moments later, all that I could add was that if any such numskull could ever write anything worth reading, maybe there was something in Christian Science too.

Three days later I got the following letter from Mencken, who had returned to Baltimore:

Dear George: Grab hold of the bar-rail, steady yourself, and prepare yourself for a terrible shock! I've just read the advance sheets of the book of that *Lump* we met at Schmidt's and, by God, he has done the job! It's a genuinely excellent piece of work. Get it as soon as you can and take a look. I begin to believe that perhaps there isn't a God after all. There is no justice in the world.

Quoted in Mark Schorer, *Sinclair Lewis: An American Life*, 1963

The novel in question was Main Street.

D. H. Lawrence · 1885–1930

In 1955 the journalist Norman Shrapnel visited Eastwood, the village where Lawrence grew up. Had he lived, Lawrence would have been 69 at the time.

The first man I spoke to in the Breach [a group of dwellings]—a young-old veteran of the pits properly dressed in flat cap and collarless shirt, 43 years a miner and twice badly injured—was swift off the mark.

'Bert Lawrence? Don't talk to me about him.' He gripped my elbow with a hard hand, and gave his judgment.

'I'd put him down as nowt. Given a tip-top education by his father—as fine a man as you'd meet in a day's march. That was on a butty's pay, pound to fifty shilling a week. Then he took all his knowledge away. Didn't give this country a penny back.'

He brooded fiercely and then went on. 'Spoke to nobody. Never had a pal in his life. Only played ring-o'-roses with young women.' At this improbable idyll of memory his spectacles shone in the afternoon sun like signal lamps across half a century.

'But his father, now there was a man. Full of life and friendliness. Big roaring carnation in his coat. They still talk about him in Eastwood.' He pointed a hundred yards up the hill as if to another world. 'He could dance, too, till his legs were broke to bits. He got buried.' This was announced with professional casualness: then he reverted to the shortcomings of the man whom the rest of the world, outside the Breach, regarded as great. 'But Bert never acknowledged him properly, not as a father should be. It was the mother. Thought that much of herself. But she was nothing.'

Norman Shrapnel, *Manchester Guardian*, 18 March 1955

D. H. LAWRENCE's irruption into Augustus John's studio is one of the incidents most deeply etched on my memory. I had been lunching with him at Queen's Restaurant in Sloane Square. Hearing I was about to sit nearby, he took it into his head to come and see my portrait.

The collision between the two Red Beards was enthralling. D. H. was in a queer, challenging mood. Why the atmosphere of a studio and the impact of a brother artist should thus have affected him, I have no idea, but whatever spiritual revolt he felt made him—strange symptom—speak in Latin, a quite uncharacteristic vagary.

With his wide-brimmed black hat in his hand, he walked into the studio like some nervous, lightfooted woodland animal on the look-out for something to shy at.

There was some minutes silence during which he prowled about the studio, gloomily, mutely surveying the finished and unfinished works of art. Then, like a clock rustily clearing its throat to strike, he muttered, 'Mortuus est. Mortuus est,' several times. Gathering volume, his voice became a tolling bell. Suddenly, raising his head, he summed up the situation with the sepulchral utterance, 'Let the DEAD PAINT THE DEAD!'

Pacing up and down, he knelled this lugubrious refrain several times.

John showed wonderful tolerance of this curious behaviour. That he had been pronounced to be dead did not seem to distress him. To one so plentifully endowed with vitality, the cap, I suppose, was too obvious a misfit to matter.

Whatever his unspoken feelings, the artist expressed great admiration for the writer's 'head,' and asked him to sit for a drawing. Lawrence consented, but unfortunately this plan never came off.

Cynthia Asquith, *Haply I May Remember*, 1950

Augustus John left his own account of this meeting:

I MET D. H. Lawrence in the flesh once only. Lady Cynthia Asquith, whose portrait I was painting, brought him round one day to my studio. Lady Cynthia would have liked me to paint Lawrence and I would have been interested to do so. But Lawrence protested that he was too ugly. I didn't agree. I never did insist on an Adonis for a model, and I thought Lawrence's features would have done very well for my purpose; even if they didn't conform to any known canon of beauty, they didn't lack character. Besides, did I not recognize in them the mask of genius? On this occasion the poet made a point of compensating himself for his physical drawbacks by a dazzling display of cerebral fireworks. Originality or Death seemed to be his motto. Lady Cynthia treated us to a box at the Opera that evening. A resplendent guardsman was of the party: Frieda Lawrence, who also was present, assured us all that her German father's uniform was much grander than that of this officer. On leaving what Sir Edwin Lutyens used to call the 'uproar', D.H.L. announced that he would like to howl like a dog.

Augustus John, *Chiaroscuro*, 1952

In the autumn of 1928 Lawrence and his American friends Earl and Achsah Brewster travelled south to Italy. They broke their journey briefly at Strasbourg:

THE twilight outside was bitter cold; Lawrence decided to keep warm with *Ben Hur* at the cinema until train time. Half an hour we watched doves fluttering around baby-faced blonde dolls, brutal Romans accursed with hearts of stone, galleys of inhuman slaves, galloping horses whizzing perilous chariots. There was no human touch, nothing resembling a reality of any phase of life we knew or could imagine. Lawrence gasped out that he was going; if we did not take him out immediately he would be violently sick; such falsity nauseated him; he could not bear to see other people there open-mouthed, swallowing it, believing it to be true.

Earl and Achsah Brewster, *D. H. Lawrence: Reminiscences and Correspondence*, 1934

IT will be remembered that when Lawrence held a show of his paintings at Dorothy Warren's Gallery in Maddox Street, the police raided the exhibition, removing such works as offended their sense of propriety, and while they were about it, carried off a number of designs by William Blake as well! The Force is nothing if not thorough.

John, *Chiaroscuro*

To a party where I meet Mrs D. H. Lawrence. She is much less *hausfrau* than I had supposed. A sharp questing little nose, a bright inquisitive impression, a sense of silliness somewhere, and excess. She talks quite naturally about Lawrence and is clearly pleased at his being the hero of a legend . . . She says that Lawrence said, 'Frieda, if people really knew what you were like, they would strangle you.' I say, 'Did he say that angrily?' She said, 'No—very quietly, after several minutes deep thought.'

Harold Nicolson, diary, 9 December 1932

EZRA POUND · 1885–1972

Homer Pound was Ezra's doting father:

THERE is a story which true or not illustrates perfectly Homer's lack of guile. It was in Rapallo in the 1930s and Homer and his son were in attendance on Max Beerbohm at his home on the road to Zoagli. Most of the time Ezra Pound talked, a barrage of historical detail and proposals for monetary reform. During a lull in which he was absent from the room, Homer leant across, and, shaking his head in wonderment, said 'You know Mr Beerbohm, there isn't a darn thing that boy of mine don't know.'

Noel Stock, *The Life of Ezra Pound*, 1970

A GROUP went to the Old Cheshire Cheese, where Yeats held forth at length on the ways of bringing music and poetry together. Pound sought attention by eating two red tulips.

William Van O'Connor, *Ezra Pound*, 1963

> *Pound isn't the only poet to have eaten a tulip. Alistair Cooke recalled an undergraduate dinner at Cambridge at which William Empson got very drunk. There was a vase of tulips on the table; Empson suddenly announced that he could see no reason why one shouldn't eat one, and proceeded to do just that, petal by petal. Shortly afterwards he threw up.*

When Pound visited Paris in 1930, he told Caresse Crosby that he wanted to savour 'the immediate flavour of Paris by night':

I TOOK him to the Boule Blanche where a remarkably beautiful and brilliant band of Martinique players were beating out hot music. We had a ringside table, Ezra was enthralled—I with my broken heart could not dance, which was perhaps just as well. As the music grew in fury Ezra avidly watched the dancers, 'These people don't know a thing about rhythm,' he cried scornfully, and he shut his eyes, thrust forward his red-bearded chin and began a sort of tattoo with his feet—suddenly unable to sit still a minute longer he leapt to the floor and seized the tiny Martiniquaise vendor of cigarettes in his arms, packets flying, then head back, eyes closed, chin out, he began a sort of voodoo prance, his tiny partner held glued against his piston-pumping knees.

The hot music grew hotter. Ezra grew hotter. One by one the uninspired dancers melted from the floor and formed a ring to watch that Anglo-savage ecstasy—on and on went the two, until with a final screech of cymbals the music crashed to an end. Ezra opened his eyes, flicked the cigarette girl aside like an extinguished match and collapsed into the chair beside me. The room exhaled a long orgasmic sigh—I too.

Caresse Crosby, *The Passionate Years*, 1955

At the end of the Second World War, during which he had broadcast on Rome Radio, Pound was charged with treason but found unfit to plead, and confined in a mental institution in Washington, DC, until 1958. After his release he returned to Italy on board the Italian liner Cristoforo Colombo*:*

THE liner called at Naples on 9 July, and Italian reporters and photographers came on board. They asked Ezra what it had been like spending twelve years in an American insane asylum. He answered: 'All America is an insane asylum.' The matter of anti-Semitism was raised. He told them: 'The Fascist dictators made a mistake in the way they persecuted the Jews. The mistake was not in fighting the Jews, but the manner in which the Jews were fought. Rather than attack them as a bloc, each case should have been examined individually.' Photographers asked him to pose, and he smilingly obliged. His shirt showing great patches of sweat from the heat, he placed his left hand on his hip, and raised his other arm in the Fascist salute.

Humphrey Carpenter, *A Serious Character: The Life of Ezra Pound*, 1988

RONALD FIRBANK · 1886–1926

(novelist: his books include *Valmouth* and *The Flower beneath the Foot*)

I USED to see him from time to time at the theatre when I was doing dramatic criticism. He often attended First Nights, in spite of an overwhelming shyness which made the presence of other people an agony to him. Sometimes the agony was so great that he would do extraordinary things that made him very conspicuous and so increased his self-consciousness, (e.g. he would get up in the middle of an act, or start rummaging under his seat). He must have derived some curious painful pleasure from his embarrassments. The last time I saw him was at Robert Nichols's wedding. We sat with various other people in the Café Royal. As I took my seat at the table opposite him, Firbank gave his usual agonised wriggle of embarrassment and said:

'Aldous—always my *torture*.'

Which must, I think, have been his spontaneous reaction to most people, at any rate at first.

Aldous Huxley, quoted in Ifan Kyrle Fletcher, *Ronald Firbank: A Memoir*, 1930

IT was at the Russian Ballet that an absurd incident occurred in which Firbank and Lady X (a well-known female eccentric) both loudly complained that the one had 'leered' at the other.

Lord Berners, in Fletcher, *Ronald Firbank*

Marianne Moore · 1887–1972

Never having found her at a loss on any topic whatsoever, I wanted to give myself the pleasure at least once of hearing her stumped about something. Certain that only an experience completely strange to her would be the thing, I invited her to a ball game at the Polo Grounds. This descent into the world of the lowbrow started beautifully. It was a Saturday afternoon and the Cubs and the Giants were scheduled for one of their ancient frays. The 'L' [elevated railway] was jammed with fans and we had to stand all the way uptown and hang on to straps. Marianne was totally oblivious to the discomfiture anyone else would have felt and, in answer to a question of mine, paraded whole battalions of perfectly marshalled ideas in long columns of balanced periods which no lurching on the part of the train or pushing on the part of the crowd disturbed. Wait till we reach the grounds, I promised myself, and Matty [the baseball player Christy Mathewson] winds up, tosses a perfect fadeaway, the batter misses it, and Marianne goes on talking.

Well, I got her safely to her seat and sat down beside her. Without so much as a glance toward the players at practice grabbing grounders and tossing fungos, she went on giving me her impression of the respective technical achievements of Mr Pound and Mr Aldington without missing a turn in the rhythm of her speech, until I, a little impatient, touched her arm and, indicating a man in the pitcher's box winding up with the movement Matty's so famous for, interrupted: 'But Marianne, wait a moment, the game's about to begin. Don't you want to watch the first ball?' 'Yes, indeed,' she said, stopped, blushed and leaned forward.

The first pitch was called a strike, and the narrator—Alfred Kreymborg—decided that it was time to try to expose Marianne Moore's ignorance.

Delighted, I quickly turned to her with: 'Do you happen to know the gentleman who threw that strike?'

'I've never seen him before,' she admitted, 'but I take it it must be Mr Mathewson.'

I could only gasp, 'Why?'

'I've read his instructive book on the art of pitching—'

'Strike Two!' interrupted the umpire.

'And it's a pleasure,' she continued imperturbably, 'to note how unerringly his execution supports his theories—'

Alfred Kreymborg, *Troubadour*, 1925

Edith Sitwell · 1887–1964

During the 1920s Edith Sitwell lived in Bayswater. Her flat was small and dingy, but many celebrated literary and artistic figures attended the tea parties she gave:

'Mrs Patrick Campbell sailed in'—and later sent Edith a dozen silver teaspoons, having been inconvenienced by the fact that these articles were not provided at 22 Pembridge Mansions. She meant it kindly. Mrs Patrick Campbell was an old friend of Lady Ida's [Lady Ida was Edith's mother], and used to say to Edith, 'You'll never have your mother's beauty—poor child! . . . But never mind! You look at one in such a nice way, it doesn't matter.' This became such a regular observation that Edith learnt to get it in first 'How d'you do, Mrs Campbell? I know I shall never have my mother's beauty, but I look at you in such a nice way, it doesn't matter.'

Victoria Glendinning, *Edith Sitwell*, 1981

> *According to John Pearson, in his joint biography of Edith and her brothers,* Façades, *at the age of 4 'Edith was seated in her perambulator when Mrs Patrick Campbell called and had the temerity to call the infant Edith "Baby". Edith hit her.'*

Katherine Mansfield · 1888–1923

One evening in 1916 Katherine Mansfield and her friends S. S. Koteliansky and the painter Mark Gertler went to the Café Royal, near Piccadilly Circus. The fullest contemporary account of what followed was in a letter which Gertler wrote the next day to Lady Ottoline Morrell—an account which among other things, in the words of Antony Alpers, 'exposes the racist attitudes of Liberal England':

Gertler's letter described how he and Kot and Katherine (a Polish Jew, a Ukrainian Jew and a Colonial), finding the café packed, were obliged to sit at a table already occupied by a coloured man—'an Indian, perhaps, but a weak type', whom they hardly noticed. After a time a 'Long Thin White Herring of a Woman with a Terrific High Bunch of Crimson Hair' came to join him, and then another coloured man made a third:

> We immediately hated all three of them. Soon to our astonishment they began to talk 'Intellectually'—they were University Blacks—using 'perfect' English very long words carefully chosen. They talked about Dostoevsky, Russia, the New Age, all in a very advanced manner. All this irritated us enough, But imagine our

Hatred and Horror when the red headed piece of dried Dung produced a Volume of Lawrence's poems and commenced to discuss Lawrence with the others, in this perfect English and carefully picked long words! We had been ragging them all the time, but now we knew something drastic must be done. We sat and thought. Suddenly Katherine leant towards them and with a sweet smile said '*Will* you let me have that Book a moment?' 'Certainly' they all beamed back—even more sweetly. Imagine their horror and utter amazement when Katherine without a word more, rose from the table, Book and all, we following calmly—most calmly we walked out of the Café!!!

Antony Alpers, *Katherine Mansfield*, 1980

D. H. Lawrence put this episode into Women in Love, *where Katherine appears as Gudrun and the Café Royal becomes 'the Pompadour'. One of the 'University Blacks' was a Bengali Muslim law student, H. S. Suhrawardy, who later became a leading politician: after Partition he served as Chief Minister of East Bengal in Pakistan.*

In 1921 Katherine Mansfield discovered that Elizabeth Bibesco had designs on her husband, Middleton Murry, and that the two of them were becoming romantically involved. After intercepting one of Elizabeth's letters to Murry, she decided to put paid to the relationship with a letter of her own:

Dear Princess Bibesco,

I am afraid you must stop writing these little love letters to my husband while he and I live together. It's one of the things which are not done in our world.

You are very young. Won't you ask your husband to explain to you the impossibility of such a situation.

Please do not make me have to write to you again. I do not like scolding people and simply hate having to teach them manners.

Yours sincerely,
Katherine Mansfield

Cited by Alpers, *Katherine Mansfield*

Mansfield's biographer Claire Tomalin comments: 'No one could possibly suspect from this letter that Katherine had once been a Bohemian and a merry adulteress herself; the queenly tone of the rebuke may well have been an echo of the voice in which her mother had addressed her in those earlier years.'

Eugene O'Neill · 1888–1953

Though he appeared to be totally recovered from tuberculosis O'Neill was not supposed to touch liquor. Yet on Cape Cod—and elsewhere—his torments of mind were such that he tempted the fates by drinking heavily. One celebrated Provincetown story pictures him at the end of a drinking bout seeing a green mouse in a corner of his room. He threw all the crockery in the place at it, but the mouse calmly remained. Then he threw all the broken bits of crockery, and all the pieces of bits. Still the green mouse placidly stared. At this point O'Neill collapsed on the bed and passed out. When he awoke the green mouse was gone, but not the mound of broken crockery.

Allen Churchill, *The Improper Bohemians*, 1961

O'Neill looked back nostalgically to his early days as a sailor:

In talking about those 'wonderful' days, O'Neill often spoke to Carlotta [his second wife] of the nickelodeons they had in the New Orleans bagnios and other low dives he had frequented. He could hum or sing many of the old tunes. In an attempt to console O'Neill in his nostalgia, Carlotta went to a music store and asked if they could provide her with a player piano of this kind. In the storage room they found the very thing. A madame in a bagnio had failed to keep up her payments and her player piano had been repossessed. It was painted green and was adorned with roses and cupids; and colored lights flashed as it played. With it came old rolls of music, including 'All Alone', 'Springtime Rag', 'That Mysterious Rag', 'Waiting at the Church', 'Alexander's Ragtime Band' and 'The Robert E. Lee'. Carlotta gave it to O'Neill for his birthday, saying that she wanted him to have all the things his heart desired.

O'Neill named the piano Rosie and kept a derby hat on top of it half filled with nickels. Many years later, he told Hamilton Basso that he was not sure playing Rosie so much was a good idea. 'I try to remember,' he said, 'a beautiful verse from Verlaine and come up with a line of "Everybody's Doing It" or "Oh, You Great Big Beautiful Doll".'

Croswell Bowen, *The Curse of the Misbegotten*, 1960

In 1943, shortly after her eighteenth birthday, O'Neill's daughter Oona married Charlie Chaplin. According to a friend, he wrote her 'a very harsh and severing letter', and she never heard from him again:

According to Nathan [the theatre critic George Jean Nathan], O'Neill was bitter about Oona's marriage and resented any reference by his friends or acquaintances to his only daughter and his new son-in-law. 'There is enough wry comedy in life as it is,' he remarked.

Bowen, *The Curse of the Misbegotten*

Sir Lewis Namier · 1888–1960

The book which made Namier's reputation, The Structure of Politics at the Accession of George III, *was published in 1929:*

The review which had the most dramatic consequences was by G. M. Trevelyan, doyen of those Whig historians for whom Namier had so little respect. Trevelyan wrote of 'the Namier way': 'Mr Namier is a new factor in the historical world.' Reading the review at tea, Professor Jacob at Manchester telegraphed at once to offer Namier the vacant chair of modern history. Namier was always grateful to Trevelyan and, characteristically, claimed to have repaid his debt by refusing ever to review Trevelyan's books.

John Cannon, in *Oxford Dictionary of National Biography*, 2004

Raymond Chandler · 1888–1959

After his wife's death in 1954 Chandler paid a number of prolonged visits to England, where he had spent much of his early life before settling in California. He was deeply troubled, and drinking heavily, but he resisted suggestions that he might find relief in psychotherapy:

When I remarked that our neuroses mostly originate in childhood, he replied with scornful, teasing gusto: 'Oh, I don't know—I pick mine up as I go along.'

But he could still be a lively companion:

An expedition to Cambridge to meet Frances Cornford [the poet] amused him. Having asked him what was his favourite expression in the American vernacular, she was visibly startled when he replied vigorously, 'Aw, turn blue.'

Natasha Spender, 'His Own Long Goodbye', in *The World of Raymond Chandler*, ed. Miriam Gross, 1977

T. S. Eliot · 1888–1965

In the spring of 1914 Bertrand Russell taught a course in symbolic logic at Harvard:

I HAD a post-graduate class of twelve, who used to come to tea with me once a week. One of them was T. S. Eliot, who subsequently wrote a poem about it, called 'Mr Apollinax'. I did not know at the time that Eliot wrote poetry. He had, I think, already written 'A Portrait of a Lady', and 'Prufrock', but he did not see fit to mention the fact. He was extraordinarily silent, and only once made a remark which struck me. I was praising Heraclitus, and he observed: 'Yes, he always reminds me of Villon.' I thought this remark so good that I always wished he would make another.

Bertrand Russell, *Autobiography*, vol. i, 1967

I. A. Richards got to know Eliot when he was working in the Colonial and Foreign Department of Lloyds Bank, in the City, and by chance he also learned the bank's view of 'our young Mr Eliot':

I CAME across a shrewd, kindly, and charming man (up at Arolla in the Swiss Alps, it was) who turned out to be a high senior official in that very Queen Henrietta Street focus of the great bank's far-flung activities. When he learned that I knew TSE, I could see that he was getting ready at once to frame a question. Something in his hesitant approach made me a little wary in my turn.

MR W. You know him, I suppose, as a literary man, as a writer and . . . er . . . and . . . er . . . as a poet?

I.A.R. Yes, he's very well known, you know, as a critic, and as a poet.

MR W. Tell me, if you will—you won't mind me asking, will you? Tell me, is he, in your judgment, would you say, would you call him, a good poet?

I.A.R. Well, in my judgment—not everyone would agree, of course, far from it, he *is* a good poet.

MR W. You know, I myself am really very glad indeed to hear you say that. Many of my colleagues wouldn't agree at all. They think a Banker has no business whatever to be a poet. They don't think the two things can combine. But I believe that anything a man does, whatever his *hobby* may be, it's all the better if he is really keen on it and does it well. I think it helps him with his work. If you see our young friend, you might tell him that we think he's doing quite well at the Bank. In fact, if he goes on as he has been doing, I don't see why—in time, of course, in time—he mightn't even become a Branch Manager.

I. A. Richards, 'On TSE', in Allen Tate (ed.), *T. S. Eliot: The Man and his Work*, 1967

ELIOT once gave a friend some obscene poems back in 1920 and never got them back. They think the friend's sister, who's a nun, saw them and burned them. It's all right if you know they're burned, but if you're not sure it's always worrisome.

W. H. Auden in *The Table Talk of W. H. Auden*, ed. Alan Ansen, 1990

When Eliot was editing the Criterion *he often asked the magazine's younger contributors to lunch with him*, à deux. *One of them was Hugh Sykes Davies:*

AMONG ourselves of course, these luncheons were a matter for tactful boasting. 'I had lunch with Eliot the other day' was a phrase which I remember hearing, and I am sure I must have uttered it too, though I remember that less clearly. The tone of voice appropriate to such an utterance was very level, unemphatic, almost a throw-away, such was the inherent force of the fact itself. Only one of us, much the most resourceful in the management of English idiom, found a way of improving on it, to 'I was lunching with Eliot the other day', and we were left to wonder whether this subtle modal meddling with the verb might not indicate a frequency of meeting denied to most of us.

Hugh Sykes Davies, 'Mistah Kurtz: He Dead', in Tate (ed.), *T. S. Eliot*

THERE was a party (I forget everybody else in the room) where Eliot broke into some chatter about a letter being misunderstood. 'Ah, letters,' he said, rather as if they were some rare kind of bird, 'I had to look into the question of letters at one time. I found that the mistake . . . that most people make . . . about letters, is that after writing their letters, carefully, they go out, and look for a pillar-box. I found that it is very much better, after giving one's attention to composing the letter, to . . . pop it into the fire.' This kind of thing was a little unnerving, because one did not know how tragically it ought to be taken; it was clearly not to be regarded as a flippancy.

William Empson, in Richard March and Tambimuttu (eds.), *T. S. Eliot: A Symposium*, 1948

SOON after the musical *New Faces* opened on Broadway, I told Eliot that the hit song, Eartha Kitt's rendition of 'Monotonous', contained the line, 'T. S. Eliot writes pomes to me.' He immediately took out his card, inscribed it to Miss Kitt, and asked me to have the florist send her roses. I happily did so, and the only indication that the flowers reached her was an item in a newspaper column to the effect that 'Eartha Kitt *claims* that

T. S. Eliot sent her a bouquet'—a line Eliot enjoyed almost as much as the one in her song.

Robert Giroux, 'A Personal Memoir', in Tate (ed.), *T. S. Eliot*

The line from the Eartha Kitt song should read, 'T. S. Eliot writes books for me'; it rhymes with 'King Farouk's on tenterhooks for me.' Later in the memoir Giroux recalls that Eliot's love of musicals and music halls was 'incurable, and his comment on My Fair Lady, *when Roger and Dorothea Straus and I took him to the original production, was characteristic: "Shaw has been greatly improved by music."'*

On 10 January 1957, at 6.15 in the morning when it was still dark, they [Eliot and Valerie Fletcher] were married at St Barnabas's Church in Addison Road, Kensington: she was thirty and he now sixty-eight . . . Quite by chance he discovered just before the ceremony that Jules Laforgue, who had exercised such a decisive influence on his youthful poetry, had also been married at St Barnabas's.

Peter Ackroyd, *T. S. Eliot*, 1984

W. N. P. Barbellion · 1889–1919

(diarist; an assistant at the Natural History Museum, South Kensington)

I have for years past received my rejected MSS. back from every conceivable kind of periodical, from *Punch* to the *Hibbert Journal*. At one time I used to file their rejection forms and meditated writing a facetious essay on them. But I decided they were too monotonously similar. My custom was when the ordinary avenues to literary fame had failed me—the half-crown Reviews and the sixpenny Weeklies—to seek out at a library some obscure publication—a Parish Magazine or the local paper—anything was grabbed as a last chance. On one of these occasions I discovered the *Westminster Review* and immediately plied them with a manuscript and the usual polite note. After six weeks, having no reply, I wrote again and waited for another six weeks. My second remonstrance met with a similar fate, so I went into the City to interview the publishers, and to demand my manuscript back. The manager was out, and I was asked to call again. After waiting about for some time, I left my card, took my departure and decided I would write. The same evening I told the publishers that the anonymous editor would neither print my article nor return it. Would they kindly give me his name and address so that I could write personally. After some delay they replied that although it was not the custom to disclose the editor's name, the following address would find her. She was a lady living in Richmond Row, Shepherd's Bush. I wrote to her at once and received no answer. Meanwhile, I had observed that no further issues of the review had appeared on the bookstalls, and the booksellers were unable to give me any information. I wrote again to the address—this time a playful and facetious letter in which I said I did not propose to take the matter into court, but if it would save her any trouble I would call for the MS. as I lived only a few minutes' walk distant. I received no answer. I was busy at the time and kept putting off executing my firm purpose of visiting the good lady until one evening as I was casually reading the *Star* coming home in the 'bus, I read an account of how some charitably disposed woman had recently visited the Hammersmith Workhouse and removed to her own home a poor soul who was once the friend of George Eliot, George Henry Lewes, and other well-known literary persons of the sixties and had, until it ceased publication a few months before, edited the once notable *Westminster Review*.

The Journal of a Disappointed Man, 1919

Ludwig Wittgenstein · 1889–1951

The friend who lent me them [a set of rooms in St John's College, Cambridge] had small reproduction drawings of Bernard Shaw and T. S. Eliot hanging in frames on one of the walls. I cannot remember any comment Wittgenstein made about Shaw, but about Eliot's face he remarked in a negative tone that it was 'a modern face'.

Theodore Redpath, *Ludwig Wittgenstein: A Student's Memoir*, 1990

He was liable to behave in a ludicrous fashion. Believing that riches were evil, he gave his own away, but only to his rich relations, on the grounds that, being rich already, they could not be further corrupted.

Anthony Quinton, *From Wodehouse to Wittgenstein*, 1998

Richard Simon · 1889–1960

(American publisher; co-founder of Simon & Schuster)

Launching a new children's book, *Dr Dan the Bandage Man*, Simon decided to include a free gift of six Band-Aids with each copy. He cabled a friend at the manufacturers, Johnson and Johnson: 'Please ship half million Band-Aids immediately.' Back came the reply: 'Band-Aids on the way. What the hell happened to you?'

Bennett Cerf, *Good for a Laugh*, 1952

Robert Benchley · 1889–1945

(American humorist; frequenter of the Round Table at the Algonquin)

From an interview with Dorothy Parker:

And Harold Ross, *The New Yorker* editor. He was a professional lunatic, but I don't know if he was a great man. He had a profound ignorance. On one of Mr Benchley's manuscripts he wrote in the margin opposite 'Andromache,' 'Who he?' Mr Benchley wrote back, 'You keep out of this.'

Writers at Work: The Paris Review *Interviews*, first series, 1958

Jean Rhys · 1890–1979

Jean Rhys was born in Dominica. At the age of 16, she was brought to England; two years later, she was working as a chorus girl:

In England my love and longing for books completely left me. I never felt the least desire to read anything, not even a newspaper, and I think this indifference lasted a long time. Years. I don't remember reading anything on tour except *Forest Lovers. Forest Lovers* was a book set in the Middle Ages, about a man and a girl who loved each other very much and who escaped into the forest to hide, but they always slept with a sword between them. All the girls in the dressing-room had read the book and the conversation about the sword was endless. 'What did they have to do that for? Why? Besides, you could easily get over the sword.'—'No you couldn't, you'd get cut.'—'Of course you wouldn't.'

Smile Please: An Unfinished Autobiography, 1979

Rhys goes on to say that 'however abominable and dull my life was, it never occurred to me to buy a book or even a newspaper, which now seems very strange to me'.

The Forest Lovers *(1898) was written by Maurice Hewlett, an author who enjoyed a considerable literary reputation in his time.*

Agatha Christie · 1890–1976

By the end of the 'thirties she was occasionally irritated because Poirot was such a favourite of her readers and publishers—particularly of the American magazine publishers at *Collier's* and the *Saturday Evening Post*, which took most of her work and paid high prices. 'Poirot is rather insufferable,' she wrote to Cork [her agent]. 'Most public men are who have lived too long. But none of them like retiring! So I am afraid Poirot won't either—not while he is my chief source of income.'

Janet Morgan, *Agatha Christie*, 1984

Poirot went marching on. In the 1960s, when one of her books was due to be filmed, Agatha Christie was horrified by talk of the detective's character being changed and brought up to date. She was afraid this meant introducing a lot more violence, something to which she was opposed on principle. And in any case, 'if people have liked Poirot for about forty years as an egocentric creep they would probably prefer him to go on that way'.

Hugh MacDiarmid · 1892–1978

(pen-name of Christopher Murray Grieve)

Apparently MacDiarmid not only drank in the White Lion [a pub in Thakenham, a village in Sussex where he lived for a few months in 1932] but occasionally wrote there. During an evening's drinking MacDiarmid announced that he wanted to commit a poem to paper. Valda [the poet's companion, later his second wife] went to the toilet and returned with several sheets of paper. Slightly inebriated and with toilet paper thus to hand, MacDiarmid noted down one of his most memorable lyrics, 'Milk-Wort and Bog-Cotton'. The first of two stanzas is an expression of MacDiarmid's affinity with the earth and shows an exquisite sense of rhythm as the lines ebb and flow around the traditional measure of the iambic pentameter:

Cwa' een like milk-wort and bog-cotton hair!
I love you, earth, in this mood best o' a' . . .

In the second stanza, returning to a theme that runs through [MacDiarmid's most famous poem] *A Drunk Man Looks at the Thistle*, the poet observes that 'deep surroonding darkness . . . is aye the price o' licht'.

Alan Bold, *Hugh MacDiarmid*, 1988

Sir Osbert Sitwell · 1892–1969

On some occasion he and Harold Nicolson were together filling embarkation forms on a Channel crossing.

'What age are you going to put, Osbert?' asked Nicolson.

'What sex are you going to put, Harold?'

Anthony Powell, *Messengers of Day*, 1978

Wilfred Owen · 1893–1918

After service on the Western Front, Owen was invalided home in June 1917. He returned to France, where he was to meet his death in action, in August 1918.

In November 1917, while he was still recovering his health, he spent a week or so near Winchester with his cousin, Leslie Gunston:

Owen wrote a few days later, adding a postscript on the envelope which only came to light when Gunston unearthed it some sixty years later: 'I travelled up from Win: to Lond: with Bottomley [Horatio Bottomley, MP, journalist, swindler, and demagogue]. But didn't intrude on his Great Thoughts.' Two of the most influential writers on the war had been brought briefly face to face. The self-satisfied editor of *John Bull* ('The Paper on Which the Sun Never Sets') probably took no notice of the unknown officer whose future fame would long outlast his own.

Dominic Hibberd, *Wilfred Owen: The Last Year*, 1992

Bottomley had recently published a shilling booklet entitled 'Great Thoughts', and Dominic Hibberd goes on to quote some of them. For example, 'The "Conscientious Objector" is a fungus growth—a human toadstool—which should be uprooted without further delay.'

E. E. Cummings · 1894–1962

In the early 1920s Cummings lived in Paris, where an evening out with his friends John Dos Passos and Gilbert Seldes ended in trouble:

Cummings asked the gendarme why he was being arrested, and the gendarme replied, 'For pissing on Paris.' Cummings pointed out that he had merely pissed on the fiacre. 'Le fiacre—c'est Paris!' exclaimed the gendarme, and took him along—Seldes and Dos Passos following. . . . Seldes overheard this colloquy between the arresting gendarme and the officer behind the desk:

'Un Américain qui pisse.'

'Quoi—encore un pisseur Américain?'

Cummings told me the dialogue that took place inside.

'Would you do that in your own country?' asked the officer behind the desk.

'Yes,' replied Cummings.

'Menteur!' screamed the sergeant of police.

'Why do you call me a liar?' asked Cummings.

'Because I know about America—I have a relative there.'

'Where?'

'In Brook-leen.'

Cummings was asked where he lived, and a gendarme went outside to check with Seldes and Dos Passos. When it was found that he had told the truth, he was permitted to leave, but with orders to report to a magistrate the next morning. . . . When Cummings showed up, he was greeted by several hastily drawn posters announcing, 'Reprieve Pisseur Américain!'

Charles Norman, *The Magic Maker: E. E. Cummings*, 1958

Aldous Huxley · 1894–1963

In spite of twenty-five years in Southern California, he remains an English gentleman. The scientist's habit of examining everything from every side and of turning everything upside down and inside out is also characteristic of Aldous. I remember him leafing through a copy of *Transition*, reading a poem in it, looking again at the title of the magazine, reflecting for a moment, then saying, 'Backwards it spells NO IT ISN(T) ART.'

Igor Stravinsky in Igor Stravinsky and Robert Craft, *Memories and Commentaries*, 2002

A group of us had gone to the pier to have dinner at a little fish restaurant, and while waiting to be served, Charlie Chaplin noticed a sign across the way that read, 'Scientific Handwriting Analysis. Ten Cents.' Charlie decided, as a joke, to try the expert out. Aldous stopped him. It would be too simple for a swami to 'read' for Charlie because his appearance was familiar to practically everyone in the world. On the other hand no one would recognize Aldous. So Charlie wrote a few words on a scrap of paper which Aldous took to the lady. He returned from his interview in a mood of deep concentration and reported what had happened. The lady had studied the writing a moment and then looked up at Aldous suspiciously, 'Are you trying to make fun of me, sir?' she asked. Aldous assured her he was not and wanted to know why she asked. She paused and studied Charlie's writing more closely. Then, still suspicious, she asked, 'Did you write this while you were in an unnatural or cramped position?' Aldous then admitted that the writing was not his own but he assured the lady that it had been done quite normally. 'Then,' said the expert, 'I don't know what to say, because if what you tell me is true, the man who wrote this is a God-given genius.' We were all duly impressed. Later Aldous came to know the handwriting lady personally; she turned out to be well versed in her trade and we consulted her frequently.

Anita Loos in *Aldous Huxley: A Memorial Volume*, ed. Julian Huxley, 1965

Robert Graves · 1895–1985

At the age of 20 Graves was serving with the Welsh Regiment on the Western Front:

In the interval between stand-to and breakfast, the men who were not getting in a bit of extra sleep sat about talking and smoking, writing letters home, cleaning their rifles, running their thumb-nails up the seams of their shirts to kill lice, gambling. Lice were a standing joke. Young Bumford handed me one. 'We was just having an argument as to whether it's best to kill the old ones or the young ones, sir. Morgan here says that if you kill the old ones, the young ones die of grief; but Parry here, sir, he says that the young ones are easier to kill and you can catch the old ones when they go to the funeral.' He appealed to me as an arbiter: 'You've been to college, sir, haven't you?'

I said: 'Yes, I have, but so had Crawshay Bailey's brother Norwich.'

The platoon treasured this as a wonderfully witty answer. *Crawshay Bailey* is one of the idiotic songs of Wales. Crawshay Bailey himself 'had an engine and he couldn't make it go', and all his relatives in the song had similar shortcomings. Crawshay Bailey's brother Norwich, for instance, was fond of oatmeal porridge, but was sent to Cardiff College, for to get a bit of knowledge. After that, I had no trouble with the platoon.

Graves, *Goodbye to All That*, 1929

Graves was given his first taste of night patrol after his arrival at Laventie. His orders involved a two-hour stomach crawl into German territory under barbed wire and enemy flares; the prize was a glass container which appeared to contain only wine dregs and rainwater. The contents were not the point. He was praised for having carried out a dangerous mission.

Miranda Seymour, *Robert Graves*, 1995

After the First World War Graves studied as an undergraduate at Oxford:

AT the end of my first term's work, I attended the usual college board to give an account of myself. The spokesman coughed, and said a little stiffly: 'I understand, Mr Graves, that the essays which you write for your English tutor are, shall I say, a trifle temperamental. It appears, indeed, that you prefer some authors to others.'

Graves, *Goodbye to All That*

In The White Goddess *(1948) Graves expounded his belief that all true poetry is inspired by a muse who in one form or another is an incarnation of the matriarchal Moon Goddess. He had trouble getting the book published:*

JONATHAN CAPE [who had published some of his previous books] rejected it and added, condescendingly, that he would give the author a dinner if he could find a publisher willing to take it on. An unnamed American publisher, having refused it, gave Graves satisfaction on another level by 'almost immediately' hanging himself in a garden, dressed in women's clothes. This, to Graves' myth-loving mind, was a clear sign that the Goddess was on his side.

Seymour, *Robert Graves*

> *The sad fate of the American publisher was recounted by Graves in a lecture. Miranda Seymour adds in a note that 'the story has proved impossible for the Author to verify'.*

EDMUND WILSON · 1895–1972

HE could be hilarious in his retentiveness, his obstinacy, his intense personal relation to any book or subject that he liked very much or disliked very much. Discussing *The Scarlet Letter* (a book that as a literary modernist he easily disliked because it belonged to the American schoolroom or too much to his own past: on his mother's side he was descended from the Mathers), he was angrily asked by a young professor of American Studies, 'May I ask when you last read the book?' 'Nineteen fifteen,' Wilson said breezily.

Alfred Kazin, *New York Jew*, 1978

Philip Rahv and William Phillips were the editors of the Partisan Review, *the distinguished literary quarterly founded in 1934. Many of its contributors, like the editors, were New York Jewish intellectuals.*

RAHV pumped me for whatever trivial incidents I had to tell, for they somehow fattened his own ego against Wilson. But there was one remark

I did not tell, though it got back to Rahv anyway. When I saw Wilson after I was back in America, I told him I had joined the staff of *Partisan Review*; he merely laughed and remarked of Rahv and Phillips 'Potash and Perlmutter.' He was citing an earlier comedy of his own playgoing years. Potash and Perlmutter are the eternal pair of bumbling Jewish businessmen, yoked together and perpetually querulous about each other, but somehow managing a business that survives by the skin of its teeth. Wilson's remark was intended to be humorous, not malicious; there was much anger but no great malice in the man that I ever noticed; but when the remark got back home it had changed coloration. I had told it secretly to Delmore, but he leaked it. And Rahv's retort on this occasion was pithy and vigorous: 'The shmuck!' he said of Edmund Wilson.

William Barrett, *The Truants: Adventures among Intellectuals*, 1982

L. P. Hartley · 1895–1972

(novelist: author of the 'Eustace and Hilda' trilogy and *The Go-Between*)

Leslie had just been obliged to sack a manservant who, like many of his predecessors, had constantly bullied, cheeked and cheated him. Here, I thought, was the ideal solution. When, a few days later, I was having luncheon with him in his eyrie in Rutland Gate, I told him of the couple: former hospital nurse and former policeman, she an excellent plain cook, he an extremely careful driver and skilled handyman and gardener, both totally honest, both utterly respectful and respectable. As I enumerated each of their virtues, Leslie looked glummer and glummer. Then he said, 'Well, I'll think about it.' I realized that what he really wanted was the dangerous excitement of yet another manservant just out of nick.

One such manservant was extremely handsome and also extremely sinister. He and Leslie would have constant rows, at the close of one of which, when I myself was present, the manservant told Leslie, 'Oh, do me a favour, will you? Just fuck off!' When the manservant had stormed out of the room, Leslie looked across at me, his eyes twinkling, clearly delighted: 'What a *very* odd thing to say!'

Francis King, *Yesterday Came Suddenly*, 1993

F. R. Leavis · 1895–1978

Leavis taught at Cambridge, but occasionally came over to give a lecture to an undergraduate society in Oxford. One of those who went to hear him was the young A. Alvarez:

The subject of his lecture was Shelley, Shelley and his moral and poetic shortcomings—a sinister combination of self-indulgence and flabby thinking that amounted, Leavis said, to 'viciousness and corruption'. Shelley, of course, was an Oxford man and a great favourite with the dons who taught us, so Leavis's swingeing attack went down a treat with his iconoclastic audience. But it was a baffling performance, not least because what he was saying seemed so much at odds with his appearance. In his shabby corduroy jacket, with his shirt wide open at the neck, he looked just like the portraits of Shelley. Like Shelley, too, he seemed weightless, all fire and nerves and literary passion. And the passion made the lecture doubly puzzling. At one point he read Shelley's famous lyric 'When the lamp is shattered' and then explained, in detail, why it was a dreadful poem. But he had read it with such understanding and feeling that the reading made nonsense of the analysis. He made the poem sound beautiful and convincing, he made it sound like a masterpiece, so that when he trampled all over it he seemed to be doing violence to himself.

A. Alvarez, *Where Did It All Go Right?*, 1999

F. Scott Fitzgerald · 1896–1940

Scott and Zelda Fitzgerald spent the first years of their marriage in New York:

Their wild and well-publicized pranks soon became notorious. Watching a comedy in the front row of a theater, they annoyed the actors by laughing appreciatively in all the wrong places. Kicked out of the Biltmore for disturbing other guests, they celebrated their move to the Commodore by spinning through the revolving doors for half an hour. Looking like a figurehead on the prow of a ship, Zelda paid a surcharge to catch the breeze on the hood of a taxi. Out of sheer exuberance they jumped into the fountain in Union Square and into the fountain near the Plaza, and achieved instant fame at the Greenwich Village Follies, whose curtain by Reginald Marsh included a picture of Zelda splashing in these urban pools. During a Hawaiian pageant in Montgomery (which they visited in March 1921), Zelda bent over, lifted her grass skirt and wriggled her pert behind. In May 1920 they rented a house on Compo Road in suburban Westport and hired a Japanese servant. Bored by the suburbs,

Zelda summoned the firemen (as she had done as a child in Montgomery). When asked where the blaze was, she struck her breast and exclaimed: 'Here!'

Jeffrey Meyers, *Scott Fitzgerald*, 1994

When they lived in France in the 1920s the Fitzgeralds' closest friends were a wealthy couple, Gerald and Sara Murphy, although the Murphys sometimes found their antics hard to take:

SCOTT's worst offense, which stretched Gerald's tolerance to the breaking point, led to temporary banishment from the Villa America. It seemed to justify Gerald's angry statement that 'he really had the most appalling sense of humor, sophomoric and—well, trashy.' Feeling that his fellow guests were not paying sufficient attention to him, Scott seemed determined to destroy the formal dinner party. He 'began throwing Sara's gold-flecked Venetian wineglasses over the garden wall. He had smashed three of them this way before Gerald stopped him. As the party was breaking up, Gerald went up to Scott (among the last to leave) and told him that he would not be welcome in their house for three weeks.' While exiled from their parties, Scott made his presence felt by throwing a can of garbage onto the patio as the Murphys were dining.

Meyers, *Scott Fitzgerald*

In 1927 Fitzgerald accepted an offer to work on a script in Hollywood. As Ian Hamilton puts it, in his book Writers in Hollywood, *'several celebrated "Scott and Zelda" horror stories issue from this venture. There is the Sam Goldwyn party story (S and Z, not invited, turned up on their hands and knees and barked until they were let in), and the "ladies' purses" story (S and Z, out to tea, collected all the ladies' purses, boiled them in a pot, and served them as tomato soup).' And then there was the surprise visit they paid one night, accompanied by the artist James Montgomery Flagg, to the home of the fashionable scriptwriter and ladies' man John Monk Saunders:*

SAUNDERS was in his pajamas and a Sulka dressing robe and sandals, smiling imperturbably and getting drinks as if nothing surprised him. He turned on his phonograph and we set about chatting, with the exception of Mrs F., who in prowling around found a pair of editor's shears and then sat down next to Saunders on a lounge, pulled open his robe and took a deep inhalation, then called: 'Scott, come here. John smells lovely!'

Scott went over and sat on the other side of Saunders and they buried their noses in his manly chest. They sighed luxuriously. Then Mrs F. remembered the shears and began gently urging her host to let her perform a quick operation on him, explaining with quiet eloquence that his earthly troubles would be over if he would submit.

James Mongomery Flagg, *Roses and Buckshot*, 1946

WILLIAM FAULKNER · 1897–1962

Faulkner explains how he started as a writer:

I WAS living in New Orleans, doing whatever kind of work was necessary to earn a little money now and then. I met Sherwood Anderson. We would walk about the city in the afternoon and talk to people. In the evenings we would meet again and sit over a bottle or two while he talked and I listened. In the forenoon I would never see him. He was secluded, working. The next day we would repeat. I decided that if that was the life of a writer, then becoming a writer was the thing for me. So I began to write my first book. At once I found that writing was fun. I even forgot that I hadn't seen Mr Anderson for three weeks until he walked in my door, the first time he ever came to see me, and said, 'What's wrong? Are you mad at me?' I told him I was writing a book. He said, 'My God,' and walked out. When I finished the book—it was *Soldier's Pay*—I met Mrs Anderson on the street. She asked how the book was going, and I said I'd finished it. She said, 'Sherwood says that he will make a trade with you. If he doesn't have to read your manuscript he will tell his publisher to accept it.' I said, 'Done,' and that's how I became a writer.

Writers at Work: The Paris Review *Interviews*, first series, 1958

There are several different versions of the legend of Faulkner's misleading request to 'work at home' when he was in Hollywood. The story has been told in connection with all three studios which employed him—MGM, Twentieth Century Fox, and finally Warner Brothers:

JERRY WALD brought him to Burbank, and I gave him a sumptuous office with two attractive secretaries, and I said: 'No one's going to bother you here, Mr Faulkner. Your time will be your own.'

'Thank you, Mr Warner,' he said, 'but if it's all the same to you, I'd rather work at home.'

'Now, we don't expect you to punch any clocks, Mr Faulkner,' I said. 'You can come and go as you please.'

'I would prefer *not* to work in an office,' he said stubbornly.

Some weeks later, when something urgent arose in connection with the script, I asked Bill Schaefer to call Faulkner.

'You know he works at home,' Bill said.

'Of course. Call him at home.'

'This is long distance. We're ready on your call to Mr Faulkner.'

'Long distance?' I almost yelled.

'Yes, sir,' the operator said. 'He's in Oxford, Mississippi.'

'Mr Faulkner, how could you do this to me? How could you leave town without letting me know? You said you'd be working at home.'

'This is my home,' Faulkner said patiently, 'I live in Mississippi.'

Jack Warner, *My First Hundred Years in Hollywood*, 1965

Nirad C. Chaudhuri · 1897–1999

Born in Bengal, Chaudhuri was 54 when he published his first book, the classic Autobiography of an Unknown Indian, *and 58 when he visited Europe for the first time. In 1970 he and his wife emigrated to England and settled in Oxford. It was there, in the 1980s, that Jeremy Lewis, who worked for his publisher, visited him in order to discuss the massive second volume of his autobiography. (The typescript ran to well over a thousand pages.)*

On arrival, Lewis found that Chaudhuri had installed 'a gigantic music centre, like an enormous metal crab':

Gesturing to me with a downward motion of his hand to stay exactly where I was, Mr Chaudhuri then darted towards a dresser in which, it seemed, he kept his large collection of gramophone records, selected several, and then—once again clasping his hands together—announced that he was going to subject me to a musical quiz. 'So,' Mr Chaudhuri announced—'So', it seemed, was as popular and as peremptory a prefix as 'Now', and much in use that day—'So, I am going to test you on music. I am going to play you a familiar piece of music, and you will please tell me what is different about this particular recording.' The music was familiar enough—*Eine Kleine Nachtmusik*—but so befuddled was I by Mr Chaudhuri's rhetorical flow, and so convinced that I would never pass the test, that I quite failed to notice that an extra movement had somehow been smuggled into Mr Chaudhuri's recording; and when I confessed, in an agony of shame, that I had no idea how or why it was any different from more conventional versions, my tormentor dashed the record to the floor with a triumphant cry, and moved on to question number two. As the morning wore on I failed on Bellini arias, and Love Songs from the Auvergne, and Spanish gypsy music; and with every failure Mr Chaudhuri let out a devilish cry and danced on the spot like Quilp in *The Old Curiosity Shop* and dashed yet another record to the ground. Every now and then he interrupted his musical examination with a literary quiz, plucking *Jane Eyre* or *Pride and Prejudice* in their leather-bound editions from the shelves above his head, making me read a selected passage and then (in vain) inviting me to explain some point of etiquette from the early nineteenth century; and book after book rained from his hand to join the other discarded cultural artefacts on the floor. All this, alas, provided shaming support for Mr Chaudhuri's loudly proclaimed view—

half gloating, half regretful—that even well-educated modern Englishmen are shockingly ignorant of their culture and history, and that this is all too indicative of a nation in decline. From time to time I tried to stem the flow by hoisting the typescript onto my knee like a neglected baby, but Mr Chaudhuri brushed such diversions aside.

After a break for lunch the quizzing resumed, though by now Chaudhuri seemed 'in mellower and more merciful mood'. Finally, at four o'clock, Lewis made his excuses and left:

I HAD, rather to my surprise, become extremely fond of my host during the day we had spent together, but my brain—which had given a predictably poor showing—could take no more.

Jeremy Lewis, *Kindred Spirits*, 1995

C. S. LEWIS · 1898–1963

Lewis aroused mixed reactions among his pupils at Oxford:

FOR every one of them who (like John Wain) managed to enjoy and to ape Lewis's forceful logic, there were at least as many who were alarmed and cowed by the heavy-handedness of his manner, combined with his general refusal to put his relationship with his pupils on anything like a personal footing. A few lapped it up, but some very nearly ran away. 'If you think that way about Keats you needn't come here again!' Lewis once roared down the stairs to a departing pupil. And on another occasion when an Australian student professed that he could never read Arnold's *Sohrab and Rustum*, and refused to admit its good qualities even after Lewis had chanted a hundred lines of it at him, Lewis declared, 'The sword must settle it!' and reached for a broadsword and a rapier which (according to J. A. W. Bennett, who was there) were inexplicably in the corner of the room. They fenced—Lewis of course choosing the broadsword—and, said Bennett, 'Lewis actually drew blood—a slight nick.'

Humphrey Carpenter, *The Inklings*, 1978

I NEVER heard Lewis speak ill of Leavis, but then he plainly preferred not to speak about him at all. It is clear he found little virtue in his writings, and the high-minded priggery of that kind of agnostic mind was never to his taste . . . I once asked him directly what he thought of Leavis. He looked very grave, as if fearful of being quoted; and then, in a half-mocking tone, he said in a low voice: 'I think he's saved.' I asked why. 'Because,' he replied with what appeared to be complete gravity, 'he isn't interested in money.' 'So you think you may meet at the Last Judgement?'

I asked, steering us out of embarrassment. 'If our names on that occasion are taken in alphabetical order, yes,' he said, and the exchange broke up in a laugh.

George Watson, 'The Art of Disagreement: C. S. Lewis', *Hudson Review*, 1995

Another observer records seeing Lewis and Leavis together:

NOT twenty years ago, in Cambridge, I was party to a conversation between F. R. Leavis and C. S. Lewis, illustrious antagonists on many famous issues and occasions, who agreed however that there could not be in any serious sense universities on American soil because—and I can't remember which of the revered elders produced this moth-eaten proposition—the United States was not a democracy but (wait for it!) a plutocracy. Sagely nodding and capping each other's observations, Leavis and Lewis would hear nothing of expostulations from me, or from another of the company lately returned from a year in the States.

Donald Davie, *These the Companions*, 1982

HART CRANE · 1899–1932

Harry and Caresse Crosby published Crane's poem The Bridge. *They also invited him to stay in their house in Paris:*

WE were aware of Hart's midnight prowlings and also aware, to our dismay, of his nocturnal pick-ups. He said he'd go out for a nightcap so it was with great relief that I heard him come in about two a.m. and softly close the stairway door. Then all was quiet. But in the morning, what a hideous awakening! Marcelle brought my morning coffee to me in hands that trembled with shock. 'Oh, Madame,' she said, '*quel malheur, quel malheur*.' I jumped from my bed and followed her downstairs to see what was the matter. By that time it was ten o'clock and Hart had already departed, probably as silently as he had entered, but he had left behind him traces of great activity. On the wallpaper and across the pale pink spread, up and down the curtains and over the white chenille rug were the blackest footprints and handprints I have ever seen, hundreds of them. No wonder, for I heard to my fury that he had brought a chimney-sweep home for the night.

Caresse Crosby, *The Passionate Years*, 1955

Noël Coward · 1899–1973

Off the stage, when did Noël act, and when was his private behaviour totally spontaneous? Given an audience, he seldom entered a room; he almost always made an entry; and I remember another occasion, this time at a house in France, where a number of English guests were assembled. Among them was the singer Olga Lynn—'Oggie' to her large affectionate circle—a remarkably short and rather stout lady, inclined to wear a very broad hat, so that she had somewhat the appearance of a perambulatory mushroom. She was then recovering from a slight stroke; but of this Noël happened to be unaware. He arrived late and, a suitable entry having been made, moved genially around the room, distributing kisses and smiles and bows, until at last he came to Oggie. 'Darling Oggie; and how are *you*?' he demanded. 'Thank you, Noël; I've been ill you see', she replied in muffled accents and patted her poor flaccid cheek. Noël dramatically threw up his hands. 'Not—a—tiny—*strokey*—Oggie—darling?' he enquired in tones of heart-felt consternation, carefully spacing out the words and lending each a poignant emphasis. We were all tempted to laugh, and quickly resisted the impulse; but although the enquiry may perhaps sound brutal, it had the right effect upon the sufferer, since it implied that a stroke was the kind of harmless minor mishap, mildly ridiculous rather than really grave, like tripping over a dog or tumbling downstairs, that might come anybody's way.

Peter Quennell, *The Wanton Chase*, 1980

Ernest Hemingway · 1899–1961

When Hemingway and his wife Hadley arrived in Paris in 1921, one of the first Americans to get in touch with them was Lewis Galantière, to whom they had forwarded a letter of introduction from Sherwood Anderson. Galantière, who knew Paris intimately, took them out to dinner in a smart restaurant:

At the outset of the meal Hemingway found him delightful, but as it became clear that Hadley felt the same way Hemingway's competitive ire was aroused. Wherefore he brought up the subject of boxing. When Galantière admitted to a slight acquaintance with the sport, Hemingway invited him back to the Jacob for a few rounds of postprandial sparring. He had two pairs of regulation boxing gloves in his trunk, so there would be no problem about proper equipment. On the way across the Atlantic, he further informed Galantière, he had fought a three-round exhibition match in the dining salon of their steamship with an Italo-American fighter from Salt Lake City and had beaten him badly. Galantière's reluctance to accept Hemingway's invitation became pronounced at this point. He didn't really like to hit other people, he explained, any more than he liked being hit himself. But Hemingway refused to take no for an answer.

In the living room of the Hemingways' suite, the two men touched gloves and commenced to circle one another, while Hadley acted as timekeeper. After a minute or two, during which time neither man threw a single punch, Galantière straightened up and laughingly said that he had had enough. After removing one glove, he put on his glasses and began to unlace the other glove. In the meantime, Hemingway had been shadow boxing, throwing lefts and rights and dancing about. Suddenly, he lunged at Galantière and hit him in the face, breaking his glasses. Luckily, no fragments flew into the victim's eyes or cut his face. Hemingway was obviously relieved about this, but he felt no contrition, in Hadley's opinion. He had effectively demonstrated his masculine superiority.

Kenneth S. Lynn, *Hemingway*, 1987

Kenneth Lynn adds that 'somehow, Galantière's wish to be friends survived the incident'.

HEMINGWAY was a great pal of Joyce's, and Joyce remarked to me one day that he thought it was a mistake, Hemingway's thinking himself such a tough fellow and McAlmon trying to pass himself off as the sensitive type. It was the other way round, he thought. So Joyce found you out, Hemingway!

Sylvia Beach, *Shakespeare and Company*, 1960

Robert McAlmon—American poet and short story writer, best known for his memoir Being Geniuses Together.

I WROTE a piece about him for 'Talk of the Town' and because he struck me as so awesomely strong and full of life I headed the piece 'Indestructible'. In the light of his miserable last years, it was just the wrong word for me to have chosen, and yet Hemingway believed it of himself at the time; and not alone of himself but of his whole family. In our talk, he outlined his theory that no Hemingway had ever died a natural death. 'That's one reason I've written so little about my family', he said. 'I can't say everything I want to say about it as long as certain people are still alive.' This was, at his request, a deliberately oblique reference to his mother, whom he hated. He told me of how she sent him the gun with which his father shot himself, and Hemingway spoke of his certainty that he would never follow in his father's footsteps.

Brendan Gill, *Here at the New Yorker*, 1975

Vladimir Nabokov · 1899–1977

ROBERT ROBINSON. First, sir, to spare you irritation, I wonder if you will instruct me in the pronunciation of your name.

VLADIMIR NABOKOV. Let me put it this way. There exists a number of deceptively simple-looking Russian names, whose spelling and pronunciation present the foreigner with strange traps. The name Suvarov took a couple of centuries to lose the preposterous middle 'a'—it should be Suvoruv. American autograph-seekers, while professing a knowledge of all my books—prudently not mentioning their titles—rejuggle the vowels of my name in all the ways allowed by mathematics. 'Nabakav' is especially touching for the 'a's. Pronunciation problems fall into a less erratic pattern. On the playing-fields of Cambridge, my football team used to hail me as 'Nabkov' or facetiously, 'Macnab'. New Yorkers reveal their tendency of turning 'o' into 'ah' by pronouncing my name 'Nabarkov'. The aberration, 'N*a*bokov', is a favourite one of postal officials; now the correct Russian way would take too much time to explain, and so I've settled for the euphonious 'Nab*o*kov', with the middle syllable accented and rhyming with 'smoke'. Would you like to try?

R.R. Mr NabOkov.

V.N. That's right.

BBC interview, 1977; reprinted in *Vladimir Nabokov: His Life, his Work, his World*, ed. Peter Quennell, 1979

In his autobiography Nabokov describes a visit which his father made to London in 1916 at the invitation of the British government, together with five other prominent representatives of the Russian press:

THERE had been an official banquet presided over by Sir Edward Grey, and a funny interview with George V whom Chukovski, the *enfant terrible* of the group, insisted on asking if he liked the works of Oscar Wilde—'dze ooarks of OOald.' The king, who was baffled by his interrogator's accent and who, anyway, had never been a voracious reader, neatly countered by inquiring how his guests liked the London fog (later Chukovski used to cite this triumphantly as an example of British cant—tabooing a writer because of his morals).

Nabokov, *Speak, Memory*, revised edition 1967

When Nabokov moved to America in 1940, he found some of his fellow Russian émigrés uncongenial:

AN émigré teacher of Russian at Columbia complimented him, as soon as he was introduced, on his magnificent aristocratic pronunciation: 'All one hears here are Yids.' At an émigré party where Nabokov was the guest of honor, he heard the host himself use the word 'Yid.' Normally extremely correct in his speech—there is not a single obscenity in his published work—Nabokov responded by swearing deliberately and forcefully. When his host reacted with astonishment, Nabokov replied, 'I thought this was the language you used in this house,' and promptly left.

Brian Boyd, *Vladimir Nabokov: The American Years*, 1992

AFTER dinner he and Véra would play a game of Russian Scrabble on a board Vivian Crespi had given them early in the year. Scrabble coincidences struck Nabokov's imagination: 'There is something of the planchette in this game,' he observed to his sister. One evening as he was collecting the tiles for the first round, he mentioned Elena's recent dream that Fyodor's dream at the end of *The Gift* had really happened. '*Zabavno* [amusing],' he reflected, and then discovered *zabavno* in his scrabble rack. A few days earlier he had been telling Véra that he had four people (*chetvero*) dining in *Ada*, and *chetvero* (seven letters in Russian) turned up in his rack. No wonder he appropriated Russian Scrabble for the theme of portents and prophecies in *Ada*.

Boyd, *Vladmir Nabokov*

IN America *Lolita* was becoming a household word and regular subject of jokes by television hosts like Steve Allen, Dean Martin and Milton Berle. The process of vulgarization would ultimately lead to such horrors as the life-size Lolita doll with 'French and Greek apertures' advertised in the mid-1970s. In 1958, standards were very different—and Nabokov's own stricter than most. He was quite shocked when a little girl of eight or nine came to his door for candy on Halloween, dressed up by her parents as Lolita, with a tennis racquet and a ponytail, and a sign reading L-O-L-I-T-A. Before the novel's publication, he had insisted to Minton [Walter Minton, his American publisher] that there be no little girl on the book's cover, and now as a *Lolita* movie looked more and more possible, he warned Minton that he 'would veto the use of a real child. Let them find a dwarfess.'

Boyd, *Vladimir Nabokov*

Despite their friendship, the seeds of Edmund Wilson's hostility to Nabokov were sown long before Wilson's attack on Nabokov's translation of Eugene Onegin*:*

WILSON came to resent Nabokov's dismissal of other writers and his unshakable self-assurance, and as early as 1945 he wrote to him of 'your insatiable and narcissistic vanity.' Nabokov played up to that image, deliberately teasing his friend. When Wilson wrote that he had begun to learn chess, for instance, Nabokov replied: 'I hope that you will soon be playing well enough for me to beat you.'

Boyd, *Vladimir Nabokov*

Nabokov eventually returned to live in Europe:

FOR a famous expatriate writer one source of contact with America was to be found in the books optimistic publishers sent him to read. After he had received *Catch-22*, Vera wrote back on his behalf that he made it a rule not to give his opinion 'since he is a harsh judge. But he agrees to make an exception in this case . . . "This book is a torrent of trash, dialogical diarrhoea, the automatic produce of a prolix typewriter." Please do not repeat this either to the author or to his publisher.'

Boyd, *Vladimir Nobokov*

ELIZABETH BOWEN · 1899–1973

ELIZABETH has been going to an Austrian psychoanalyst to be cured of her stammer (which is so much part of her). So far it seems to me that she has told him nothing while he has told her the story of his life. This hardly surprises me.

Charles Ritchie, May 1942; in *The Siren Years: Undiplomatic Diaries*, 1974

Bowen's husband Alan often seemed to play a secondary role in her life:

THE guests at Clarence Terrace were almost all Elizabeth's friends, not Alan's; it was for Elizabeth they came, not for Alan. The young Oxford dons, the London critics, the writers, had little to say to him. There were exceptions. But some of them were very naughty, very rude. They talked across him, they ignored him, while accepting his hospitality . . .

Apocryphal stories grew up about Alan and the clever friends, perhaps the most graphic being that about a party at Bowen's Court where a guest, blundering off to look for a lavatory, opened a door to find Alan alone in a small room eating his supper off a tray. Apocryphal stories have a poetic if not a historical truth; they express what a sufficient number of people feel to have been the truth. And the truth is that to an outside observer Alan seemed to be having rather a thin time.

Victoria Glendinning, *Elizabeth Bowen*, 1977

C. L. R. James · 1901–1989

(born in Trinidad; historian, political activist, and writer on cricket; author of *The Black Jacobins* and *Beyond a Boundary*)

James spent his last years in London, in a house in Brixton, above the offices of the magazine Race Today. *For a time one of the other occupants of the house was a young Jamaican poet, Mikey Smith, who had come to Britain on a reading tour. Smith attracted enthusiastic crowds: the BBC made a television programme about him, and invited James and the Jamaican-British poet Linton Kwesi Johnson (who had helped arrange the tour) to join him in a conversation about poetry:*

The cameras follow Mikey through several of his public performances and they record interviews with him. Then comes the day of the tripartite discussion. It is held in the old man's room with the two young black poets in attendance. They discuss the nature of Jamaican dialect. Mikey adopts the stance of the grass roots man, the illiterate, suffering genius who knows no language but the spontaneous revelations of his verse. One can also see the old man becoming increasingly impatient with the stance, asking him to repeat phrases in plain English. This inhibits the progress of the conversation and gets the cameras to stop and start but doesn't deter CLR who seems determined to extract some clarity from Mikey and refuses to bolster the falsehood he believes him to be creating.

The game is blown wide open when, with a sneer, Mikey alludes to 'Shak-uss-peeree. Or whatever he is called.' A sneer too far. The old man calls him to order.

'Now hold on. I have lived most of my life in the Caribbean, I know Jamaica and Jamaican people and I have never heard Shakespeare's name pronounced like that.'

He refuses to let Mikey wear ignorance on his sleeve as a badge of his rebellion. It's the wrong kind of rebellion. He recommends, on or off camera, I can't remember, though I am present at the interview and stand behind the bright camera lights tripod, that Mikey read some Wordsworth and some Shelley.

Mikey stares defiantly but has been corrected. The last scene of the documentary features Mikey standing in the dawn on Westminster Bridge and rendering Wordsworth's sonnet about the scene in a very moving way.

Farrukh Dondy, *C. L. R. James*, 2001

Stevie Smith · 1902–1971

Occasionally Stevie's impatience with sentimentality could make her seem hard and intolerant. Moreover, if at a dinner party the conversation did not interest her she simply threw it aside and darted elsewhere or sang one of her poems, her tremulous, atonal chant shattering the ongoing discussion. When her stories went on rather long, in a giggly sort of way, she could be accused of monomania by an unsympathetic listener. Even her friend and admirer, Sir John Lawrence admits: 'She wasn't going to be bored. She wasn't disagreeable about it, but she wasn't going to have it.'

Frances Spalding, *Stevie Smith*, 1988

Langston Hughes · 1902–1967

Hughes was a leading figure in the 'Harlem Renaissance' of the 1920s. During the mid-20s he spent two years in Washington. His contacts with poor blacks in the city reinforced his passionate devotion to black music ('its strength like the beat of the human heart, its humor, its rooted power'), and many of his poems employ the rhythms and techniques of the blues:

The blues poems I would often make up in my head and sing on the way to work. (Except that I could never carry a tune. But when I sing to myself, I think I am singing.) One evening, I was crossing Rock Creek Bridge, singing a blues I was trying to get right before I put it down on paper. A man passing on the opposite side of the bridge stopped, looked at me, then turned around and cut across the roadway.

He said: 'Son, what's the matter? Are you ill?'

'No,' I said. 'Just singing.'

'I thought you were groaning,' he commented. 'Sorry!' And went his way.

So after that I never sang my verses aloud in the street any more.

Langston Hughes, *The Big Sea*, 1940

David Cecil · 1902–1986

(critic and biographer)

In the early 1950s A. Alvarez was working on a thesis at Oxford, though a year at Princeton had made him restless:

Maybe I was too full of America. Soon after I got back to Oxford, Lord David Cecil invited me to dinner at New College, where he taught English. Cecil was Oxford's ultimate appreciative critic, all fine feeling and sensibility. His face was long and delicate, like a borzoi's, he wore beautifully cut tweeds and a velvet waistcoat, he spoke in sudden bursts and with a lisp. I got to know him just after I founded the Critical Society, when he invited me to join his weekly seminar on practical criticism, and to our mutual astonishment and Freddie's scorn we got along just fine. [*'Freddie' was Alvarez's old Oxford tutor, F. W. Bateson.*]

Over dinner that evening I told him a long-winded story about a Princeton friend who spent a summer climbing in the Bugaboos, in British Columbia, ran out of money, and had to hitch-hike back to New York with $5 in his pocket. It was a difficult trip all the way, but his worst moment was at three in the morning, in the middle of the Panhandle desert, when he had to use his clasp-knife to fight off a homosexual truck driver. It was a good story but I was over-dramatizing it, trying to impress Lord David with this macho new world I had discovered. He listened wide-eyed, as a good host should, until I had finished. Then he said, 'Good heaventh, I would have thuccumbed!'

A. Alvarez, *Where Did It All Go Right?*, 1999

George Orwell · 1903–1950

(pen-name of Eric Blair)

Orwell was at the preparatory school St Cyprian's with Cyril Connolly. The school appears in Connolly's account of it under the name of 'St Wulfric's':

The remarkable thing about Orwell was that alone among the boys he was an intellectual and not a parrot for he thought for himself, read Shaw and Samuel Butler and rejected not only St Wulfric's but the war, the Empire, Kipling, Sussex, and Character. I remember a moment under a fig-tree in one of the inland boulevards of the seaside town, Orwell striding beside me and saying in his flat, ageless voice: 'You know, Connolly, there is only one remedy for all diseases.' I felt the usual guilty tremor when sex was mentioned and hazarded, 'You mean going to the lavatory?' 'No—I mean Death!' He was not a romantic, he had use neither for the blandishments of the drill-sergeant who made us feel character was identical with boxing nor for the threats of the chaplain with his grizzled cheektufts and his gospel of a Jesus of character who detested immorality and swearing as much as he loved the Allies. 'Of course, you realise, Connolly,' said Orwell, 'that, whoever wins this war, we shall emerge a second-rate nation.'

Cyril Connolly, *Enemies of Promise*, 1938

Connolly later admitted that he had made this account of Orwell's views too dramatic by dating them too early—that they actually reflect Orwell as he was at Eton (where Connolly was also a pupil) three or four years later.

ONE thing all Orwell's friends were agreed upon was that his accent was upper-class . . . 'Markedly Old Etonian,' thought his young friend Michael Meyer, by which he meant simultaneously high-pitched and drawling. No doubt Orwell was aware of his elevated tone. The young George Bowling, joining a west London tennis club in *Coming Up for Air*, listens to its middle-class suburban members calling out the score in voices that are 'a passable imitation of the upper crust'. His creator's was the real thing, ripe for modification if he thought the social circumstances demanded it. There were occasional forays, for example, into the style known as 'Duke of Windsor cockney'. A BBC colleague once heard him assuring an Asian contributor that skin tone played no part in their relationship: 'The fack that you're black and I'm white has *nudding woddever to do wiv it.*'

D. J. Taylor, *Orwell: The Life*, 2003

RICHARD REES recalled a curious exchange on the subject of his *nom de plume*: seeing his name in print gave him an unpleasant feeling, Orwell explained, because 'how can you be sure your enemy won't cut it out and work some sort of black magic on it?' This was whimsy, Rees thought, while noting that on occasions of this sort one could never be sure if Orwell was being serious or not.

Taylor, *Orwell*

ORWELL was once arguing with a Communist sympathizer about the true nature of Stalin's Russia. Forced to concede that there might be *some* political repression, his opponent fell back on what was then a much-favoured cliché.

COMMUNIST SYMPATHIZER. Well, you can't make an omelette without breaking eggs.

ORWELL. Where's the omelette?

Reported in conversation

DAVID ASTOR asked him once what the Marxists thought of him. Orwell itemised some choice pieces of invective. 'A Fascist hyena . . . A Fascist octopus.' There was a pause. 'They're very fond of animals.'

Taylor, *Orwell*.

IN a friendly, and even affectionate, way [Malcolm] Muggeridge and [Anthony] Powell would often lure Orwell away from sensible empiricism to wild flights of political fantasy, like his view that the Labour

Government should, in honesty, try to convert the British electorate to the idea that they should accept a lower standard of living in order to get rid of the evils of colonialism. 'Freedom for the Colonies, and a Lower Standard of Living for all', that would have been his election rallying cry. It was impossible not to respect the integrity of his ideas and the seriousness with which they were put forward, inevitable that Muggeridge and Powell should see him primarily as an English eccentric with a great fund of out-of-the-way knowledge, and strongly held opinions about such matters as the proper way of making tea and of cooking steak and kidney pudding. His eccentricity manifested itself in his actions as well as in his arguments. Thus he took a tremendous, almost childish, pleasure in bringing back from Germany a ball-bearing pen, at a time when they were not obtainable in England, and he appeared one day in an extraordinary garment with which he was greatly delighted, an old army greatcoat dyed mud brown, of which he said proudly (and wrongly): 'You won't guess what *this* is.' He was anxious always to get clothes such as he thought a workman might wear, and when Muggeridge was going to Washington for the *Daily Telegraph* Orwell asked him to send over a pair of boots. Whether it was that he had a low opinion of the leather used in England then, or whether he found it difficult to get a pair of boots to fit him—he took size twelve—I don't remember, but Muggeridge's failure to send these boots became a distinctly sore point with him. 'Have you heard anything from Malcolm? He hasn't sent me any boots', he would say each time I met him, only partly as a joke. Did he ever get the boots? I can't remember.

Julian Symons, *Critical Occasions*, 1966

Evelyn Waugh · 1903–1966

According to his son Auberon, Waugh's chief defect was his greed:

On one occasion, just after the war, the first consignment of bananas reached Britain. Neither I, my sister Teresa nor my sister Margaret had ever eaten a banana throughout the war, when they were unprocurable, but we had heard all about them as the most delicious taste in the world. When this first consignment arrived, the socialist government decided that every child in the country should be allowed one banana. An army of civil servants issued a library of special banana coupons, and the great day arrived when my mother came home with three bananas. All three were put on my father's plate, and before the anguished eyes of his children, he poured on cream, which was almost unprocurable, and sugar, which was heavily rationed, and ate all three. A child's sense of justice may be defective in many respects, and egocentric at the best of times, but it is no less intense for either. By any standards, he had done wrong. It would be absurd to say that I never forgave him, but he was permanently marked down in my estimation from that moment, in ways which no amount of sexual transgression would have achieved.

Auberon Waugh, *Will This Do?*, 1991

WHEN I met Mr Waugh, in New York in February 1949, his popping blue eyes looked askance at me, and I soon found that the cutting edge in the books was even sharper in the person: he was not an endearing character. I admired his talent for dialogue and the naming of characters (Dr Kakaphilos, Father Rothschild SJ), and in person I admired, even while suffering from, the agility with which he caused my remarks to boomerang. But whether Mr Waugh was disagreeable, or only preposterously arch, I cannot say. I addressed him in French at first, and he replied that he did not speak the language. His wife contradicted him charmingly, and was harshly rebuked. I asked whether he would care for a whisky and was told, 'I do not drink whisky before meals', stated as a universal fact I should have known. I made an admiring remark about the Constitution of the United States and was reminded that Mr Waugh is a Tory. I used the word 'music' and was told that music is physical torment to him. We talked at length only about US burial customs, and here his impressive technical knowledge suggested that he was gathering material for a doctorate on mausoleums. (After reading *The Loved One*, I visited Forest Lawn and the Hollywood Pet Cemetery.) At dinner I recommended the chicken, but this was a new *gaffe*. 'It's Friday.' But by the time the meatless meal was over and he had peeled, sucked and blown a cigar, the clipped conversation was succeeded by some almost amiable sentences.

Igor Stravinsky in Igor Stravinsky and Robert Craft, *Memories and Commentaries*, 2002

LUNCHEON at the Beefsteak. I have had a letter from Evan Tredegar asking me to join a committee consisting of himself, Marie Stopes, an unknown B.Litt., and 'we hope Harold Nicolson', to proclaim Alfred Douglas the greatest sonneteer since Shakespeare. I replied that considering Milton and Wordsworth I could not agree with the judgement and that anyway I thought Marie Stopes a preposterous person to propose it. At the Beefsteak I met Harold. He said he had replied to Evan saying that considering Milton and Wordsworth he could not agree with the judgement and that anyway he thought Marie Stopes a preposterous person to propose it. Am I developing a Beefsteak mind?

Evelyn Waugh, diary, 26 April 1946

Cyril Connolly · 1903–1974

As an undergraduate at Oxford, Connolly was taken up by the celebrated don Maurice Bowra:

He would introduce me to some of his older friends like Philip Ritchie with a genial, 'This is Connolly. Coming man. (Pause.) Hasn't come yet.'

Cyril Connolly in *Maurice Bowra: A Celebration*, ed. Hugh Lloyd-Jones, 1974

For a number of years the author John Lehmann ran his own publishing firm. When it closed down, a lunch was given for him:

It was in a private room at the Trocadero and it was organised by Henry Green, who told me he had done some research and discovered that this was the first time writers had banded together to honour an editor since Leigh Hunt had come out of prison for libelling the Prince Regent. We were in a room opposite one in which the members of an ironmongers' trade association were lunching, and ironmongers kept drifting into our luncheon as we did into theirs. I recall nothing of the lunch which cost 18/6, except that Forster was present and didn't speak, that T. S. Eliot did and made it seem that as poet, editor and publisher Lehmann was altogether his superior, and that towards the end of the meal Cyril Connolly complained loudly: 'We've had the sixpennyworth. When do the eighteen shillings' begin?'

Walter Allen, *As I Walked Down New Grub Street*, 1981

In 1939 Connolly founded his magazine Horizon, *with Stephen Spender as associate editor:*

Bertrand Russell, feeling that the young men—at thirty-seven, Cyril was the eldest of the three—deserved every encouragement, sent them an unsolicited offering. It arrived one morning when Cyril got to the mail first at Stephen's flat out of which they were operating. He read it. He did not like it. He found it too politically earnest and rejected it apologetically. The grounds he gave for the rejection were that 'Spender didn't like it'. A blatantly untrue comment which he forbore from divulging to the one supposed to have made it; who, indeed, did not even know of the manuscript's existence. Spender, understandably, was puzzled and dismayed to find himself the innocent target of hard looks from Russell whenever they met thenceforth. It was quite some time before the truth came out. In the telling of the tale Spender somehow managed to make it sound slanted against him while approving of Cyril's oneupmanship.

Michael Luke, *David Tennant and the Gargoyle Years*, 1991

Nathanael West · 1903–1940

(pen-name of Nathan Weinstein; novelist, author of *Miss Lonelyhearts* and *The Day of the Locust*)

The day after Scott Fitzgerald's death, on December 22, 1940, Nathanael West and his wife, Eileen, were killed in a car accident as they traveled back from a hunting weekend in Mexico. The 'world's worst driver,' West had over the years been involved in many an auto wreck—he habitually drove fast, was known to make U-turns across six lanes of rush-hour traffic, and was more or less color blind. He was also famous for day-dreaming at the wheel; several of his friends refused to drive with him. When 'bluntly warned' by one of them that 'some day he would be killed if he did not keep his eyes on the road ahead,' his answer was always the same scornful laughter. On the day of his death, West skidded out of a side road onto the main northbound boulevard and hit the first oncoming car: he had not noticed a red light, or he noticed it too late and was traveling too fast.

Ian Hamilton, *Writers in Hollywood*, 1990

Frank O'Connor · 1903–1966

(pen-name of Michael O'Donovan; Irish author, critic, and translator, best known for his short stories)

I accompanied him to London for the very first broadcast of his Irish poetry translations. Well before the scheduled time, around eleven at night, we were there waiting, and a more jittery Michael I had seldom seen. As he was about to enter the studio, a young man with alarm in his face burst into the room jabbering something about a hitch and an important announcement. Poor Michael almost crumpled at the knees. We waited, and then over the speaker beside us came the dramatic news that Chamberlain was returning unexpectedly from his meeting with Hitler at Munich. I shall never forget his anguish as that official returned to take him to the studio, leaving me to hear a stunned nation being told that Frank O'Connor would now read some medieval Irish verses.

Dermot Foley in *Michael/Frank*, ed. Maurice Sheehy, 1969

Christopher Isherwood · 1904–1986

In May 1935 Thomas Mann's daughter Erika learned that the Nazis were about to deprive her of her German citizenship. She asked Isherwood to marry her, so that she could acquire a British passport, but he reluctantly refused—partly to avoid exposing his German lover, Heinz, to damaging publicity, and partly, as he later put it, because of 'his rooted horror of marriage'. ('To him, it was the sacrament of the Others; the supreme affirmation of their dictatorship.')

Instead, he suggested that he should write to Auden, explaining the situation and asking if he was willing. Erika agreed; Auden cabled back 'Delighted', and he and Erika were married on 15 June—by chance, the very day Goebbels announced that she was no longer a German.

Erika subsequently went to America. So, in due course, did Auden and Isherwood:

In 1939, not long after their arrival in the United States, Wystan and Christopher visited Thomas and Katia Mann, who were then living at Princeton with Erika, Klaus and some of their other children. A photographer from *Time* happened to be present. Thomas asked Wystan and Christopher to pose with them for a group portrait. 'I know Mr Auden's your son-in-law,' said the photographer, 'but Mr Isherwood—what's his relation to your family?' Thomas's prompt reply made everybody laugh but the photographer, who didn't understand German: 'Family pimp.'

Christopher Isherwood, *Christopher and his Kind*, 1977

Graham Greene · 1904–1991

Greene, I think, by temperament hated anyone who was his boss, and his boss at this time was Wilson Harris, who besides being editor of the *Spectator* was an independent member of parliament supporting the Churchill government. Greene always spoke of him with dislike, as of someone especially sanctimonious and mealy-mouthed, and took much pleasure in persecuting him. Thus when Frank Harris, who was best known as a pornographer and whose antecedents were mysterious, died, Graham sent a paragraph pseudonymously and on Authors' Club writing paper to the Londoner's Diary of the *Evening Standard* to the effect that it was not generally known that the late Frank Harris, author of *My Life and Loves*, was the cousin of Mr Wilson Harris, MP, editor of the *Spectator*. It was, alas, not used.

On this occasion, he had planned to telephone the Reform Club, where Harris lunched daily with his cronies, announce that he was speaking from the Cabinet Office, and request the telephone operator to inform Mr Wilson Harris immediately that he was to call at 10 Downing Street at 3.30.

Walter Allen, *As I Walked Down New Grub Street*, 1981

In the early 1970s the jazz musician John Chilton took temporary charge of a small bookshop in Bloomsbury belonging to his wife. One day a customer came in whom he immediately recognized as Graham Greene:

I WANTED to make a gift of the book he'd chosen, *Ezra Pound in Kensington*, but he insisted on paying for it. I pulled a copy of *Our Man in Havana* from a shelf and asked if he'd mind signing it. He asked my name and wrote a warm inscription. I thanked him and mentioned film criticism, which led to him reeling off a string of yesteryear stars, including Harold Lloyd. I commented that Lloyd had named one of his characters Harold Diddlebock only to find that the real Mr H D had jumped up and demanded an apology. Greene smiled and said, 'I always make a special point of avoiding any name that might be recognised.'

We shook hands and he buttoned his excessively long black overcoat and left. Some while later I read Greene's novel *The Human Factor* and saw that the author had named a character (who appears once) Chilton.

I Once Met: Fifty Encounters with the Famous, ed. Richard Ingrams, 1996

ANTHONY POWELL · 1905–2000

After coming down from Oxford, Powell took a job in publishing. He also joined the Territorial Army:

THE unit he chose was a Gunner regiment, reckoning that what was good enough for Tolstoy was good enough for him. Two evenings a week he slogged out to their headquarters in Brixton, where he rode round and round a dusty shed and learnt the rudiments of gun-aiming. Aware that he had practically nothing in common with the other officers, many of whom were City types who referred, in a Woosterish way, to their 'mater' and their 'guv'nor', he said little and swore a lot. To no avail. One evening he was introduced to an officer he hadn't met before. 'This is Powell,' said the Adjutant. 'He's a Senior Wrangler or something.' After that he packed it in.

Michael Barber, *Anthony Powell: A Life*, 2004

In the New Year Honours of 1988 Powell was made a Companion of Honour, and in February of that year he went to Buckingham Palace to receive the decoration. Presenting it to him, the Queen said, 'It's a nice light decoration to wear round the neck':

AFTER we sat down the Queen asked if I was writing anything now. Thinking it best not to mention a Diary, I replied only odds and ends of memoirs, possibly to be published at the discretion of my heirs and successors, not before my own demise. She enquired exactly what I had written, saying: 'You have written so many books, Mr Powell.' I provided a rough adumbration of *Dance* [*to the Music of Time*], adding the sequence was becoming very generally translated into European languages, among which I was particularly amused that two of the three war volumes were going into Bulgarian, doubted if they would attempt the third, as the Katyn massacre was mentioned. HM then spoke of the Iron Curtain, saying whenever she went to Berlin efforts were made to make her look at the Wall, but she would not go. I asked if she had ever seen it, she replied, 'Once', but it gave her such horrors she never wanted to see it again . . .

She asked where I lived. I replied in Somerset on the Wiltshire border, invoking Longleat as a reference point she at once took. The Queen enquired about our garden and said she had picked twenty-seven varieties of flower the previous day in Buckingham Palace garden (like the Queen in *Cymbeline* to distil poisons?), thereby probably making the gardener extremely cross. I am totally ignorant on all horticultural matters and said we had many stretches of snowdrops. HM asked: 'Have you aconites?' Having no idea of the answer to that, I replied guardedly: 'Only a few, Ma'am,' which V [Powell's wife] later confirmed as correct. This more or less closed the audience . . .

Anthony Powell, *Journals 1987–1989*, 1996

ARTHUR KOESTLER · 1905–1983

THE Blitz continued to drive me back and forth; and, finally, I came to rest at a studio occupied by Cyril Connolly, where a fellow tenant was Arthur Koestler, whose extraordinary novel *Darkness at Noon* had already earned him wide acclaim. As a novelist, I greatly admired Koestler; as a human being I sometimes found him a little touchy and suspicious; and an absurd squabble presently broke out, followed by an irate correspondence, because I was alleged to have told a girl we both knew that in bed he wore a hair-net; and he protested that I had gravely injured his chances of securing her affections. 'Like every civilized Continental', he said, he wore a hair-net only when he was going to his bath.

Peter Quennell, *The Wanton Chase*, 1980

John O'Hara · 1905–1970

(novelist: his books include *Appointment in Samarra* and *Pal Joey*)

O'Hara is buried in Princeton. The inscription on his gravestone reads: 'Better than anyone else, he told the truth about his time, the first half of the twentieth century. He was a professional. He wrote honestly and well.'

This epitaph was composed by O'Hara himself.

The story of the inscription is cited in Brendan Gill, *Here at the New Yorker*, 1975

Samuel Beckett · 1906–1989

In 1928 Beckett went to Paris as lecteur d'anglais *at the École Normale Supérieure:*

At the École Normale, weird, nocturnal wailings could often be heard emanating from Beckett's room. Richard Aldington was alluding to this when he wrote that Beckett 'wanted to commit suicide, a fate he nearly imposed on half the faculty of the École by playing the flute.' Jean Coulomb, who had a room near Beckett, objected to the nocturnal serenading when he was trying to sleep. In fact, it was not a flute that he played at all: 'I used to play a tin whistle,' said Beckett. 'A rusty old tin whistle. I had a tin whistle and I used to tweetle on it.'

James Knowlson, *The Life of Samuel Beckett*, 1996

Not long after arriving in Paris he got to know James Joyce, and agreed to help him with his work. He read aloud to him and occasionally took dictation:

Writers on Beckett and Joyce have often spoken about Beckett's contribution to *Finnegans Wake*. He is said to have taken down as dictation the words 'Come in', when someone knocked at the door and, when Joyce insisted that the phrase should be included, let it stand. Yet it has proved hard for scholars to find the unintended words in the finished text.

Knowlson, *Life of Samuel Beckett*

A French writer, Claude Jamet, provides a glimpse of Beckett in the 1950s:

I knew Beckett by sight. At two in the morning—the bars closed late, especially in Montparnasse—at a bar called the Rond-Point . . . Beckett was having a drink at the bar. There were a few lost intellectuals like

Beckett and myself, and a few tramps. One of the tramps standing by Beckett said to him: 'My word, that's a fine jacket you're wearing, a lovely jacket.' And I saw Beckett take off his jacket and give it to the tramp. Without emptying the pockets either.

Quoted in Knowlson, *Life of Samuel Beckett*

CLANCY SIGAL told Beckett one day how Doris Lessing, with whom Sigal was living in the late 1950s, had introduced him as an identifiable character, 'Saul Green', a macho kind of American, into several of her books. He explained to Beckett what a disturbing experience this had been. 'Beckett shook his magnificent head. "Identity is so fragile—how did you ever survive?" He looked at me more closely. "Or did you?" '

Knowlson, *Life of Samuel Beckett*

R. K. NARAYAN · 1906–2001

(novelist; his books include *The Bachelor of Arts* and *A Tiger for Malgudi*)

MY free-lance efforts at Madras bore fruit to the extent that I was given a book to review. Its title was *Development of Maritime Laws in 17th-Century England*. A most unattractive book, but I struggled through its pages and wrote a brief note on it, and though not paid for, it afforded me the thrill of seeing my words in print for the first time. The same journal also accepted a short story and paid ten rupees less money-order charges. My first year's income from writing was thus about nine rupees and twelve annas (about a dollar and a quarter). In the second year there was a slight improvement, as *The Hindu* took a story and sent me eighteen rupees (less money-order charges); in the year following, a children's story brought me thirty rupees. I handed this cheque to my father and he was delighted. He remarked, 'Your first and last cheque, I suppose!' I objected to his saying 'last' and he at once apologized. 'I don't know what made me say "last." Don't mind it.'

R. K. Narayan, *My Days*, 1975

Narayan's memoirs include an account of his 11-year-old grandson:

THREE years ago, when he was convalescing after an appendix operation, he was interested in writing. I lent him my portable typewriter, and he sat up in bed and typed away all day with two fingers. Sometimes he copied from a storybook, and sometimes spun out an original story. One such was called 'Grand' (he would not explain why), and I give it below:

'Once upon a time there was a man and his father. They were so poor.

No one to help them. One day his father's birthday came. Then that man became very rich. Then his son became poor. Then another day his uncle came. His father's son's birthday came. Then his uncle became so rich. Give me the monies, said the man. Then the uncle became so poor. Then his father told uncle, Go to R. K. Narayan and take some monies. Then he will be so poor.'

I liked the story for the ease with which it conveys in one sweep the complexities, muddles, and demands of kinship, and the ups and downs of man's fortunes—enough substance to fill a novel; above all my name involved in it afforded me a refreshingly objective view of myself. Recently I confronted my grandson with his composition. (Not easy to get his attention nowadays even for a few minutes, but I caught him in the passage as he came in from school and before he could run out to play.) He glanced through it indifferently and shook his head disapprovingly: 'I wrote it so long ago! I was young then. Throw it away, please.' I explained that I couldn't. He remained thoughtful for a moment, and said, 'That uncle is not a real uncle, but only a next-house man. They all spent their monies too much on birthday parties, buying hundreds of ice-creams, sweets, and what not, and so had no money at the end. They should not ask you for money. They should ask others. Put in these corrections . . .'

Narayan, *My Days*

William Empson · 1906–1984

After 1961 he never saw a book through the press. Revision claimed him. He had to revise until his prose ceased to bore even him. 'I still have to put in the careless ease,' he once remarked, sitting by the pond in his Hampstead garden, when I reproached him gently for not collecting his essays. 'The careless ease always goes in last.'

George Watson, 'William Empson: Prophet against God', *Hudson Review*, 1996

John Betjeman · 1906–1984

Office life [at the *Architectural Review*] in Queen Anne's Gate was enlivened too by his mercurial personality and his pose of disrespect for authority. He practiced at that time an undergraduate style of exhibitionism which was tolerable because accompanied by wit and good humour. I remember, as an example of the kind of prank he took a pride in, his boasting to me one day that he had just come from the Geological Museum, then housed in a dusty, unvisited red-brick building in Piccadilly, and had contributed an exhibit of his own. 'Do go and look,' he said. So I went, and there indeed beneath the glass of one of the show-cases, which someone had I suppose carelessly left unlocked, was a small brown object with a neatly lettered card reading 'Horse chestnut picked up in Bushey Park. Donated by J. Betjeman Esquire.' I believe it remained unnoticed and undisturbed until the building was demolished in 1935 to make way for Simpson's store.

J. M. Richards, *Memoirs of an Unjust Fella*, 1980

In 1934 John and Penelope Betjeman, who had got married the previous year, moved into a house in the village of Uffington, in Berkshire. Among the friends who came to stay with them there were Cyril Connolly and his wife:

IN one of the Connollys' visits John and Penelope had a violent row in which they rampaged over the house yelling at each other, passing straight through the bathroom where the Connollys were taking a bath together.

Bevis Hillier, *John Betjeman: New Love, New Fame*, 2002

W. H. AUDEN · 1907–1973

Gabriel Carritt was a friend of Auden at Oxford:

A RATHER odd aspect of him which I am told he retained in later life, was his belief in fate and that he could intervene with the Almighty. Once, when we were walking on the downs, he discovered that he had lost three pounds which he had stuffed loose into his trouser pocket. 'Never mind,' he said. 'We will pick them up on the way back.' Four hours later, in the dusk, as we followed the ridgeway above Letcombe Bassett, we saw three notes fluttering along the grass. He picked them up, put them back loose in the same pocket, and said nothing.

On another occasion we were walking along the Roman wall and late at night were reluctantly received at a small inn. When we went to our room, Wystan found under his crumpled pillow a half-full bottle of brandy. He took a drink as if he had just ordered it and passed it on.

Gabriel Carritt, 'A Friend of the Family', in Stephen Spender (ed.), *W. H. Auden: A Tribute*, 1975

I TOOK part in what I think was the first public reading of *The Ascent of F6*, at one of the [Birmingham] University English Club's fortnightly meetings. Auden took charge, distributed the scripts and allotted the parts. We read at sight. I remember how astonished and impressed we were when, the reading ended, Auden went round the tiny audience of perhaps forty undergraduates literally with a hat, saying that the labourer was worthy of his hire and that nothing should ever be given free. It is conceivable he pocketed fifteen shillings.

Walter Allen, *As I Walked Down New Grub Street*, 1981

AUDEN had total self-confidence, of course. He just thought that he was cleverer than anyone else, but without arrogance, really, just out of his own judgement . . . He knew exactly what he was doing, and he was totally indifferent about what anyone said about it. And then being a 'psychoanalyst' helped him a great deal. For instance, when he was so attacked by Randall Jarrell in 1947 or so, he said, 'He must be in love with me; I can't think of any other explanation.' He was genuinely puzzled. He didn't think it was a damaging attack in any way.

Stephen Spender in *Writers at Work: The* Paris Review *Interviews*, sixth series, 1985

Truman Capote's In Cold Blood *prompted a discussion between Auden and Robert Craft on capital punishment, in which Craft asked the poet whether he thought a death sentence was ever justifiable:*

'WELL, there *have* been people on whom I can picture it being carried out. Brecht for one. In fact, I can imagine doing it to him myself. It might even have been rather enjoyable, when the time came, to have been able to say to him, "Now, let's step outside." But of course I'd have given him a good "last meal".'

Robert Craft, *Stravinsky: Chronicle of a Friendship*, 1972

To record an obituary for someone and then have him die a month later—which happened to me in the case of T. S. Eliot—makes you feel as if you were in some way responsible.

W. H. Auden, quoted in Igor Stravinsky and Robert Craft, *Memories and Commentaries*, 2002

AUDEN was surprised to learn from a third party that Mike de Lisio, his sculptor friend, wrote poetry in his spare time and had had some of his verses published in the *New Yorker*. 'How nice of him never to have told me,' he said.

Willard Espy, *An Almanac of Words at Play*, 1975

LOUIS MACNEICE · 1907–1963

I REMEMBERED the story of the set-to between Louis and the swashbuckling Roy Campbell. Louis had reproached Campbell in some pub or other for having struck a poet, a man weaker than himself. 'It was only a bit of a pat, like this,' Campbell had replied, tapping Louis lightly. 'I don't believe you,' Louis had said. 'I think it was a real swipe, like this.' And he had slapped Campbell's face, hard.

Dan Davin, *Closing Times*, 1975

Roy Campbell: poet, satirist, and translator, notorious for his pro-Fascist sympathies during the Spanish Civil War.

Ian Fleming · 1908–1964

Fleming initially made his reputation as a journalist. In the years after the Second World War he also toyed with the idea of writing a thriller, though he might not have had the confidence to try his hand at one without the encouragement of his closest friend in publishing, the poet and novelist William Plomer:

Having written his book, Fleming chose to make a characteristically convoluted approach to Plomer. On 12 May 1952 he was having lunch with Plomer in a London restaurant when he changed the course of their conversation to ask Plomer, 'How do you get cigarette smoke out of a woman once you've got it in?' Plomer, who delighted in the grotesque caprices of the human race, speculated rapidly on what he later called 'this intimate-sounding injection'. Fleming then explained that one could not use a word like 'exhales', while 'puffs it out' sounded silly to his ears. At this point Plomer looked up sharply: 'You've written a book!' And Fleming, with a great show of reluctance, admitted that he had, and consented to let Plomer read it. The book was *Casino Royale*.

Peter F. Alexander, *William Plomer*, 1989

Plomer, who read for Jonathan Cape, foresaw great things for the book, and in the face of strong opposition from some of his colleagues, he persuaded Cape to take it on.

Malcolm Lowry · 1909–1957

In 1948 Malcolm Lowry's friend, the writer James Stern, gave a party in his flat in New York to celebrate the publication of Lowry's novel Under the Volcano*:*

I've read stories about this party, where forty or fifty people were supposed to have come. That's quite impossible because they couldn't have got in. I expect there were fifteen perhaps. Malc just stood by the door while people came in and shook his hand and said a few kind words. And he was speechless. Whether he was drinking more then, or had drunk more then, I don't know. After about an hour, as people began to move away, he disappeared. But he couldn't disappear very far without leaving the flat. He had nowhere to go but the bathroom. So I went to the bathroom and there I found him. He had a habit of staring at himself in the mirror, and there he was staring at himself in the mirror, blood pouring out of his nose. He was wiping this blood off his face and throwing it all over the bathroom. He was convinced that he had TB, and he looked rather pleased about it, snorting with laughter. He was a hideous sight and so was the bathroom. He was taken straight to a doctor.

James Stern in Gordon Bowker (ed.), *Malcolm Lowry Remembered*, 1985

Isaiah Berlin · 1909–1997

Between 1942 and 1945 Berlin worked out of the British Embassy in Washington, monitoring American opinion. Churchill was impressed by his dispatches (which were sent in the name of the ambassador), and asked who was responsible for them.

In February 1944 the songwriter Irving Berlin was in London, and Mrs Churchill asked her husband whether he could see him to thank him for his war work. She had had in mind only the briefest of meetings, but to her surprise Churchill said that he must come to lunch—an imposing occasion, as it turned out, attended by a number of senior figures:

At the head of the table, Churchill kept up a steady stream of talk about the war situation. At the end of lunch, Churchill turned and said, 'Now, Mr Berlin, tell us what in your opinion is the likelihood of my dear friend, the President, being re-elected for a fourth term.' Berlin, who spoke in a heavy Brooklyn accent, said he felt sure that Roosevelt's great name would ensure him victory. He added for good measure, 'But if he won't stand again, I don't think I'll vote at all.'

'You mean,' asked Churchill, 'that you think you'll have a vote?'

'I sincerely hope so.'

Churchill muttered that it was a good sign of Anglo-American co-operation if the Professor had a vote in America. Churchill's subsequent questions about the state and volume of war production in the States elicted only vague and noncommittal replies. Churchill, growing exasperated, asked Berlin when he thought the war would end. 'Mr Prime Minister, I shall tell my children and grandchildren that Winston Churchill asked *me* that question.' By now thoroughly confused, Churchill asked what was the most important thing that Mr Berlin had written. He replied, 'White Christmas'.

Sensing social disaster, Clementine Churchill said gently that they should all be grateful to Mr Berlin because he had been so generous. 'Generous?' her husband growled, looking about him in consternation . . .

Shortly thereafter the lunch broke up. Berlin returned to the hotel where he was staying with the producer Alexander Korda. He reported that it had been a puzzling lunch. He did not exactly seem to hit it off with the Prime Minister.

Michael Ignatieff, *Isaiah Berlin*, 1998

This is the authentic version of the most famous of Isaiah Berlin anecdotes. Various apocryphal versions also circulated: according to one of them, after Irving Berlin had left Churchill observed. 'That man writes much better than he talks.'

Nelson Algren · 1909–1981

(American novelist, author of *A Walk on the Wild Side* and *The Man with the Golden Arm*)

INTERVIEWER. How about this movie, *The Man with the Golden Arm*?

ALGREN. Yeah.

INTERVIEWER. Did you have anything to do with the script?

ALGREN. No. No, I didn't last long. I went out there for a thousand a week, and I worked Monday, and I got fired Wednesday. The guy that hired me was out of town Tuesday.

Writers at Work: The Paris Review *Interviews*, first series, 1958

William Golding · 1911–1993

In the 1980s the book dealer Rick Gekoski, who was working on a bibliography of William Golding, paid a number of visits to Golding and his wife at their home in Cornwall. One morning Golding took him to his bank and produced 'a remarkably homely object' from a safe deposit box—the manuscript of Lord of the Flies *(it was written in school exercise books), which he asked Gekoski to inspect with an eye to valuation:*

I WAS rather surprised that he would consider selling it, but he was tormented, in his later years, by anxiety about money. So acute was this that Lady Golding begged me, one evening, to reason with him about it.

'It's all right for you,' he remarked grumpily, 'you're a rich man.'

I offered, sight unseen, to swap financial positions with him, before suggesting to him that his worries were symbolic. 'What's it *really* about?' I asked: 'loss of power or control? Declining hold on things? It's quite common to feel that way at your time of life.'

He glared at my impertinence. 'Don't be so bloody stupid,' he said, 'it's about *money*.'

His financial concerns were, he admitted, exacerbated by the terror that he might go to jail for tax evasion.

'I have nightmares about it,' he said.

'Talk to Rick about it,' urged Ann. 'He'll tell you how silly it all is.'

'In 1961,' Golding said, 'I visited Canada, and did a series of lectures. Well, one of the universities gave me a cheque for $100.' He paused, distressed at having to remember and speak of it.

'And?'

'I cashed it in Canada, and spent it.'

'And?'

'That's all.'

'It never happened again?'

He shuddered. 'Certainly not! I lie awake at night worrying that Inland Revenue will catch up with me, and put me in jail.'

I was careful not to laugh. 'Well,' I said judiciously, 'I don't suppose you find that many Nobel Prize winners in jail for tax evasion.'

'Lester Piggott was sent to jail!'

'He was a jockey, and it was for a VAT fraud,' I said. 'The figure was apparently four million pounds.'

'The principle is the same,' said Bill, with conviction.

So he had come, I think, to regard the manuscript of *Lord of the Flies* as a little nest egg, and was receptive to the idea of cashing it in. He was a man of many doubts, but he had never doubted, from the moment of its inception, the value of *Lord of the Flies*, as either text or object. When he finished the first draft, he announced to his family that one day it would 'win him the Nobel Prize'. And, though the prize is given for lifetime achievement and not for a single work, he was right.

He also had little doubt as to its exact financial value. Though he had asked me to value it, he had a figure in mind.

'If you can find a nice rich American or Japanese,' he said, with an attempt at worldly offhandedness utterly foreign to his nature, 'I would take a million for it.'

'A million what?' I asked, maybe a little puckishly.

He seemed to consider.

'Pounds, of course!' (As if I had insulted the Queen.)

'But Bill,' I said, as reasonably as I could, 'the only twentieth-century manuscript to have fetched anything remotely like that sort of figure is Kafka's *The Trial*.'

He nodded his head, as if this confirmed his view.

'Anyway,' I said, 'there is no buyer out there at that sort of price.'

'Surely there's got to be some super-rich collector who would be dying to have it!'

'In my experience you don't get to be super-rich by not caring what you pay for things. Value for money is the only way the rich can protect themselves.'

He glared at me. Clearly I was a rotten dealer.

'Get me a million,' he said, 'and you can have 5 per cent.'

When Gekoski consulted a number of leading dealers, their estimates of the manuscript's value ranged from £50,000 to £250,000. When he conveyed his information to Golding, 'he snorted with contempt'.

Gekoski concludes:

I suppose the latter figure is now closer to the mark, if you could find a rich American or Japanese. After all, the manuscript of *On The Road* recently fetched over two million dollars, because that novel had a special place in the heart of at least one rich American. Who knows? Maybe *Lord of the Flies* does too.

Rick Gekoski, *Tolkien's Gown*, 2004

Patrick White · 1912–1990

Of all the quarrels and displays of rage which punctuated White's career, few were more spectacular than his falling-out with Sidney Nolan. The two men had been friends for many years, and although White began to develop doubts about Nolan after the artist's wife Cynthia committed suicide in 1976, he continued to maintain a show of friendship. Certainly nothing prepared Nolan for what White had to say in Flaws in the Glass, *the volume of memoirs he published in 1981:*

Charles Osborne, arts bureaucrat, biographer and Australian Londoner, received a review copy from the *Financial Times* and was so startled by White's account of Cynthia Nolan's suicide that he rang the painter and read the passage to him. Nolan had no inkling that White's feelings towards him had shifted so fundamentally. He had seemed sympathetic when they met, quite unchanged since Cynthia's death. Now he heard Osborne read: 'What I cannot forgive is him flinging himself on another woman's breast when the ashes were scarcely cold, the chase after recognition by one who did not need it, the cameras, the public birthdays, the political hanky-panky . . . all of which, and the Athenaeum Club, would contribute to the death of any painter.'

Nolan tried to stop the book. He consulted two London lawyers, Lord

Goodman and the playwright-barrister John Mortimer, who, he says, advised him the book was defamatory, but urged him not to take action because the case would be expensive and very painful. Nolan claims also to have been told by one of the editors at Cape that White was prevented by the publishers from saying even worse things about him. Whatever may have been said to mollify the painter, this does not appear to have been the case. Greene [the publisher Graham Greene] and White insist that no cuts were made to *Flaws in the Glass* before its publication. Nolan took his own revenge. He sent a diptych out to Australia called *Nightmare*, which had an ashen-faced White in a pale blue cap (inmate? prisoner? magician?) standing by a dog's arse. A line on the animal's haunch might be a tail curled back or a map of its bowel. A crucifix is painted on the dog's belly and its head bears a crude likeness to Manoly Lascaris [White's lover]. Nolan also sent out some drawings based on the *Divine Comedy* in which White is thrust into the sodomites' circle of hell. When these went on exhibition, Nolan told the press, 'I'm a good hater . . . I'll bury him . . . He doesn't understand much about life does he? He's just lived with a man for forty years.' White began to claim he had never much liked or been impressed by Sid Nolan. 'It was far more Cynthia. He's done far more harm to himself than he has to me. I didn't like what he said about Manoly and Manoly was very upset. But anyway, he will bite the dust. He already has as far as his talent goes.'

David Marr, *Patrick White: A Life*, 1991

Shortly before White died Nolan sent a message through a go-between saying that he would welcome a reconciliation, but White rejected the idea with scorn and what David Marr calls 'a muted tirade'.

Nigel Dennis · 1912–1989

(novelist; author of *Cards of Identity*)

As a young man Dennis worked as secretary to the psychologist Alfred Adler, who had come to Britain as a refugee:

Nigel Dennis was at a sherry party Adler was giving and was in a depressed state. He was involved in a romance with a woman older and smarter than he was and he did not know where to turn to retain her affection by providing the kind of expensive pleasures to which she was accustomed. Adler's glance lighted on Dennis for a moment and he said, 'Oh look, Nigel is down in the mouth. I know what he needs. He needs a cheque.' He took out his cheque book and wrote one out.

Nigel Dennis recalled that incident to confirm his claim of Adler's brilliance as a diagnostician.

Anthony Quinton, *From Wodehouse to Wittgenstein*, 1998

Robertson Davies · 1913–1995

(Canadian novelist, playwright, teacher, and, for many years, full-time journalist)

You ask me for the story I have always wanted to write. Like most newspapermen I know a lot of stories that it would have been an exquisite pleasure to write—if one had intended to suspend publication the following day. But what is the point of grieving for them now? I have written what had to be written.

Very early in my newspaper experience I was given the job of writing an obituary notice of a priest who had died in a rural community within the circulation range of the newspaper I was working for; the facts available made one slim paragraph, and I had to piece it out, somehow, to respectable length. Nobody seemed to know anything about Father Blank, and so, in despair, I wrote a description of a perfect priest, ascribing all the virtues to him, and tacked it on the end of my story. Within the week after it was published I received several warm commendations on the skill with which I had captured Father Blank's character. I had, it appeared, described him to a T.

'Confessions of an Editor', in *The Enthusiasms of Robertson Davies*, 1990

George Barker · 1913–1991

Barker published his first volume of poems in 1933, when he was only 20:

The most beautiful story in the whole Barker legend is how, when as a very young man, on arriving home for tea one day, his invalid Irish grandmother, tightly gripping her constant companion, a thin ebony stick with a silver handle, pulled herself up on to her mass-going feet and bowed to him as he entered. In her struggle to rise the book she had been reading dropped to the floor. It was Yeats's *Oxford Book of Modern Verse*; and the youngest poet there included was the grandson who had to kneel in order to pick it up for her.

Paul Potts, *Dante Called You Beatrice*, 1960

Barbara Pym · 1913–1980

Although Barbara Pym was already a well-established novelist, in 1963 her novel An Unsuitable Attachment *was rejected by her regular publishers and by a number of other publishing houses. A subsequent novel was similarly rejected, and over the next fourteen years it began to look as though she might never again find a publisher. In 1973 she wrote a letter to the magazine* The Author *about the publication problems novelists faced. She reported the result the following year, in another letter, to her friend Philip Larkin:*

It's rather discouraging to go on writing with so little hope of publication but I try not to think about that. By the way, the letter I wrote to *The Author* about not getting published was never published, which seems to be the final accolade of failure.

A Very Private Eye: The Diaries, Letters and Notebooks of Barbara Pym, 1984

In January 1977 Barbara Pym's luck turned. The Times Literary Supplement *published a symposium in which well-known literary figures were asked to nominate the most underrated writer of the century, and she was the only living writer chosen by two people (Philip Larkin and Lord David Cecil). From this point on publishers expressed a strong interest in her work, and her reputation soared.*

Dylan Thomas · 1914–1953

Another story he told was of himself, while standing at the bar of a pub, being approached by a huge and minatory navvy, who said with a leer—'Wouldn't think I was a pansy, would you, mate?' To which Dylan replied, as quick as a whistle, 'And you wouldn't think I wasn't, would you?'

Pamela Hansford Johnson, *Important to Me*, 1974

He had a reputation as a thief, and I believe that it was, in some measure, justified. As early as the spring of 1941, when a guest at Laugharne Castle, he was writing to Bertram Rota, the bookseller, offering him first editions of modern novels. They may, of course, have been his father's. Later, after the war, many people were to complain that objects were missing when Dylan had been to stay. In 1943, Theo [Constantine FitzGibbon's wife] did once catch him walking out of our little Godfrey Street house with her electric sewing machine. This was a rather valuable instrument of which she was almost inordinately proud and which he would have regarded as quite useless and fit only for the pawnshop. She told him to put it down, which he did, and with the expression of the Swansea schoolboy caught cheating at maths and in a ham actor's tones of outraged innocence, he asked:

'Are you accusing me of *stealing*?'

'Yes,' she said.

'Well!' he replied, and bore no ill feeling.

Constantine FitzGibbon, *The Life of Dylan Thomas*, 1965

In 1946 Rosamond Lehmann attended a dinner given by Edith Sitwell at the Sesame Club following a poetry reading at the Wigmore Hall:

'DYLAN THOMAS and his wife both arrived wildly drunk, fought and hit each other, and altogether presented a painful problem to Edith and all the distinguished guests, as they could neither be disposed of nor tamed,' Rosamond related. 'I shall never forget Mrs Thomas shoving a drunken elbow into her ice cream, then offering the elbow to T. S. Eliot & telling him to "lick it off".'

Selina Hastings, *Rosamond Lehmann*, 2002

WILLIAM BURROUGHS · 1914–1997

In 1951 Burroughs went to a private drinking session in an apartment above a bar in Mexico City, carrying a bag with a gun in it—a .38 automatic—which he wanted to sell. His wife Joan (aged 27) and his small son Billy were with him; those present also included a young man, Lewis Marker, with whom he had become obsessed:

DURING a gap in the conversation, Burroughs took the .38 out of the bag and said to Joan, as if it was an old party trick (though he claimed never to have suggested it before): 'I guess it's about time for our William Tell act.'

Joan placed an object on her head and turned sideways-on to her husband, who was sitting six feet away. He fired, shooting her through the temple. Marker, the reluctant lover, said: 'Bill, I think you've killed her.'

(*Fadeout to* New Year, 1965: Burroughs in his home town of St Louis is being interviewed for the *Paris Review*. He speaks at length about one of his favourite topics, the falsehoods perpetrated by the print media. Then he says: '. . . that terrible accident with Joan Vollmer, my wife. I had a revolver that I was planning to sell to a friend. I was checking it over and it went off—killed her. A rumour started that I was trying to shoot a glass of champagne from her head William Tell style. Absurd and false.')

Was it a champagne glass? Elsewhere, Burroughs described the putative target as a 'highball glass'. Carl Solomon, who may have got his information from Ginsberg, also called it a 'champagne glass', although unreliability is suggested by his dating the scene to 1950.

Edward de Grazia, a lawyer who was later to defend the work of Burroughs in court against the charge of obscenity, recounted the incident in his book about censorship, *Girls Lean Back Everywhere*: 'He aimed too low at a whiskey glass.' In a footnote, de Grazia qualified this assertion with proper lawyerly caution: 'variously also reported to have been a champagne glass . . . an apricot, an orange'. The publisher Barney Rosset once pointed out Burroughs to Alain Robbe-Grillet, with the recommendation that he was 'a very important writer'. 'Ah, yes?' said Robbe-Grillet. 'What has he done?' Rosset replied: 'He put an apple on his wife's head and killed her.' One of the witnesses, Marker's friend Eddie Woods, recalled that Joan had been drinking gin, and that when Burroughs came out with his William Tell quip, 'she balanced her glass on her head'. A *New York Post* reporter filled it up and made it 'a glass of gin'.

A historian of the Beat Generation, Steven Watson, called it a water glass, a more temperate view backed up by a recent collective biography of Beat women. The source of the detail could be a Burroughs biographer, Barry Miles, who described it with more precision as 'a six-ounce water glass'. A Kerouac biographer, Steve Turner, turned it into 'a wine glass'. Kerouac's publisher, Robert Giroux, who heard the news in New York soon after he had rejected the scroll *On the Road*, called it 'an old tin can'.

Billy junior was present throughout. Aged four at the time, he did not register what was on his mother's head as his father took aim, but his testimony has a poetry lacking in any of the others: 'she placed an apple or an apricot or a grape or myself on her head and challenged my father to shoot'.

James Campbell, *This Is the Beat Generation*, 1999

Burroughs left Mexico; he was convicted of criminal negligence and given a two-year suspended sentence, in absentia.

John Berryman · 1914–1972

The 'phantom mistress' referred to in the following passage is the seventeenth-century American poet Anne Bradstreet, the subject of Berryman's first major poem, Homage to Mistress Bradstreet, *and the object of fantasies in which he dreamed of seducing her:*

In Paris, where John and I stayed at the Hôtel des Saints Pères for ten days on our arrival at the end of April 1953, there had been a scene that was a trope for our marriage. I wakened in the middle of the night in panic: Where was John? I had heard him come in hours before and crash into the armoire that jutted out from the wall before dropping into bed. Now his bed was empty. The French windows, which opened onto a narrow balcony, were ajar. In the glaucous moonlight, I could just make out his pajamaed figure, poised on the balustrade. Suppressing an impulse to cry out, I went as quickly as I could to his side and said his name. Without a word, he took the hand I held up to his, as he had done on his mother's terrace, and allowed me—eyes open or closed? I could not see—to lead him back to bed. When his breathing became deep and regular, I locked the window. The remainder of the night, I sat in a chair thinking.

John's life had become a high-wire act. He was flirting with his subtle foe in the certainty that there was an invisible net, held by me, which would catch him should he lose his footing. The job of net-holder had exhausted me. More important, I realized that by making myself available in this way I had been encouraging him to be more and more incautious, less vigilant against the current that was always threatening to suck him under. By morning I knew that I could not, should not, hold up the net much longer.

Early the next day we left Paris for Autun. John complained of a hangover. 'Idiot that I am, I sat up in a café drinking brandy, brooding over the mistakes I've made in the management of my life during the fourteen years since I was last in Paris.' As was so often the case, he remembered having drunk too much, but had forgotten what he'd done while drinking. As was also often the case, I was unable to forget. It seemed to me, as we wandered through central France and down to the Riviera, that John's phantom mistress (whom, having done with, he was now desperate to shake) rarely gave us a moment's peace. During his 'three-day drunk at the fête of St. Tropez,' he recited 'Homage' nonstop to whomever would lend an ear. The final night of the fête, when the last of the revelers had gone to bed, he cornered the local bakers trapped at their ovens, and recited to them. Covered with flour from the dough they were kneading, perplexed by their strange visitor who pushed his eyeglasses up onto the bridge of his nose as he declaimed:

> How long with nothing in the ruinous heat,
> clams & acorns stomaching, distinction perishing,

they listened with wonder and awe, understanding only that the passion behind the lines was trying to burn itself out so that the exhausted poet could, like the carefree revelers, get some sleep.

Eileen Simpson, *Poets in their Youth*, 1982

Berryman committed suicide in 1972, jumping to his death from a bridge above the Mississippi River.

Saul Bellow · 1915–2005

'I write from about eight o'clock in the morning until one,' he once told a reporter: 'Then I go out and make my mistakes.'

James Atlas, *Bellow*, 2000

Bellow was a close friend of the sociologist Edward Shils, a colleague on the Committee on Social Thought at the University of Chicago, but they eventually fell out:

Shils was later mordant on the subject of Bellow . . . When October, Nobel month, rolled round a few years after they had become estranged, Shils warned a colleague on the committee, 'Better watch out for Saul today; he's in a bad mood. The Nobel Prize is being announced, and you can't win twice.'

Atlas, *Bellow*

Arthur Miller · 1915–2005

Arthur Miller and Marilyn Monroe were married from June 1956 to January 1961. On 5 August 1962 Monroe was found dead in her home in Los Angeles:

Monroe's New York public relations representative, Arthur Jacobs, called Miller to personally deliver the news of her death. His terse response was, 'It's your problem, not mine.' Jacobs replied, 'Arthur, you always were a shit,' and hung up. Miller didn't attend the funeral at the Westwood Village Memorial Chapel in Los Angeles but his father did. Isadore Miller had tried, he said, to call Marilyn on the day before she died but couldn't reach her. The last time he had spoken with her, a week and a half earlier, 'She sounded happy,' he said, but when 'she wanted help . . . nobody was near her.'

Arthur didn't send flowers either. His only recorded reaction, in a letter written to a friend, was that 'The earth shocks for a moment [but] her life-death will not enlighten many.'

Martin Gottfried, *Arthur Miller*, 2003

Roald Dahl · 1916–1990

In the 1970s Kingsley Amis and Roald Dahl were fellow guests at a party outside London, at which Dahl arrived by helicopter:

I COULD not imagine why this form of transport had been thought necessary on a perfectly normal fine day, a Sunday as I remember, nor was any explanation proffered. At some stage, not by my choice, I found myself closeted alone with him.

First declaring himself a great fan of mine, he asked, 'What are you working on at the moment, Kingsley?'

I started to make some reply, but he cut me short. 'That sounds marvellous,' he said, 'but do you expect to make a lot of money out of it however well you do it?'

'I don't know about a lot,' I said. 'Enough, I hope. The sort of money I usually make.'

'So you've no financial problems.'

'I wouldn't say that either exactly, but I seem to be able to—'

Dahl was shaking his head slowly. 'I hate to think of a chap of your distinction having to worry about money at your time of life. Tell me, how old are you now?' I told him and it was much what he or anybody else would have expected. 'Yes. You might be able to write better, I mean even better, if you were financially secure.'

I was hating to think of a number of things, but one that eluded me was how to turn the conversation. I must have mumbled something about only knowing how to write in the way I always had. Never mind—what had *he* got on the—

He was shaking his head again. 'What you want to do,' he said, 'is write a children's book. That's where the money is today, believe me.' ('Today', as I said, was quite some time back.)

'I wouldn't know how to set about it.'

'Do you know what my advance was on my last one?' When he found I did not, in fact had no idea, he told me. It certainly sounded like a large sum.

'I couldn't do it,' I told him again. 'I don't think I enjoyed children's books much when I was a child myself. I've got no feeling for that kind of thing.'

'Never mind, the little bastards'd swallow it.'

Many times in these pages I have put in people's mouths approximations to what they said, what they might well have said, what they said at another time, and a few almost-outright inventions, but that last remark is verbatim.

'Well, I suppose you'd know,' I replied, 'but I can't help feeling they'd see through me. Children are supposed to be good at detecting insincerity and such, aren't they? Again, you're the man who understands about all that.'

When he seemed to have no more to say for the moment I went on with more on previous lines, boring him a good deal, it seemed, but that was perfectly all right with me. At length he roused himself.

'Well, it's up to you. Either you will or you won't. Write a children's book, I mean. But if you do decide to have a crack, let me give you one word of warning. Unless you put everything you've got into it, unless you write it from the heart, the kids'll have no use for it. They'll see you're having them on. And just let me tell you from experience that there's nothing kids hate more than that. They won't give you a second chance either. You'll have had it for good as far as they're concerned. Just you bear that in mind as a word of friendly advice. Now, if you'll excuse me, I rather think I'll go in search of another drink.'

And, with a stiff nod and an air of having asserted his integrity by rejecting some particularly outrageous and repulsive suggestion, the man who put everything into the books he wrote for the kids left me to my thoughts. I felt rather as if I had been looking at one of those pictures by Escher in which the eye is led up a flight of stairs only to find itself at the same level as it started at.

I watched the television news that night, but there was no report of a famous children's author being killed in a helicopter crash.

Kingsley Amis, *Memoirs*, 1991

Robert Lowell · 1917–1977

The nickname 'Cal', which Lowell stuck to all his life, was part Caligula and part Caliban. Indeed, it appears that the Caliban came first, after a class reading of *The Tempest* [at St Mark's, the boarding school in Massachusetts which he attended], and that Lowell somehow had it transmuted to the (to him) more glamorous Roman tyrant. His classmates considered both models thoroughly appropriate.

Ian Hamilton, *Robert Lowell*, 1983

Lowell's last major breakdown took place in London. He was admitted to a private hospital, where a friend went to see him:

I went to visit Cal one afternoon and met one of those gangly mental patients hanging around in the corridors. I asked him where Mr Lowell was, and he said, 'Oh, you mean the Professor. He's going around with his piece of steel. He's got this very important piece of steel.' Anyway, I found Cal wandering out on the lawn, carrying what looked like a piece of motor car engine, or part of a central heating system, and Cal was standing there holding it up and saying, 'The Chief Engineer gave me this. This is a present from the Chief Engineer.' I said, 'Oh yes.' And he said, 'You know what this is? This is the Totentanz. This is what Hitler used to eliminate the Jews.' I said, 'Cal, it's not. It's a piece of steel. It's nothing to do with the Jews.' And then this awful sad, glazed look in his eyes, and he said something like 'It's just my way. It's only a joke.'

Jonathan Raban, quoted in Hamilton, *Robert Lowell*

Later Lowell was released from hospital. At a restaurant in Soho, according to Hamilton's account, he disobeyed doctor's orders and drank some wine. Then he 'tried to enlist help from the waiters and from strangers lunching at adjoining tables—help in compiling an "anthology of world poetry". He told them he was king of Scotland but that the anthology's selection process would be wholly democratic.'

The pianist and wit Oscar Levant was introduced to Lowell by a mutual friend. Like the poet, Levant suffered from periodic spells of mental illness:

WE all had dinner in the Oak Room at the New York Plaza Hotel. Lowell was slightly sloshed and garrulous, but he looks the way a poet should look . . .

'I've been committed to twelve sanitariums,' he announced with an air of triumph. 'How about you?'

Who counts? 'Ten,' I said at random. I didn't want a contest.

Oscar Levant, *The Unimportance of Being Oscar*, 1968

ANTHONY BURGESS · 1917–1994

(pen-name of John Anthony Burgess Wilson)

MR BURGESS grew up in a world where, as he says, education and educated people were the enemies, and later, when he was conscripted into the army, he found that this attitude was not confined to Manchester or to the lower orders. 'I remember cleaning out the latrines at Newbattle Abbey, and being asked by the visiting general what I had done in civilian life. I told him and he said: "At last you're doing something useful." ' Mr Burgess had been a student of English literature at Manchester University.

Robertson Davies, *The Enthusiasms of Robertson Davies*, 1990

Carson McCullers · 1917–1967

(novelist; her books include *The Heart is a Lonely Hunter* and *The Ballad of the Sad Café*)

The American novelist William Goyen recalled that when he first knew her Carson McCullers 'had great vitality and she was quite beautiful in that already decaying way':

GOYEN. She was like a fairy. She had the most delicate kind of tinkling, dazzling little way about her . . . like a little star.

INTERVIEWER. What sort of people interested her?

GOYEN. She had a devastating crush on Elizabeth Bowen. She actually got to Bowen's Court: she shambled over there and spent a fortnight. I heard from Elizabeth that Carson appeared at dinner the first night in her shorts, tennis shorts: that poor body, you know, in tennis shorts and she came down the stairs; that was her debut. It didn't last long. But that was Carson.

Writers at Work: The Paris Review *Interviews*, sixth series, 1985

Muriel Spark · 1918–

Christina Kay was one of Muriel Spark's teachers at James Gillespie's School in Edinburgh. She was (in large measure) the original of Jean Brodie in The Prime of Miss Jean Brodie*:*

Christina Kay was an experimental teacher. Once, she separated us according to our signs of the zodiac: she had read somewhere that children of the same zodiacal sign had a special, mysterious affinity. For a time I was separated from Frances, a Capricorn, and put beside a boring Aquarian. What happened as a result of this experiment was nothing. But even that nothing Miss Kay somehow made into an interesting, a triumphant discovery.

Her father had died when she was still a girl. It had fallen to her to manage affairs for her widowed mother. She told us of the day she had to go and query a bill at the Edinburgh gas office. Our class of girls, incipient feminists, was totally enthralled by Miss Kay's account of how the clerks tittered and nudged each other: a *female* desiring to discuss the details of a gas bill! 'But', said Miss Kay, 'I went through that bill with the clerk, point by point. He at first said he couldn't see any mistake. But when I asked to see the manager he had another look at the bill. He consulted with one of his colleagues. Finally he came to me with a very long face. He admitted there had been an error in calculation. I made them amend the bill, and I paid it then and there. *That*', said Miss Kay, with her sweet, wise smile, 'taught them to sneer at a businesslike young woman.'

Miss Kay always had the knack of gaining our entire sympathy, whatever her views. She could tolerate, even admire, the Scottish aristocracy (on account of their good manners), but the English no. She made a certain amount of propaganda against English dukes, who, she explained with the utmost scorn, stepped out of their baths every morning into the waiting arms of their valets, who stood holding the bath-towels and who rubbed them dry. This made us all laugh a lot. And, in fact, we often had cause for general mirth in Miss Kay's class.

Muriel Spark, *Curriculum Vitae: An Autobiography*, 1992

Iris Murdoch · 1919–1999

As an undergraduate at Oxford, Iris Murdoch was a leading member of the Labour Club. The club at the time was heavily Marxist in complexion, which eventually led to a split: some 400 members broke away to form a rival organization, the Democratic Socialist Club. The treasurer of the new group was Roy Jenkins:

The main duty that I remember going with this office was that of engaging in a long and unrewarding correspondence with Iris Murdoch, my opposite number in the old club, about the sharing of its assets and/or liabilities. Both our different ideological positions and the arm's-length nature of our negotiations were indicated by our respective salutations. 'Dear Comrade Jenkins,' she began. 'Dear Miss Murdoch,' I replied. Forty-seven years later I compensated by giving her an Oxford honorary degree.

Roy Jenkins, *A Life at the Centre*, 1992

A. N. Wilson reports on a party in Oxford in 1978:

I got there early but not so early as IM, who thinks that when he puts 6.30 on an invitation card, the host will be even more pleased if guests turn up at 6.20. She is wearing a rich royal-blue 'top', ski-pants and lace-up shoes, slightly misshapen, from Marks & Sparks. As I approach her, she raises her glass with a radiant smile, and says, 'You've heard the news?' 'No . . . What?' 'A Polish Pope—they've elected a Polish Pope!'

'How exciting—who is he?'

'He's the Archbishop of Cracow, he's an intellectual, oh, this is simply the best news for years in the Roman Church.'

John Fuller standing by suggests that Poles are even more conservative than Italians when it comes to religious matters . . .

'But no, no—this is marvellous news. I love Poland, I love Poles . . .'

'But it doesn't mean that the Roman Church will change . . .'

'Of course it won't, in one sense . . . but I don't know! It HAS to. It is bound eventually to accept women priests, for instance.'

'You think a Polish Pope will ordain women?'

'I don't see why not. The Roman Church has changed much more radically in many ways than the Anglican Church, than my Church, if I can call it that . . .'

'Do you think that the Polish Pope will ordain women before they ordain women in the Church of England?' I ask.

IM is swigging the white wine very fast and has already put away about half a litre of the stuff when she asserts, 'Certainly!' (Sortunlah!)

'Like to bet?'

'I'll bet on it, yes!' She shakes my hand. 'No, no, I see the whole of Christianity making great changes. It's vital, vitally important that we should all have access to this—stuff!'

John Fuller asks, 'What stuff?'

'To religion,' she answers shortly.

A. N. Wilson, *Iris Murdoch as I Knew Her*, 2003

SHE admired Frank Kermode's learning, but thought him a bit dour, like the Scots. When I said he came from the Isle of Man, she added that that was even worse, for their ancestors were all 'elves or something'.

Jeffrey Meyers, *Privileged Moments*, 2000

J. D. SALINGER · 1919–

ONE day Salinger's mother came to visit the school [Valley Forge Military Academy, which Salinger attended between 1934 and 1936]. She commented on the red flashes that some of the boys wore on their caps (these were awarded for meritorious conduct of one sort or another). Salinger told her that she must at all costs avoid speaking with these boys. The flashes, he said, were worn as punishment for using profane language.

Ian Hamilton, *In Search of J. D. Salinger*, 1988

DORIS LESSING · 1919–

I AM walking down Church Street, Kensington, with Donald Ogden Stewart, and we are going to have dinner, his suggestion. He must be sixty or so, a lean, balding, freckly, sandy man, and I am thirty-something.

He says to me, 'I ought to tell you that these days I am more interested in food than in sex.' I was absolutely, coldly furious. That it was so graceless—well, what did one expect? meaning, specifically, from Americans; but there had never been, not for one second, any suggestion of a physical attraction, and anyway he was old. Now I see this as a quite sensible (if graceless) way of dealing with the situation. After all, he had come from Hollywood, and from the Left in America, and probably had had affairs by the dozen. To his contemporaries he must have seemed an attractive man. None of us find it easy to know that we are not as attractive as we once were. He had thought, I'm not going to sit through the whole dinner while she is wondering if I'm going to make a pass.

Doris Lessing, *Walking in the Shade*, 1997

Donald Ogden Stewart (1894–1980) was a well-known American playwright and screenwriter. A Communist sympathizer, he lived in England in the latter part of his life.

My most bizarre sexual encounter was with Ken Tynan. I had gone with him to the theatre and then to some party of actors winding down after a performance. Ken was the star, shedding witticisms and benevolent advice and criticism. Then it was very late, and he suggested I stay the night in Mount Street. The young of every generation have to imagine they have invented casual ways, but the innocent sharing of beds did not begin in the sixties. Not once, nor twice, have I spent a friendly night with some man because we haven't finished our conversation or because he missed the last train. Never, not for the slice of a second, had there been sexual attraction between Ken and me. I cannot imagine two human beings less likely to make each other's pulses flutter. I had often been in the Tynan bedroom, because it was where we left coats during parties. I came back from the bathroom to get into bed beside companionable Ken, and suddenly the bedroom walls had been grotesquely transformed, for on them were arranged every sort of whip, as if in a whip museum. Now, you'd think, wouldn't you, that Ken would say, 'Are you wondering what all those whips are doing there?' Or I would say, 'Now, about those whips, Ken?' Not at all; there we lay, side by side, conversing agreeably about a hundred things, but certainly politics, because that was our favourite subject. I used to tell him he was romantic, not to say sentimental, and ignorant, and he complained I was cynical and lacking faith in humanity. I remember an occasion when he summoned me to a meeting to discuss how to protest about something, I forget what, with several prominent people. I said I found this business of celebrities 'sitting down' in public to fast as a protest absurd and laughable, because everyone knew that the moment the 'fast' was over we would all be off to a five-star restaurant. Ken thought I was lacking in any instinct for publicity, and he was afraid I often showed reactionary tendencies.

And so we fell asleep and were woken by a female menial bringing breakfast on two trays. (Ken refused to cook, and so did Elaine Dundy [Tynan's wife at the time]. Neither knew how to boil an egg, they proudly claimed, and they always ate in restaurants. Even breakfast was brought in.) Then she tidied away the whips.

Lessing, *Walking in the Shade*

A SCENE: A famous American feminist is visiting London, and I go to see her with a man who has consistently taken a feminist position, and long before it was fashionable. As we walk through the hotel she deliberately slams one door after another in his face.

Lessing, *Walking in the Shade*

D. J. ENRIGHT · 1920–2002

LONG ago, a letter from a male person was forwarded by *The Listener*, which went like this: 'Dear D. Enright, Can you be the vivacious Dorothy Enright I met on a cruise to South Africa five years ago? Do you remember those nights on deck, gazing at the moon? . . . You didn't tell me you wrote poems, but I should have guessed . . .', et—somewhat embarrassingly—cetera.

Enright, *Interplay*, 1995

KURT VONNEGUT · 1922–

Vonnegut was being held as a prisoner of war during the fire-bombing of Dresden in February 1945:

OUR guards were noncoms—a sergeant, a corporal, and four privates—and leaderless. Cityless, too, because they were Dresdeners who'd been shot up on the front and sent home for easy duty. They kept us at attention for a couple of hours. They didn't know what else to do. They'd go over and talk to each other. Finally we trekked across the rubble and they quartered us with some South Africans in a suburb. Every day we walked into the city and dug into basements and shelters to get the corpses out, as a sanitary measure. When we went into them, a typical shelter, an ordinary basement usually, looked like a streetcar full of people who'd simultaneously had heart failure. Just people sitting there in their chairs, all dead. A fire storm is an amazing thing. It doesn't occur in nature. It's fed by the tornadoes that occur in the midst of it and there isn't a damned thing to breathe. We brought the dead out. They were loaded on wagons and taken to parks, large, open areas in the city which weren't filled with rubble. The Germans got funeral pyres going, burning the bodies to keep them from stinking and from spreading disease. One hundred thirty thousand corpses were hidden underground. It was a terribly elaborate Easter egg hunt. We went to work through cordons of German soldiers. Civilians didn't get to see what we were up to. After a few days the city began to smell, and a new technique was invented. Necessity is the mother of invention. We would bust into the shelter, gather up valuables from people's laps without attempting identification, and turn the valuables over to guards. Then soldiers would come in with a flame thrower and stand in the door and cremate the people inside. Get the gold and jewelry out and then burn everybody inside.

Writers at Work: The Paris Review *Interviews*, sixth series, 1985

Philip Larkin · 1922–1985

Glyn Lloyd and Philip Larkin were fellow pupils and friends at a preparatory school in Coventry which Larkin began attending in 1928, at the age of 6. Like most of the other boys, Lloyd was a passionate collector of cigarette cards:

In late 1929 or early 1930 a new series of cards was issued consisting of international rugby footballers. I had collected about half the set and kept the cards in an album specially designed for them. One day when I was about to add new cards to my collection, I discovered that at least half were missing. I was distraught and let out a bellow of tearful rage, alerting the rest of the family to the situation. Circumstantial evidence pointed to Philip as prime suspect. My mother was emphatic: he had been looking through the album only recently when on a lunchtime visit.

How to obtain proof or, more importantly, retrieve the cards was another matter. The family were sympathetic but perhaps did not appreciate the full magnitude of my loss. My best friend Peter, who was also collecting the series, was more understanding. He was nearly a year older and, at the age of eight and a half, capable of righteous indignation. He overcame my diffidence and together we called at the Larkin house, accusing Philip of taking the cards, and demanding them back. He did return them. Unfortunately they had been defaced: all the beautiful red, white, blue and green shirts had been obliterated beneath a pattern of fine cross-hatching in blue-black ink! Decades later, in memorable English, Philip laid much blame on his mum and dad. I wouldn't know about that; but certainly in terms of f—king things up, he did a Grade A job on my cigarette cards.

I Once Met: Fifty Encounters with the Famous, ed. Richard Ingrams, 1996

In 1950 Larkin joined the staff of Queen's University, Belfast, as a sub-librarian. One of his friends in Belfast was a newly appointed junior lecturer in Spanish in the university, Arthur Terry:

ONE could see what he meant when he referred to his taste for 'deprivation': my own austere digs in Wellesley Avenue became for him a source of unbelievable richness—sheer fantasy, of course, as were our mutual speculations concerning the secret lives of my landlady and fellow-lodgers. Such fantasies, certainly, did much to enliven the minor hazards of a fairly uneventful life: in our early days, for instance, we both sent our laundry to the Good Shepherd Laundry, an establishment housed in a convent up the Ormeau Road; each week our socks came back twice their normal length, elongated, or so we imagined, by jovial Irish nuns who placed stones in their toes when hanging them out to dry.

Arthur Terry, 'Larkin in Belfast', in George Hartley (ed.), *Philip Larkin: A Tribute*, 1988

In the course of a journey Larkin came across a village in Cumbria called Kaber. The name moved him to send a limerick to his editor at Faber and Faber, Charles Monteith:

There was an old fellow of Kaber,
Who published a volume with Faber:
When they said 'Join the club?'
He ran off to the pub—
But Charles called, 'You must *love* your neighbour.'

The somewhat obscure third and fourth lines Philip explained as 'fillers' to be replaced more specifically as occasion demanded. For example:

When they said, 'Meet Ted Hughes',
He replied, 'I refuse',

or

When they said, 'Meet Thom Gunn',
He cried, 'God, I must run',

and so on.

Charles Monteith, 'Publishing Larkin', in Anthony Thwaite (ed.), *Larkin at Sixty*, 1982

KINGSLEY AMIS · 1922–1995

KINGSLEY AMIS to luncheon . . . His new novel, *Difficulties with Girls*, was out last week . . . Its newspaper coverage is being extensive, on the whole good, with one or two violent exceptions. Kingsley brought off a notable double by having an obsequious piece written about him by John Mortimer in one Colour Supplement, and Kingsley himself being egregiously rude to Mortimer in another on the same day. Among other things, Mortimer stated in his interview that Kingsley 'hit his son with a hammer', when in fact Kingsley had said he 'hit his thumb with a hammer'.

Anthony Powell, *Journals 1987–1989*, 1996

Norman Mailer · 1923–

In 1948 I was out of the army and in college, it was final exam time, and I was flipping through the back pages of *Time* magazine and saw a picture of Norman with a smoking cigarette in his hand—a sort of sophisticated picture—and my first thought was, Oh, my God, Norman's been arrested for rape.

I laugh when I recall this, but my response wasn't completely crazy, I assure you, because when I'd first met him in basic training at Fort Bragg, North Carolina, he was going around the barracks asking all the men about their sex lives. This was the first or second week, and he was taking notes, operating like an interviewer, going from individual to individual asking the same questions as if conducting a research survey. He was asking if they went in for foreplay, and, as I recall, most of them said they didn't. In fact, that's why I remember another guy in the group who'll go unnamed, an Italian, who told Norman, 'I just get on and off my wife,' which was probably the consensus of everyone he talked to, that sex in those days was tapping your wife on the shoulder and saying, 'I'm gonna jump on you.'

Nobody got angry at him. It was like a matter-of-fact type of thing—'Here's this guy asking me these questions.' He wasn't far out about it or showing off, and he wrote people's responses down on what I remember was more like a yellow pad than a notebook. Now, after all these years, I assume he was doing it to get information for something he was going to write, to get the feel of people's attitudes. He hadn't talked about his own wife, Bea, but sex always seemed very much on his mind. Hence my reaction to the *Time* photograph. Obviously this didn't make any sense given the kind of picture it was, so then I turned back a page and saw it was a review of *The Naked and the Dead.*

Clifford Maskovsky in Peter Manso, *Mailer: His Life and Times*, 1985

Brendan Behan · 1923–1964

While staying in New York, Behan suffered a series of seizures. With the help of a doctor, Max Tasler, he was admitted to a semi-private ward in the University Hospital, but he was an unwilling patient. When his wife Beatrice and a friend, George Kleinsinger, went to visit him, they found him wandering around with his lower half naked. (He had discarded his pyjama trousers.) He was convinced that he was in a mental hospital, and desperate to get out:

BRENDAN had started ringing for the elevator, which didn't arrive because he was pressing the 'up' instead of the 'down' button. George had grabbed another patient in the corridor and entreated him to tell Brendan he was not in a psychiatric unit.

'Sure you're not', said the patient to Brendan. 'This ain't no nuthouse. It's just a hospital, Mister, and I'm just a patient like you.'

'It's a fucking puzzle factory', wept Brendan.

Max Tasler arrived. Although he endeavoured to convince Brendan that the University was a general hospital he was no more successful than the rest of us had been.

'Look, Brendan,' he said, 'we'll give you a nice quiet room to yourself where you can read, and there'll be no other patients to disturb you.'

He took us in the elevator to an upper floor and showed us a room with a splendid view of New York City. Brendan said he would stay if Dr Tasler got him a drink.

'Okay,' agreed Tasler, 'I'll get you a beer.'

Brendan changed course again. 'I don't want your fucking beer. I just want out of here.'

He was beyond persuasion. Max Tasler just shrugged his shoulders and told one of the staff to fetch Mr Behan's clothes.

When Brendan had dressed we went down in the elevator with him. It was crowded and suddenly Brendan glimpsed, behind the passengers, a patient lying on a stretcher. He screamed at the attendant to stop the elevator. We scrambled out at the cafeteria floor.

Brendan, followed by George, went looking for a drink, but only soft drinks were served in the cafeteria.

'Give him anything', whispered George to the woman behind the counter.

She was about to pour an apple juice when Brendan caught sight of a waitress filling a vinegar jar from a pitcher. He grabbed the pitcher from her hand and drank the contents down.

'Jeez,' she exclaimed, 'look what he's done!'

Brendan was pulling a face. 'It's kind of bitter, George.'

Dr Tasler had followed us into the cafeteria, and I told him what had happened. 'Gosh,' he said, 'he's got a stronger stomach than I thought.'

We got Brendan into a cab and drove back to the Chelsea. But before we could escort him into the hotel he made a sharp turn left in the direction of the Oasis.

'No, Brendan!' I cried.

But there was no restraining him. He was still talking incoherently, but as soon as he had taken a shot of Napper Tandy, his term for a brandy, he came lucid and began to talk sensibly.

Beatrice Behan, *My Life with Brendan*, 1973

Truman Capote · 1924–1984

An Atlantic crossing on the Queen Mary *in 1948. Capote's companion during the voyage was Tennessee Williams:*

We had scarcely left Southampton when Truman began to notice that a portly and bibulous bishop was popping up unexpectedly almost everywhere Truman went. I began to notice it, too. We would hardly sit down at a bar on the ship when in would come the Bishop, less steadily than the calm ocean and the seaworthy vessel could possibly account for. He would cast a glazed and anxious look about the bar. Then his eyes would light up as he spotted little Truman crouching before the bar, hoping to escape the attention of this eminent churchman. No luck, never, none, whatsoever. The Bishop would invariably spot us, the gloom would disappear from his round face and he would fairly plunge at the nearest bar stool, close to those occupied by Truman and me. Or if we were at a table or at a seat in the movie auditorium, he would plump himself down (quite uninvited, needless to say) or would heave into an adjoining seat. So it went for half the crossing.

A dreadful confrontation between the Bishop and Truman was unmistakably impending and down it came like a bolt from heaven.

Truman and I were seated vis-à-vis at a table for two in the dining salon. With apparitional abruptness, the Bishop had drawn up a chair between us and started to engage us in conversation. His motive was not of an evangelistic nature. I mean not in the usual sense. Truman had declared himself quite uninterested in any church of any denomination.

On this evening, Truman began to stare at the Bishop's massive ring.

'You know,' he drawled sweetly to the Bishop, 'I've always wanted to have a bishop's ring.'

The Bishop chuckled indulgently.

'A bishop's ring is only available to a bishop,' I think was his answer.

'Oh, I don't know,' countered Truman, 'it occurred to me that maybe I might find one in a pawnshop. You know, one that had been hocked by a defrocked bishop.'

He drawled out 'defrocked bishop' in a way that left no doubt of his implication. The bishop turned redder than usual and excused himself from the table and we were not disturbed by his persistent approaches for the rest of the voyage.

Tennessee Williams, *Memoirs*, 1976

James Baldwin · 1924–1987

At the age of twenty-four Baldwin left New York and went to live in Paris, where he took a room in the Hotel Verneuil in Saint-Germain-des-Prés. Mary Keen was one of a group of expatriates living in the Verneuil with whom he became friendly. Most of them were aspiring writers. All of them were white:

Mary Keen claims that Baldwin's friends in the hotel and at the Café de Flore, where they spent many evenings, did not think of him as a black person. But although Baldwin made no show of being the odd one out, he was forced to see himself as black and incorporated the self-deprecatory tricks of the inferiority trade into his wit. Mary Keen remembers that strangers assumed he was a jazz musician—their definition of a black man in Paris—and one of the mock titles for a book she and Baldwin concocted for fun was 'Non, nous ne jouons pas la trompette' ('No, we don't play the trumpet').

Words commonly used to describe Baldwin by those who knew him during this period are 'intense', 'unreliable', 'comical'. Another acquaintance of the time recalls him as being 'very ugly': 'Put a bone through his nose and it would've made sense,' says Ann Birstein, herself now a novelist in New York, then a frequent visitor, like Baldwin, to the literary gatherings held in the rue de Verneuil apartment of Eileen and Stanley Geist. 'If there was bad luck going, he would get it. But Jimmy was laughing all the time. He was very funny.' The business of dreaming up titles for books that would not get written seems to have been popular. 'I remember,' says Birstein, 'that the one we thought of for Jimmy was "A Negro looks at Henry James", which was a big joke at the time.'

More of a joke for some than others. Baldwin laughed along, giving a public show of acceptance of himself as a figure of fun, no doubt perceiving beneath the jests a genuine affection. But he was also making the effort to be released from the description 'young Negro writer', and even 'young Negro'. Unsympathetic perceptions of him as a savage with a bone through his nose could only fortify the category . . .

James Campbell, *Talking at the Gates: A Life of James Baldwin*, 1991

Gore Vidal · 1925–

1 March 1948, Rome. Gore Vidal, a young American novelist, is staying at the Eden and we lunched together today . . . GV was not shy: which I always find rather agreeable. 'What would you say the colour of my hair was?' he inquired. 'The colour of stale marron glacé,' I replied, feeling that I might as well say what I really thought. 'Yes, but in the summer it's straw blonde,' he rejoined, adding '—and my body gets the colour of old mahogany: it's sensational.'

Roger Hinks, *The Gymnasium of the Mind*, 1984

Allen Ginsberg · 1926–1997

By the 1980s, Beat Studies had become a popular component of many English Literature curricula, and Ginsberg began to take a scholar's interest in the detail of his own career. Much of the early history of the Beats was the history of who did what to whom. Did Jack ever do it to Bill, or Bill to Jack, or Neal to Peter, and so on.

One thing was sure: Allen did it to them all, and he was determined that history should get it right. To this end, says his biographer Barry Miles, he 'kept all the sixty-thousand-plus letters he received throughout his life, and he has saved his manuscripts, journals, notebooks and doodles. Since the 1970s he has frequently taped his lectures, his conversations with relatives and friends and, on occasion, his telephone conversations.' Shortly before Ginsberg's death in 1997, a profilist visited his office on Union Square: 'a proper office with three Apple Macs, a cuttings library, Ginsberg's massive photographic archive, a photocopier and multiple phone lines. It acts as a "servicing organization", helping poets with hand-outs from Ginsberg's Committee on Poetry—a charitable foundation set up in 1965 to avoid paying taxes to a war-mongering government—or for "stuff like fixing their teeth or an emergency of some kind". More than 100 poets have benefited from Ginsberg's redistribution of his earnings.'

Ian Hamilton, *Against Oblivion*, 2002

John Ashbery · 1927–

From an interview with Mark Ford:

MARK FORD. Your first poem was 'The Battle', which you wrote when you were how old?

JOHN ASHBERY. Eight. Actually, one influence on it might have been the movie of *A Midsummer Night's Dream*, made in 1935, with Mickey Rooney as Puck. I remember boning up on Lamb's version before seeing this movie in which there were lots of fairies sliding down moonbeams and so on.

MF. Well, your poem—which is about a conflict between fairies and bunnies—has the lines:

> The fairies are riding upon their snowflakes,
> And the tall haystacks are great sugar mounds.
> These are the fairies' camping grounds.

Very Shakespearean . . .

JA. Yes! And at the time it seemed quite perfect to me. It even ended up being read by the best-selling author in America at the time, Mary Roberts Rinehart. She mainly wrote mystery stories, a number of which featured a female detective named Tish. She was very famous, and lived on Fifth Avenue—though I'd never been to New York City [Ashbery grew up in a small farming community near Rochester, NY], I'd heard of Fifth Avenue. Anyway, her son married my mother's cousin, and on Christmas Day, so the story goes, this poem was read aloud in her apartment to great acclaim. Alas, I wasn't there, and in fact I didn't get to New York City until I was seventeen years old.

John Ashbery in Conversation with Mark Ford, 2003

Dan Jacobson · 1929–

(Novelist and short-story writer; his books include *The Price of Diamonds* and *The Rape of Tamar*)

In 1950 Dan Jacobson arrived in London from South Africa, knowing no one in the city. On his journey he had read a book containing a collection of letters between Virginia Woolf and Logan Pearsall Smith, and one of the first sights he sought out was Virginia's Woolf's house in Tavistock Square—but when he got there, all he found was a bomb-site:

THE house Virginia Woolf had written those letters from was no longer there, and I was disappointed to see this. But the rest of the square was presumably much as it had been when she had been alive and had written her letters to Logan Pearsall Smith. He and she had exchanged elaborate, self-conscious mock-insults about 'Chelsea', which he was supposed to represent, and 'Bloomsbury', which of course had been hers. Part of what they had meant by Bloomsbury I saw to be these trees and houses, the glimpses above them of some of the buildings of London University, the traffic in Southampton Row. Was there nothing else? Within the disappointment that the house should have been scooped out of the square another began to grow. So this was it. I had seen it. True, I had not seen, and thought it unlikely I would ever see, any of the people who had made up the Bloomsbury society; but the physical Bloomsbury was about me. The disappointment was not with its appearance, which was black enough, and severe enough, and imposing enough; it arose from the very fact of my having seen it. The half-conscious, always-unfinished guess-work which had been so inextricably an aspect of my reading, throughout my childhood and adolescence in South Africa, the dreamlike otherness or remoteness in the books I had read, which I had valued more than I had supposed, were being taken from me, bit by bit. Here was one bit of it gone. I would never again be able to visit a Bloomsbury of my own imagination—a district vaguer and therefore more glamorous than the reality; one less hard and angular and self-defining. I would not have exchanged my glimpse of the Bloomsbury of brick and tar, of tree-trunk and iron railing, for anything I might have been able to imagine; but still, there was a loss.

Another loss I knew was my own imagination of myself in Bloomsbury, or anywhere else in London. Coming to London had not—not yet, at any rate—changed me, transformed me, made a new man of me. Bloomsbury was what it had been before I had seen it. So was I.

'Time of Arrival', in *Time and Time Again*, 1985

John Osborne · 1929–1994

While the first production of Look Back in Anger *was in rehearsal, the English Stage Company found Osborne extra work*:

I BECAME play-reader for £2 a week, taking home nightly some thirty or forty scripts. When I once complained of the burden to Tony [Richardson, the director of *Look Back in Anger*], he said, his voice rising to its most imitable pitch, 'But you don't *read* them? Not all *through*?' I ventured some pious pretence about talent being missed through hasty scanning. He picked up a few scripts from my bag and went through half a dozen. Some took twenty seconds, some half a minute, two minutes at most, a high-pitched, awesome Geiger counter. '*There*, that's how you read a play.'

Almost a Gentleman, 1991

Ted Hughes · 1930–1998

In later readings of his poem 'The Thought-Fox', he often gave an account of the strange dream that prompted his abandoning the study of English Literature [while an undergraduate at Cambridge] as an academic subject. He had spent all evening struggling to complete an essay of literary criticism. In his dream that night, a fox appeared that was the size of a wolf, and placed its paw, which seemed to be a bleeding human hand, flat palm-down on the blank space of Hughes's page, saying, 'Stop this—you are destroying us.' As it lifted the hand away from the page, Hughes saw the blood-print glistening wet. Hughes understood that mark as an image of his own pain at forcing himself to go against his nature. The poem was written two years after the dream, but the meaning was clear to him as he woke.

Elaine Feinstein, *Ted Hughes: The Life of a Poet*, 2001

Derek Walcott · 1930–

In 1989 Walcott travelled to London to receive the Queen's Gold Medal for Poetry. A native of St Lucia, he was the first Commonwealth citizen to be awarded the medal:

Previous winners included Auden, Christopher Fry, Robert Graves, Philip Larkin and Stephen Spender. Walcott later claimed that he and the Queen talked about 'how Americans speak Shakespearean verse': ' "Ma'am," I said, "you know Sly Stallone. Well, his version of Hamlet goes, To be *or what*." She just cracked up.'

Bruce King, *Derek Walcott; A Caribbean Life*, 2000

Harold Pinter · 1930–

Pinter's early play The Hothouse *had its origins in personal experience:*

'I went along in 1954 to the Maudsley Hospital in London,' Pinter now recalls, 'as a guinea-pig. They were offering ten bob or something for guinea-pigs and I needed the money desperately. I read a bona fide advertisement and went along. It was all above board, as it seemed. Nurses and doctors all in white. They tested my blood-pressure first. Perfectly all right. I was put in a room with electrodes. They said, "Just sit there for a while and relax." I'd no idea what was going to happen. Suddenly there was a most appalling noise through the earphones and I nearly jumped through the roof. I felt my heart go . . . BANG! The noise lasted a few seconds and then was switched off. The doctor came in grinning and said, "Well, that really gave you a start, didn't it?" I said, "It certainly did." And they said, "Thanks very much." There was no interrogation, as in the play, but it left a deep impression on me. I couldn't forget the experience. I was trembling all over. And I would have been in such a vulnerable position if they had started to ask me questions. Later I asked them what it was all about and they said they were testing levels of reaction. That mystified me. Who exactly were they going to give this kind of shock-treatment to? Anyway, *The Hothouse* was kicked off by that experience. I was well aware of being used for an experiment and feeling quite powerless.'

Michael Billington, *The Life and Work of Harold Pinter*, 1996

Alan Ayckbourn first met Pinter when he was a 20-year-old actor appearing in a production of The Birthday Party*:*

WHEN he arrived in Scarborough he was in a very defensive, not to say depressed state. We had probably three weeks to rehearse. I remember asking Pinter about my character. Where does he come from? Where is he going to? What can you tell me about him that will give me more understanding? And Harold just said, 'Mind your own fucking business. Concentrate on what's there.'

Billington, *Life and Work*

CHINUA ACHEBE · 1930–

In 1957 Achebe spent several months in London. He had already completed a draft of his first novel, Things Fall Apart, *but felt that it needed further work; he took the manuscript back to Lagos, where he worked for the Nigerian Broadcasting Service, and finished revising it there:*

WHEN I was in England, I had seen advertisements about typing agencies; I had learned that if you really want to make a good impression, you should have your manuscript well typed. So, foolishly, from Nigeria, I parceled my manuscript—handwritten, by the way, and the only copy in the whole world—wrapped it up and posted it to this typing agency that advertised in the *Spectator*. They wrote back and said, 'Thank you for your manuscript. We'll charge thirty-two pounds.' That was what they wanted for two copies, and which they had to receive before they started. So I sent thirty-two pounds in British postal order to these people, and then I heard no more. Weeks passed, and months. I wrote and wrote and wrote. No answer. Not a word. I was getting thinner and thinner and thinner. Finally, I was very lucky. My boss at the broadcasting house was going home to London on leave. A very stubborn Englishwoman. I told her about this. She said. 'Give me their name and address.' When she got to London she went there! She said, 'What's this nonsense?' They must have been shocked, because I think their notion was that a manuscript sent from *Africa*—well, there's really nobody to follow it up. The British don't normally behave like that. It's not done, you see. But something from Africa was treated differently. So when this woman, Mrs Beattie, turned up in their office, and said, 'What's going on?' they were confused. They said, 'The manuscript was sent but customs returned it.' Mrs. Beattie said, 'Can I see your dispatch book?' They had no dispatch book. So she said, 'Well, send this thing, typed up, back to him in the next week, or otherwise you'll hear about it.' So soon after that, I received the typed manuscript of *Things Fall Apart*. One copy, not two. No letter at all to say what happened.

Interview in *Paris Review*, 1994

In his biography of Achebe, Ezenwa-Ohaeto quotes the novelist's response to a friend who asked what his reaction would have been if the manuscript had been stolen: 'he said that he would have died'.

Anthony Thwaite · 1930–

The poet and critic Anthony Thwaite has always enjoyed the Sherlock Holmes stories. Who doesn't love the pipe, the teasing of trusty old Watson, the devilishly clever deductions? If only one were half as clever oneself.

Mr Thwaite is now entitled to think he is. You remember the opening lines of *The Memoirs of Sherlock Holmes*: ' "I am afraid, Watson, that I shall have to go," said Holmes . . .' Mr Thwaite has received in the post an unsolicited copy of the *Memoirs* which opens, ' "I am afraid, Watson, that I shall have to go," said Thwaite, as we sat down together to our breakfast one morning'. The book is called *The Memoirs of Anthony Thwaite*, and is published by Customized Classics of Toronto.

'Dear Anthony,' they write chummily, 'Customized Classics is a company that believes in promoting literacy by bringing new life to much-loved classic books.' New life has been brought to Conan Doyle's work by replacing each mention of 'Sherlock Holmes' with 'Anthony Thwaite'. Even the blurb positions our familiar poet in unfamiliar mode: 'Follow Thwaite as he chases after criminals through the foggy gas-lit streets of Victorian London and uncovers sinister secrets.' Mr Thwaite is apt to find it sinister each time he glimpses himself retiring to Baker Street and preparing to give himself a shot in the arm.

J.C. in the NB column in *Times Literary Supplement*, 2001

Tom Wolfe · 1931–

(novelist and social commentator; author of *The Bonfire of the Vanities*)

When I wrote *Radical Chic*, about a party for the Black Panthers at Leonard Bernstein's apartment, I noticed that the platters upon which the Panthers were being served Roquefort cheese balls were gadrooned. They had this little sort of ribbing around the edges of the trays. You may think that's a small point, but I think that small points like that can really make a piece, particularly at the beginning. There's something about a gadrooned platter being served to the Black Panthers that really gives a piece a bite, particularly at the beginning. It doesn't matter if your audience doesn't know what a gadrooned platter is. Often people are flattered to have an unusual word thrust upon them. They say, 'Well, that author thinks I know what he's talking about!'

Interview in *Paris Review*, 1991

V. S. Naipaul · 1932–

Naipaul's father wrote short stories and dreamed of a literary career. For much of his life he worked on a newspaper, the Trinidad Guardian, *but in the 1930s, not long after Naipaul was born, he had a breakdown which compelled him to give up his job for several years:*

Admiration of the craft stayed with him. In 1936, in the middle of his illness—when I would have been staying at my mother's family house—he sent me a little book: *The School of Poetry*, an anthology, really a decorated keepsake, edited by Alice Meynell. It had been marked down by the shop from forty-eight cents to twenty-four cents. It was his gift to his son of something noble, something connected with the word. Somehow the book survived all our moves. It is inscribed: 'to Vidyadhar, from his father. Today you have reached the span of 3 years, 10 months and 15 days. And I make this present to you with this counsel in addition. Live up to the estate of man, follow truth, be kind and gentle and trust God.'

'Prologue to an Autobiography', 1982

A STORY used to be told of him by West Indian friends. Asked on the telephone whether he was coloured, by an English landlady to whom he was applying in his youth for a room, he replied: 'Hopelessly.' This is not a story which shows him sorrowing or apologizing; the reply is a patrician joke which may (if uttered) have meant, among other things, that there wasn't much hope for the landlady.

Karl Miller, *Dark Horses*, 1998

SYLVIA PLATH · 1932–1963

In October 1962 Ted Hughes wrote to his friends William and Dido Merwin to tell them that he had left Sylvia Plath. Not long afterwards Dido saw him in London:

HAVING conscientiously condoned and paid lip-service to his loyal excuses and camouflages in the past, I asked him as the first question on that first evening—partly to mark and partly to test out a new, and presumably uncensored, dispensation of things—what had been hardest to take during the time he and Sylvia were together. His answer was simply to recount the beginnings of what had by then become his highly successful broadcast series.

The head of the [BBC] Schools Broadcasting Department, Moira Doolan—a lady of a certain age—had telephoned to arrange a meeting. Sylvia had answered and decided that the timbre and lilt of the voice on the line boded Shared Experience beyond the call of duty. Ted returned half an hour late for lunch (having secured the job he was after) to find that she had torn up all his work in hand: manuscripts, drafts, notebooks, the lot. As a final, gratuitous act of pure spite, she had also gralloched his complete Shakespeare. Only the hard spine and the end boards had stood up to the onslaught. The text had been more or less reduced to 'fluff'. There were just a few scraps of Ted's work that he managed to salvage and stick back together with Scotch tape.

Dido Merwin, 'Vessel of Wrath: A Memoir of Sylvia Plath', printed as an appendix in Anne Stevenson, *Bitter Fame: A Life of Sylvia Plath*, 1989

Dido Merwin is a hostile witness—there is a somewhat sardonic account of her role in Janet Malcolm's book about Sylvia Plath's posthumous reputation, The Silent Woman *(1994)—but of course her hostility does not necessarily mean that the events she reports didn't occur as she describes them.*

John Updike · 1932–

In myself I observe the very traits that used to irritate me in men of late middle age whom I have known: a forgetfulness, a repetitiveness, a fussiness with parcels and strings, a doddery deliberation of movement mixed with patches of inattention and uncertainty that make my car-driving increasingly hazardous and—other, younger drivers indicate with gestures and honking—irritating to others. I feel also an innocent self-absorption, a ruminativeness that makes me blind and deaf and indifferent to the contemporary trends and fads that are so crucial to the young, invested as these passing twitches are with their own emerging identity and sexuality. My brain cells have accepted their program and are full. I used to find it difficult to talk to my first wife's father, an intelligent and sensitive man, because he didn't seem to be *up* on anything. Now, as I look over *The New Yorker*, its cartoons and 'The Talk of the Town' bristle with allusions I don't quite catch, and a psychic music that isn't mine, any more than Thurber's and White's was mine . . .

Also like my late Unitarian father-in-law am I now in my amazed, insistent appreciation of the physical world, of this planet with its scenery and weather—that pathetic discovery which the old make that every day and season has its beauty and its uses, that even a walk to the mailbox is a precious experience, that all species of tree and weed have their signature and style and the sky is a pageant of clouds. Aging calls us outdoors, after the adult indoors of work and love-life and keeping stylish, into the lowly simplicities that we thought we had outgrown as children. We come again to love the plain world, its stone and wood, its air and water. 'What a glorious view!' my father-in-law would announce as we smirked in the back seat of the car he was inattentively driving. But in truth all views have something glorious about them. The act of seeing is itself glorious, and of hearing, and feeling, and tasting. One of my dead golf partners, Ted Lucas, said once within my hearing to another dear departed fellow golfer, John Conley, 'Life is bliss.' The remark had come about by I forget what circuitry, but I assume John must have somehow raised the contrary possibility; this was unlike him, for he was a good Catholic as well as a good golfer in his prime, with a smooth takeaway and sound hip motion. Ted also, on another occasion, while we were floundering around in the sunshine on a little friendly nine-hole course called Cape Ann, suddenly exclaimed, 'Ah, to be alive, on a June day, in Ipswich, Massachusetts!' The course was actually in Essex, but I knew what he meant—a happiness above and beyond any particular cause for it. I was relatively young, and Ted and John were relatively old, and I was alert, during our Wednesday afternoons together, for what wisdom might fall to me. Ted came originally from New York City and, after what I gathered to have been a rakish early life, converted to Bahaism, and died in an instant, of a heart attack, while making a telephone call from the hospital to say he was being released.

Self-Consciousness, 1989

Geoffrey Hill · 1932–

Diana Athill was Geoffrey Hill's editor at the publisher Andre Deutsch:

Geoffrey was a difficult writer to work with because of his anxiety: he was bedevilled by premonitions of disaster, and had to be patiently and repeatedly reassured although my own nerves, worked on by his, would be fraying even as I spoke or wrote my soothing words. Once something frightening happened. A book of his—I think it was *Mercian Hymns*—had been read in page-proof by him and me, and I had just passed it to the production department to be sent to press. That same afternoon he telephoned apologetically, saying he was aware of how neurotic he was being and would I please forgive him, but he had suddenly started to worry about whether the copyright line had been included in the preliminary pages. I knew it had been, but I also knew how tormenting his anxieties were, so instead of saying 'Yes, of course it's there,' I said: 'Production probably hasn't sent it off yet, so hold on and I'll run down and check so that we can be a hundred per cent sure.' Which I did, and the line was there, and Geoffrey was comforted. And when the printed book was delivered to us there was no copyright line.

Diana Athill, *Stet: A Memoir*, 2000

Michael Frayn · 1933–

This year, for various reasons, four different works of mine have reached the point where they need titles, and I've reached the point where I need hospitalisation. It's not that I can't write titles. I've written far more titles than anything else in my life. For one of these four projects I have 107 titles. For another—74. For the third—134. 134 titles! For one short book! 134 pretty good titles, though I say so myself. The trouble is you don't want 134 pretty good titles. You want one perfect title.

No titles at all so far for the fourth project, but this is because I haven't written the thing yet. Though after the agonies I've had with the other three I'm starting to wonder if I shouldn't write the title of this one first, then dash down a few thousand words to fit it.

The curious thing is that you usually do have a title first. You have the working title, that you put on the front of the file when you begin work, just so that you know which file's which. The working title, as its name suggests, works. That's to say, it actually succeeds in telling you which file's which, and it does it without being pretentious, or facetious, or unintentionally obscene. But the publisher, or the producer, or whoever it is, doesn't like it. Your agent doesn't like it—your partner doesn't like it. No one likes it. This may be because they don't know about it—you haven't told them. You know you can't use the working title. Life has to be harder than that.

One of the troubles with a list of 134 titles is that it offers odds of at least 133 to 1 against getting it right. I've got it wrong many times in the past. There's only one novel of mine that anyone ever remembers—and for all practical purposes it's called *The One About Fleet Street*, because even the people who remember the book can't remember the title I gave it. I wrote another book called *Constructions*. I think I realised even before publication that I'd picked a dud here, when my own agent referred to it in the course of the same conversation once as *Conceptions* and once as *Contractions*.

Speak after the Beep, 1995

Joe Orton · 1933–1967

Disinfection proceeds apace. Back in 1962 Joe Orton and Kenneth Halliwell served six months in prison for stealing or 'wilfully damaging' books belonging to Islington public libraries. Orton had enhanced some of the books with spoof blurbs. In 1995 these 'works' were put on display in the same libraries, the borough librarian explaining that in those far-off days no one was to know etc, but 'over the years we have become proud of Joe Orton as a leading literary figure with local associations'.

D. J. Enright, *Play Resumed*, 1999

Wole Soyinka · 1934–

(playwright and novelist; the first African writer to be awarded the Nobel Prize for Literature)

One evening, after Joan Littlewood of the Theatre Workshop had become interested in putting on one of his plays, Soyinka (or Maren, as he calls himself in his memoirs) was taken by Joan Littlewood to an East End pub controlled by the notorious Kray twins. Ronnie and Reggie Kray were both present, and he was introduced to them:

It was no ordinary night at the pub; indeed, a section of the pub was closed to the general public that night, and that was where the party was taking place. He was pleased to meet the parliamentarian Tom Driberg again; he had not seen him since his efforts on behalf of Anthony Enahoro. Maren was not particularly curious about the party, but he did observe that a smallish individual appeared to be the toast of the crowd. He received frequent pats on the back and had glasses clinked with his more than anyone else. Was that the celebrant, Maren wanted to know? Joan Littlewood revealed in a strangely conspiratorial whisper that he was indeed; an auntie of his had just died and had left him a fortune.

Pointless to query whether it was the death of the aunt that the centre of attraction was celebrating, or the welcome inheritance, or both. Maren expressed himself content with the fact that the East Enders appeared to celebrate death like most Africans. Judging by the quantity of champagne that was going down, not to mention oysters, caviar and canapés, he remarked that the lady must have passed on at a very ripe old age, since that would be the yardstick by which his own people would lavish such extravagance on death festivities. Joan corrected him in an amused whisper: no one had really died—well, in a sense, the man had made a killing but there was no corpse. He had pulled off a job—a jewellers' shop—and the haul had been substantial. The gang was celebrating his success.

Wole Soyinka, *Ibadan: A Memoir*, 1994

In the 1960s Soyinka attended a month-long theatre festival in Cuba:

In Habana once, a middle-aged man looked at him with disapproval, the cause of offence being the miserable tuft on his chin. Why, he demanded, was he wearing a beard? Did he see anyone in Cuba with a beard except Fidel? In deference to the leader, and to stamp him with distinction everywhere, the revolution had decided that only Fidel was permitted to exercise the privilege of a beard.

Maren was flabbergasted. What are you going to do, he asked him?

Place a barber at the immigration posts and insist that your visitors shave before they are granted entry? Do you really feel that this straggle of hair on my chin constitutes the slightest threat to the hirsute triumph in which your leader's face is camouflaged? But the man remained unimpressed by any arguments. As a young, and seemingly intelligent fellow, Maren should not be seen with a beard on the streets of Habana. At the Casas de las Americas, where he recounted the experience, the man was dismissed as a crank, but Maren did observe, for the first time, that no one he encountered in Habana did wear a beard.

Soyinka, *Ibadan*

Beryl Bainbridge · 1934–

In 1989 Beryl Bainbridge published one of her best-known novels, An Awfully Big Adventure. *For several years before that, very little had been heard from her:*

I did some journalism. But I was getting uneasy about not doing any proper writing. One night I was a bit tight, and I thought I would put the books in order upstairs. So, tiddly and humming away in the middle of the night, I tripped against a table and knocked myself out for about twenty seconds. When I came to, I went downstairs and rang my mother. Now, my mother had been dead for twenty years, or more. I dialed what I thought was her number, and a voice said. 'The time sponsored by Acurist is two thirty-five and ten seconds.' It was a man's voice, and the next morning I remembered that it used to be a woman, and that she was always known as the Girl with the Golden Voice.

I rang up the archives of the British Telecom and they were very helpful and sent me a lot of material on the Girl with the Golden Voice, who had come from Liverpool [Beryl Bainbridge's home town]. It emerged that she had become a member of the BBC's rep for a little while, and in 1939 had disappeared to America. She was now living in an old people's home in Croydon. They sent me a photograph of her. So I thought, What if your mother had left you but you knew she was alive. And what if you knew that she was the Girl with the Golden Voice? I thought it was a super plot, and it came to me so easily . . .

Interview in *Paris Review*, 2000

Simon Gray · 1936–

In The Smoking Diaries *Gray describes receiving a letter from 'a troublesome fan', a woman who was eager to let him know that he owed his success entirely to a talent for 'brown-nosing'—first through university, then into the theatre:*

It's an odd letter to get, it seems to me, even from a fan—although it's true that I have little experience of fans—and going strictly by results she's on pretty shaky ground, in fact I sometimes find myself thinking that if only I'd had a gift for what she calls 'brown-nosing', or even basic diplomacy—that if only I hadn't said that to this one, this to that one, or hadn't drunk so very much through my late forties, throughout my fifties, I might have—well, what? at least have got my plays returned more speedily by Trevor Nunn, for instance, possibly bits of them actually read by his predecessor at the National, Richard Eyre, to whom I never actually sent them, on the grounds that every time I met him he seemed to wince, in a noble and kindly sort of way, and I felt it would be wrong to trouble him with parcels of plays through the post or with phone calls from my agent—and as for the smaller subsidized houses, oh, the Donmar, now I come to think of it, in the form of young Sam Mendes, when he was even younger Sam Mendes, his face as yet unmarked by appearing regularly in the press, once sent a message through my agent that he was eager to do something of mine and so—fatally for me—asked if we could meet, to discuss it. I told him over lunch about the play I was working on, which I intended very shortly to confer on him—it involved an abandoned wife kidnapping her husband's mistress and keeping her chained in an outhouse, it should be a very well-appointed outhouse, I explained, where she would give her captive rival a literary and moral education, and—as is so often the way with teachers and taught—they would fall in love with each other and—and so forth—I said I thought the basic situation was pretty sexy, didn't he think? especially if we got a really pretty girl to chain—I suspect I gave the impression we'd do it together, find the girl, purchase the chain, one of us wind it about her waist, the other snap the padlock—with the prospect of paying customers, too—naturally I didn't say anything along those lines, explicitly, but perhaps he heard things in my voice, lubricious and salacious things, and saw stuff in my eyes, overfocused and red-rimmed—anyway, he parted from me no doubt hoping our paths would never cross again, and they haven't, although since his Oscar I've sent him an idea for a film, just a few lines, but written out in neat and sober handwriting, to which he replied courteously, in a loose sort of scrawl, but then why should he be careful with his handwriting, he has no need to be. And why rake over these old ranklings, when there are older ranklings that I still haven't finished raking over like—what? The dawn is upon us. Let me greet it with a sleeping pill.

The Smoking Diaries, 2004

Tom Stoppard · 1937–

In the mid-1960s David Stafford was living in a block of mansion flats off Vauxhall Bridge Road:

One of the denizens of this Edwardian sepulchre was a lean young man, barely older than myself, who scurried in and out at odd hours dressed in a black velvet jacket and trousers that aged noticeably over the months. Pale and intense, with raven hair that curled wildly around his pallid features, he was obviously drawn by some unseen force that propelled him along the corridors like the March Hare. Sometimes he would be seen with a small child, or a woman, or both. The three lived directly above us, and often we would hear the child crying. Rumour had it that he was artistic.

At this time, as a noviciate in the Foreign Office, I kept gentleman's hours, which meant that crises never happened before ten o'clock and a full reading of *The Times*. So everyone else had left for work when there was a knock at the door and I opened it to find the black velvet suit. Its occupant smiled, apologised for the intrusion, and asked if we might do him a favour. He had, he explained, noted that we were out during the daytime. As a writer whose concentration was distracted by a crying infant, could he possibly use our kitchen table to write on during the day, when everyone was out? I should explain that the table was a bit of a sore point. For some mystical reason one of my flatmates, an expert on medieval theology, had ordered one that was eight feet square. The result was no floor space and a table that could seat the twelve disciples. It definitely needed more using. So to get rid of the eccentric scribbler I said yes. I didn't even bother with his name.

For the next few months I saw nothing of him. The only reminder of his existence was the coffee cup he always left unwashed in the sink and the unending litter of crumpled paper he threw into the wastepaper basket. Once I inspected it, only to find that every sheet was blank. This confirmed me in my pin-striped view that he was a wastrel, and I went about my own business of saving the world with an increased sense of purpose.

Then, one evening, he called to say he had completed his manuscript. 'Manuscript?' I echoed, not quite believing my ears and thinking of the forests he'd massacred in our kitchen. 'Oh, yes,' he smiled, 'I've been writing a play.' He must have seen the disbelief on my face. 'It's about a couple of characters from Shakespeare,' he explained, 'what happens behind the scenes.' Deranged, I thought, but felt compelled to be polite. 'Oh, who?' I asked. 'Rosencrantz and Guildenstern,' he replied, 'from Hamlet'. I looked at the decayed velvet suit and his big black eyes staring at me from his mop of hair. Then I knew he was crazy.

I Once Met: Fifty Encounters with the Famous, ed. Richard Ingrams, 1996

LAST Saturday the *Guardian* published a long profile of the playwright, Sir Tom Stoppard . . . It quoted from a piece about Stoppard written by Kenneth Tynan in 1977 for the *New Yorker* magazine: 'For Stoppard, art is a game within a game, the larger game being life itself, an absurd mosaic of incidents and accidents in which (as Beckett, whom he venerates, says in his aptly titled *Endgame*) "something is taking its course".'

The interviewer then went on to write: 'Underpinning all his work and increasingly apparent in his later plays, however, is an attempt to come to terms with the characteristic Beckettian view that "I am a human nothing".' Sir Tom may be modest, but not so modest as to consider himself 'a human nothing'. In a letter to yesterday's *Guardian*, he pointed out that this was 'a mistranscription from the tape of a talk I gave over thirty years ago, published at the time in the *Sunday Times*. As the paper explained a week later, the phrase should have read, "I am assuming nothing". Such are the pitfalls of the clippings library'. As a journalist, I feel quite sorry for the author of the piece, for that is the kind of pitfall that catches all of us from time to time. But it might have been wiser not to have described the phrase as a 'characteristic Beckettian view'.

Alexander Chancellor, *Daily Telegraph*, 25 June 2002

LES A. MURRAY · 1938–

(Australian poet)

I ALMOST managed to get right through high school without any serious engagement with poetry. I had read *The Rime of the Ancient Mariner* with some fascination in fourth year; also I had read *Paradise Lost*—indeed, all of Milton—in a single long weekend sometime in my teens, but that was for the science-fiction. I remember being irritated by the wordy, cumbrous manner of the story's telling; the poetry stuff seemed to make it stiff and preachy. In the end, I enjoyed *Samson Agonistes* more. That was a yarn I had enjoyed in the Bible, about a God-favoured Big Bloke who tore the gates off towns and slew enemies wholesale, and ended up as one prepared to pull the factory down rather than work.

'On Being Subject Matter', in *The Paperbark Tree*, 1992

Murray grew up in a remote farm in New South Wales and learned to read at home. 'I didn't go to school or meet a teacher till I was nine,' he has written. 'But it was a teacher who opened my eyes to poetry just before I left school, to such effect that I was set on the course of life I would follow.'

HUMAN cruelty only began to come my way as a dreamy fat hillbilly kid at my next and final school, Taree High. That was the first place I learned the nicknames that are used to punish obesity, and the peculiar cultural rituals of townspeople *vis-à-vis* countryfolk. In my own culture, I had never been persecuted for being fat, or for anything else. Now, almost every sentence addressed to me referred to my figure, and many were uttered only for the derisive nicknames they contained. This went on for two straight years, and I learned to regard as a friend any boy who derided me only in public, to protect himself, and was sensible in private. One miraculous friend, called Colin McCabe, never derided me at all, and even mostly called me by my first name. No girl was ever a friend in any sense; it was made clear, with ornamentations of contempt and frost even by those who didn't go in for loud jeering, that this was unthinkable in my case. It was a firm training in self-sufficiency, and immunized me against any herd-animal leanings I might have developed.

'From Bulby Brush to Figure City', in *The Paperbark Tree*

IAN HAMILTON · 1938–2001

Hamilton cast a spell on other writers in his circle which can't altogether be explained by his achievements—notable though they were—as poet, critic, and editor:

I AM standing on the corner of Bayswater Road and Gloucester Terrace just by the Lancaster Hotel with Ian. We are looking for a taxi. I propose a competition. Let's see who has the pulling-power to conjure a taxi: it is nearly rush hour and none seems to be about. I wave, gesture, move into the road, but all the taxis are occupied or those which seem empty ignore me. It's then Ian's turn. He raises his hand and three unoccupied taxis appear at his side. Much the same happens in bars. Perhaps it would too if he were feeding the ducks or scattering crumbs to goldfish.

Peter Porter in David Harsent (ed.), *Another Round at the Pillars: Essays, Poems and Reflections on Ian Hamilton*, 1999

Margaret Atwood · 1939–

In the early 1970s Margaret Atwood was taken by her two aunts to a nearby town to meet an author called Ernest Buckler. Years before he had written a novel called The Mountain and the Valley: *it had had some success in the States but had been virtually suppressed in his native Canada once his Toronto publishers realized that it contained what Atwood's mother referred to as 'goings on'.*

Atwood herself had read it as an adolescent, and been greatly impressed. By the time she was taken to see Buckler she had moved on, and had published several books herself, but she still remembered it with fondness:

Ernest Buckler lived in a house that could not have been changed for fifty years. It still had a horsehair sofa, antimacassars, a woodstove in the living room. Ernest himself was enormously likeable and highly nervous, and anxious that we be pleased. He hopped around a lot, talking a mile a minute, and kept popping out to the kitchen, and popping back again. We talked mostly about books, and about his plans to scandalize the neighbourhood by phoning me up at my grandmother's house, on the party line, and pretending we were having an affair. 'That would give the old biddies something to talk about,' he said. Everyone listened in, of course, whenever he had a call, but not just because he was a local celebrity. They listened in on everyone.

After we left, my Aunt J. said, 'That was something! He said you had a teeming brain!' (He had said this.) My Aunt K.'s comment was, 'That man was oiled.' Of the three of us, she was the only one who figured out why Mr Buckler had made such frequent trips to the kitchen. But it was understandable that he should have been secretive about it: in the Valley there were those who drank, and then there were decent people.

Also: there were those who wrote, and then there were decent people. A certain amount of writing was tolerated, but only within limits. Newspaper columns about children and the changing seasons were fine. Sex, swearing and drinking were beyond the pale.

'Great Aunts', in *Curious Pursuits*, 2005

Seamus Heaney · 1939–

Heaney recalls the gestation of his poem 'The Guttural Muse':

One evening, I went fishing with a friend of mine called Barrie Cook, tench fishing. They're a toothless fish and they send up bubbles—they love the slime and the mud, and you fish for them in the dark. There's this kind of slimy goodness about them; they told me they were called a doctor fish because there was a superstition that the slime upon them healed wounded fish—pike and so on—that touched them as they went past. Then later on I was in a hotel up around County Monaghan one night, feeling strange and poetically barren, and there was a dance on, a lot of country kids listening to pop music, and at about half past one they came out over the car park, and these absolute dialect voices came bubbling up to me. It was like a vision of the kind of life I had in the fifties, going to dances and so on, and I felt the redemptive quality of the dialect, of the guttural, the illiterate self.

Viewpoints: Poets in Conversation with John Haffenden, 1981

Alan Ayckbourn · 1939–

At the age of 20 Ayckbourn faced the prospect of doing National Service. It was not one he relished:

Eventually the time came for his medical examination. They took some blood from his earlobe and he fainted as promised [in conversation with a recruiting officer]. He had also fainted on the parade ground when the buckle of his braces dug into his chest; he thought it was a rib sticking out. Next he was to join one of four queues for the doctors conducting personal medicals: a lottery. Alan saw a man with two perforated eardrums and a host of other ailments passed fit for service and his heart sank, knowing that he had nothing wrong with him except a slight knee injury he was hoping to play up. He joined a queue at random and met a well-spoken young doctor with the sort of assistant then labelled an 'oik' by the officer classes.

DOCTOR. Strip orf. Stand on the glass mat. Got anything to report?
ALAN. Very peculiar knee, sir.
DOCTOR. Oh yes? (*Pause*) Oh. I see you write.
ALAN. Well yes, I do a bit of writing. I've written a couple of plays.
DOCTOR. I'm writing. I'm writing my memoirs.

ALAN. Oh right. (*Thinks*: He's writing his memoirs at 23?)
DOCTOR. Have you got a good agent? Anyone you think I could send it to?
ALAN. Well, you could send it to my agent. (*Thinks*: See where sending it to Peggy Ramsay will get you.)
DOCTOR. Thanks very much. D'you really want to do this?
ALAN. No.
DOCTOR. Tell me about the knee again.
ALAN. Well, it's—
DOCTOR. Well, I haven't examined it, but I can tell you from here I don't like the look of it.
ALAN. Really?
DOCTOR. No, no, not at all. Could you walk to that wall, unaided?
ALAN. I'll have a go for you, sir, but—
DOCTOR. I don't think you could.
ALAN. I think I might sort of fall down round about that chair.
DOCTOR. I've got some bad news for you. I'm afraid we can't take you. Because what'll happen is, you'll be marching around on the first day, and that knee's going to give way and we're going to be paying you a pension for the rest of your life. I can't allow the RAF into that sort of financial obligation.
ALAN. Oh, damn.
DOCTOR. I'm sorry. Absolutely not.
OIK. Nobody ever did anything like that for me.
DOCTOR. Because you're an oik, Wilkins, and what possible use are you out in the real world? You're better off in here. Well, thank you, I'll expect my cheque in the morning.
ALAN. Thank you very much, sir.
(*Exit, limping heavily.*)

Paul Allen, *Alan Ayckbourn*, 2001

J. M. Coetzee · 1940–

(novelist: his books include *The Life and Times of Michael K* and *Disgrace*)

Coetzee's paternal grandfather was an Afrikaans farmer who made sure that his family spoke English and who hoisted a Union Jack outside his house on the King's birthday. As a child, Coetzee heard his father and uncles reminiscing about the old man, and laughing—' 'n Ware ou jintleman en 'n ware ou jingo!', '*a real old gentleman and a real old jingo!*':

What of himself? If the grandfather he reveres was a jingo, is he a jingo too? Can a child be a jingo? He stands to attention when *God Save the King* is played in the bioscope and the Union Jack waves on the screen. Bagpipe music sends a shiver down his spine, as do words like *stalwart, valorous*. Should he keep it a secret, this attachment of his to England?

He cannot understand why it is that so many people around him dislike England. England is Dunkirk and the Battle of Britain. England is doing one's duty and accepting one's fate in a quiet, unfussy way. England is the boy at the battle of Jutland, who stood by his guns while the deck was burning under him. England is Sir Lancelot of the Lake and Richard the Lionheart and Robin Hood with his longbow of yew and his suit of Lincoln green. What do the Afrikaners have to compare? Dirkie Uys, who rode his horse till it died. Piet Retief, who was made a fool of by Dingaan. And then the Voortrekkers getting their revenge by shooting thousands of Zulus who didn't have guns, and being proud of it.

There is a Church-of-England church in Worcester, and a clergyman with grey hair and a pipe who doubles as Scoutmaster and whom some of the English boys in his class—the proper English boys, with English names and homes in the old, leafy part of Worcester—refer to familiarly as Padre. When the English talk like that he falls silent. There is the English language, which he commands with ease. There is England and everything that England stands for, to which he believes he is loyal. But more than that is required, clearly, before one will be accepted as truly English: tests to face, some of which he knows he will not pass.

Boyhood, 1997

Bruce Chatwin · 1940–1989

(travel writer and novelist)

In the exalted mood induced by his final illness, Chatwin constantly lavished exotic presents on his friends. His fabled 'eye' for rare artefacts hadn't deserted him, but it had begun to play him false:

When Jonathan Hope visited him he was presented with a parting gift. 'It's an Aboriginal subincision knife,' said Bruce, as he lay on the bed, with his wife massaging his wasted legs—and held out a small round object with sharpened edges. He had found it in the Bush and correctly identified it as an instrument designed to be used in an Aboriginal initiation rite in which the underside of the urethra is slit open. Then he held it up to the light. 'It's obviously made from some sort of desert opal,' he said: 'It's a wonderful colour, almost the colour of chartreuse.' A few weeks later the Director of the Australian National Gallery arrived at Hope's house to look at some Indonesian textiles. He picked up the opal from the table, and in his turn held it up to the light: 'Hmmm. Amazing what the Abos can do with a bit of an old beer bottle.'

Susannah Clapp, *After Chatwin*, 1997

Bob Dylan · 1941–

Walter Yetnikoff was head of CBS Records for nearly twenty years. One of the stars on the CBS label during his time in charge was Bob Dylan (formerly Robert Zimmerman), and when Dylan performed at Madison Square Garden in the 1980s Yetnikoff gave a dinner for him afterwards:

As much as you could deal with Dylan, I dealt with him. I understood how hard he worked to protect his mystique. He was entitled. I saw him as a master poet, master folk rocker, voice of a generation, American icon and a guy who still sold a shitload of records. If he wanted to sulk in the corner, let him sulk in the corner.

After the concert, I hosted a private dinner for him at a swanky restaurant. We planned to eat at midnight. By 2 A.M. he still hadn't arrived. I was about to go home—the hell with him—when, just like that, he and his entourage walked through the door. His entourage surprised me. I was expecting Bohemian groupies and scruffy musicians. Instead he arrived with his family—his Jewish uncles, his Jewish cousins, his Jewish mother, Mrs Zimmerman, his Jewish girlfriend Carol Childs and his Jewish dog, an oversized mastiff.

Sitting next to Bob and his mother, I was astonished by their dialogue. The mysterious poet suddenly turned into little Bobby Zimmerman.

'You're not eating, Bobby,' said Mom as his girlfriend Carol was cutting up his food as though he were an infant.

'Please, Ma. You're embarrassing me.'

'I saw you ate nothing for lunch. You're skin and bones.'

'I'm eating, Ma, I'm eating.'

'And have you thanked Mr Yetnikoff for this lovely dinner?'

'Thank you, Walter.'

'You're mumbling, Bobby. I don't think Mr Yetnikoff heard you.'

'He heard me,' Dylan said sarcastically.

'Bobby, be nice.'

'Does your son always give you this much trouble?' I asked.

'Bobby? God forbid. Bobby gives me such naches. He's a good boy, a regular mensch. He calls, he writes, he listens to his mother. Every mother should have such a son.'

'Stop, Ma,' said Bob. 'You're embarrassing me.'

'You *should* be embarrassed,' I said to Dylan. 'You're a fraud.'

He looked at me quizzically. I explained, 'Aren't you the guy who wrote, "And don't criticize/what you can't understand/your sons and your daughters/are beyond your command . . ."? So why are you whining to your mother?'

'I wrote that a long time ago. Is it okay with you if I love my mother?'

'That's wonderful. I understand you've done the definitive version of "My Yiddishe Momma." '

He smiled.

Walter Yetnikoff with David Ritz, *Howling at the Moon*, 2004

John Irving · 1942–

Until the success of his novel The World According to Garp, *Irving supported himself partly as a wrestling coach, partly by teaching Creative Writing. In his memoirs, he stresses the limitations that young writers whom he taught imposed on themselves when they stuck too closely to their own experience. But that doesn't mean that their attempts to escape from autobiographical fiction were necessarily successful either:*

A STUDENT of mine at Iowa—a brilliant fellow, academically; he would go on to earn a Ph.D. in something I can't even pronounce or spell—wrote an accomplished, lucid short story about a dinner party from the point of view of the hostess's fork.

If you think this sounds fascinating, my case is already lost. Indeed, the young writer's fellow students worshiped this story and the young genius who wrote it; they regarded my all-too-apparent indifference to the fork story as an insult not only to the author but to all of them. Ah, to *almost* all of them, for I was saved by a most unlikely and usually most silent member of the class. He was an Indian from Kerala, a devout Christian, and his accent and word order caused him to be treated dismissively—as someone who was struggling with English as a second language, although this was not the case. English was his first language, and he spoke and wrote it very well; the unfamiliarity of his accent and the cadence, even of his written sentences, made the other students regard him lightly.

Into the sea of approval that the fork story was receiving, and while my 'but . . .' was repeatedly drowned out by the boisterous air of celebration in the class, the Indian Christian from Kerala said, 'Excuse me, but perhaps I would have been moved if I were a fork. Unfortunately, I am merely a human being.'

That day, and perhaps forever after, *he* should have been the teacher and I should have given my complete attention to him. He is not a writer these days, except on the faithful Christmas cards he sends from India, where he is a doctor. Under the usual holiday greetings, and the annual photograph of his increasing family, he writes in a firm, readable hand: 'Still merely a human being.'

On my Christmas cards to him, I write: 'Not yet a fork.'

The Imaginary Girlfriend, 1996

Craig Raine · 1944–

Craig Raine's collection of poems, Rich, *also contains a childhood memoir. In the course of it he recalls his early film-going and reading, beginning with the films which made the greatest impression*—Apache, *for instance, and* The Egyptian*:*

At the same time, I had begun to read books. Aged nine, I joined the library and was introduced by a boy called Sid Staveley to the photographs in Lord Russell of Liverpool's *The Scourge of the Swastika*, a bulging book bound in jaundiced polythene which was kept in the adult section. Its atrocities escaped me completely. And the moral polemic. I remember still, though, a photograph of nude, overweight women being made to run through a wet courtyard. One, nearest the camera, was blurred. I remember being unable to connect those grainy breasts and pubic hair with anything in my own life—flesh, for instance—but the image gave me a mysterious frisson which I mistakenly took for sex. The books I actually borrowed from the library—the bad-tempered bump of the date stamp dying in my ears—were adventure stories. I read two a day for two years and forgot them.

The most important book I possessed was not, strictly speaking, a book at all. On the back of the *Topper*, a comic I read at the time, was a serial of Robert Louis Stevenson's *Kidnapped*, told almost entirely in pictures. Beneath each frame there was a scrap of token text which I suppose I must have read. I saved up these back pages until I had a complete set and my mother sewed them together on her treddle-operated Singer machine. This 'book' was where I spent most of my childhood. Thirty years later, I can still recall particular images—Alan Breck's silver button set on a wooden cross and placed as a sign in the window of a but and ben; redcoats prodding the heather with their bayonets while Breck and David Balfour sweltered out the day on the top of a huge granite boulder; Breck lowering his belt so that Balfour could scramble up; a chieftain's hide-out somehow built using the trees. To this day I have never read Stevenson's text.

'A Silver Plate', in *Rich*, 1984

August Wilson · 1945–2005

(dramatist; his plays include *Ma Rainey's Black Bottom* and *Fences*)

Wilson studied the language his characters use at first hand:

The language is defined by those who speak it. There's a place in Pittsburgh called Pat's Place, a cigar store, which I read about in Claude McKay's *Home of Harlem*. It was where the railroad porters would congregate and tell stories. I thought, Hey, I know Pat's Place. I literally ran there. I was twenty-one at the time and had no idea I was going to write about it. I wasn't keeping notes. But I loved listening to them. One of the exchanges I heard made it into *Ma Rainey's Black Bottom*. Someone said, 'I came to Pittsburgh in '42 on the B & O,' and another guy said, 'Oh no, you ain't come to Pittsburgh in '42 . . . the B & O Railroad didn't stop in Pittsburgh in '42!' And the first guy would say, 'You gonna tell *me* what railroad I came in on?' 'Hell yeah I'm gonna tell you the truth!' Then someone would walk in and they'd say, 'Hey, Philmore! The B & O Railroad stop here in '42?' People would drift in and they'd all have various answers to that. They would argue about how far away the moon was. They'd say, 'Man, the moon a million miles away.' They called me Youngblood. They'd say, 'Hey, Youngblood, how far the moon?' And I'd say, '150,000 miles,' and they'd say, 'That boy don't know nothing! The moon's a *million* miles.' I just loved to hang around those old guys—you got philosophy about life, what a man is, what his duties, his responsibilities are . . .

Occasionally these guys would die and I would pay my respects. There'd be a message on a blackboard they kept in Pat's Place: 'Funeral for Jo Boy, Saturday, one P.M.' I'd look around and try to figure out which one was missing. I'd go across to the funeral home and look at him and I'd go, 'Oh, it was *that* guy, the guy that wore the little brown hat all the time.'

I used to hang around Pat's Place through my twenties, going there less as the time went by. That's where I learned how black people talk.

Interview in *Paris Review*, 1999

Salman Rushdie · 1947–

In the radio programme 'Desert Island Discs' celebrity interviewees are invited to choose one book and a luxury item in addition to the eight records they would like to hear if marooned on an imaginary atoll. Salman Rushdie appeared on the programme on 8 September 1988 as part of the pre-publication publicity attending *The Satanic Verses*, his first novel for five years. Given his Indian Muslim background and his fondness for fabulous, phantasmagorical narratives, his choice of book was not surprising: *The Thousand and One Nights*, that great collection of tales which, as he said, 'contains all other stories'. His choice of luxury was much more unexpected: 'I would like to have an unlisted radio telephone,' he said. 'That would allow me to ring up anybody else, without anyone ringing me.' Not the least of the many ironies accompanying the Rushdie Affair is that within six months of that interview Rushdie's wish, in this regard at least, had been fulfilled. On 16 February 1989, after the Ayatollah Khomeini had issued a *fatwa* or legal ruling declaring Salman Rushdie an apostate from Islam and one whose blood must be shed, the Indo-British novelist and his wife were obliged to 'go underground' for their own protection. From the 'safe houses' where armed Special Branch officers are presumed to guard his person day and night, he can telephone his agents, publishers, associates and friends with whom he makes occasional, closely-guarded sorties. They cannot phone him, and few of them know where he is.

Malise Ruthven, *A Satanic Affair*, 1990

Ian McEwan · 1948–

McEwan's story of Cold War espionage, The Innocent, *was published in 1990:*

INTERVIEWER. Did you do medical research for *The Innocent*?

MCEWAN. I went to have dinner with Michael Dunnill, who was the University Lecturer in Pathology at Merton. I told him I was planning a scene in which an inexpert and frightened man cuts up a body—

INTERVIEWER. And he said, 'Oh, you must be Ian McEwan.'

MCEWAN. He said something even more frightening. When I asked him how long would it take to saw through an arm, he invited me to one of his regular early Monday morning autopsies. 'You come along,' he said, 'and we'll cut an arm off and see.' I said, 'But what about the relatives?' And he said, 'Oh, my assistant will sew it back on and it won't show at all.'

I began to have serious doubts about this Monday morning appointment. I felt the writing was going well and I didn't want to be blown off course. At the same time, I felt it was my novelist's duty to go. Then, very fortunately, I had supper with Richard Eyre, who thought I was crazy to go. He said, 'You'll invent it much better than you'll describe it.' Immediately he said this, I knew he was right. Later, I showed my scene to Michael Dunnill, and he passed it. Had I gone to the autopsy, I would have had to become a journalist—and I don't think I'm a good journalist. I can describe accurately the thing that I imagine far better than the thing I remember seeing.

Interview in *Paris Review*, 2002

Martin Amis · 1949–

On a tube train to Earls Court I saw a young man reading *The Rachel Papers* [Martin Amis's first novel], about a week after its publication. He was enjoying the book, and in the best possible way: a reluctant smile, an unreluctant smile, a reluctant smile, and so on. I still regret that I didn't go up to him. But I told myself: listen, this will be happening all the time—get used to it. I need hardly add that it didn't happen again for about fifteen years (someone in a headset, on an aeroplane, scowling at *The Moronic Inferno*). When my first novel won the Somerset Maugham Award I told myself the same sort of thing: get used to it. And that *never* happened again.

Experience, 2000

Carol Ann Duffy · 1955–

At a poetry reading somewhere in England last year, I read the first poem in *Mean Time*; a poem whose longish title gave me A Certain Quiet Pride—'The Captain of the 1964 *Top of the Form* Team'. I had, unquestionably, made this up. The poem is about a person—in this case, a man—who has never recovered from not being fourteen any more. During the interval of the reading, a middle-aged woman approached me in a friendly way. 'Do you know,' she said with a recognizable glee, 'you've really upset my husband.' Her husband, she went on to tell me over a glass of Regional Arts Association Red, had actually been the real-life captain of a *Top of the Form* team in the sixties. What's more, she reckoned that he was just like the poem. He was its eponymous hero. One of the lines in the poem tells how the boy owned a Gonk [a blob-like toy with rudimentary features] which he kept as a lucky mascot. After the reading, I got to meet the man in question. 'Now then,' he said keenly, 'I don't think we had Gonks in 1964.'

In Clare Brown and Don Paterson (eds.), *Don't Ask Me What I Mean*, 2003

Top of the Form *was a radio quiz for schoolchildren.*

Craig Brown · 1957–

(satirist and essayist)

In his essay 'Dread Phrase', Craig Brown discusses some of the perils of writing parodies, including the danger that life will catch up with art:

I ONCE wrote a *Private Eye* parody of Norman Tebbit. In it, Tebbit voiced his suspicions that Cherie Blair was not all-white. He was particularly worried about her Christian name. 'Sounds foreign to me. Cherry, yes. Cherie, no. To my ordinary English ear, the word has a peculiar, almost Eastern ring to it. Frankly, it wouldn't surprise me to find it had pitched up from India or even Pakistan . . . Of course, if the trendy new Prime Minister of this once-great country chooses to run around with an Indian wife, that is his own concern. But doesn't it get on your goat that the so-called People's Prime Minister can't come clean about his predilections? A word in your ear, Blair. Isn't it high time you forced your missus into a sari? Oh, and don't forget to lock up those valuables when she finds her way indoors!' Spookily, *Private Eye* came out on a Wednesday; in that Thursday's newspaper, Cherie Blair was photographed wearing a sari.

This Is Craig Brown, 2003

Jeanette Winterson · 1959–

(novelist; her books include *Oranges are not the Only Fruit* and *Sexing the Cherry*)

Jeanette Winterson's parents were Pentecostal evangelists:

MY parents owned six books between them. Two of those were Bibles and the third was a concordance to the Old and New Testaments. The fourth was *The House At Pooh Corner*. The fifth, *The Chatterbox Annual 1923* and the sixth, Malory's *Morte d'Arthur*.

I found it necessary to smuggle books in and out of the house and I cannot claim too much for the provision of an outside toilet when there is no room of one's own. It was on the toilet that I first read Freud and D. H. Lawrence, and perhaps that was the best place, after all. We kept a rubber torch hung on the cistern, and I had to divide my money from a Saturday job, between buying books and buying batteries. My mother knew exactly how long her Ever Readys would last if used only to illuminate the gap that separated the toilet paper from its function.

Once I had tucked the book back down my knickers to get it indoors again, I had to find somewhere to hide it, and anyone with a single bed, standard size, and paperbacks, standard size, will discover that seventy-seven can be accommodated per layer under the mattress. But as my collection grew, I began to worry that my mother might notice that her daughter's bed was rising visibly. One day she did. She burned everything.

Art Objects, 1995

J. K. Rowling · 1965–

In a crime worthy of Voldemort himself, two men were caught yesterday attempting to spill the beans on the eagerly awaited next instalment of the adventures of Harry Potter.

They were arrested after a shot was fired during a meeting in which it is believed they were trying to sell stolen copies of *Harry Potter and the Half-Blood Prince*, the sixth book in J. K. Rowling's best-selling series.

The book, which is published on July 16, has sparked massive interest since the author's revelation that a major character would be killed off.

Bookmakers were forced to suspend betting on the victim's identity late last month amid fears that the text had been leaked.

Yesterday the plot thickened in true J. K. Rowling fashion when the police received reports of gunfire in a street in Kettering, Northamptonshire, where a reporter and photographer from the *Sun* newspaper had met two men allegedly purporting to have copies of the book for sale. The reporter, John Askill, had apparently arranged to meet the men after they claimed that they were prepared to sell a copy for £50,000.

The newspaper said that a shot was fired over Askill's head after he grabbed the novel and tried to escape.

Spokesmen for the *Sun* and the *Daily Mirror* said both had been contacted by someone claiming to have the new book.

Northamptonshire police said last night that two men from Kettering had been charged over the incident. A police spokesman said a 37-year-old man had been charged with possession of an offensive weapon and handling stolen property, 'namely a copy of the new Harry Potter novel'.

A man aged 19 was charged with theft of the book and possession of an imitation firearm with intent to cause fear and violence.

Early today J. K. Rowling was granted a High Court injunction against the two men to stop them leaking details of the book. Security surrounding the tale has been extremely tight.

Daily Telegraph, 4 June 2005

It is hard to imagine a comparable incident taking place in the past—prompted by the imminent appearance of a new work by Lewis Carroll, say, or Beatrix Potter, or Kenneth Grahame. Perhaps the love of literature is growing more intense.

ACKNOWLEDGEMENTS

Peter Ackroyd: from *T. S. Eliot* (Hamish Hamilton, 1984), copyright © Peter Ackroyd 1984, reprinted by permission of Penguin Books Ltd.; and from *Dickens* (Sinclair Stevenson, 1990), copyright © Peter Ackroyd 1990, reprinted by permission of The Random House Group Ltd. and Sheil Land Associates Ltd. on behalf of the author.

Peter F. Alexander: from *William Plomer* (OUP, 1989), reprinted by permission of Oxford University Press.

Gay Wilson Allen: from *The Solitary Singer* (John Calder, 1955), reprinted by permission of the Calder Educational Trust Ltd.

Paul Allen: from *Alan Ayckbourn* (Methuen, 2001), reprinted by permission of the publishers.

Walter Allen: from *As I Walked Down New Grub Street* (Heinemann, 1981), reprinted by permission of David Higham Associates.

Anthony Alpers: from *Katherine Mansfield* (Jonathan Cape, 1980), copyright © Anthony Alpers 1989, reprinted by permission of Johnson & Alcock Ltd.

Al Alvarez: *Where Did It All Go Right?* (Bloomsbury, 2000), copyright © Al Alvarez 1999, reprinted by permission of Gillon Aitken Associates.

Kingsley Amis: from *Memoirs* (Hutchinson, 1991), copyright © Kingsley Amis 1991, reprinted by permission of The Random House Publishing Group and Jonathan Clowes Ltd., London, on behalf of the Literary Estate of Kingsley Amis.

Martin Amis: from *Experience* (Jonathan Cape, 2000), reprinted by permission of The Random House Publishing Group.

Charles Angoff: from *H. L. Mencken: A Portrait from Memory* (Thomas Yoseloff, 1956); copyright holder not traced.

Noel Annan: from *The Dons* (HarperCollins, 1999), copyright © Noel Annan 1999, reprinted by permission of HarperCollins Publishers Ltd.

F. Anstey: from *A Long Retrospect* (Oxford, 1936), reprinted by permission of The Society of Authors as the Literary Representative of the Estate of F. Anstey.

Newton Arvin: from *Longfellow: His Life and Work* (Little, Brown, 1963), copyright © Newton Arvin 1963, reprinted by permission of Little, Brown and Co., Inc.

John Ashbery: from *John Ashbery in Conversation with Mark Ford* (BTL, 2003), reprinted by permission of the publishers, Between the Lines.

Cynthia Asquith: from *Haply I May Remember* (James Barrie, 1950), reprinted by permission of Roland Asquith.

Diana Athill: from *Stet: A Memoir* (Granta, 2000), copyright © Diana Athill 2000, reprinted by permission of Granta Books and Grove/Atlantic, Inc.

James Atlas: from *Bellow* (Faber, 2000), reprinted by permission of the publishers, Faber & Faber Ltd.

Margaret Atwood: in the UK from *Curious Pursuits* (Virago Press, 2005), reprinted by permission of the Time Warner Book Group UK; in the USA from *Writing with Intent: Essays, Reviews, Personal Prose, 1983–2005*, copyright © 2004, 2005 by O. W. Toad Ltd., reprinted by permission of the publisher, Carroll & Graf Publishers, a division of Avalon Publishing Group; and in Canada from *Moving Targets*, reprinted by permission of the publishers, House of Anansi Press.

W. H. Auden: from *The Table Talk of W. H. Auden, in conversation with Alan Ansen*, edited by Nicholas Jenkins (Sea Cliff, 1989), reprinted by permission of Curtis Brown Ltd.; and from Igor Stravinsky and Robert Craft, *Memories and Commentaries* (Faber,

2002), reprinted by permission of the publishers, Faber & Faber Ltd. and Farrar, Straus & Giroux, LLC.

Stanley Ayling: from *Edmund Burke* (John Murray, 1988).

Constance Babington-Smith: from *John Masefield* (OUP, 1978), reprinted by permission of PFD (www.pfd.co.uk) on behalf of the author.

Michael Barber: from *Anthony Powell: A Life* (Duckworth, 2004), reprinted by permission of Gerald Duckworth & Co. Ltd.

William Barrett: from *The Truants: Adventures Among Intellectuals* (Anchor Press/ Doubleday 1982); copyright holder not traced.

J. M. Barrie: from the Dedication (1928) to *Peter Pan*, copyright © 1937 Great Ormond Street Hospital for Children, London, reprinted by permission of The Great Ormond Street Hospital for Children's Charity.

Georgina Battiscombe: from *Christina Rossetti* (Constable, 1981), reprinted by permission of Constable & Robinson Ltd.

Sylvia Beach: from *Shakespeare and Company* (Harcourt Brace, 1959; Faber, 1960).

Thomas Beer: from *The Mauve Decade* (Knopf, 1926), reprinted by permission of Random House, Inc.

Max Beerbohm: from 'From Bloomsbury to Bayswater' (1942) and from 'A Point to be Remembered by Very Eminent Men' (1918), in *Mainly on Air* (Heinemann, 1942); and from 'From a Brother's Viewpoint', in Max Beerbohm and others, *Henry Beerbohm Tree* (Hutchinson, 1920).

Beatrice Behan: from *My Life with Brendan* (Leslie Frewen, 1973), reprinted by permission of the Sayle Literary Agency.

S. N. Behrman: from *Conversations with Max* (Hamish Hamilton, 1960), copyright © S. N. Behrman 1960, reprinted by permission of Penguin Books Ltd. and Brandt and Hochman Literary Agents, Inc.

Vanessa Bell: from 'Notes on Virginia's Childhood', copyright © 1961 the Estate of Vanessa Bell, reprinted by permission of Henrietta Garnett.

E. F. Benson: from *As We Were* (Longmans, 1930); and from *Final Edition* (Longmans, 1940), reprinted by permission of A. P. Watt Ltd. on behalf of the Executors of the Estate of K. S. P. McDowall.

Lord Berners: quoted in Ifan Kyrle Fletcher, *Ronald Firbank: A Memoir* (Duckworth, 1930), reprinted by permission of the Berners Trust.

Michael Billington: from *The Life and Work of Harold Pinter* (Faber, 1996), reprinted by permission of the publishers, Faber & Faber Ltd. and Farrar, Straus & Giroux, LLC.

Robert Birley: from *Sunk Without Trace* (Hart-Davis, 1962); copyright holder not traced.

Claude Blagden: from *Well Remembered* (Hodder, 1953).

Paula Blanchard: from *Margaret Fuller* (Delacorte Press, 1978).

Dirk Bogarde: from *A Postilion Struck by Lightning* (Chatto, 1977), copyright © Dirk Bogarde 1977, reprinted by permission of PFD (www.pfd.co.uk) on behalf of the author's Estate.

Alan Bold: from *Hugh MacDiarmid* (John Murray, 1988).

Croswell Bowen: from *The Curse of the Misbegotten* (Hart-Davis, 1960); copyright holder not traced.

C. M. Bowra: from *Memories* (Weidenfeld, 1966), reprinted by permission of the publisher, Weidenfeld & Nicolson, an imprint of The Orion Publishing Group Ltd. and Wadham College, Oxford.

Brian Boyd: from *Vladimir Nabokov: The American Years* (Chatto & Windus, 1992), copyright © Brian Boyd 1990, 1991, reprinted by permission of The Random House Group Ltd. and Princeton University Press.

Constantin Brancusi: 'Symbol of Joyce' (1929), copyright © ADAGP, Paris and DACS, London 2005, reproduced with permission.

Peter Brazeau: from *Parts of a World: Wallace Stevens Remembered* (Random House, 1983), copyright © 1977, 1980, 1983 by Peter Brazeau, reprinted by permission of Alfred A. Knopf, a division of Random House, Inc.

Earl and Achsah Brewster: from *D. H. Lawrence: Reminiscences and Correspondence* (Secker & Warburg, 1934); copyright holder not traced.

Van Wyck Brooks: from *The Times of Melville and Whitman* (J. M. Dent, 1947); copyright holder not traced.

Craig Brown: from *This is Craig Brown* (Ebury Press, 2003), reprinted by permission of The Random House Group Ltd.

Frank Budgen: from *James Joyce and the Making of Ulysses* (Indiana University Press, 1934), reprinted by permission of the publisher.

James Campbell in the *Times Literary Supplement*, 2001, reprinted by permission of the *TLS*; from *This is the Beat Generation* (Secker & Warburg, 1999), copyright © James Campbell 1999, reprinted by permission of The Random House Group Ltd. and Gillon Aitken Associates; and from *Talking at the Gates: A Life of James Baldwin* (Faber, 1991), copyright © James Campbell 1991, reprinted by permission of Gillon Aitken Associates.

Humphrey Carpenter: from *A Serious Character: The Life of Ezra Pound* (Faber, 1988), reprinted by permission of the publishers, Faber & Faber Ltd.

Gabriel Carritt: from 'A Friend in the Family', in *W. H. Auden: A Tribute*, edited by Stephen Spender (Weidenfeld, 1975), reprinted by permission of the publisher, Weidenfeld & Nicolson, an imprint of The Orion Publishing Group.

Catherine Carswell: from *Robbie Burns* (Duckworth, 1933), reprinted by permission of Gerald Duckworth & Co. Ltd.

David Cecil: from *Max* (Constable, 1964), reprinted by permission of Constable & Robinson Ltd.; and in *Recollections of Virginia Woolf*, edited by Joan Russell (Peter Owen, 1979), reprinted by permission of Peter Owen Ltd., London.

Bennett Cerf: from *At Random* (Random House, 1977) copyright © Random House, Inc., 1977, reprinted by permission of Random House, Inc.; and from *Good for a Laugh* (Random House, 1952); copyright holder not traced.

Alexander Chancellor: from 'Guardian Profile of Tom Stoppard', in the *Daily Telegraph*, 25 June 2002, reprinted by permission of the Telegraph Group Ltd.

Richard Chase: from *Emily Dickinson* (Methuen, 1952), reprinted by permission of Taylor & Francis Group.

Susan Chitty: from *That Singular Person Called Lear* (Weidenfeld & Nicolson, 1988), reprinted by permission of The Orion Publishing Group Ltd.

Allen Churchill: from *The Improper Bohemians* (Cassell, 1961), copyright © Allen Churchill 1959, reprinted by permission of Dutton, a division of Penguin Group (USA) Inc., and of International Creative Management.

Susannah Clapp: from *After Chatwin* (Jonathan Cape, 1997), reprinted by permission of the author, c/o Rogers, Coleridge & White Ltd., 20 Powis Mews, London W11 1JN.

M. L. Clarke: from *Richard Porson* (CUP, 1937), reprinted by permission of Cambridge University Press.

J. M. Coetzee: from *Boyhood* (Secker & Warburg, 1997), reprinted by permission of David Higham Associates.

Cyril Connolly: in *Maurice Bowra: A Celebration*, edited by Hugh Lloyd-Jones (Duckworth, 1974); and from *Enemies of Promise* (Routledge, 1938), copyright © Cyril Connolly 1938, reprinted by permission of the author, c/o Rogers, Coleridge & White Ltd., 20 Powis Mews, London W11 1JN.

Jessie Conrad: from *Joseph Conrad as I Knew Him* (Heinemann, 1926), reprinted by permission of the Jessie Conrad Estate, c/o Penningtons Solicitors.

Thomas Copeland: from *Edmund Burke: Six Essays* (Cape, 1950).

Robert Craft: from *Stravinsky: Chronicle of a Friendship* (Victor Gollancz, 1972).

Rupert Croft-Cooke: from *The Unrecorded Life of Oscar Wilde* (W. H. Allen, 1972).

Caresse Crosby: from *The Passionate Years* (Ecco Press, 1979), reprinted by permission of HarperCollins Publishers, Inc.

Donald Davie: from *These the Companions* (Cambridge University Press, 1982), reprinted by permission of Mrs Doreen Davie.

Hugh Sykes Davies: from 'Mistah Kurtz: He Dead', in *T. S. Eliot: The Man and His Work*, edited by Allen Tate (Chatto, 1967); copyright holder not traced.

Robertson Davies: from *The Enthusiasms of Robertson Davies*, edited by Judith Skelton Grant (Viking, 1990), copyright © Judith Skelton Grant 1990, reprinted by permission of Viking Penguin, a division of Penguin Group (USA) Inc.

Dan Davin: from *Closing Times* (OUP, 1975), reprinted by permission of David Higham Associates.

Farrukh Dhondy: from *C. L. R. James* (Weidenfeld, 2001), reprinted by permission of David Higham Associates.

Emily Dickinson: Letter 78 to Emily Fowler (Ford), copyright © 1958, 1986, The President and Fellows of Harvard College; 1914, 1924, 1932, 1942 by Martha Dickinson Bianchi; 1952 by Alfred Leete Hampson; 1960 by Mary L. Hampson (included in Alfred Habegger, *My Ways are Laid Away in Books*), from *The Letters of Emily Dickinson*, edited by Thomas H. Johnson (The Belknap Press of Harvard University Press, 1986), reprinted by permission of the publishers.

E. R. Dodds: from Preface to *Journal and Letters of Stephen McKenna* (Constable, 1936), reprinted by permission of the Bodleian Library.

Carol Ann Duffy: in *Don't Ask Me What I Mean*, edited by Clare Brown and Don Paterson (Picador, 2003), reprinted by permission of Macmillan Publishers.

Irvin Ehrenpreis: from *The Personality of Jonathan Swift* (Methuen, 1958), reprinted by permission of Taylor & Francis Group.

Richard Ellmann: from *Oscar Wilde* (Hamish Hamilton, 1987, Penguin Books, 1988), copyright © The Estate of Richard Ellmann 1987, reprinted by permission of Penguin Books Ltd. and Alfred A. Knopf, a division of Random House, Inc.; and from *James Joyce* (OUP, 1959), reprinted by permission of Oxford University Press, Inc.

William Empson: in *T. S. Eliot: A Symposium* edited by Richard March and Tambimuttu (Editions Poetry, 1948), copyright © William Empson 1948, reprinted by permission of Curtis Brown Group Ltd., London, on behalf of the Estate of William Empson.

D. J. Enright: from *Play Resumed* (OUP, 1999), reprinted by permission of Oxford University Press; and from *Interplay* (OUP, 1995), reprinted by permission of Watson, Little Ltd. for the author.

Jacob Epstein: from *Epstein: An Autobiography* (Hulton Press, 1955); copyright holder not traced.

St John Ervine: from *Bernard Shaw* (Constable, 1956), reprinted by permission of the Society of Authors as the Literary Representative of the Estate of St John Ervine.

Willard Espy: from *An Almanac of Words at Play* (Clarkson Potter, 1975); copyright holder not traced.

Anne Fadiman: from *Ex Libris: Confessions of a Common Reader* (Penguin Press, 2000), copyright © Anne Fadiman 2000, reprinted by permission of Penguin Books Ltd.

Elaine Feinstein: from *Ted Hughes* (Weidenfeld, 2001), reprinted by permission of the author c/o Rogers, Coleridge & White, 20 Powis Mews, London W11 1JN.

Elliott Felkin: from 'Days with Thomas Hardy', in *Encounter*, 1962, reprinted by permission of the heirs of Elliott Felkin.

Constantine Fitzgibbon: from *The Life of Dylan Thomas* (Dent, 1975).

James Montgomery Flagg: from *Roses and Buckshot* (Putnam, 1946); copyright holder not traced.

Dermot Foley: in *Michael/Frank*, edited by Maurice Sheehy (Macmillan, 1969); copyright holder not traced.

Ford Madox Ford: from *Return to Yesterday* (Victor Gollancz, 1931), and from *Joseph Conrad: A Personal Remembrance* (Duckworth, 1924), reprinted by permission of David Higham Associates.

E. M. Forster: from *Selected Letters*, volume ii (Collins, 1985), reprinted by permission of The Provost and Scholars of King's College, Cambridge and The Society of Authors as the Literary Representatives of the E. M. Forster Estate.

Michael Frayn: from *Speak After the Beep* (Methuen, 1995), reprinted by permission of the publisher and of Greene & Heaton Ltd.

P. N. Furbank: from *E. M. Forster: A Life*, volume ii (Secker & Warburg, 1978), reprinted by permission of The Random House Group Ltd.

Hamlin Garland: from *Afternoon Neighbours* (Macmillan, 1934), reprinted by permission of Victoria Doyle-Jones.

Edward Garnett: from an article in *Century* magazine (1928), reprinted by permission of Richard Garnett.

William Gaunt: from *The Aesthetic Adventure* (Cape, 1945), reprinted by permission of A. P. Watt Ltd. on behalf of the Estate of William Gaunt.

Rick Gekoski: from *Tolkien's Gown* (Constable, 2004), reprinted by permission of Constable & Robinson Ltd.

Winifred Gérin: from *Emily Brontë* (OUP, 1971), reprinted by permission of Oxford University Press.

Monk Gibbon: from *The Masterpiece and the Man: Yeats as I Knew Him* (Hart-Davis, 1959); copyright holder not traced.

Carola Giedion-Welcker: from 'Meetings with Joyce', in *Portraits of the Artist in Exile*, edited by Willard Potts (Wolfhound, 1979), reprinted by permission of the University of Washington Press.

Brendan Gill: from *Here at the New Yorker* (Michael Joseph, 1975).

Robert Giroux: from 'A Personal Memoir', in *T. S. Eliot: The Man and His Work*, edited by Allen Tate (Chatto, 1967); copyright holder not traced.

Victoria Glendenning: from *Jonathan Swift* (Hutchinson, 1998); from *Edith Sitwell* (Weidenfeld, 1981); and from *Elizabeth Bowen* (Weidenfeld, 1977), reprinted by permission of David Higham Associates.

Martin Gottfried: from *Arthur Miller* (Faber, 2003), reprinted by permission of the publishers, Faber & Faber Ltd. and Da Capo Press.

Fiona Govan: from 'Harry Potter and the Kettering Gunfight', *Daily Telegraph*, 4 June 2005, reprinted by permission of the Telegraph Group Ltd.

Robert Graves: from *Goodbye to All That* in *The Complete Poems in One Volume*, edited by Beryl Graves and Dunstan Ward (Carcanet, 2000), reprinted by permission of Carcanet Press Ltd.

Robert Graves and Alan Hodge: from *The Long Weekend* (Faber, 1950), reprinted by permission of Carcanet Press Ltd.

Simon Gray: from *The Smoking Diaries* (Granta, 2004), copyright © Simon Gray 2004, reprinted by permission of the publishers, Granta Books and Carrol & Graf Publishers, a division of Avalon Publishing Group.

S. J. Greenblatt: from *Sir Walter Raleigh* (Yale University Press, 1973), reprinted by permission of the author.

James Grossman: from *James Fenimore Cooper* (Methuen, 1950), reprinted by permission of Taylor & Francis Group.

Alfred Habegger: from *My Ways are Laid Away in Books* (Random House, 2002), reprinted by permission of Random House, Inc.

Gordon S. Haight: from *George Eliot* (OUP, 1968); copyright holder not traced.

Ian Hamilton: from *Against Oblivion* (Viking, 2002), copyright © Ian Hamilton 2002, reprinted by permission of Penguin Books Ltd.; from *In Search of J. D. Salinger* (Heinemann, 1988), copyright © Ian Hamilton 1988; from *Writers in Hollywood* (Heinemann, 1990), copyright © Ian Hamilton 1990, reprinted by permission of Gillon Aitken Associates on behalf of the Literary Estate of Ian Hamilton; and from *Robert Lowell* (Faber, 1983), copyright © Ian Hamilton 1983, reprinted by permission of the publishers, Faber & Faber Ltd. and of Gillon Aitken Associates on behalf of the Literary Estate of Ian Hamilton.

Arthur Hannah: from *Irish Literary Portraits*, edited by W. R. Rodgers (BBC, 1972); copyright holder not traced.

Pamela Hansford Johnson: from *Important to Me* (Macmillan, 1974), reprinted by permission of Macmillan Publishers.

Florence Emily Hardy: from *The Early Life of Thomas Hardy* (Macmillan, 1928), and from *The Later Years of Thomas Hardy* (Macmillan, 1930), reprinted by permission of Macmillan Publishers.

Rupert Hart-Davis: from *Hugh Walpole* (Macmillan, 1952), reprinted by permission of Duff Hart-Davis.

Selina Hastings: from *Rosamond Lehmann* (Chatto, 2002), reprinted by permission of The Random House Group Ltd.

E. S. P. Haynes: from *The Lawyer: A Conversation Piece* (Eyre & Spottiswoode, 1950), reprinted by permission of The Random House Group Ltd.

William Hayter: from *Spooner* (W. H. Allen, 1977).

Seamus Heaney: in *Viewpoints: Poets in Conversation with John Haffenden* (Faber, 1981), reprinted by permission of the publishers, Faber & Faber Ltd.

Dominic Hibberd: from *Wilfred Owen: The Final Year* (Constable, 1992), reprinted by permission of the author.

Bevis Hillier: from *John Betjeman: New Fame, New Love* (John Murray, 2002).

Tim Hilton: from *Ruskin: The Early Years* (Yale University Press, 1985), copyright © Tim Hilton 1985, and *Ruskin: The Later Years* (Yale University Press, 2000), copyright © Tim Hilton 2000, reprinted by permission of Yale University Press.

Roger Hinks: from *The Gymnasium of the Mind* (Michael Russell, 1984), reprinted by permission of the publisher.

John Holden: from A. J. A. Symons, *The Quest for Corvo* (Cassell, 1934); copyright holder not traced.

Vyvyan Holland: from *Son of Oscar Wilde* (OUP, 1988), reprinted by permission of Merlin Holland.

Michael Holroyd: from *Lytton Strachey* (Chatto, 1994), reprinted by permission of A. P. Watt Ltd. on behalf of Michael Holroyd.

Park Honan: from *Matthew Arnold* (Weidenfeld & Nicolson, 1981), copyright © Park Honan 1981, reprinted by permission of The Orion Publishing Group Ltd. and Pollinger Ltd. for the proprietor.

Sidney Hook: from *Out of Step* (Harper & Row, 1987), reprinted by permission of the copyright proprietor, Ernest B. Hook, c/o Writer's Representatives, LLC. All rights reserved.

Langston Hughes: from *The Big Sea* (Pluto Press, 1986), reprinted by permission of Harold Ober Associates and Farrar, Straus & Giroux, LLC.

Aldous Huxley: from Ifan Kyrie Fletcher, *Ronald Firbank: A Memoir* (Duckworth, 1930).

Julian Huxley: from *Memories* (Penguin, 1972), copyright © Estate of Julian Huxley 1970, reprinted by permission of PFD (www.pfd.co.uk) on behalf of the Estate of Julian Huxley.

Michael Igniateff: from *Isaiah Berlin* (Chatto & Windus, 1998), copyright © Michael Igniateff 1998, reprinted by permission of The Random House Group Ltd. and Henry Holt & Company.

Richard Ingrams: from *I Once Met: Fifty Encounters with the Famous* (Oldie Publications, 1996).

William Irvine & Park Honan: from *The Book, the Ring and the Poet* (Bodley Head, 1975), reprinted by permission of Pollinger Ltd. for the proprietors.

John Irving: from *The Imaginary Friend* (Bloomsbury, 1996), copyright © Garp Enterprises Inc. 1996, reprinted by permission of the publisher and the author.

Christopher Isherwood: from *Christopher and His Kind* (Methuen, 1977), copyright © Peter Matthiessen 1970, reprinted by permission of The Random House Group Ltd. for the Estate of Christopher Isherwood and Donadio & Olson, Inc.

Dan Jacobson: from 'Time of Arrival', in *Time and Time Again* (Deutsch, 1985), reprinted by permission of the author.

Roy Jenkins: from *A Life at the Centre* (Macmillan, 1992), reprinted by permission of Macmillan Publishers.

Augustus John: from *Chiaroscuro* (Jonathan Cape, 1952), reprinted by permission of David Higham Associates.

Kathleen Jones: from *Catherine Cookson: The Biography* (Constable, 1999), reprinted by permission of Constable & Robinson Ltd.

Stanislaus Joyce: from *My Brother's Keeper* (Faber, 1960), reprinted by permission of the publishers, Faber & Faber Ltd.

Garson Kanin: from *Remembering Mr Maugham* (Hamish Hamilton, 1966); copyright holder not traced.

Justin Kaplan: from *Mr Clemens and Mark Twain: A Biography* (Simon & Schuster, 1966).

Alfred Kazin: from *New York Jew* (Secker & Warburg, 1978), copyright © Alfred Kazin 1978, reprinted by permission of The Random House Group Ltd. and the Wylie Agency.

Richard Kennedy: from *A Boy at the Hogarth Press* (Whittington Press, 1972), reprinted by permission of Rachel Ansari.

R. W. Ketton-Cramer: from *Thomas Gray* (CUP, 1955), reprinted by permission of Cambridge University Press.

James Kilroy: from *The 'Playboy' Riots* (Dolmen Press, 1971); copyright holder not traced.

Bruce King: from *Derek Walcott: A Carribean Life* (OUP, 2000), reprinted by permission of Oxford University Press.

Francis King: from *Yesterday Came Suddenly* (Constable, 1993), reprinted by permission of Constable & Robinson Ltd.

Rudyard Kipling: from *Something of Myself* (Macmillan, 1937), reprinted by permission of A. P. Watt Ltd. on behalf of The National Trust for Places of Historic Interest or Natural Beauty.

James Knowlson: from *Damned to Fame: The Life of Samuel Beckett* (Bloomsbury, 1996), copyright © James Knowlson 1996, reprinted by permission of the publishers, Bloomsbury and Grove/Atlantic, Inc.

Alfred Kreymborg: from *Troubadour* (Sagamore, 1957); copyright holder not traced.

J. W. Lambert and Michael Ratcliffe: from *The Bodley Head* (The Bodley Head, 1987), reprinted by permission of The Random House Group Ltd.

Philip Larkin: limerick in Charles Monteith, 'Publishing Larkin', in *Larkin at Sixty*, edited by Anthony Thwaite (Faber, 1982), reprinted by permission of Faber & Faber Ltd.

Frieda Lawrence: from *Memoirs and Correspondence*, edited by E. W. Tedlock (Heinemann, 1961), reprinted by permission of Pollinger Ltd. for the proprietor.

Mary Lawton: from *A Lifetime with Mark Twain: The Memories of Katy Leary* (Fredonia Books, 2003), reprinted by permission of the publisher.

Stephen Leacock: from *The Boy I Left Behind Me* (Bodley Head, 1947); copyright holder not traced.

James Lees-Milne: from *A Mingled Measure: Diaries 1953–1972* (John Murray, 1994/2000).

Shane Leslie: quoted in W. B. Stafford and R. S. McDowell, *Mahaffy* (Routledge, 1971), reprinted by permission of Sir John Leslie, Bt.

Doris Lessing: from *Walking in the Shade* (HarperCollins, 1997), copyright © Doris Lessing 1997, reprinted by permission of HarperCollins Publishers Ltd. and Jonathan Clowes Ltd., London, on behalf of Doris Lessing.

Oscar Levant: from *The Unimportance of Being Oscar* (Putnam, 1968); copyright holder not traced.

Edith Lewis: from *Willa Cather Living* (Alfred A. Knopf, 1953), reprinted by permission of the publishers.

Philip Lindsay: from *The Haunted Man* (Hutchinson, 1953); copyright holder not traced.

Anita Loos: from *Aldous Huxley: A Memorial Volume*, edited by Julian Huxley (Chatto, 1965); copyright holder not traced.

Susan Lowndes: from *Diaries and Letters of Marie Belloc* (Chatto & Windus, 1971), reprinted by permission of The Random House Group Ltd. and the author.

Percy Lubbock: from *Portrait of Edith Wharton* (Jonathan Cape, 1947), reprinted by permission of The Random House Group Ltd. and the Sayle Literary Agency.

Michael Luke: from *David Tennant and the Gargoyle Years* (Weidenfeld, 1991), reprinted by permission of the publisher, Weidenfeld & Nicolson, an imprint of The Orion Publishing Group.

Kenneth S. Lynn: from *Hemingway* (Simon & Schuster, 1987).

Hugh MacDiarmid: from *The Scottish Eccentrics* (Carcanet, 1993), reprinted by permission of Carcanet Press Ltd.

Roger McHugh: from *Irish Literary Portraits*, edited by W. R. Rodgers (BBC, 1972); copyright holder not traced.

Ian McIntyre: from *Dirt & Deity: A Life of Robert Burns* (HarperCollins, 1995), copyright © Ian McIntyre 1995, reprinted by permission of HarperCollins Publishers Ltd.

Maynard Mack: from *Alexander Pope* (Yale University Press, 1985), copyright © Maynard Mack 1985, reprinted by permission of Yale University Press.

J. W. Mackail: from *The Life of William Morris* (Constable, 1995), reprinted by permission of Selina Thirkell.

Compton Mackenzie: from *My Life and Times* (Chatto, 1965), reprinted by permission of the Society of Authors as the Literary Representative of the Estate of Compton Mackenzie.

Leslie Marchant: from *Byron: A Portrait* (John Murray, 1971).

David Marr: from *Patrick White* (Jonathan Cape, 1991), reprinted by permission of The Random House Group Ltd. and Australian Literary Management.

Edward Marsh: from *A Number of People* (Wm. Heinemann, 1939), reprinted by permission of David Higham Associates.

Arthur Marshall: from *Girls Will Be Girls* (Hamish Hamilton, 1974), reprinted by permission of P. A. Kelland for the Estate of Arthur Marshall.

Robert Bernard Martin: from *With Friends Possessed: A Life of Edward Fitzgerald* (Faber, 1985), reprinted by permission of the publishers, Faber & Faber Ltd.; and from *Gerard Manley Hopkins* (HarperCollins 1991), copyright © Robert Bernard Martin 1991, reprinted by permission of HarperCollins Publishers Ltd.

John Masefield: from *Synge: A Few Personal Recollections* (Cuala Press, 1915), reprinted by permission of The Society of Authors as the Literary Representative of the Estate of John Masefield.

Clifford Maskovsky: in *Mailer: His Life and Times*, edited by Peter Manso (Penguin, 1985); copyright holder not traced.

W. Somerset Maugham: from *In Vagrant Mood* (Heinemann, 1952), reprinted by permission of The Random House Group Ltd. and A. P. Watt Ltd. on behalf of the Royal Literary Fund.

James R. Mellow: from *Charmed Circle: Gertrude Stein and Company* (Phaidon Press, 1974), copyright © James R. Mellow 1974, reprinted by permission of the publisher.

Dido Merwin: from 'Vessel of Wrath: A Memoir of Sylvia Plath', in Anne Stevenson, *Bitter Fame: A Life of Sylvia Plath* (Viking, 1989); copyright holder not traced.

Jeffrey Meyers: from *Privileged Moments* (University of Wisconsin Press, 2000), reprinted by permission of the publisher; from *Edgar Allan Poe: His Life and Legacy* (John Murray, 1992); and from *Scott Fitzgerald* (Macmillan, 1994), reprinted by permission of Macmillan Publishers.

C. C. Hoyer Millar: from *George Du Maurier and Others* (Cassell, 1937); copyright holder not traced.

Karl Miller: from *Dark Horses* (Picador, 1968), reprinted by permission of Macmillan Publishers.

Charles Monteith: from 'Publishing Larkin', in *Larkin at Sixty*, edited by Anthony Thwaite (Faber, 1982), reprinted by permission of Faber & Faber Ltd.

Janet Morgan: from *Agatha Christie* (Collins, 1984), reprinted by permission of David Higham Associates.

Timothy Mowl: from *William Beckford* (John Murray, 1998).

Malcolm Muggeridge: from *Night and Day* magazine, November 1937, reprinted by permission of David Higham Associates.

Les A. Murray: from 'On Being Subject Matter' and from 'From Bulby Brush to Figure City', in *The Paperbark Tree* (Carcanet, 1992), reprinted by permission of Carcanet Press Ltd., Margaret Connolly & Associates, and Farrar, Straus & Giroux, LLC.

Vladimir Nabokov: from *Speak, Memory: An Autobiography Revisited* (revised edition, Weidenfeld, 1967), reprinted by permission of the Estate of Vladimir Nabokov c/o Smith/Skolnik Literary Management. All rights reserved.

V. S. Naipaul: from 'Prologue to an Autobiography' (1982), in *Literary Occasions* (Picador, 2004), copyright © V. S. Naipaul 1982, reprinted by permission of Gillon Aitken Associates.

Zdzisław Najder: from *Joseph Conrad: A Chronicle* (Cambridge University Press, 1983); copyright holder not traced.

R. K. Narayan: from *My Days* (Chatto, 1975), copyright © 1973, 1974 by R. K. Narayan, reprinted by permission of the Wallace Literary Agency, Inc.

Eveleigh Nash: from *I Liked the Life I Lived* (John Murray, 1941).

George Jean Nathan: from Mark Schorer, *Sinclair Lewis: An American Life*

(Heinemann, 1963), reprinted by permission of Patricia Angelin, Literary Executrix, The George Jean Nathan Estate.

Harold Nicolson: from *Tennyson* (Constable, 1923), reprinted by permission of Constable & Robinson Ltd.; and from *Diaries and Letters 1930–1939* (Collins, 1966), reprinted by permission of Juliet Nicolson for the Harold Nicolson Literary Estate.

Charles Norman: from *The Magic Maker: E. E. Cummings* (Little, Brown, 1972); copyright holder not traced.

Simon Nowell-Smith: quoting Henry Dwight Sedgwick, in *The Legend of the Master* (OUP, 1985), reprinted by permission of Geoffrey Nowell-Smith as Literary Executor.

Frank O'Connor: on Shaw, copyright © Frank O'Connor 1972, from *Irish Literary Portraits*, edited by W. R. Rodgers (BBC, 1972), reprinted by permission of PFD (www.pfd.co.uk) on behalf of Frank O'Connor.

William Van O'Connor: from *Ezra Pound: University of Minnesota Pamphlets on American Writers*, no. 26 (University of Minnesota Press, 1963), copyright © William Van O'Connor 1963, reprinted by permission of the publisher.

Sean O'Faolain: from *Newman's Way* (Longmans, 1952), reprinted by permission of the author, c/o Rogers, Coleridge & White Ltd., 20 Powis Mews, London W11 1JN

Edith Olivier: from *Without Knowing Mr Walkley* (Faber, 1938), reprinted by permission of Johnson & Alcock Ltd.

John Osborne: from *Almost a Gentleman* (Faber, 1991), reprinted by permission of the publishers, Faber & Faber Ltd. and The Argon Foundation c/o Gordon Dickerson.

Vincent O'Sullivan: from *Aspects of Wilde* (Constable, 1936): copyright holder not traced.

Fintan O'Toole: from *A Traitor's Kiss: The Life of Richard Brinsley Sheridan* (Granta, 1997), reprinted by permission of A. P. Watt Ltd. on behalf of Fintan O'Toole.

Michael St John Packe: from *J. S. Mill* (Secker & Warburg, 1954); copyright holder not traced.

Jay Parini: from *Robert Frost* (Heinemann, 1998), reprinted by permission of The Random House Group Ltd.

Hershel Parker: from *Herman Melville* (Johns Hopkins University Press, 1996), copyright © Herschel Parker 1996, reprinted by permission of the publisher.

Hesketh Pearson: from *Conan Doyle: His Life and Art* (Methuen, 1943); from *Tom Paine* (Hamish Hamilton, 1937); from *The Smith of Smiths* (Hamish Hamilton, 1934); from *Bernard Shaw* (Collins 1942, Unwin 1987); and from a letter to Malcolm Muggeridge in *About Kingsmill* (1951), reprinted by permission of A. P. Watt Ltd. on behalf of Michael Holroyd.

Samuel Pepys: from *The Diary of Samuel Pepys: A New and Complete Translation* by Robert Latham and William Matthews, copyright © The Master, Fellows and Scholars of Magdalene College, Cambridge, the Estate of Robert Latham and the Estate of Lois Emery Matthews 1974, reprinted by permission of PFD (www.pfd.co.uk) on behalf of The Master, Fellows and Scholars of Magdalene College, Cambridge, the Estate of Robert Latham and the Estate of Lois Emery Matthews.

Peter Porter: from *Another Round at the Pillars: Essays, Poems and Reflections on Ian Hamilton* edited by David Harsent (Cargo Press, 1999), reprinted by permission of Peter Porter.

Paul Potts: from *Dante Called You Beatrice* (Eyre & Spottiswoode, 1960); copyright holder not traced.

Reginald Pound: from *Arnold Bennett* (Heinemann, 1952); copyright holder not traced.

Anthony Powell: from *Journals 1987–1989* (Heinemann, 1996), reprinted by permission of The Random House Group Ltd. and David Higham Associates; from *Messengers of Day* (Heinemann, 1978), reprinted by permission of David Higham Associates.

Barbara Pym: from *A Very Private Eye: The Diaries, Letters and Notebooks of Barbara Pym*, edited by Hazel Holt and Hilary Pym (Macmillan, 1984), reprinted by permission of Macmillan Publishers.

Peter Quennell: from *The Sign of the Fish* (Collins, 1960), copyright © Peter Quennell 1960, and from *The Wanton Chase* (Weidenfeld, 1980), copyright © Peter Quennell 1980, reprinted by permission of Curtis Brown Group Ltd., London on behalf of the Estate of Peter Quennell; from an interview with Vladimir Nabokov in *Vladimir Nabokov: His Life, His Work, His World*, edited by Peter Quennell (Weidenfeld, 1979), copyright © Peter Quennell 1979, reprinted by permission of the publisher, Weidenfeld & Nicolson, an imprint of The Orion Publishing Group and of Curtis Brown Group Ltd., London, on behalf of the Estate of Peter Quennell.

Anthony Quinton: from *From Wodehouse to Wittgenstein* (Carcanet, 1998), reprinted by permission of Carcanet Press Ltd.

Craig Raine: from 'A Silver Plate', in *Rich* (Faber, 1984), reprinted by permission of David Godwin Associates.

Theodore Redpath: from *Ludwig Wittgenstein: A Student's Memoir* (Duckworth, 1990), reprinted by permission of Gerald Duckworth & Co. Ltd.

Jean Rhys: from *Smile Please* (André Deutsch, 1979), copyright © Jean Rhys 1979, reprinted by permission of Sheil Land Associates Ltd. on behalf of the Estate of Jean Rhys.

Grant Richards: from *Author Hunting* (Hamish Hamilton, 1934); copyright holder not traced.

Ivor Armstrong Richards: from 'On TSE', in *T. S. Eliot: The Man and His Work*, edited by Allen Tate (Chatto, 1967), reprinted by permission of Dr R. Luckett for the Literary Estate of D. E. P. and I. A. Richards, c/o Magdalene College, Cambridge.

J. M. Richards: from *Memoirs of an Unjust Fella* (Weidenfeld, 1980), reprinted by permission of the publisher, Weidenfeld & Nicolson, an imprint of The Orion Publishing Group.

Charles Ritchie: from *The Siren Years: Undiplomatic Diaries* (Macmillan, 1974), reprinted by permission of Macmillan Publishers.

W. Graham Robertson: from *Time Was* (Hamish Hamilton, 1931, 1945); copyright holder not traced.

William Rothenstein: from *Men and Memories 1872–1900* (Faber, 1931); and from *Men and Memories 1900–1922* (Faber, 1932), reprinted by permission of The Bridgeman Art Library.

Constance Rourke: from *American Humor: A Study of the National Character* (Harcourt, 1931), copyright © 1931 by Harcourt, Inc. and renewed 1958 by Carl E. Shoaff, Jr., reprinted by permission of the publisher.

Bertrand Russell: from *Autobiography* (Routledge, 1998), reprinted by permission of Taylor & Francis Books and the Bertrand Russell Peace Foundation; from *Portraits from Memory* (Allen & Unwin, 1956); and from *The Amberley Papers*, edited by Bertrand and Patricia Russell (The Hogarth Press, 1937), reprinted by permission of The Bertrand Russell Peace Foundation Ltd.

Malise Ruthven: from *A Satanic Affair* (Chatto & Windus, 1990), reprinted by permission of The Random House Group Ltd.

Edward Sackville-West: from *A Flame in Sunlight* (Bodley Head, 1974), copyright © Edward Sackville-West 1974, reprinted by permission of Curtis Brown Group Ltd., London, on behalf of the Estate of Edward Sackville-West.

Samuel Schoenbaum: from *Shakespeare's Lives* (OUP, 1991), reprinted by permission of Oxford University Press.

Norman Schrapnel: from an article on D. H. Lawrence in the *Manchester Guardian*, 18 March 1955, copyright © Guardian Newspapers Ltd. 1955, reprinted by permission of Guardian Newspapers Ltd.

Miranda Seymour: from *Robert Graves* (Doubleday, 1995), reprinted by permission of David Higham Associates.

Bernard Shaw: from a letter to Ellen Terry, 1897, and from an article in *The Star*, 1890, reprinted by permission of The Society of Authors on behalf of the Bernard Shaw Estate.

Jack Simmons: from *Southey* (Collins, 1945).

Eileen Simpson: from *Poets in Their Youth* (Random House, 1982).

Edith Sitwell: from *Coming to London*, edited by John Lehmann (Phoenix House, 1957), reprinted by permission of David Higham Associates.

Osbert Sitwell: from *Noble Essences* (Macmillan, 1950), reprinted by permission of David Higham Associates.

Logan Pearsall Smith: from *Unforgotten Years* (Constable, 1938), reprinted by permission of the London Library.

Wole Soyinka: from *Ibadan: A Memoir* (Methuen, 1994), copyright © Wole Soyinka 1994, reprinted by permission of the publisher and of Melanie Jackson Agency, LLC.

Frances Spalding: from *Stevie Smith* (Faber, 1988), reprinted by permission of the author.

Muriel Spark: from *Curriculum Vitae: An Autobiography* (Constable, 1992), reprinted by permission of David Higham Associates.

Natasha Spender: from 'His Own Long Goodbye', in *The World of Raymond Chandler*, edited by Miriam Gross (Weidenfeld & Nicolson, 1977); copyright holder not traced.

R. W. Stallman: from *Stephen Crane* (George Braziller, 1972); copyright holder not traced.

Gertrude Stein: from *The Autobiography of Alice B. Toklas* (Bodley Head, 1933) reprinted by permission of David Higham Associates and Random House, Inc.

James Stern: from *Malcolm Lowry Remembered*, edited by Gordon Bowker (BBC/Ariel Books, 1985), reprinted by permission of Imrie & Dervis Literary Agents.

James Stevens: in *James, Seumas & Jacques: Unpublished Writings* (Macmillan, 1964).

J. I. M. Stewart: from *Myself and Michael Innes* (Gollancz, 1987), reprinted by permission of A. P. Watt Ltd. on behalf of Michael Stewart.

Noel Stock: from *The Life of Ezra Pound* (Routledge, 1970), reprinted by permission of the publishers, Taylor & Francis Group.

Igor Stravinsky: from Igor Stravinsky and Robert Craft, *Memories and Commentaries* (Faber, 2002), reprinted by permission of the publishers, Faber & Faber Ltd. and Farrar, Straus & Giroux, LLC.

L. A. G. Strong: from *Green Memory* (Methuen, 1961), copyright © Estate of L. A. G. Strong 1961, reprinted by permission of PFD (www.pfd.co.uk) on behalf of the Estate of L. A. G. Strong.

Julian Symons: from *Critical Occasions* (Penguin, 1966), copyright © Julian Symons 1966, reprinted by permission of Curtis Brown Group Ltd., London, on behalf of the Estate of Julian Symons.

D. J. Taylor: from *Thackeray* (Chatto & Windus, 1999), copyright © D. J. Taylor 1999, reprinted by permission of The Random House Group Ltd. and the author, c/o Rogers, Coleridge & White Ltd., 20 Powis Mews, London W11 1JN; and from *Orwell: The Life* (Chatto & Windus, 2003), copyright © D. J. Taylor 2003, reprinted by permission of The Random House Group Ltd. and Henry Holt & Company.

Sir Charles Tennyson: from 'Memories of My Grandfather', in *The Listener*, October 1969, reprinted by permission of Hallam Tennyson.

Arthur Terry: from 'Larkin in Belfast', in *Philip Larkin: A Tribute*, edited by George Hartley (Marvell Press, 1988); copyright holder not traced.

Claire Tomalin: from *The Life and Death of Mary Wollstonecraft* (Weidenfeld & Nicolson, 1974), copyright © Claire Tomalin 1974, reprinted by permission of The Orion Publishing Group Ltd. and David Godwin Associates Ltd.; and from *Samuel Pepys: The Unequalled Self* (Viking, 2002), copyright © Claire Tomalin 2002, reprinted by permission of Penguin Books Ltd. and Alfred A. Knopf, a division of Random House, Inc.

Jenny Uglow: from *Elizabeth Gaskell: A Habit of Stories* (Faber, 1993) reprinted by permission of the publishers, Faber & Faber Ltd., and Farrar, Straus & Giroux, LLC.

John Updike: from *Self-Consciousness: Memoirs* (Penguin, 1990), copyright © John Updike 1989, reprinted by permission of Penguin Books Ltd.

Edward Wagenknecht: from *Harriet Beecher Stowe* (OUP, 1965), copyright © 1965 by Edward Wagenknecht, renewed 1993, from *Nathaniel Hawthorne: Man and Writer* (OUP, 1961), copyright © 1961 by Edward Wagenknecht, renewed 1989, and from *Mark Twain: The Man and His Work* (University of Oklahoma Press, 1961), copyright © 1935 by Edward Wagenknecht, renewed by the University of Oklahoma Press 1961, 1981; all reprinted by permission of Russell & Volkening as agents for the author.

Maisie Ward: from *Robert Browning and His World: The Private Face* (Cassell, 1967); and from *Chesterton* (Penguin, 1958); copyright holder not traced.

Jack Warner: from *My First Hundred Years in Hollywood* (Random House, 1965).

George Watson: from 'The Art of Disagreement: C. S. Lewis (1898–1963)', *Hudson Review*, 48/2 (Summer 1995), copyright © 1995 The Hudson Review, Inc.; from 'Prophet Against God: William Empson (1906–84)', *Hudson Review*, 49/1 (Spring 1996), copyright © 1996 The Hudson Review, Inc.; and from 'Forever Forster: Edward Morgan Forster (1879–1970)', *Hudson Review*, 55/4 (Winter 2003), copyright © 2003 The Hudson Review, Inc., reprinted by permission of *Hudson Review*.

Auberon Waugh: from *Will This Do?* (Century, 1991), reprinted by permission of PFD (www.pfd.co.uk) on behalf of The Estate of Auberon Waugh.

Evelyn Waugh: from *Rossetti: His Life and Works* (Duckworth, 1928), copyright © The Evelyn Waugh Settlement Trust 1928, reprinted by permission of PFD (www.pfd.co.uk) on behalf of the Evelyn Waugh, Settlement Trust; and from *The Diaries of Evelyn Waugh* edited by Michael Davie (Weidenfeld, 1976), reprinted by permission of the publishers, Weidenfeld & Nicolson, an imprint of The Orion Publishing Group and Little, Brown and Co., Inc.

Edith Wharton: from *A Backward Glance* (Appleton, 1934), reprinted by permission of the Estate of Edith Wharton and the Watkins/Loomis Agency.

Tennessee Williams: from *Memoirs* (W. H. Allen, 1976).

A. N. Wilson: from *Iris Murdoch as I Knew Her* (Hutchinson, 2003), copyright © A. N. Wilson 2003; and from *Hilaire Belloc* (Hamish Hamilton, 1984), copyright © A. N. Wilson 1984, 1996, reprinted by permission of PFD (www.pfd.co.uk) on behalf of the author.

Angus Wilson: from *The Strange Ride of Rudyard Kipling* (Secker & Warburg, 1977), copyright © Angus Wilson 1977, reprinted by permission of Curtis Brown Group Ltd., London, on behalf of the Estate of Angus Wilson.

Edmund Wilson: from *Letters on Literature and Politics* (Routledge, 1977).

Jeanette Winterson: from *Art Objects* (Jonathan Cape, 1995), reprinted by permission of The Random House Group Ltd. and the author.

Percy Withers: from *A Buried Life* (Jonathan Cape, 1940), reprinted by permission of The Random House Group Ltd.

P. G. Wodehouse: from *Performing Flea* (Herbert Jenkins, 1953); from *Over Seventy* (Herbert Jenkins, 1957); and from Introduction to *The World of Jeeves* (1967), reprinted by permission of The Random House Group Ltd. and A. P. Watt Ltd. on behalf of The Trustees of the Wodehouse Estate.

Alexander Woollcott: from *The Letters of Alexander Woollcott*, edited by Beatrice Kaufman (Cassell, 1941); copyright holder not traced.

Marjorie Worthington: from *Miss Alcott of Concord* (Doubleday, 1958), reprinted by permission of Random House, Inc.

W. B. Yeats: from *The Trembling of the Veil: The Autobiography of William Butler Yeats* (T. Werner Laurie, 1922), copyright 1916, 1936 by the Macmillan Company, copyright © renewed 1944, 1964 by Bertha Georgie Yeats, reprinted by permission of Scribner, an imprint of Simon & Schuster Adult Publishing Group and of A. P. Watt Ltd. on behalf of Michael B. Yeats.

Walter Yetnikoff: from Walter Yetnikoff with David Ritz, from *Howling at the Moon* (Abacus, 2004), copyright © Walter Yetnikoff 2004, reprinted by permission of the Time Warner Book Group UK and Broadway Books, a division of Random House, Inc.

Extracts from the *Oxford Dictionary of National Biography*: P. F. Strawson quoting Gilbert Ryle (1986), Vincent Carretta (2004), and John Cannon (2004), reprinted by permission of Oxford University Press.

Extracts from interviews with the following, from *Writers at Work: The Paris Review* (Secker & Warburg): Chinua Achebe (1994); Nelson Algred (1st series, 1958); Beryl Bainbridge (2000); William Faulkner (1st series, 1958); Robert Frost (2nd series, 1963); William Goyen (6th series, 1985); Ian McEwan (2002); Dorothy Parker (1st series, 1958); Stephen Spender (6th series, 1985); Kurt Vonnegut (6th series, 1985); August Wilson (1999); Tom Wolfe (1991).

Although every effort has been made to trace and contact copyright holders prior to publication this has not been possible in the cases indicated. If notified, the publisher will be pleased to rectify any errors or omissions at the earliest opportunity.

INDEX OF NAMES

Main entries are indicated in **bold** type.